FORM AND MEANING IN LANGUAGE

CSLI Lecture Notes
Number 228

CHARLES J. FILLMORE

Form and Meaning in Language
Volume III: *Papers on Linguistic Theory and Construction*

Preface by
Lily Wong Fillmore

edited by
Pedro Gras, Jan-Ola Östman & Jef Verschueren

CSLI Publications
*Center for the Study of
Language and Information
Stanford, California*

Library of Congress Cataloging-in-Publication Data

Names: Fillmore, Charles J

Title: Form and Meaning in Language : Papers on Linguistic Theory and
  Construction / Charles J. Fillmore

Description: p. cm. – (CSLI Lecture Notes ; v. 228) | Includes bibliographical
  references and index.

Identifiers: LCCN 2002156118 (print) | LCCN 2002156118 (ebook) |
      ISBN 9781684000579 (ebook) |
      ISBN 9781684000562 (paperback : alk. paper)

Subjects: 1. Linguistics. I. Title. II. Series

Classification: LCC P121.F4786 2003 | DDC 410-dc21

LC record available at `https://lccn.loc.gov/2002156118`

CIP

CSLI Publications is located on the campus of Stanford University.

Visit our web site at
`http://cslipublications.stanford.edu/`
for comments on this and other titles, as well as for changes
and corrections by the author and publisher.

Contents

Preface

LILY WONG FILLMORE

Pedro Gras, Jan-Ola Östman, and Jef Verschueren have done a favor for scholars and researchers who are interested in the evolution of Charles Fillmore's linguistic ideas by hunting down and putting together some papers for this volume that have not been easy to access by those who are interested in reading them.

The papers in this compilation span the three and a half decades in which Fillmore's view of how to represent semantic information in a grammar evolved from case frames (works which were republished as the first volume of this series, Fillmore 2003), to frame semantics, to construction grammar, and eventually to building a frame-based lexicon through the FrameNet Project, a huge effort which engaged him in linguistic research to the end of his life. In that project, the lexicon is taken as a "vast inventory of the words, multiword phrases, and grammatical constructions that speakers of a language have to know outright, as contrasted with those abilities speakers have for generating or interpreting language by building on the things they already know" (Fillmore 2006).

Fillmore's interest in language and linguistic research which eventually led to theorizing about the role of semantics in grammar and the conceptual structures that frame language understanding and grammar was grounded in data, although that perspective went against the long-held conviction by linguists that intuitions and introspection are ample enough evidence in such research. As he worked with frame semantics, he realized that the analyses of words such as *revenge* or *risk* called for keeping track of myriad details of what speakers are aware of and can call on, in interpreting sentences in which such words appear. "The idea behind frame semantics is that speakers are aware of possibly quite complex situation types, packages of connected expectations, that go by various names—frames, schemas, scenarios, scripts, cultural narratives, memes—and the words in our language are understood with such frames as their presupposed background" (Fillmore 2012). He saw the advantage of computer-aided corpus-based research in which these details might be richly annotated in multi-layered sets of analyses for study, and became an enthusiastic practitioner in computational linguistic research, or as he once described it, "computer-aided armchair linguistics" (this volume, chapter 13).

Construction grammar, in Charles Fillmore's and Paul Kay's framework (Fillmore & Kay 1996), was an effort to unite a formal description of general grammatical processes with the detailed syntactic, semantic, and pragmatic feature structures of frame semantics necessary to account for the meaning and use of constructions. Fillmore characterized the theory underlying his formulation of Construction Grammar as differing from other frameworks, "first in its insistence that syntactic patterns are often tightly associated with interpretation instructions, but secondly in that it takes as a major part of its assignment the task of accounting for the workings of complex grammatical constructions as well as simple ones" (this volume, chapter 7). Ultimately, the goal was to represent as fully as feasible the linguistic and contextual knowledge speakers of a language must have and apply to use the language effectively and successfully. That work remained unfinished, although many others have taken up the challenge and developed it further, expanding its reach into areas of linguistic inquiry such as language change, typology, and language acquisition (Fried 2015).

The relationship between Construction Grammar and the development of Fillmore's FrameNet research was in direct line with his belief in a continuity between grammar and the lexicon. Once he and his colleagues began assembling "a database for recording the meanings and the semantic and syntactic combinatorial properties of lexical units" and a set of procedures for analyzing them, Fillmore became convinced that the effort would require the inclusion of grammatical constructions and means for "annotating sentences by noting which parts of them are licensed by which specific constructions" in a "constructicon" (this volume, chapter 15). The work involved the analysis of various idioms and multiword constructions, going beyond multiword units such as phrasal verbs and particles, and words with selected prepositional complements, etc., that were already included in the FrameNet database. The attempt to design procedures for describing and annotating constructions and their components turned out to be more difficult than anticipated, but Fillmore and his colleagues found the advantages of including constructional and lexical information in the same database to be worth continued effort, and that being the case, he worked on it to the end.

The FrameNet Project that Fillmore founded at Berkeley continues its work in building a machine- and human-readable lexical database in English at the International Computer Science Institute in Berkeley, and on-going FrameNet projects in French, Spanish, German, Swedish, Brazilian Portuguese, Chinese, Japanese, and Korean continue at locations around the world (see https://framenet.icsi.berkeley.edu/fndrupal/ for information about FrameNet and references to Fillmore's work on frames and the lexicon, which are not included in this collection).

References

Fillmore, Charles J. 2003. *Form and Meaning in Language, Vol. I: Papers on Semantic Roles*. Stanford, CA: CSLI Publications.

Fillmore, Charles J. 2006. Frame Semantics. *Encyclopedia of Language & Linguistics* (Second Edition, Volume 4), ed. K. Brown, 613–620. Oxford: Elsevier.

Fillmore, Charles J. 2012. Encounters with Language. *Computational Linguistics* 38(4): 701–718.

Fillmore, Charles J. & Paul Kay. 1996. *Construction Grammar Coursebook*. Unpublished Manuscript, University of California at Berkeley, Department of Linguistics.

Fried, Mirjam. 2015. Construction Grammar. In *Syntax—Theory and Analysis. An International Handbook* (Handbooks of Linguistics and Communication Science 42:1–3), ed. T. Kiss & A. Alexiadou, 974–1003. Berlin: Mouton de Gruyter.

Acknowledgments

The editors wish to express their gratitude to CSLI Director Dikran Kara-gueuzian and CSLI Editorial Associates Dana Kendra Peters and Sarah Weaver for encouraging and guiding this publication project.

Acknowledgment is made for the following permissions to reprint:

- from The Ohio State University's Linguistics Department,
  - ❖ for the 1970 article "On Generativity," *Working Papers in Linguistics* 6: 1–19
  - ❖ for the 1987 article "Varieties of Conditional Sentences," Published in *ESCOL III: Proceedings of the Third Eastern States Conference on Linguistics*, ed. by Fred Marshall, 163–182. The Ohio State University
- from the Berkeley Linguistics Society,
  - ❖ for the 1979 article "Innocence: A Second Idealization for Linguistics," *Proceedings of the Fifth Annual Meeting of the Berkeley Linguistics Society*, 63–76
  - ❖ for the 1985 article "Syntactic Intrusions and the Notion of Grammatical Constructions," *Proceedings of the Eleventh Annual Meeting of the Berkeley Linguistics Society*, 73–86
  - ❖ for the 1988 article "The Mechanisms of 'Construction Grammar'," *Proceedings of the Fourteenth Annual Meeting of the Berkeley Linguistics Society*, 35–55
  - ❖ for the 1994 article "Under the Circumstances (Place, Time, Manner, etc.)," *Proceedings of the Twentieth Annual Meeting of the Berkeley Linguistics Society*, 158–172
- from The MIT Press, for the 1984 article "Some Thoughts on the Boundaries and Components of Linguistics," published in *Talking Minds: The Study of Language in Cognitive Science*, ed. by Thomas G. Bever, John

M. Carroll & Lance A. Miller, 73–108. Cambridge, Mass.: The MIT Press

♦ from Elsevier, for the 1989 article "Grammatical Construction Theory and the Familiar Dichotomies," published in *Language Processing in Social Context*, ed. by Rainer Dietrich & Carl F. Graumann, 17–38. Amsterdam: North-Holland

  ♦ from the Chicago Linguistic Society, for the 1992 article (from the 1990 CLS meeting) "Epistemic Stance and Verbal Form in English Conditional Sentences," *Papers from the 26th Regional Meeting of the Chicago Linguistic Society,* 137–161

  ♦ from Mouton de Gruyter, for the 1992 article "'Corpus Linguistics' or 'Computer-aided Armchair Linguistics'," published in *Directions in Corpus Linguistics: Proceedings of Nobel Symposium 82, Stockholm, 4–8 August 1991,* ed. by Jan Svartvik, 35–60. Berlin: Mouton de Gruyter

  ♦ from Taylor & Francis for the 1996 article "The Pragmatics of Constructions," published in *Social Interaction, Social Context, and Language: Essays in Honor of Susan Ervin-Tripp,* ed. by Dan Isaac Slobin, Julie Gerhardt, Amy Kyratzis & Jiansheng Guo, 53–69. Mahwah, NJ: Lawrence Erlbaum

  ♦ from John Benjamins Publishing Company, for the 2002 article "Minigrammars of some time-when expressions in English," published in *Complex Sentences in Grammar and Discourse: Essays in Honor of Sandra A. Thompson,* ed. by Joan Bybee & Michael Noonan, 31–59. Amsterdam: John Benjamins

  ♦ from the Universitat Pompeu Fabra's Institut de Lingüística Aplicada, for the 2008 article "Border Conflicts: FrameNet Meets Construction Grammar," published in *EURALEX XIII: Proceedings of the 13th International Congress,* ed. by Elisenda Bernal & Janet DeCesaris, 49–68. Barcelona: Universitat Pompeu Fabra.

CSLI Publications is itself the copyright holder of the 1999 article "Inversion and Constructional Inheritance," published in *Lexical and Constructional Aspects of Linguistic Explanation,* ed. by G. Webelhuth, J.-P. Koenig & A. Kathol, 113–128. Chapter 4 of this volume, the 1990 article "The Contribution of Linguistics to Language Understanding" was published in Santiago by the Universidad de Chile in *Proceedings of the First Symposium on Cognition, Language and Culture: Crossdisciplinary Dialog in Cognitive Sciences,* ed. by Aura Bocaz, 109–128. Repeated attempts to trace the current copyright holder (including through the Copyright Clearance Center) did not yield any results.

The editors also acknowledge the generous support of the University of Antwerp Linguistics Department, which enabled their editorial assistant, Ellen Todts, to devote a significant amount of time to the conversion of (mostly scanned) original texts in many different formats into the CSLI style required for this publication.

Introduction

PEDRO GRAS, JAN-OLA ÖSTMAN & JEF VERSCHUEREN
University of Antwerp & University of Helsinki

In 2003 Charles J. Fillmore (1929–2014) published *Form and Meaning in Language, Volume I: Papers on Semantic Roles*. In this book Fillmore gathered a collection of his papers published between 1969 and 1978 that gave rise to a new grammatical theory known as Case Grammar. The chapters were preceded by short notes in which Fillmore contextualized them, not only synthesizing the main points, but especially giving precious information on the intellectual context in which they were written, and even with references to how Fillmore himself taught the contents of these papers to his students.

Fillmore had planned to add further volumes to *Form and Meaning in Language*, as attested by the indication '*Volume I*' in the title and the fact that he had already sent some papers to the director of CSLI, Dikran Karagueuzian, to be included in these volumes. Unfortunately for us readers, Fillmore was, as always, very busy with several other projects, an activity he continued until the end of his life—especially so with FrameNet and its extension into a Constructicon (Fillmore 2012). Thus, he did not find the time to complete the collection with new volumes dedicated to his diverse areas of interest in the study of language.

Charles Fillmore's contribution to the field of linguistics cannot be overemphasized. He was one of those renaissance-type scholars who had a solid understanding and knowledge of virtually every field in linguistics—and he was always willing to share his thoughts with his colleagues, students, and the international community of linguists. He published a lot, but because he always got new ideas, he never managed to finish his books–in–the–making on semantics, or on Construction Grammar. Many of his ideas found publication in other scholars' works, not seldom without proper attribution to him; but when asked how he felt about this, he said: "Ideas are cheap—you always get new ones!". Words of a true scholar.

The editors of *Form and Meaning in Language, Volumes II & III,* owe many inspirational ideas to Charles Fillmore: Jan-Ola Östman and Jef Verschueren count themselves amongst his PhD students at UC Berkeley, and Pedro Gras trained himself as a construction grammarian with the help of Fillmore's writings (and he was fortunate to attend a course that Fillmore taught at the University of Bergen in 2008). Some of the papers that are collected in these two volumes have been published in outlets not so readily available, while they are clearly of high importance for the field, not only from the point of view of the history of linguistics, but specifically because the findings and arguments in them are still very relevant today. With this in mind—and with the support of Lily Wong Fillmore and Dikran Karagueuzian—we have put together two further volumes under the same general heading of *Form and Meaning in Language*, continuing Fillmore's *Volume I* collection.

Two areas in which Fillmore's work has been extremely influential are not covered in these three volumes. The first is his work on deixis, available as *Lectures on Deixis* (1997a). The second is the area of frame semantics, readily to be found through a bibliography on the FrameNet website (https://framenet.icsi.berkeley.edu/). Volume II covers Fillmore's work on *Discourse and Pragmatics,* and volume III deals with *Linguistic Theory and Constructions.* We are convinced that, together with what is easily accessible elsewhere (e.g. in international journals like *Language*), these volumes make Fillmore's oeuvre much more accessible. One caveat needs to be mentioned, though. There are many manuscripts and other unpublished analyses and articles that Fillmore readily distributed to his colleagues and students, and that are in that respect 'available'—and indeed referred to in the discipline. We have, however, decided not to publish studies that Fillmore himself presumably did not think of as ready for publication in their present shape.

We will not here try to give a synopsis of Fillmore's life and of his contribution to the field of linguistics and of his huge influence on his students, colleagues and on other scholars. In addition to several shorter and personal obituaries published after his death, the overview of his contribution to linguistics by Ackerman, Kay & O'Connor (2014) published in *Language* well summarizes his achievements, as does his own reflection of his relation to linguistics in Fillmore (2012). We would, however, like to point out some aspects that made Fillmore a model of academic work: clarity, honesty and integrity, and the balance between theory and practice.

As to the first feature—as the reader him/herself will have the possibility to discover—the papers to be found in these volumes were written in an exceptionally clear and even entertaining style, full of examples and detailed explanations, which allow the author's position to be accurately expressed. In an academic context, in which obscurity of expression and excessive formalization are often practiced, Fillmore's sustained effort to bring forth a particularly clear message is not only remarkable but most welcome—a model to be followed.

This quest for clarity is closely related to Fillmore's honesty and integrity. Instead of presenting his own position as the only one possible, rather than describing alternative positions as completely wrong or simply ignoring them, Fillmore is especially careful to describe clearly and accurately his own position, explicitly pointing out to what extent it moves away from alternative positions and what advantages it may bring. Again, this attitude contrasts with the frequent practice, in linguistics as elsewhere, to ignore or even revile 'rival' theories.

Finally, Fillmore's intellectual production shows a remarkable balance between theory and practice. He liked to call himself an ordinary working linguist (OWL), whose main goal was to explain the intricate properties of the grammar and lexicon of natural languages. To that end, he came up with several theories that have turned out to be highly influential in different areas of linguistics: Case Grammar, Frame Semantics, Construction Grammar and a variety of contributions to linguistic pragmatics. (An additional, complementary characteristic of Fillmore was his modesty: he rarely himself talked about his approaches to language as full-fledged 'theories'.)

It is important to note also that in Fillmore's work, theory making and model construction was always the outcome of an attempt to get the facts right; data were not there simply in order to serve as justification for an elegant theory. In addition to the range of theoretical contributions he made, he devoted an important amount of attention to 'applied' linguistics. Quite a number of papers included in these volumes deal with lexicography, computational linguistics, second language acquisition, language pedagogy or forensic linguistics.

The present volume on *Linguistic Theory and Constructions* brings together Fillmore's most important articles on how his notion of "grammatical construction" grew into an internationally recognized approach to linguistic

analysis and to the understanding of language structure and language function. The articles in this volume have been organized under four headings,
out of which three focus specifically on constructions as such, and one section
starts the volume with three pre-constructional articles displaying Fillmore's
deep understanding of, and interest in the organization of linguistic
knowledge generally.

The studies included in Part 1, entitled *On the organization of linguistic
knowledge*, are not specifically framed in Construction Grammar terms, but
they point to some of the key aspects that gradually led to a constructional
model of language. The first chapter, "On generativity" (1972), continues his
early work on phonology and on the cyclic application of rules in generative
grammar (Fillmore 1962, 1963), here taking the perspective of Chomsky's
(1965) Standard Theory. The chapter discusses "what it takes for something
to be a generative grammar" from the perspective of an 'ordinary working
grammarian,' whose main goal is to describe the grammatical properties of
the sentences of a language, and he identifies two main problems. The first
has to do with the concept of relative grammaticality. According to Chomsky
and Miller (1963), a generative grammar can be defined as a device that contains the grammatical sentences of a language and assigns them a structural
description, and it can also assign degrees of grammaticality to strings of
words. However, as Fillmore argues, the kind of decisions needed to assign
such degrees are hard to operationalize, due to several factors that go beyond
the capacities of an 'ordinary working grammarian'. As a second point, Fillmore points to the existence of areas of grammar in which speakers cannot
decide what is the (best) grammatical version of a sentence (if any), like question tags with *somebody* as their antecedent (*Somebody's out there, {isn't
there/isn't he/aren't they?}*). To deal with cases like this, he suggests that
grammars do not need to be complete, but should be left open in some areas
"just for those situations in which the creative part of a grammar sets up
something which the interpretive part cannot cope with".

In "Innocence. A Second Idealization for Linguistics" (1979), Fillmore
discusses the tension between theoretical idealizations and actual linguistic
use in explaining meaning. In addition to the idealization of the "ideal
speaker/hearer in a homogenous speech community" generally assumed in
generative grammar, Fillmore suggests that there is a second idealization operating in most traditions of semantics, that of the *innocent speaker/hearer*:
"It knows the morphemes of its language and their meanings, it recognizes
the grammatical structures and processes in which these morphemes take
part, and it knows the semantic import of each of these". The study points to
some of the areas of language that defy a purely compositional analysis—

lexical and phrasal idioms, collocations, register appropriateness, metaphorical language, indirect communication or discourse function—and reviews
some of the solutions proposed to deal with these. On this basis, Fillmore
concludes that, even though some idealization is needed in semantic theory,
there are aspects of language use that defy a purely compositional analysis.
Interestingly, one of these are grammatical constructions, referred to as structural formulas in the study: "For the structural formulas that I have in mind,
the grammatical form and possibly one or two lexical items are fixed, but the
class of substitutions is open but constrained by semantic and pragmatic considerations."

In "Some Thoughts on the Boundaries and Components of Linguistics"
(1984), Fillmore attempts to present a global overview of the organization of
language science that can give a proper account of both ends of speech communication: sound and meaning. In this long and detailed study, Fillmore
presents a descriptive framework that recognizes different levels of analysis—word, sentence, discourse—and relationships between them: part to
whole, taxonomic, hierarchical, instrumental, internal regular and external
regular. He devotes some sections to discussions of the kinds of decisions
needed to account for the sound aspect of human communication, including
the relationship between phonetics and phonology, and the boundaries between word and sentence phonology. The rest of the chapter is devoted to the
analysis of meaning, where he discusses the differences between linguistic
and encyclopedic meaning as well as the boundaries between meaning and
context of use. In the later sections of the study, Fillmore refers to his approach of Frame Semantics and also points to what will be later defined as
grammatical constructions: "we will have to recognize a level of representation that provides syntactically structured lexical material together with semantic information that can be associated with particular lexical items,
phrasal items (where necessary), and particular syntactic forms (where necessary)".

The fourth and final chapter of this section is entitled "The Contribution
of Linguistics to Language Understanding" (1990) and it is based on a paper
presented at a Symposium on Cognition, Language and Culture organized by
the University of Chile. Here Fillmore addresses the role of lexical and grammatical meaning in the process of language understanding. He starts out by
referring to a debate between Ivan Sag and Roger Schank, in which Schank
proposed that syntax made a minimal contribution to language understanding, one percent of the whole. According to Schank, language understanding
is mostly based on what speakers know about the entities being referred to by
means of words, knowledge shared by participants, and general inferencing
mechanisms. By contrast, Fillmore defends the view that linguistic meaning

plays a central role in language understanding. In the rest of the study, Fillmore argues that "a great many of the lexical and grammatical resources in a language are best described in terms of the manner in which they shape, in expression and comprehension, the conceptual structures that organize linguistic messages". In order to sustain this claim, he analyzes a set of linguistic phenomena from the point of view of their meaning potential: the frames evoked by lexical items as well as their combinatorial properties, the semantics of prepositions, tense and time, negative quantifiers, and grammatical constructions, with a special section dedicated to conditional constructions.

The four studies in Part 2, *The Foundations of Construction Grammar*, constitute—together with Fillmore, Kay & O'Connor (1988) and Kay & Fillmore (1999), both published in *Language*—the founding texts of Construction Grammar. Chapter 5, "Syntactic Intrusions and the Notion of Grammatical Construction" (1985), deals with the analysis of two grammatical phenomena of English that cannot be properly explained from a purely derivational perspective: redundant *have* in past counterfactual clauses (*If you had've eaten it, you would have died*) and the insertion of interjections after clause-initial wh-words (*What the heck did you see?*). After providing evidence that these two phenomena require reference to specific syntactic environments (counterfactual conditional clauses and interrogative clauses headed by a wh-word (except *which*)), Fillmore argues in favour of a grammatical model that takes grammatical constructions as basic units of analysis, rather than considering them the product of derivation (cf. Chomsky 1981).

In the next chapter, "The Mechanisms of 'Construction Grammar'" (1988), after situating Construction Grammar against transformational and phrase-structure grammars, Fillmore introduces the fundamental technical notions of what has become known as Berkeley Construction Grammar (Fillmore 2013): the distinction between internal and external properties of a construction, the use of nested boxes as a notation system, the use of attribute–value pairs for feature structure representation, and the mechanisms of unification and inheritance to explain the combination of constructions.

The following chapter, "Grammatical Construction Theory and the Familiar Dichotomies" (1989), is also an introduction to Construction Grammar, but instead of focusing on the formal apparatus of the theory, Fillmore here discusses the implications of the framework for some generally adopted distinctions in linguistics, especially the competence versus performance dichotomy. A substantial part of the study is dedicated to presenting a sample of grammatical constructions that put into question "the separability of the inner structure of language from a study of its use". The sample includes different types of constructions: conditional, comparative, presentational, information structure constructions and bare noun binomials. They all pair some (semi-)schematic syntactic form with non-compositional meaning, including conventional aspects of discourse and pragmatic context. The analyses of these constructions are then used as evidence to question some idealizations that have characterized generative approaches to language: competence and performance, social and individual aspects of linguistic structure, lexicon and grammar, syntax and semantics, grammar and pragmatics, meaning and understanding, and synchrony and diachrony.

Finally, in "Inversion and Constructional Inheritance" (1999) Fillmore focuses on the concept of constructional inheritance through an analysis of the English Subject-Auxiliary Inversion (SAI) construction. The chapter starts with a definition of the notion of construction—"a set of formal conditions on morphosyntax, semantic interpretation, pragmatic function and phonology that jointly characterize or license certain classes of linguistic objects"—and offers a typology of grammatical constructions: phrasal, lexical and linking constructions. Next, the chapter focuses on the notion of inheritance: "If construction C inherits construction D, then C shares all the conditions of D while adding some of its own". The chapter further describes the ancestors of SAI, the abstract phrasal constructions of English that are inherited by the SAI construction, such as the Head Feature Construction (HFC) and the Verb Headed Phrase (VHP), among others. As Fillmore notes, "neither SAI nor any of its ancestors is provided with semantic or pragmatic information. [...] Whether SAI itself has a pragmatic or functional component shared by all of its inheritors is something on which I do not take a stand". The rest of the chapter is devoted to the analysis of some of the non-interrogative constructions that inherit the SAI construction, and which encode rich semantic-pragmatic information, including blessings, wishes and curses, exclamations, the negative contraction construction, emphatic negative imperatives, auxiliary conditionals and correlative conditionals.

The studies in Part 3, *Constructional Analyses*, contains different kinds of applications to the grammar of English of the theoretical framework described in detail in Part 2. Chapters 9 and 10 are dedicated to the analysis of conditional sentences focusing on different aspects of their formal and interpretive features, while chapters 11 and 12 analyze the properties of adjuncts and temporal expressions.

"Varieties of conditional sentences" (1987) proposes a constructional account of the whole family of conditional constructions in English, dealing simultaneously with their syntactic form, their semantic interpretation and their use. The chapter starts with an analysis of correlative conditionals of the type *The bigger they come, the harder they fall*, showing their main syntactic, semantic and pragmatic features, arguing that "any successful description of these phenomena require us to assemble *for this single construction* an organized body of facts which cannot simply be taken for granted as following from other facts independently knowable about the grammar of English." The rest of the chapter is dedicated to a detailed analysis of the properties of conditionals as constructions, with a particular focus on conditional constructions having clausal antecedents and clausal consequents.

In "Epistemic Stance and Verbal Form in English Conditional Sentences" (1992), the focus switches to the semantic and pragmatic principles that govern the selection of verbal forms in conditional constructions. The goal of the study is "to explain the permitted verbal clusters in the protasis and apodosis clauses of conditional sentences, the compatible and incompatible combinations of verbal forms across the two clauses, and the semantic interpretations that accompany each permitted pairing". In order to do so, the study relies on a notion of concord where both clauses express the same epistemic stance. The key notions of the proposed analysis are the following three: (i) epistemic stance: "the epistemic relationship which the speaker has to the world represented by the conditional sentence: the speaker might regard it as the actual world, might regard it as distinct from the actual world, or might not know whether the alternative world represented in the conditional sentence is the actual world or not"; (ii) relative time: "the relative positions in time of states of affairs P, and Q, and the time of speaking", and (iii) interest: "whether or not the speaker puts a positive evaluation on the alternative situation in which P holds". The analysis makes use of diagrams that represent the features of relative time and epistemic stance in different types of conditional constructions.

In "Under the Circumstances (Place, Time, Manner, etc.)" (1994), which was presented at a Berkeley Linguistics Society Meeting dedicated to the contributions of Fillmore on the occasion of his 65th anniversary, Fillmore himself provides a chronological overview of the treatment of circumstantial adverbials in contemporary syntactic theory. The chapter opens with Tesnière's (1959) distinction between *actants* and *circonstants* and various interpretations of this distinction in cognitive-functional theories, including Frame Semantics, and moves on to the treatment of circumstantial adverbials in the Standard Theory of Generative Grammar (Chomsky 1965), and the reactions to this model by Generative Semantics and Case Grammar. This overview is used to raise some questions relating to the notion of subcategorization, and its alternative treatment in Construction Grammar. The constructional analysis proposed consists of identifying different sorts of constructions that project the valence of the verb into the VP and allows incorporation of any circumstantial adverbs in context-sensitive ways, taking into account their role in the frame evoked by the verb: frame-internal (obliques) or frame-external (adjuncts).

The last chapter in this section, "Mini-grammar of some time-when expressions in English" (2002), proposes a constructional analysis of two semantically defined types of adverbial expressions in English that indicate the time at which some events occur, referred to as the target. In the first type, the Vector Construction, "the target is understood as situated at a particular distance earlier than or later than some explicit or implicit temporal landmark", e.g. *three years before the war*. The second family of constructions "have to do with locating a temporal target in respect to segmentations of the time flow of the kind provided by diaries and calendars", e.g. *last spring*. The analysis is framed in Construction Grammar Lite, a simplified notation of Berkeley Construction Grammar. Following standard practice in Fillmore's analysis, the study examines the specific features of the constructions under analysis while pointing to generalizations in other areas of English grammar where relevant.

The studies in the final section, Part 4, have been given the title *Constructions and Language Use*. These studies extend constructional analyses in three different directions: Pragmatics, Corpus Linguistics and Computational Linguistics. In "The Pragmatics of Constructions" (1996), Fillmore discusses the role of pragmatics in the analysis of grammatical constructions. He starts by making a distinction between a grammar-external and a grammar-internal view of pragmatics. The first might include general mechanisms of language use, such as politeness principles or common-sense inferencing (i.e. conversational implicatures). These principles are relatively independent of the specific linguistic resources employed by speakers. By contrast, a grammar-internal view of pragmatics seeks to explore the specific contextual information encoded in the grammar and the lexicon of a language. This view regards "the pragmatic dimension as an inherent part of every grammatical construction". Through an analysis of the pragmatic aspects associated with different grammatical constructions, Fillmore illustrates the difficulty of deciding when pragmatic information should be regarded as encoded in a grammatical construction: "For a structurally complex structure, we need to ask whether its interpretation can be analyzed as a compositional product of its constituent parts, or whether it is an instance of a complex structure with its own status as a separately functioning grammatical construction".

In "'Corpus Linguistics' or 'Computer-aided Armchair Linguistics'" (1992), Fillmore seeks to reconcile two separate—and often opposed—methodologies in linguistic studies: the use of corpora (corpus linguistics) and the recourse to introspection (armchair linguistics). Instead of aligning himself with one of these seemingly opposite approaches, he defends the convenience of combining the use of corpora and native speakers' intuitions: "My conclusion is that the two kinds of linguists [armchair and corpus] need each other. Or better, that the two kinds of linguists, wherever possible, should exist in the same body." The study focuses on the analysis of the English words *risk* and *home*, combining insights from Frame Semantics and Corpus Linguistics. Though not explicitly framed in Construction Grammar terminology, the analysis substantiates the Construction Grammar principle according to which a complete analysis of a lexical item consists of the set of constructions in which the word can occur, specifying for each construction both the formal features of its constituents and the conventional aspects of its meaning. Fillmore shows that the use of corpora offers a systematic method for obtaining the data the analyses have to account for, including very specific contexts that are difficult to access through introspection. On the other hand, he also points to the need for using evidence that is not readily available in a corpus, like the use of negative evidence: "a corpus cannot tell us what is not possible."

The last chapter in this section "Border Conflicts: FrameNet Meets Construction Grammar" (2008) explores the possibility of creating a *constructicon* of English—a record of grammatical constructions—building on the methodology of FrameNet, a database of the semantic and syntactic combinatorial properties of words. The chapter starts by describing the theoretical and methodological basis of FrameNet and its extension to create full text annotation. It is precisely the attempt of annotating full texts that opens the door for including grammatical constructions as linguistic resources that contribute to the meaning of texts. The research project described in this paper consists of creating an inventory of 'minor grammatical constructions' in English and to develop a procedure for annotating instances of them. After signaling the similarities between the annotation of lexical items and that of constructions and the specific difficulties that grammatical constructions pose for annotation, Fillmore briefly describes the varieties of minor constructions included in the project. These range from argument structure constructions to constructions that include specific lexical items (e.g. the *way* construction, as in *She pushed her way through the crowd*) or are restricted to limited sets of lexical items (e.g. plural-noun reciprocals as predicates, as in *I was best friends with him at school*).

The present collection focuses on making available publications by Charles Fillmore that have previously not been easily accessible. The volume focuses on his work on Construction Grammar, publications that paved the way for this model, and how it has been put to use and how it can be combined with FrameNet and general constructicon building. Fillmore's colleagues and students have continued his work, refined it, and even split up into different types of construction grammars, focusing on e.g. cognitive, formal, interactional, typological etc. aspects. (For a general overview of the historical and intellectual background to Construction Grammar, see Fried & Östman 2004).

The volume does not include all of Charles Fillmore's publications in the area of "Linguistic Theory and Constructions" that are not easily accessible. In particular, we want to mention his 1997 article in Japanese (Fillmore 1997b), on corpus analysis and construction grammar. In this study, Fillmore analyzes the constructions needed in order to understand the sentence *Bunka to iu kotoba ni wa, iroiro na imi ya tukaikata ga aru* 'The word "culture" has various meanings and usages,' a sentence from a book written by the anthropological linguist Takao Suzuki. Even though most of Fillmore's studies are analyses of details in English grammar, he had a keen and solid interest in other languages, and thus of making Construction Grammar a grammar with universal impact. Fillmore had, for instance, studied at Kyoto University while he was teaching English in Japan. In the brief summary in English of the 1997b article (pp. 63–64), he refers to the launch of a project to investigate the structure of Japanese that "should eventually result in a body of knowledge concerning the principle constructions in Japanese grammar, not just from a syntactic perspective, but from a semantic and pragmatic one as well" and he wants to be able "to find how the use of constructions can be used to characterize particular styles of language use." All these visions were later entered into by Fillmore himself and his colleagues and students in their analyses, and constructions in a large number of languages have been analyzed and constructicons and FrameNets for specific languages have been developed and keep intriguing scholars of different credos and in all parts of the world.

References

Ackerman, Farrell, Paul Kay & Mary Catherine O'Connor. 2015. Charles J. Fillmore. *Language* 90(3): 755–761.

Chomsky, Noam. 1965. Aspects of the Theory of Syntax. Cambridge, Mass.: MIT Press.

Chomsky, Noam. 1981. *Lectures on Government and Binding: The Pisa Lectures*. Holland: Foris Publications.

Noam Chomsky & George A. Miller. 1963. Introduction to the Formal Analysis of Natural Languages. *Handbook of Mathematical Psychology*, Volume II, ed. R. Duncan Luce, Robert R. Bush & Eugene Galanter, 269–321. New York & London: John Wiley and Sons.

Fillmore, Charles J. 1962. *A System for Characterizing Phonological Theories*. Ann Arbor: University of Michigan dissertation.

Fillmore, Charles J. 1963. The Position of Embedding transformations in a Grammar. *Word* 19(2): 208–231.

Fillmore, Charles J. 1997a. *Lectures on Deixis*. Stanford, CA: CSLI Publications.

Fillmore, Charles J., 1997b. Corpus Analysis and Construction Grammar. *New Directions in Linguistics and the Japanese Language* (Proceedings of the Second International Symposium), 53–64. Tokyo: National Language Research Institute. [The text is in Japanese, with a brief abstract in English.]

Fillmore, Charles J. 2003. *Form and Meaning in Language, Vol. I: Papers on Semantic Roles*. Stanford, CA: CSLI Publications.

Fillmore, Charles J. 2012. Encounters with Language. *Computational Linguistics* 38(4): 701–718.

Fillmore, Charles J. 2013. Berkeley Construction Grammar. *The Oxford Handbook of Construction Grammar*, ed. Thomas Hoffmann & Graeme Trousdale, 112–132. Oxford: Oxford University Press.

Fillmore, Charles J., Paul Kay & Mary Catherine O'Connor. 1988. Regularity and Idiomaticity in Grammatical Constructions: The Case of *Let Alone*. *Language* 64(3): 501–538.

Fried, Mirjam & Jan-Ola Östman, 2004. Historical and Intellectual background of Construction Grammar. *Construction Grammar in a Cross-Language Perspective*, ed. Mirjam Fried & Jan-Ola Östman, 1–10. Amsterdam: John Benjamins.

Kay, Paul & Charles J. Fillmore. 1999. Grammatical Constructions and Linguistic Generalizations: The *What's X Doing Y?* Construction. Language 75(1): 1–33.

Tesnière, Lucien. 1959. *Éléments de syntaxe structurale*. Paris: Klincksieck.

Part 1

On the Organization of Linguistic Knowledge

1

On Generativity

1972

CHARLES J. FILLMORE

1.

For some time I have been striving to understand just exactly what it takes for something to be a generative grammar. The nature of my concern with this question is not that of a metatheoretician within the discipline, not that of a philosopher of science looking at our field from the outside; it is rather that of an easily confused 'ordinary working grammarian' who is trying to be minimally clear about what it is that he is doing.

The ordinary working grammarian of whom I speak has fairly special and fairly limited ways of troubling himself with the problems I will be discussing, and he has special and limited reasons for being pleased or displeased with a theory. For example, when the ordinary working grammarian is told that a generative grammar of a language is a recursive device which demarcates exhaustively and exclusively the unlimitedly large set of sentences in the language, what that means to him is that he has a test for knowing whether what he has done, in describing a certain language, has been successful: if he discovers sentences in the language which his grammar fails to recognize, or if he notices sequences which his grammar allows but the language does not, then he knows that his efforts have fallen short of complete success.

If the ordinary working grammarian is told that he can capture generalizations that would otherwise escape him only by adopting a particular notation or a particular set of conventions regarding the form and interpretation of grammatical rules, what that means to him is that the grammatical descriptions he writes should be simpler if he uses these notations and conventions than if he does not, and that grammars written by people who adhere to the same conventions will be interpretable to him.

Similarly, when the ordinary working grammarian is told that the model of grammar with which he should work must contain in its notation or in an auxiliary set of conventions a body of assumptions about language universals, he is willing to accept this, not so much because he is pleased that in this way the theory abstracts properties of the basic human psychic apparatus for language out of the cultural diversity of individual languages, but because this decision makes it possible for him not to have to remember all the things he believes to be true about language in general: to the extent that his beliefs about language universals are embedded in the notations he uses, he will always know when to be surprised by new evidence which contradicts one or another of these beliefs. He knows that when he encounters linguistic facts which he cannot articulate with the notational and conceptual apparatus at his disposal, he has correctly detected a crisis in the theory and is now in a position to revise his beliefs about language.

Our grammarian, we have seen, is essentially lazy, and, indeed, almost 'practical' in his views about what theories are for.

I am going to claim that the ordinary working grammarian is confused about what it takes for something to be a generative grammar. Before I go on to explain myself, I must report immediately that we do not find him guilty of the much-discussed confusion between *generate* as a stative verb used to relate a grammar and the sentences of the language it is a grammar of, and *generate* as an active verb used of a human being and the utterance he produces. The ordinary working grammarian knows and is careful about these distinctions.[1]

I must explain also, before I go on, that the ordinary working grammarian I have in mind finds himself fairly solidly within the generative camp. His doubts about generative grammar do not arise from any assumptions about the superiority of the research goals of the taxonomists or distributionists of a decade or two ago. To him, the data do not determine the conceptual base of the theory; they constitute, rather, the phenomenon which the theory has to explain. And this was something he learned from the generativists.

---

[1] It is not so easy to keep these notions distinct in one's unconscious, I must admit. I continually find that I am attracted to 'generative semantics' or back again to 'interpretive semantics' depending on whether I have recently been more impressed with my experiences of wanting to say things I do not know how to express, or with my experiences of having said things which I cannot understand. In the former mood I am convinced that the mechanism inside me for constructing well-formed messages is intact, and that what is malfunctioning is the component which maps messages into utterances; when I am in the latter state I feel that the mechanism for producing grammatical sentences is intact, and that what is defective is the apparatus for assigning meanings to them.

For the sake of younger readers, let me interpret my allusions. I am old enough to remember the days when, as a typical classroom demonstration of analytic procedures in linguistics, the professor presented a pair of linguistic forms, showed on the basis of the distribution of the constituent elements that they are analogously constructed, and then continued by pointing out that their external distribution proves them to be distinct. I contribute the following examples to this discussion: the pair *maternity dress* and *paternity suit*. It is easy to believe that there are distributional parallels in English-language texts between *maternity* and *paternity*, and that the distributional properties of *dress* and *suit* are analogous. However, on examining the external distribution of the two-word expressions, we would discover that they are in fact quite distinct, in that they occur in vastly unlike total context sets. Some of my teachers took the trouble to say that when a linguist claims that two forms are grammatically distinct, what he means, precisely, is that their total context sets are distinct.

Today reasonable people are much more likely to say that there is something about what these expressions *are* which accounts for the different distributions, rather than the other way around; and such reasonable people might be said to be taking the generativist position. To the challenge that these two ways of talking about the facts amount to the same thing, I reply that in the development of a generative description, one would notice the internal similarity of *maternity dress* and *paternity suit* only by accident; in the development of a distributionist account, the comparison of these forms is a necessary step in the individual description.

2.

My topic, then, is the way in which a 'generative' linguist conceives the relation between a grammar and the objects which the grammar is designed to identify and describe, i.e., the 'grammatical' sentences of the language in question.

In the earliest discussions of generative grammars, a comparison was suggested between writing a grammar and specifying the set of well-formed formulas in a mathematical system. In Chomsky (1957: 13) we read:

> The fundamental aim in the linguistic analysis of a language L is to separate the 'grammatical' sequences which are sentences of L from 'ungrammatical' sequences which are not sentences of L and to study the structure of the grammatical sequences. The grammar of L will thus be a device that generates all of the grammatical sequences of L and none of the ungrammatical ones.

A generative grammar recognizes certain strings of symbols as well-formed sentences in the language, but not others, much in the manner of the formation rules in a mathematical system.

This function of a grammar is interpretable as being identical to one of the unarticulated goals of the traditional grammarians, the difference being that a generative grammar is one in which the characterization of the totality of well-formed sentences is made explicit. To mention an aspect of such a suggestion which comes quickly to mind, it seems quite likely that some traditional grammarians, and many classroom grammarians, may indeed have been willing to think of a grammar as analogous to the system of formation rules in a mathematical system—that is, in the quite literal sense that in both cases the rules were devised by wise and rational creators, for the creators' own purposes, and that the admission or rejection of a presented formula or sentence was to depend on whether or not it was in conformity with these independently valued rules. A mathematical system and a system of grammatical rules upheld by proponents of the doctrine or correctness are both, after all, manmade.

Explicit generative grammars appeared on the scene, fortunately, at a time when the question of the membership of a sentence in a language was taken as an empirical issue. On the *de facto*, as opposed to the *de jure*, theory of grammaticality, the speaker is the source of the language, and a successful generative grammar is one which conforms in its predictions to certain kinds of judgments made by speakers of a language about the sentences in their language. A proposed grammar can be shown to be incorrect by a demonstration that the set of sentences in the language is not the same as the set of sentences recognized by the grammar.

That, at least, was the goal which grammarians learned to set for themselves. In the face of the first requirement, it is clear that what the ordinary working grammarian needs to *find* out is the identity of the set of *de facto* grammatical sentences, and what he needs to *figure* out is whether the grammar he constructs puts the good sentences in and rules the bad ones out. We shall soon see that this requirement is a difficult one.

In addition to this requirement that a grammar identify each of the grammatical sentences of language, the concept of generative grammar comprises the further condition that it associate with each of the sentences it generates a structural description—a display of all the grammatical information about the sentence which the speakers of the language can be said to possess. As these first two requirements are phrased in Katz (1966: 123), the rules of a linguistic description must not only be capable of producing an infinite list of formal objects, but the formal objects on the list must be the sentences of the language under study and the list must exclude any string in the vocabulary of the language that is not a sentence in the language. Furthermore, these rules must somehow specify all the information about the sentences that a speaker utilizes to produce and understand them.

The second requirement does not commit us to anything new in the actual workings of a grammar. The very rules which play a part in the successful generation of the sentences of the language can be used, *via* a structure–assigning algorithm taken to be part of linguistic theory, to provide the correct structural descriptions. As stated in Thorne (1968: 302), "The set of rules involved in the generation of a sentence is equivalent to an analysis of it."

With the concept of generative grammars thus elaborated to contain the notion 'correct structural description,' the relation between a grammar and the set of linguistic objects it generates is subtler than was apparent at first. The native-speaker judgments to which the analyst needs to appeal for convincing himself that his work is adequate involve not only acceptance or rejection of sentences, but also assent to various kinds of assertions about the sentences that are accepted.

Our ordinary working grammarian looks at this new responsibility and sees two problems: first, whether he can determine what the correct structural descriptions of the sentences in the languages are; and second, whether the rules needed for generating the sentences in the first sense are indeed precisely those which will succeed in assigning correct structural descriptions. The ordinary working grammarian worries, in other words, about whether there really is a definitional relation between a description of everything speakers know about the sentences of their language and grammatical rules of the type he has learned.

From the beginning, but only with seriousness in work later than Chomsky (1957), the concept of generative grammar has been further enriched by the requirement that it be capable of ranking sentences along a dimension ranging from the fully grammatical to the totally unstructured. It was apparently believed by Chomsky that for this new role there need be no new requirements on the form and operation of the generative apparatus itself. In Chomsky and Miller (1963: 291) we read that a generative grammar, *defined as* a device which enumerates the grammatical sentences of a language and which assigns structural descriptions to each of these, may also be *regarded as* a device which assigns to any string presented to it a relative-grammaticality index. What is needed, apparently, is some system of conventions which governs the way in which the structure-assigning apparatus is to be consulted for determining, for any nonsentence, its degree of departure from full grammaticality.

The ordinary working grammarian, confronting this added responsibility, sees now three things to worry about. The first is whether he or anyone he trusts knows how to rank sentences according to their degree of deviation from full grammaticality; the second is whether there is a general way of determining, from the rules of grammar, a ranking of sentences which conforms to these judgments. His third problem is that he fails to understand why knowing what is wrong with each of two sentences should entail knowing whether one of them is worse off than the other.

One final enrichment of the concept of generative grammar is found in the view that a grammar which a grammarian constructs is a claim about something which speakers of the language have inside their skins and which makes them able to produce and comprehend the sentences, and many of the near-sentences, of their language (see Chomsky 1965: 3–9). With this addition the study of grammar takes on a new interest and importance, naturally; but with this addition one finds it particularly difficult to imagine in advance the precise nature of criteria for success. I will argue, nevertheless, that the most intelligible view of grammatical research sees it as the attempt to discover the internal rules which account for the rule-guided aspect of human linguistic abilities.

3.

The most simply conceived goal of a generative grammar, to go back to the beginning, is that of determining, for any sequence of elements in the vocabulary of the language, whether it is grammatical or ungrammatical.

The details of the technical side of this task are of little real interest to the ordinary working grammarian. He knows that to the extent that any genuine generative grammar is an effective theory, it will always be possible to tell, *if* a sentence is generated by the grammar, *that* it is generated by the grammar: one tries out the rules, using whatever heuristic tools one has at hand, until one finds the sentence in question, and declares that it is in the language. There is, to be sure, another issue—that of knowing for certain that a presented string is ungrammatical according to the grammar—but that question is related to subtle properties of grammars that are of little concern to the ordinary working grammarian. He is willing to assume that an interpreter of a generative grammar, given wit, luck, and patience, will be able to find out one way or another whether a given sentence is in or out.

What does concern him is the nontechnical problem of knowing whether the sentences that get in are the good ones and whether the sentences that get left out are the bad ones—whether, in other words, the grammar and the speakers make the same choices. He sees this as a problem because he knows that judgments about grammaticality are subject to all sorts of confusions between grammaticality and significance, acceptability, or intelligibility; he knows that even when speakers say they understand that they are to make judgments about grammaticality rather than these other things, they still disagree; he knows that sometimes people change their minds about whether a sentence is grammatical; and he finds the appeal to unending idiolectal variation somewhat unsatisfying.

There was a time when these uncertainties would not have bothered our grammarian: a decade or so ago there was little reason to doubt the 'clear cases principle' proclaimed in Chomsky (1957: 13–14). On this principle, native-speaker judgments are criteria of grammar constructing success only with respect to the clear cases. The grammarian begins by considering sentences like *I like ice cream* that are clearly grammatical and sequences like *Ice cream me the* that are clearly ungrammatical, and he constructs the simplest grammar which generates all the incontrovertibly grammatical sentences and fails to generate all the incontrovertibly ungrammatical sentences. The grammar, then, and not the grammarian, makes the decision about the unclear cases.

Today's grammarian finds little comfort in this principle, because he knows, if he has read Ross's thesis (Ross 1967), that the kinds of arguments that seem to bear very crucially on the nature and operation of syntactic systems involve him in grammaticality decisions that are extremely difficult to make. If he has seen studies of speech variation by Elliott, Legum, and Thompson (1969), he knows that properties of grammars and sentence configurations figure importantly in the description of idiolectal and stylistic differences, but not at all in a way that gives any primacy to a simple distinction between being in the language or out, being generated or not generated by the grammar.

The simplest criterion of success, which was to consist of checking the identity of being 'in the language' to being 'generated by the grammar,' does not do, in short, what our ordinary working grammarian had hoped it would do for him.

4.

But let us turn to another problem, that of designing a grammar capable of assigning degrees of grammaticality. Chomsky's theory of relative grammaticality (Chomsky 1965: 148–54) takes roughly the following form. The grammar generates the set of fully grammatical sentences in a more or less straightforward way. For a string of words not found among the fully grammatical sentences, its degree of deviation from full grammaticality can be computed by comparing it with the grammatical sentences to which it is in some ways similar.

The procedure may be thought of as including something like the following steps. For each deviant string one identifies the set of sentences maximally similar to it. One identifies the properties which the deviant and grammatical sentences have in common, and in doing that one isolates just those properties which are 'out of place.' If an 'out–of–place' element is a constituent of a major category not found in that position in the grammatical sentences, the deviation is particularly serious—we may say that the string loses three points. Where an out–of–place element is of an appropriate category but has grammatical properties not found in that position in any of the fully grammatical sentences, the deviation is of minimal seriousness—the string loses one point. Where an out–of–place element is of an appropriate major category according to part of its context but ordinarily requires a categorial environment of a type not found in the string in question, the offense is of medium seriousness—the string loses two points. The degree of deviance of the string as a whole might be registered, in the most simple-minded rendering of this procedure, as the sum of the values of these various offenses.

The deviance-computing procedure I have just sketched, as well as subtler variations on it, has to be based on the assumption that it is in principle possible to identify, for a deviant string, just those lexical items or features which are out of place, or just those orderings of elements which are inappropriate. Even if we agree to allow multiple ways of recognizing the out–of–place elements—that is, even if we are willing to record certain strings as ambiguously deviant—we still must face the ill-defined problem of determining which portion of a deviant string provides the framework within which the rest can be described as out of place.

For any attempt to deal with this task, we have to distinguish between a deviant string of words taken in the abstract and a deviant or mistaken utterance. We shall find for the former that there is simply no possibility of determining in any absolute way its degree of departure from full grammaticality. In the latter case, an account of deviant utterances must take two cases into account: mistakes, as in the speech performance of children, drunkards, and foreigners (and the rest of us when we are off our guard), where what is of interest is a comparison between what was intended and what was said; and figurative speech, where what is of interest is the structural type which the speaker wants the hearer to perceive as a framework upon which the hearer's 'construing' abilities can impose some sort of interpretation—hopefully the intended interpretation.

To see what is involved for strings of words considered *in vacuo*, we can take the most favorable case—that of strings which happen to be identical to sentences generated by a grammar which differs in minor ways from the grammar which provides the measure. Suppose, for example, that we wish to say something about the sentences produced by a speaker of a nonstandard dialect of English and suppose that we wish to determine whether it makes sense to talk about the degree of deviation of his sentences from those of the standard dialect.

Given sentence (1), what we need to know first of all is whether it is to be compared with (2) in the standard dialect or with (3).

(1) I seen it.

(2) I have seen it

(3) I saw it.

Depending on which of the latter two is taken to be the basis of comparison, sentence (1) is deviant either by virtue of an omission or by virtue of a substitution. If the index we need is something which grades strings of words along the grammaticality dimension, it must be a meaningful question to ask whether the string comes out as more ungrammatical under one of these interpretations than under the other, and it must likewise make sense to ask whether the intuitions of native speakers of the standard dialect can be called on to decide which interpretation is correct. Such inquiry, surely, does not lead to an understanding of where (1) fails with respect to the standard dialect.

Of course, in order to know which comparison is the 'right' one, we need to know whether the rules of the dialect from which we have taken our sample allow the perfect auxiliary *have* to be contracted to zero (where the standard dialect requires retention of the final fricative), or whether these rules specify *seen* as the preterite form of *see*. In case the source dialect has nothing corresponding to the standard dialect contrast between (2) and (3), our problem is more serious still: are we to say that the dialect has only the perfect form, with the auxiliary deleted; that it has only the preterite form, realized phonologically as *seen*; or that, having the two constructions distinct at some level of analysis, the rules neutralize them in surface sentences? The answers to these questions involve detailed comparison of the grammatical rules of the separate dialects, but can in no meaningful way, as far as I can tell, be expressed as information about (1) as viewed from the standard dialect.

With (1) we have the simplest possible case, and yet there were these uncertainties. The situation with random word sequences is totally beyond hope. That becomes obvious as soon as we realize that the possibilities available for matching any one of these with a set of grammatical sentences include the operations of order change, insertion, deletion, or replacement of elements, and unrestricted combinations of these.

For utterances that are deviant by mistake, the relevant comparison is between the actual utterance and the intended utterance; but in this case, (*a*) it is not always possible to know what the intended utterance is, and (*b*) it does not matter whether the actual occurring utterance is, in the abstract, grammatical or not.

What is needed is some apparatus for pairing any string of words with any structural description, and providing some index of the degree of fit between the description and the string, the value of this index determined by an operation which relates the lexical information associated with the individual words of the string with the structural description. Such a device is what we find elaborated in Lakoff (1965). By Lakoff's procedure, any string will have an indefinitely large number of grammaticality values according to the infinite number of structural descriptions that can be brought into association with it. For a fully grammatical sentence there will be at least one structural description which it satisfies completely. An ambiguous grammatical sentence will show perfect fit with two or more structural descriptions—one for each of its possible interpretations. Working out the details requires giving different weight to distinct types of 'poor fit.' All such decisions will involve appeals to native-speaker judgments of some sort, but technically the thing seems feasible.

But notice what happens to our understanding of the working of a generative grammar when we adopt Lakoff's device. The syntactic component specifies the set of well-formed structural descriptions. The dictionary component associates with each lexical item a set of syntactic, semantic, and phonological properties, the syntactic properties understood as including information about insertability into deep-structure configurations and sensitivity to grammatical rules. The relative-grammaticality algorithm automatically assigns a grammaticality index to each ordered pair in which the first clement is a sequence of lexical items and the second is a structural description.

Under Lakoff's proposal a generative grammar can do what I think Chomsky suggested a generative grammar ought to do, i.e., serve as a grammaticality-index assigning mechanism. But the whole thing depends crucially on having correct information about the lexical items of the language. How are we to discover, our ordinary working grammarian asks, what are the correct lexical properties of the words and morphemes of a language? Can it be, he frets, that the difficulties of knowing correctly the grammar and semantics of lexical items are of the same order of magnitude as those of determining the grammaticality of sentences?

These worries of his are, I think, justified. Presumably, we are to determine the grammatical properties of lexical items by comparing deviant with nondeviant uses of them. We know that *resemble* is unpassivizable, for example, because speakers of English tell us that while (4) is grammatical, (5) is not.

(4)   John resembles a horse.

(5)   A horse is resembled by John.

But, of course, there are in fact some speakers of English who tell us that the passive sentence is not ungrammatical. That means that when we observe a seemingly deviant use of a lexical item, we must ask whether this usage constitutes a departure from conventions provided by that speaker's language, whether the speaker's language differs in relevant ways from the language we have been considering, or whether his judgments on grammaticality are sometimes inaccurate. In other words, we must be able to ask whether the speaker regularly uses the word in ways of which the observed usage is an instance, or whether in this situation he made a mistake.

Two examples will demonstrate the difficulty in knowing what the facts are. The first is an elementary case of figurative speech. Although it is certainly possible to come up with clear cases, it is frequently in practice impossible to know, even in one's own speech, whether a word has been used figuratively, in the creative sense, or whether it is simply polysemous in the needed way. The use of the word *bitch* in referring to an unpleasant adult female human was clearly figurative in its first instance, but when we find people who hesitate to use the word when speaking of a female dog, it is apparent that for them the insulting sense of the word does not draw on their creative abilities. A description of this state of affairs in terms of the marking of deviance would run like this: somebody whose lexicon contains only the literal interpretation of the noun but who is observed to use it nevertheless when referring to human beings has made a creative extension of the scope of the word that is accounted for by reference to the knowledge that participants in our civilization use attributions to human beings of nonhuman animal properties for pejoration; somebody who does not use the word when referring to female dogs lacks the original sense and has a lexical entry for *bitch* with the pejorative sense built in rather than acquired by a construal principle.

Unfortunately, an empirically indistinguishable account is found in the claim that some speakers have two descriptions of the word, others only one. On this interpretation, the acquisition of the nonliteral sense is an event in the history of the language. I know of no reasonable proposals for evaluating these alternative accounts.

For a second example, I turn to the fact that some speakers of English do not use *convince* in the same ways they use *persuade*. They allow themselves to say (6) but not (7).

(6) We persuaded him to come.

(7) We convinced him to come.

Suppose, knowing that, we hear our informant say (7). We may say that his internal grammar makes the distinction just mentioned, but that he has generalized the infinitive complement construction to the verb *convince* this one time; or that he is in the process of acquiring the more generalized rule; or that he was imitating speakers of a lesser dialect; or that he mistakenly produced this utterance by choosing the word *convince* when he intended *persuade*; or, of course, we might simply say that in his lexicon *convince* and *persuade* are given, apart from their phonology, identical descriptions.

There are, then, uncertainties about the proper way of interpreting apparently different uses of lexical items and uncertainties about the accessibility of correct lexical information in general. Appeals to introspection, the compilation of questionnaire results, and claims about idiolectal variation seem not always to point to the truth. Grammatical theory needs instead to consider deviance marking as a precise formal problem, and this it can do by applying to lexical descriptions something akin to Lakoff's proposal for computing relative grammaticality. The lexicon is a device which characterizes well-formed lexical entries but fails to associate phonological material (i.e., 'lexical items') with lexical descriptions. Grammatical theory can now be thought of as providing a way of registering the degree of grammaticality of word strings with respect to structural descriptions *if the lexical descriptions of the words are known.* This is accomplished by associating any sequence of clusters of lexical features—minus the phonological content—with any structural description. The grammar is able to assign indices of relative grammaticality, but only to ordered pairs of lexical description sequences and structural descriptions. The grammar says, in effect: if you can find strings of words that have such–and–such properties, then I can tell you exactly how well they fit any structural description.

If this is what a generative grammar is to do, it has managed to get as far as possible from its initial goal of specifying the well-formed sequences of words. The fact is, of course, that we have by this time completely lost the attention of our ordinary working grammarian. He wants to know just what these deviance markings are for, and he has serious doubts about whether the speaker's intuitive judgments on grammatically deviant sentences can be accounted for in general in terms of misordering errors and category substitutions of the sort he sees this device capable of detecting. Our grammarian knows first of all that the construal principles for a great many instances of metaphor involve understandings about objects and events rather than properties of the linguistic elements which give expression to these objects and events. More than that, he can think of many cases of what he insists on considering deviant uses of language but which cannot be described by any of the grammar-bound plans for characterizing deviance that have been proposed.

I have in mind a situation like the following. Journalists these days have been made conscious of the jeopardy to justice (or at least the danger of a libel suit) that results from public assignment of guilt to their fellow citizens. They have been instructed to heed certain rules of thumb that are supposed to keep them out of trouble, and among these, I assume, are the following: 'Never say of a person who committed a crime that he did it, only that he *allegedly* did it.' 'Never call the person who committed the crime the culprit, or the murderer, or the burglar, until after the trial; call him instead the *suspect.*'

As a result of sincere obedience to these injunctions, journalists (perhaps most noticeably in Columbus, Ohio) have acquired odd uses of the adverb *allegedly* and the noun *suspect*. Recently I heard on the evening news in Columbus:

(8) Six members of the Students for a Democratic Society were charged with allegedly distributing inflammatory literature.

(I am assuming, incidentally, that they were charged with *actually* distributing inflammatory literature; if they were only charged with allegedly doing this, then they were surely guilty, and my point is lost.) In a report on the burglary of a milk store in my city, the local evening newspaper reported:

(9) The police have no clues as to the identity of the suspect.

There was of course no suspect: they had no clues on the identity of the burglar.

These are assuredly deviant uses of the words in question, and I believe they would be recognized as such by their authors if they had had time to edit what they had written. But it seems to me that a correct description of the nature of the deviance is not the sort of thing that can be provided by a generative grammar rigged to assign grammaticality indices. I may be wrong, but I find it difficult to imagine how such an algorithm could successfully mark the two sentences I came across as being more acceptable in journalese than such technically equally odd sentences as (10) and (11).

(10) He wanted the children to allegedly rob the flower girl.

(11) I hope no suspect burns our house down while we're on vacation.

The deviant uses I have been discussing simply do not involve category errors of familiar kinds.

Uncertainties about the ways in which lexical items figure in the operation of a deviance-marking apparatus brings one face to face with the question of analogy in speech behavior. Although I have agreed with and once contributed to the body of unkind words people have directed toward a little book called *State of the Art* (Hockett 1968), I find myself convinced that in the description of changes in the lexicon, the appeal to changes in the content of grammatical rules faces a number of serious difficulties. Consider the recent popularity of event nouns used in the context of social protest in which the first element is a verb and the second element is the preposition *in*, as in *sit-in*, *love-in*, etc. I believe I am correct in my understanding that *sit-in* was the first of these. The ordinary working grammarian in me wonders how we are to describe what happened when *sit-in* became a part of the English lexicon. Were there changes in the derivational rules of the language? Was it registered as an unanalyzed lexical item? Or what?

If *sit-in* entered the language as an unanalyzed lexical item, then it had no influence on the rules, since only generative rules assign structural descriptions. If the word did have an analysis, then there either must be some supplementary apparatus for assigning structure to lexical items, or it must be taken as being generated by a possibly newly created generative rule.

Suppose we take this last position, since it is the only one that is intelligible within the framework of generative grammar. What is the nature of this newly created rule? If the rule is stated as one which takes any verb, shall we say that *sit* was marked, for a while, as the only verb to which it could apply? Shall we say that the scope of the rule was perfectly general, and merely observe as a fact about the history of usage that nobody bothered to use it for anything but the verb *sit* for the first few months after the introduction of the rule? (If the answer to this second question is yes, then we must understand the occurrence of the later words in the way that we understand the constructibility of novel sentences.)

But if the original rule was an exceptional one, applying only to *sit*, then what are we to say about such later additions as *wade-in*, *pray-in*, and *strip-in*? Are we to say that at the later stage the rule became generalized so as to include any verb, or any of a certain type of verb, or are we to say that the grammar became more complicated by virtue of having the relevant exception features added to the verbs *wade*, *pray*, *love*, and the rest? If we accept that the rule was originally general enough to include any verb, in some strict

sense of 'verb,' was it in fact general enough to include the later hippie creation, *be-in*? If not, with the extension to *be* are we to say that the rule was
further generalized or that it was made more specific so as to include *be*?

These are all, quite obviously, senseless questions. It would never occur
to anyone today to line up all these alternatives and to worry seriously about
which is to be preferred, if only because we remember how silly certain older
works seem in which we are taught five alternative analyses of the word *took*.
We have here one of those cases where we might indeed agree to say, with
Hockett, that somebody made up a word, the word caught on, other people
apprehended a pattern and made up some new words on the same pattern. A
reconstruction of this history in the form of a sequence of changes in systems
of generative rules would strike the ordinary working grammarian as nothing
more than allegiance to a ritual form. However we eventually manage to deal
with descriptive problems of this sort, it is at least very clear that in none of
this inquiry would it have been of any help to have available to us a metric of
relative grammaticality.

5.

I have said that it is difficult to see how a generative grammar can be required
to demarcate all and only the grammatical sentences of a language in view of
some rather serious questions about the empirical determinability of that set;
and I have said that it is impossible to imagine any way in which a generative
grammar can assign grammaticality indices to deviant sentences. I turn now
to a brief consideration of the ways in which a grammar assigns structural
descriptions to the sentences which it generates.

The theory of transformational grammar makes available for structural
descriptions of sentences (1) the categories of the base rules; (2) the domination relations that are defined initially by the rules of the base and are adjusted
by the transformations; (3) the left–to–right sequence of elements; (4) information about permitted cooccurrences in particular structures; and (5) information found in the lexicon regarding (*a*) insertability into deep-structure
configurations, (*b*) sensitivity to grammatical rules, and (*c*) the semantic
structure of lexical items. A grammar is judged as adequate in one important
respect if it describes sentences in ways which match certain sorts of intuitive
judgments on the part of native speakers, if it captures certain aspects of their
knowledge about the sentences.

One specific descriptive problem, ordinarily taken to be the easiest, is
that of knowing whether a grammar gives the correct constituent-structure
analysis to the surface sentence. Considering the variety of ways in which
complex verbal expressions in English get parsed, I am ready to assume that

native-speaker intuitions about constituent structure are among the least important criteria for judging the adequacy of proposed descriptions.

But it is also likely that there are a great many facts about the grammatical interpretation of sentences which the devices of categories and sequence and domination fail to capture altogether, yet which must be a part of the generative grammarian's added burden if the goal of achieving descriptive adequacy is to be seriously sought after. I have in mind a number of descriptive problems connected with the treatment of focus, topicalization, reference, deep-structure cases, presuppositions, and illocutionary-act potential. The brute-force method of incorporating all these matters into the theory is to let assertions about them find their place in proposed underlying structures for sentences. Consider sentence (12) in this connection.

(12) Did I give you the other book?

The people called generative semanticists have been accumulating arguments according to which the underlying linguistic structure of (12) will ultimately have to be something which, when rendered into English, would read like (13).

(13) There is a set of books that both you and I know about and the cardinality of that set is some number n and you and I have just had in mind a subset containing $n-1$ of those books and I am now calling your attention to the remaining nth book. There was a time when I had that book in my possession and I am now asking you to tell me whether I did anything in the past which would count as causing that book to be in your possession

The speech-act function of the sentence is made explicit in the part about the speaker's requesting an answer from the hearer; the presuppositions are captured in the clauses preceding the operative clause; the category of definiteness is reconstructed as a set of assumptions about what the speaker believes the hearer to be 'having in mind'; and so on.

When the ordinary working grammarian sees such demonstrations, he is properly overwhelmed, but he has trouble believing that the principles by which these maximally abstract representations are to be mapped into the sentences of his language are principles that today's grammarians are equipped to discover. He feels, in fact, that he finds himself in the age of what we might call the New Taxonomy, an era of a new and exuberant cataloguing of the enormous range of facts that linguists need eventually to find theories to deal with. The attempt to capture fully the native speaker's intuitions about the structure and content of his sentences has led to observations which make it extremely difficult to believe in the simple and comforting things we believed in, about grammatical theory, just a few years ago.

6.

I see in much recent work a shift of interest away from the properties of an apparatus needed solely for generating the proper set of sentences, toward the mechanisms which speakers of a language can be shown to have, on the basis of any evidence within reach, which account for their ability to do what they do when they communicate with each other using their language. This switch of emphasis to the system itself, and away from the in–or–out judgments associated with the strict notion of generative grammar, makes it possible to ask new kinds of questions. Let me give an example of what I mean.

When grammar construction is seen as a purely formal task, one of the desiderata of a grammar must be its completeness. In evaluating a grammar which is to generate all and only the sentences of a language, we cannot tolerate a situation in which symbols are introduced at one point and never interpreted or operated on by later rules. It is possible, I want to suggest, that a grammar which exhibits the workings of a natural language cannot meet such a requirement.

It may be that an earlier portion of a grammar allows the introduction of a structure even though the remaining rules of the grammar fail to assign it an acceptable surface form. For types of phenomena that have concerned Perlmutter (in Perlmutter 1968), such a failure is to be accounted for in terms of surface-structure constraints. Surface-structure constraints, however, make up a fairly clearly defined segment of the grammar itself, and their justification is based on their contribution to the task of isolating grammatical from ungrammatical strings. The issue I am about to bring up is different.

In general, tag questions in English are constructed by adding to any assertive sentence an interrogative piece which contains as subject a pronoun which matches the surface subject of the main sentence, and a pro-verb-phrase which corresponds to the predicate of the main sentence and which is negative in case the main sentence is affirmative, and vice versa. What we need to be able to say about English is that a tag question formative can be chosen with any assertive sentence but the rules for constructing tag questions out of such combinations fail to cover all cases.

People have trouble with tag questions after such sentences as (14), (15), (16), and (17).

(14) Somebody's out there.

(15) Somebody tried to get in.

(16) I'm competent to do that.

(17) One of us could go.

The rule for forming the tag question requires the selection of an appropriate pronoun. *Somebody* is human and singular and unmarked for gender. *It* is nonhuman, *he* and *she* are marked for gender, and *they* is plural. There is no pronoun which matches it. From the paraphrasability of (14) with (18) many people say (19), but others end up with (20) or (21) and still others give up.

(18) There's somebody out there.

(19) Somebody's out there, isn't there?

(20) Somebody's out there, isn't he?

(21) Somebody's out there, aren't they?

For a sentence like (15) some people say (22), and others give up, I have heard myself say (23).

(22) Somebody tried to get in, didn't they?

(23) Somebody tried to get in, didn't there?

For (16) some people accept (24), a great many allow themselves to say (25), but many others simply do not know what to say.

(24) I'm competent to do that, aren't I?

(25) I'm competent to do that, ain't I?

For (17) the best thing is to make a joke out of it:

(26) *One* of us could go, couldn't you?

Our grammar sometimes fails us.

Observations like these are certainly familiar, and for illustrating my point I could just as well have considered the rules for subject-verb agreement and their failure to yield grammatical sentences corresponding to (27) and (28).

(27) Either he or I is always on duty.

(28) Either he or I am always on duty.

The recognition of problems of this sort is the recognition of what people try to say, how their grammars fail them, and how eventually they invent a new form, they go ahead and say something they feel is ungrammatical, or they give up. To account for such situations we must allow grammars to be 'incomplete' in just the right ways, that is, for just those situations in which the creative part of a grammar sets up something which the interpretive part cannot cope with.[2]

7.

The ordinary working grammarian learns what he can about the grammatical processes which are available to the producers of sentences, and he uses what he knows of these processes for describing these sentences. He welcomes Chomsky's discussions of the nonaccessibility of correct grammaticality judgments, because without the 'clear cases principle' to guide him, he knows of no way to bring to his task of writing a grammar the evidence of grammaticality judgments. He wants to know what sorts of things can go wrong in the production of an utterance, and what kinds of freedom creative users of language have for constructing sentences or near-sentences in their language. He does not want to be responsible for a relative grammaticality ranking of utterances or utterance-description pairs.

He will be glad if he can be reassured that his success as a grammarian will not be measured on the basis of his ability to demonstrate that his grammar does everything that generative grammars have been said to have to do. I believe he deserves such reassurance.

Knowing what he does not have to do will not give him reliable insights into what he does have to do, unfortunately, but that is because the ordinary working grammarian I have in mind is exactly as confused as I am about that. If he is a practitioner of the New Taxonomy, he is having a good time. It is possible to remain happy, for a while, without well-defined goals.

---

[2] It should be pointed out, incidentally, that the discovery of this sort of operative failure in a grammar offers no comfort to those persistent spokesmen for the inherent vagueness of grammars. Grammars may indeed have areas of unimprovable vagueness, but the facts about English that I have been discussing can be made totally explicit. What gives the native speaker the impression of vagueness is his uncertainty about knowing what to do when he wants to say something which his grammar—in ways unknown to him—fails to allow him to say.

References

Chomsky, N. 1957. *Syntactic Structures*. The Hague: Mouton.

Chomsky, N. 1965. *Aspects of the Theory of Syntax*. Cambridge. M.I.T. Press.

Chomsky, N., and Miller, G. A. 1963. Introduction to the formal analysis of natural languages. *Handbook of Mathematical Psychology, vol. 11*, ed. R. D. Luce et al., 269–321. New York: Wiley.

Elliott, D, Legum S., and Thompson, S. A. 1969. Syntactic variation as linguistic data. *Papers from the 95th Regional Meeting of the Chicago Linguistic Society*, ed. R. Binnick et al., 52–59. Chicago: University of Chicago Linguistics Department.

Hockett, C. F. 1968. *The State of the Art*. The Hague: Mouton.

Katz, J. J. 1966. *The Philosophy of Language*. New York: Harper & Row.

Lakoff, G. 1965. On the Nature of Syntactic Irregularity. Ph.D. dissertation Indiana University.

Perlmutter, D. 1968. Deep and Surface Structure Constraints in Syntax. Ph.D. dissertation, M.I.T.

Ross, J. R. 1967. Constraints on Variables in Syntax. Ph.D. dissertation, M.I.T.

Thorne, J. P. 1968. Grammars and machines. *Language*, ed. R. C. Oldfield and J. C. Marshall, 293–306. New York: Penguin.

2

Innocence: A Second Idealization for Linguistics

1979
CHARLES J. FILLMORE

1.

The nature of the fit between predictions generated by a theory and the phenomena within its domain can sometimes be assessed only when different
sources of explanation can be isolated through one or more idealizations. One
such idealization is the simplifying assumption, for the laws of Newtonian
mechanics, that the physical bodies whose movements fall within their scope
are (or can be treated as) dimensionless particles, not subject to distortion or
friction. The empirical laws of elasticity and friction are themselves best formulated against this background idealization.

The most frequently discussed idealization in linguistics in recent years
has been that of the *ideal speaker/hearer in a homogeneous speech community* (Chomsky 1965:3). By means of this idealization, through which we have
learned a distinction between *competence* and *performance*, we are in principle able to separate out of the heterogeneous and disorderly data of speech,

(i)   the systematic knowledge native speakers have about their gram-
        mars,
(ii)   variation in the details of such linguistic systems from person to
        person, and
(iii)   the effects on speech of fluctuations in speakers' attentiveness to
        their own texts, memory breakdowns in the course of a text's plan-
        ning, any of the various kinds of speech defects, and interruptions
        from the surrounding world.

I am going to suggest that there is a second idealization operating in linguistics, one which underlies most traditions of semantics, and which I think it would be well to bring out into the open for careful discussion. This second idealization involves what I shall call the *innocent speaker/hearer*. In the way that, under the familiar idealization, the general theory of linguistic competence can be thought of as more or less equivalent to a theory of language perfomance on the part of an *ideal speaker/hearer*, we might say of certain theories of semantics that they are theories of the language understanding abilities of the innocent speaker/hearer.

I characterize the innocent language user as follows. It knows the morphemes of its language and their meanings, it recognizes the grammatical structures and processes in which these morphemes take part, and it knows the semantic import of each of these. As a decoder, or hearer, the innocent language user calculates the meaning of each sentence from what it knows about the sentence's parts and their organization. It makes no use of past calculations: each time a structure or sentence reappears, it is calculated anew. As an encoder, or speaker, the innocent language user decides what it wishes its interlocutors to do or feel or believe and constructs a message which expresses that decision as directly as possible. There are no layers of inference between what it says and what it means.

The innocent speaker/hearer is in principle capable of saying anything sayable, given enough time. That is, its semantic system satisfies Jerrold Katz's condition of Effability and hence qualifies as a full-fledged natural language system (Katz 1972:18). But the discourse of innocents tends to be slow, boring, and pedantic.

One early statement of our idealization is in Bloomfield's discussion of *sememes* and *episememes*. The smallest meaningful units of lexical form are morphemes, and their meanings, we learn, are sememes; the smallest meaningful units of grammatical form are tagmemes, and their meanings are episememes. Formally any utterance can be described as a collection of lexical and grammatical forms; semantically any utterance can be described as an assembly of its sememes and episememes[1] (Bloomfield 1933:166).

In more recent work the semantic capabilities of an innocent speaker/hearer have come to be spoken of in terms of *compositionality*, a term first used, I think, in Katz and Fodor's 1963 paper on the structure of a semantic theory (Katz and Fodor 1963:171). More recently still John Searle has equated the idea of a compositional semantics with an assumption about the determination of a sentence's 'literal meaning.' In his formulation of that

---

[1] Bloomfield insists, I should point out, that any effort to characterize the sememes and episememes substantively belongs outside of linguistics proper. He seems to be saying that *if* we knew what these things were, we would know, as linguists, what to do with them.

assumption '[T]he literal meaning of a sentence is entirely determined by the meanings of its component words (or morphemes) and the syntactical rules according to which these elements are combined' (Searle 1978:207).

The model of semantic competence which fits this idealization is one which contains a lexicon, a way of characterizing grammatical structures, and a set of semantic integration rules. The model is not embarrassed by ambiguity, synonymy, homonymy or vagueness. A necessary characteristic of the model is that the meaning of a sentence in a given context is a selection from a set of meanings which the sentence has out of context. Any semantic theory which treats the determination of sentence meaning in context by a meaning constructing rather than a meaning selecting process goes beyond the powers of the innocence model.

2.

An innocent speaker/hearer can do all of the things I said it can do, but it has several important limitations:

(1) It does not know lexical idioms, that is, lexical forms whose meanings could not be determined by somebody who knew merely their morphological structure and the meanings of their constituent morphemes. Knowing *jail* and *prison* and all possible uses of the *-er* suffix could not enable an innocent to figure out the difference in meaning between *jailer* and *prisoner*.[2]

(2) The innocent language user does not know phrasal idioms. If you were to go up to it and say, *your goose is cooked!*, it would feel worried if it had a pet goose, grateful if it had just brought a goose carcass home for dinner, or puzzled if it had no goose at all. But it would lack the idiomatic interpretation that the rest of us are able to give the expression.

(3) The innocent language user does not know *lexical collocations that are not based on necessary meaning relations*. If it knows the expression *blithering idiot* at all, it has to assume that *blithering* is a form of the verb *blither* and that it can be used of anything that 'blithers.' Understanding only the meanings of the words, it has no reason to know that *blithering* is limited to the context in which it modifies *idiot*.[3]

---

[2] My phrase 'the *-er* suffix' represents an implicit synchronic judgment about the structure of these words. The etymologically sophisticated will find the *jailer/prisoner* examples unfair. The claim, however, is simply that ordinary speakers will see these words as made up of stem plus *-er*.

[3] There is a problem, of course, in deciding what it is to 'know the meaning of' a word that has such tight collocational requirements, especially since the expression is almost never used in

(4) It lacks the ability to judge the appropriateness of fixed expressions to specific types of situations. It has no situational associations with such expressions as *this hurts me more than it hurts you* or *this is where I came in*, to say nothing of such semantically opaque locutions as *knock on wood* or *speak of the devil*.

(5) It possesses no construal principles for metaphorical language use, nor, in fact, does it have any reason to believe that language can be used metaphorically. It is accordingly ignorant of the conventional images that provide grounding for metaphoric interpretation in its language. Suppose we induced it to try to interpret the metaphoric utterance, *I'll stand behind you*. It has no basis for preferring the image of a person falling backwards, an image which would allow the utterance to be taken as comforting, over that of a person falling forwards, in which case the expression could be taken as threatening.[4]

(6) In general the innocent language user lacks any interpretive mechanisms for indirect communication, that is, for meaning one thing while saying another, or principles of text coherence that would allow it to 'read between the lines' in a text. If we can suppose that it enjoys being flattered, then it will indeed be flattered if we say to it, *you have a very lovely left eye*.[5]

(7) The innocent one has no background of understanding for what might be called text structure. That is, it is unable to 'situate' pieces of text within slots defined for given kinds of texts. One of the clearest examples of the kind of 'situating' I have in mind is provided by a convention in Japanese letter writing. Personal letters in Japan are expected to begin with a preamble which contains comments on the current season. The innocent, on reading at the beginning of a letter that its Japanese correspondent's garden floor is covered with leaves will not realize that this remark serves to satisfy that convention.[6]

---

what might be called its 'literal' meaning. Until just a few days ago, I myself believed that *blithering* meant 'drooling.'

[4] This example is borrowed from George Lakoff.

[5] It does not know Oswald Ducrot's 'loi d'exhaustivité' (Ducrot 1972:170) or Paul Grice's 'Quantity maxim' (Grice 1975:45).

[6] Nor is the innocent in a position to appreciate the following facts: (i) that urgent letters in which the seasonal remarks are left out usually begin with an apology, one version of which is the word *zenryaku*, an abbreviation of a larger expression which means 'apology for omitting the preamble'; and (ii) that the Kenkyusha Japanese–English dictionary defines *zenryaku* as 'I hasten to inform you that …'.

Summarizing, the innocent speaker/hearer does not know about lexical idioms, phrasal idioms, lexical collocations, situational formulas, indirect communication, or the expected structures of texts of given types. The collections of things the innocent language user does not know gives us a catalogue of the kinds of uses of and responses to language that fall outside of the ideal of a pure compositional semantics. The innocence idealization is in fact frequently thought of as establishing the boundary between semantics proper and such neighboring concerns as pragmatics, rhetoric, logic, and language comprehension. I will be showing below that in this purest form the idealization has proved to be incompatible with the territorial urges of some semantic theorists.

3.

But first I need to introduce some new distinctions. The semantics of innocence is a compositional semantics, but I need to say more now about just what that means. I would like to begin by reviewing a distinction that is sometimes ignored, that between compositionality proper and motivation. An expression can be spoken of as motivated if the speakers of the language see it as having the form it has by virtue of some (possibly vaguely perceived) word-forming or phrase-forming principles. *Poet, poem* and *poetry* appear to be constructed out of partly identical material in a way that reflects their semantic commonality, and such words as *jailer* and *prisoner* have components that speakers see as related to their meanings. On the other hand, when we say that an expression's interpretation is compositional, we mean that the expression is more than merely 'motivated'; but what is that additional element?

To be clear about this we need to make another distinction. Here, as in many areas of linguistics, I think it is important to distinguish the *decoding*, or hearer's point of view from the *encoding*, or speaker's point of view. Applying these two perspectives in the case of compositionality, we can talk about *semantic transparency* in the decoding case, and *semantic productivity* in the encoding case. An expression is semantically transparent if we can rely on compositional semantics to figure out what it means once we encounter it. A set of syntactic-semantic rules is semantically productive if by relying on them we can succeed in producing fully natural ways of saying what we mean. The distinction I am making between the two 'directions' of compositionality bears on the distinction between two senses of the English adjective *idiomatic*. In the one case, were I to say that your speech is 'idiomatic' I would mean that it contains expressions which the innocent language user could not interpret. In the other case, in describing your speech as idiomatic, what I would mean is that it is what an accomplished native speaker would naturally say, and that means that it is not likely to be what an innocent would have chosen to say. The distinction I have just drawn is essentially the distinction between what Adam Makkai calls *idioms of decoding* and *idioms of encoding* (Makkai 1972).

4.

The problems linguists have in dealing with the innocence idealization have been in connection with fixed expressions, collocations, idioms, indirect communication, and the differences I have just been discussing regarding motivation and compositionality. Many theoretical moves that semanticists have made seem to be directed toward increasing the domain of semantics while *preserving innocence*. The goal is to reformulate semantic observations in such a way that the innocence idealization fits cases it didn't fit before the reformulation, thus reducing the need to look for new sources of explanation. Compositional semantics, after all, is dependable and formally easy to cope with: the more that can be brought into its scope the better off we are. Or so it is sometimes thought.

(1)   One of the innocence preserving moves that I have in mind involves the context restriction of the senses of a polysemous word. What may have looked like a lexical or phrasal idiom will turn out to fit a purely compositional semantics if we allow ourselves to say that some of the morphemes have senses that just happen to be limited to this specific context. Zellig Harris has a beautiful formulation of this principle, using *blueberry* as his key example. He states, "the meaning of an element in each linguistic environment is the difference between the meaning of its linguistic environment and the meaning of the whole utterance (i.e. the whole social situation). Thus the meaning of *blue* in blueberry might be said to be the meaning of *blueberry* minus the meaning of *berry* and of the '– – morpheme: *blue* here therefore does not mean simply a color, but the observable differentia of blueberries as against other berries." (Harris 1951:347). Instead of saying that the word *blueberry* is a composite word which somebody in the history of the English-speaking people invented as a name for a particular genus of berries, a formulation which departs from innocence, we can now be pleased to realize that the word contains exactly the right morphemes and that these together, by completely regular rules, designate exactly this genus of berries.

(2)   The Hungarian semanticist László Antal preserves innocence in a far different way: he does so by insisting on a sharp distinction between *meaning* and *content*. To Antal, every morpheme has a unique

meaning, and every expression composed of morphemes has a meaning exactly represented by that assembly of morphemes. Content, by contrast, appears only with sentences and texts, not with words, and can be described only by using knowledge of facts that are clearly outside of linguistics. Meaning and content, Antal says, "differ from each other in that the former is broken down into smaller parts, while content manifests itself as an undivided whole." This, he goes on, "is because the meaning of the sentence is made up of the meanings of the individual morphemes that occur in it." Antal would say that the meaning differences separating *Peter lost his way*, *Peter lost his mind*, *Peter lost his job* and *Peter lost his patience* are to be found precisely and unambiguously in the meaning differences separating *way*, *mind*, *patience* and *job*.[7] Their differences in content are not so orderly; but that, according to Antal, is not the semanticist's concern (Antal 1964:23).

(3) A third move for preserving innocence is that taken by Charles Hockett; it is a decision by which expressions which might appear to some people to be morphologically complex and semantically irregular turn out to be primary linguistic units and hence to offer no challenge to compositional semantics. One way of accomplishing this kind of redefinitional solution would be to extend the range of the term morpheme to include lexical and phrasal idioms. At the lexical level this would be to say that such words as *refer*, *prefer*, *recede* and *precede* are synchronically four separate undivided morphemes whose internal structures have only etymological relevance. Hockett's choice, by contrast, was to generalize the term *idiom* to make it include morphemes. If an idiom is a linguistic form whose meaning is not built up out of the meanings of its constituent parts, then morphemes are idioms. Having made this terminological choice, Hockett can then claim that "any utterance consists wholly of an integral number of idioms. Any composite form which is not itself idiomatic consists of smaller forms which are." (Hockett 1958:173). We are left, then, with a uniform class of primary meaning bearing elements, and no troublesome distinction between morphemes and idioms.

This decision appears to leave us with the problem of not being able to recognize that certain expressions are simultaneously fixed expressions *and* semantically motivated. One possible solution—I don't know whether this would be Hockett's solution—is to regard

---

[7] Antal's examples include only *patience* and *job*, not the other two. It is clear from the context, however, that he would accept the statement I made about the four sentences.

what I see as a descriptive problem as simply involving the distinction between a pure synchronic description of a language on the one hand and on the other hand whatever knowledge or beliefs speakers may have of the motivational basis of given linguistic forms at the time they were introduced into the language.

(4) A fourth common move to preserve innocence is one which claims a sharp distinction between knowledge about shared meanings and knowledge about the world. By distinguishing, as it is sometimes put, a dictionary and an encyclopedia, we can allow ourselves to say that the innocent speaker/hearer can know everything about the meaning of a sentence independently of knowing anything at all about what the world is like.

The relevance of such a decision to the question of innocence is that it allows a distinction between two kinds of judgments about the acceptability of sentences, the one having to do with true semantic compatibility and the other with truth or plausibility. The semantic integration principles operate by accepting well-formed semantic complexes and rejecting ill-formed ones. This task is a more cleanly determined one if the meaning vs. world distinction is maintained. The analyst is left facing a number of decisions, however, that are extremely hard to make: to borrow a favorite example of John Searle's, we might wonder what could possibly be the difference between a description of an oscilloscope and a statement of the meaning of the noun *oscilloscope*.[8]

(5) A fifth move to preserve innocence is that of minimizing the appearance of polysemy in semantic description and formulating invariant meanings for all uses of a morpheme or word. Rather than describing the phrase *cut the cards*, in the sense of dividing and restacking a deck of playing cards, as an idiom, we could simply try to formulate the meaning of the verb *cut* in such a way that it included all of the uncontested uses of the verb plus the use we see in this expression.

A commitment to the formulation of invariant or 'core' meanings, a position associated in general with Dwight Bolinger (Bolinger 1977) and with respect to grammatical morphemes in the work of Roman Jakobson (Jakobson 1936) and William Diver (Diver 1964), puts its holders into an essentially unassailable position. My argument against it is that when you have captured the core

---

[8] There is no doubt that for a great many cases such a distinction is necessary, but there is clearly a problem of knowing where to draw the line. For a typical statement, see Leech (1974: 87).

meanings of everything, you have no basis for knowing which combinations of words have which meanings. The core-meaning linguist insists that morphemes have just the meanings that they have, and that people who see a problem in constructing composite meanings out of component meanings are confused about the difference between meaning and comprehension.

(6) One final innocence preserving strategy is the one which posits a finite number of possible relations that can link together the elements that make up a compound word.[9] Given this decision, we can say that the noun compounds *horse shoes* and *alligator shoes*, to use examples from Katz and Fodor (1963), are each ambiguous in many ways, and in the same ways. Each can designate shoes that are worn by the animal named, that are made out of that animal's skin, that are made in the shape of the animal, and so on. The fact that each of these has been lexicalized in English, conventionalized as a composite name with a specific assigned sense, can be taken as proper to the study of language use rather than semantics; and the fact that in detail the kinds of relationships we sense linking the parts of compounds do not appear to be neatly classifiable is merely to be taken as evidence for the abstractness of the underlying relationships (cf. Bolinger 1965:568).

5.

The innocence idealization has served linguistics well, at least as a heuristic for making linguists aware of the various modes of signifying; and in one form or another it is a necessary core of any theory capable of coping with the reality that speakers and hearers do indeed create and comprehend novel sentences. But I feel that the desire to generalize it has backed semanticists into analytical corners that they would have done well to stay out of. In particular, I believe that the facts which lie outside of anything the innocence model is capable of handling are so pervasive and powerful that nothing really important is gained by distorting the idealization in the way the innocence preservers have chosen to do. I am not arguing that the idealization be abandoned; only that it should be kept pure. There are three characteristics of the semantic systems of real speakers and hearers that seem absolutely critical in this connection.

The first of these is what might be referred to as the 'layering' of conventionality in language. With Jerry Morgan we can say that while we need to

---

[9] For a treatment exemplifying this approach as applied to the special class of 'complex nominals,' see Levi (1978).

recognize from the start the conventional or arbitrary nature of the relations between elementary signs and their meanings, we must also recognize conventional pairings of contexts with meanings-to-convey-in-those-contexts, as well as conventional pairings between contexts and particular expressions by which conventionalized meanings get conveyed in those contexts (Morgan 1978).

A second characteristic is the inescapable participation of context and background in constructing the meanings of utterances in actual use. Pamela Downing (Downing 1977), Herbert and Eve Clark (Clark and Clark 1978) and Geoffrey Nunberg (Nunberg 1977) have all given us an awareness of classes of expressions–in–use which have the following properties: they are not semantically transparent, they do not have conventionally assigned meanings, and they cannot be seen as instances of metaphoring acts of the usual kind; they are expressions for whose interpretation we *require* a detailed understanding of the participants' shared engagement in an experiential context. Once the operation of context is made clear in these obvious cases, it becomes possible for us to ask what role it plays in cases that used to appear to satisfy the idealization. I suspect that we will sometimes be surprised.

A third important characteristic of real language use is found in what I shall call *structural formulas*. A language's free phrases are limited only by the grammar and what people choose to say; fixed expressions have most of their lexical and grammatical, and maybe even their prosodic, properties fixed by convention. For the structural formulas that I have in mind, the grammatical form and possibly one or two lexical items are fixed, but the class of substitutions is open but constrained by semantic and pragmatic considerations. As an example, consider expressions of the form 'Someone plays Something to Someone's Something', as in *She played Desdemona to my Othello*, which I could use in reporting shared theatrical experiences she and I have had. As a second example, consider 'X in and X out' where X can be a word designating a cyclic calendric term, as in *day in and day out, year in and year out*, etc. (cf. Kiparsky 1976). Or consider the colloquial formula 'WATCH Something Happen', a very flexible construction beginning with 'imperative' *watch* and followed by an infinitive clause indicating a surprise which fate might have in store. (Examples: I've been insisting that you're too young to carry such a big tray of fruit, and I take it away from you. Then I say, *now watch me drop it*. We've been planning on a picnic for many days, and have just invested a lot of money in getting the supplies for it; I say, *now watch it rain*.[10]

---

[10] These expressions cannot be thought of merely as *uses* of imperative sentences with the normal embedding verb *watch*, since some of these expressions contain clausal elements that could not normally serve as complements of *watch*. I once heard an adolescent girl, who had

I expect that there are lots of structural formulas like this, each with its own private semantic interpretation rules. If the number and frequency of such constructions is very great, there might some day be semanticists who feel that the standard form of compositional semantics can be undermined altogether, by having its principles absorbed into the list of pairings of such formulas and specific semantic interpretation rules. It is conceivable that the central principle of truth conditional semantics could be introduced, in such a system, as an interpretation rule for a structural formula called 'indicative sentence.'

The argument that this last proposal is not altogether absurd must be saved for another occasion. For now let me just hope to have convinced you of the importance of distinguishing real innocence from pretended innocence.

---

been fretting at some length about how unimpressive her blind date was probably going to be, say *Now watch him be real handsome.*

References

Antal, L. 1964. *Content, Meaning and Understanding*. Mouton.

Bloomfield, L. 1933. *Language*. Holt, Rinehart and Winston.

Bolinger, D. 1965. The atomization of meaning. *Language* 41:555–573.

Bolinger, D. 1977. *Meaning and Form*. Longman.

Chomsky, N. 1965. *Aspects of the Theory of Syntax*. MIT Press.

Clark, H. H. and Clark, E. V. 1978. *When nouns surface as verbs*. ms.

Diver, W. 1964. The system of agency of the Latin noun. *Word* 20:178–196.

Downing, P. 1977. On the creation and use of English compound nouns. *Language* 53:810–842.

Ducrot, O. 1972. *Dire et ne pas dire. Principes de Semantique Linguistique*. Collection Savoir.

Harris, Z. S. 1951; 1960. *Structural Linguistics*. Phoenix.

Grice, H. P. 1975. Logic and conversation, *Syntax and Semantics Vol. III: Speech Acts*, eds. P. Cole and J. Morgan, 41–58. Academic Press.

Hockett, C. F. 1958. *A Course in Modern Linguistics*. Macmillan.

Jakobson, R. 1936; 1966. Beitrag zur allgemeinen Kasuslehre. TCLP 6.240–288; reprinted in Hamp, E., Householder, F., and Austerlitz, R. eds., *Readings in Linguistics II*. University of Chicago Press. 51–89.

Katz, J. J. 1972. *Semantic Theory*. Harper and Row.

Katz, J. J. and Fodor, J. A. 1963. The structure of a semantic theory. *Language* 39:170–210.

Kiparsky, P. 1976. Oral poetry: some linguistic and typological considerations. *Oral Literature and the Formula*, eds. B. A. Stolz and R. S. Shannon. University of Michigan.

Leech, G. 1974. *Semantics*. Penguin.

Levi, J. 1978. *The Syntax and Semantics of Complex Nominals*. Academic Press.

Makkai, A. 1972. *Idiom Structure in English*. Mouton.

Morgan, J. L. 1978. Two types of convention in indirect speech acts. *Syntax and Semantics Vol. IX: Pragmatics*, ed. P. Cole. Academic Press.

Nunberg, G. 1977. *The Pragmatics of Reference*. Ph.D. Dissertation, C.U.N.Y.

Searle, J. 1978. Literal meaning. *Erkenntnis* 13:207–224.

3

Some Thoughts on the Boundaries and Components of Linguistics

1984

CHARLES J. FILLMORE

1.

Anybody familiar with discussions in and around linguistics these days is accustomed to hearing people say things such as:

♦ 'We've got to distinguish the properties of the language faculty in the species from facts about individual languages. What you've just presented as a fact about English is really a fact about Language.' or
♦ 'Those are not questions of grammar; they're questions of usage.' or
♦ 'Why do you persist in giving structuralist explanations for facts that have only social-historical explanations?' etc.

I want to examine two closely related problems here. The first is that of deciding what does belong to a properly constituted science of language and what does not. The second is that of deciding how the components or subdomains of such a science need to be separated from one another. In general, my approach is to look at certain classes of facts and to ask what are the proper sources of explanation for such facts. In many cases my problem seems analogous to that of deciding, for a given piece of furniture, whether it fits well in one room rather than in another, or whether we ought to throw it away or give it to someone else.

I do not intend, except in one or two cases, to try to resolve these border-drawing questions, but I at least wish to examine the ways in which such issues have been discussed in recent years by linguists and their allies. The questions that need to be asked are:

♦ What kinds of observation fall within the scope of a given discipline?
♦ What methodological choices seem appropriate for a given discipline or subdomain of a discipline?
♦ What is the accepted explanatory base—that is, the standard form for statements of explanation—that a given scientific theory makes available to its disciples?

It is well known that scholars working in what might broadly and vaguely be called 'the science of language' differ importantly in respect to the cleanness with which they choose to define a central core of concern with language as such as opposed to questions about the use or context of language. Many linguists are motivated to make the circle small, liking to feel that they have closed off a territory that can be safely defended, around which a secure wall can be built, and within which everything can be known and labeled.[1] Many non-linguists too would like linguistics to be made clean and small, because that would make their own work more readily definable: if linguists could tell them precisely what 'language' or 'linguistic competence' is, then they in their turn could ask questions about how it is learned, how it is used, how it fits its contexts, and so on.[2] Linguists who choose to make the circle big, by contrast, might do so because their vision is grand, or because they enjoy the risk and excitement of having so many more things to keep track of.[3] Among those who draw the circle big are many who would not call themselves linguists at all, but are rather people who either work within a larger theory in which a science of linguistics is a proper part, or who hold to a theory that purports to deal with the data linguists concern themselves with but which finds no need for a well-defined science of linguistics within it.[4]

---

[1] See, for example, Bloch's and Trager's (1942:6) reasons for excluding meaning from linguistic inquiry, as well as Chomsky's (1982) differently motivated circumscription of 'core grammar'.

[2] See the discussion of the effect of generative linguistics on psycholinguistic research in Greene (1972).

[3] One important 'wide circle' linguist is Dell Hymes, whose 'ethnographic' position is laid out most clearly in Hymes (1974). Dwight Bolinger's 'wide circle' view of meaning is presented in Bolinger (1977). Perhaps the strongest statement favoring a widening of the field of linguistics is the 'Preamble' to the Ablex *Language and Being* series by G. P. Lakoff and J. R. Ross (first appearance in (1979, vii–viii).

[4] The language scientist best known for his independence from mainstream linguistics is perhaps Roger Schank. Numerous statements of this independence can be found in Schank (1975).

For ease of exposition, I shall refer to this broadly conceived 'science of language' as 'linguistics,' including, just for now, even the work of those who explicitly reject 'establishment linguistics' as a potential source of wisdom on the workings and structure of language.

My own interest in the resolution of these boundary drawing questions does not come from territorial urges on my part, nor does it arise from a desire for neatness, from a love of tidily labeled boxes. Rather, I feel we need to ask: Are we free to draw borders in and around linguistics according to our taste, our generosity, or the grandness of our vision—or are there empirical bases for making the boundaries go one way rather than another? That is, we need to recognize the difference between the esthetic act of drawing a boundary—in ways determined by such measures as our sense of symmetry or the reach of our arms—and the scientific act of discovering a seam in nature and tracing its course. Using a different image, we need to distinguish the perspective of a butcher from that of an anatomy student, each confronting a pig's carcass. The anatomy student, in disassembling the pig, traces a muscle from one of its moorings to the other, because he is interested in learning how the animal is put together. The butcher, by contrast, makes his segmentations of the animal in accordance with the prevailing practices of local meat eaters and his own inner urges. The point is that we need to decide whether the conceptual framework within which we articulate our beliefs about the workings of language follows the realities of language itself. In fact, we need to find out if there is such an object whose realities are in principle discoverable.

2.

The problem of boundaries for the science of language is that of finding the proper sources of explanation for the various kinds of facts connected with human communication. The problem of sorting out these various sources of explanation can be equated with that of identifying the abstractions and idealizations legitimate to a science of language. The articulation of the full set of needed idealizations provides the makings of a theory of levels that may be more complex than anything ordinarily considered in linguistics. One of my goals is to try to begin to make explicit the outline of such a theory of levels.

Human speech communication gives us one of the most compelling cases of a domain of facts requiring multiple sources of explanation. Language as we know it is learned, and learnable, only by human beings: many of the facts of human language are doubtless to be explained from the reality that its users are all members of our species. Language is learned and used in a structured but changing matrix of social activity: the purposes and institutions of groups of social beings affect language behavior in ways obvious to everyone; they are bound to have a shaping effect on linguistic structure as well. Language is transmitted from person to person in such a way that output (the utterances) produced by one generation of speakers provides, in a context of personal engagement, the data out of which the next generation constructs for itself an equivalent or near-equivalent system: the interaction of the nature of language and the nature of the human language faculty must determine both the course of this transmission and the tolerance for transmission failures of the kind that, accumulated, result in the profound changes in language form that we see across the centuries. Language is both enabled and limited by the productive, memorial, perceptual, imaginal, and processual capabilities of human beings. And it is used by people who move in, and interact with, what we sometimes call the real world. The shape of language, and the facts about its employment, must be determined in many ways by each of these realities.

3.

Let us imagine an indefinitely large *record* of the various kinds of facts we can gather about a given *speech sample*. We can say that this record is a set of *representations* of the speech sample, that the elements of each representation are determined by a set of *criteria*, and that each set of criteria characterizes a *level* of representation. We can, following Halliday (1961:241–292), define *rank size* as the size of the speech sample over which the criteria are to be applied, such as word or sentence or discourse.

I intend these notions to be taken as broadly as possible, assuming nothing in advance about which facts are linguistic or about which level defining criteria are going to turn out to be linguistically relevant. By my definitions, then, one conceivable representation of a text is a tracing of all the places at which the speaker yawned while producing it. Another is a detailed phonetic representation using just the contrasts implicit in some given segmental or featural notation system. Another is a tracing of pitch contours for the sample. It is less easy to find explicit criteria for what might be called a cognitive representation—defined according to the kinds of images, associations, awareness of fit with real world situations, etc.—that could be assumed to appear in the comprehension of an ideal interpreter.

Let us assume, then, that we can have an unlimitedly large and detailed set of representations of speech samples, or texts, in any language. We can then assume that a great many of the questions that need to be answered if we are to construct a science of language can be asked about this set. For example,

- What determines the occurrence of phenomena at given levels of representation?
- What determines the structuring of the phenomena at given levels of representation?
- Which questions get answered differently for different languages?
- Which questions get answered in the same way for all languages?

In some cases, the questions might get answered by a straightforward appeal to phenomena on another level. Thus the reason the speaker used the phoneme /m/ in a particular place in a particular English utterance is that he used the word MOTHER, as shown in the lexemic representation of the same utterance, and the word MOTHER 'contains' the phoneme /m/. Some other questions can be answered only by appealing to a language specific set of formation rules—mastery of which can be imputed to the speakers of that language—governing the kinds of structures to be found in representations at a particular level. English phonotactics allows word-initial /kr/, but does not allow word-initial /kt/. Still other questions require the discovery of sets of rules for linking one level of representation with another, in the way that a linguistic-phonetic representation can be predicted or derived from a phonological representation of the same text. And many other answers will come from knowledge of either constant or changing aspects of the context of use.

4.

As a way of exploring some of these questions, I would like to set up various distinct kinds of articulations or relationships between different levels of representation. In many cases we will be able to see a nonrandom relationship between the phenomena and structures on one level of representation and those on another level.

A first type of relation—called *part to whole*—is between representations of the same text. Here one representation of an utterance is part of another representation of the same utterance. A trivial example can be seen in the relation between a record of all the vowels in an utterance and a record of all the phonetic segments in the utterance.

A second kind of relationship—*taxonomic*—links units to categories of those units. The relationship between a representation showing word tokens and one showing part–of–speech tokens of the same utterance is taxonomic.

A third kind of relationship—*hierarchical*—is the one most commonly discussed. In it, sequences of units on one level correspond to individual units on another level. Morphemic and lexemic representations have this kind of relationship, since a 'lexeme' or word is made up of a sequence of (one or more) morphemes. Lexemic and phrasal representations are related in the same way.

In a fourth kind of relationship we can say that the units on one level provide the tools, or the means, for units on another level. Here I would like to say that the nature of the relationship is *instrumental*. Thus a level of syntactic representation might be said to have an instrumental relationship to a level of representation of *illocutionary acts*. Linguists and speech act theorists who are careful about this relationship encourage us to use a different terminology for each level, as when they distinguish 'interrogative sentence' from 'question,' 'indicative sentence' from 'statement,' etc. Thus, if we regard a relationship as instrumental, we can say that at such–and–such a point the speaker *used* an interrogative sentence *as* a question.

My fifth and sixth types of relationships, which show systematic rule-like relationships, differ in the structure of their rules. In the fifth relationship, the rules are 'autonomous'—that is, they are independent of external influences. We can regard one level as an *idealization* of the other level, an idealization from which the influences of external factors—noise, production, disturbances, etc.—have been taken away and can be resupplied once those factors are again taken into account. In the sixth relationship, we can regard one level as an *abstraction* of the other level, an abstraction from which the details, the redundancies, have been removed and to which they can be supplied by a completely regular systems of rules.

I refer to the one as *internal-regular* and to the other as *external-regular*, for want of more perspicuous terms. I see an internal-regular relationship between a phonological and a linguistic-phonetic representation, with linking rules of the standard allophonic type. I see an external-regular relationship between a linguistic-phonetic representation and what might be called an absolute phonetic representation, in which certain distortions in the signal can be seen as explainable by the facts that, say, the speaker was a young boy who yawned during the first ten seconds of the utterance and was being tickled during the final three seconds.

These notions do not exhaust the possibilities, since several different representations might well be jointly responsible for the phenomena in another representation. In explaining one representation, we might say that other representations, in a cluster, *interact*, and that the relationship between the one representation and the cluster might be either internal-regular or external-regular. One view of the prosodic contours in English is that they are determined by an interaction among phonological, lexical, syntactic, semantic, and pragmatic representations.

5.

Many issues in the organization of the science of language can be formulated within my descriptive framework. We can examine the usual kind of embedding hierarchy for linguistics by which, for example,

♦ units at the morphemic level combine hierarchically to determine units at the lexemic level,
♦ recursive combinations at the lexemic level define a hierarchical articulation between lexemic and syntactic representations, and so on.

The theory of deep structures and meaning preserving transformations provides two syntactic levels of representation linked in an internal-regular way.

We can ask whether the relationship between traces of prosodic features in English and morphemic representations is of a part-to-whole type, as would correspond to the theory of grammaticized intonation contours and stress superfixes,[5] or whether, as seems the more current view, phonological representations containing prosodic information are derived from phonological representations in which such information interacts with syntax at least, and doubtless with semantics and pragmatics as well (e.g. Halle & Keyser 1971).

If there is such a thing as semantic representation, we could ask if its relation to a cognitive representation of the utterance is instrumental or external-regular—that is, whether semantic structures provide tools for the comprehension process or stand as idealizations of it.

And we can ask certain extremely important questions about the relation between sentences and texts. If the relationship is hierarchical, then sentences are the constituents of texts, and it makes sense to talk about a grammar of texts;[6] but if the relationship is instrumental, then a text can be seen as an activity in which the producers of the text are engaged, and the sentences can be seen as the means of performing certain acts within that activity.

6.

At this point I would like to take up a number of boundary issues in linguistics, beginning with the speech end of 'speech communication,' and discuss

---

[5] See the section on 'pitch morphemes' and 'superfixes' in the Morphemics chapter of Hill (1958).

[6] One branch of linguistics that has most deliberately maintained a continuity view of sentence structure and discourse structure is the tagmemics school, especially under the hand of Robert Longacre. See, for example, Longacre (1976 Part I:1–8).

the questions of the proper treatment within the conceptual framework introduced above.

The raw observations of speech are made up of the actions of the bodies of the communicating partners, the acoustic events that accompany those actions, and the perceptual experiences, on the hearers' part, that follow from those actions and events. As a first-level abstraction, then, we need to separate the patterns that belong to human speech from those of other noise creating events such as belching, laughing, crying, sneezing, whistling, and coughing.

Events of these types may occur independently of speech, in which case we can, so to speak, resplice the tape after cutting out these events, thus ignoring them completely. When they occur simultaneously with speech, we will not look to our science for an explanation of their occurrence, but we may indeed be interested in examining their signal-distorting effect in mapping out the external-regular relationship between a linguistic-phonetic representation and an absolute phonetic one. (A sustained yawn markedly affects vowel quality.) The controlled performance of some of these events can be used as part of a conventional communicative act, as when one clears one's throat to draw attention to some impropriety; but we will doubtless find that this conventionalized use fails to articulate in a general way with the more clearly linguistic levels of representation, and that the orderliness we find in the occurrence of these events or in their acoustic effect can be explained (if at all) by principles quite different from those we independently need for a science of language.

A second but related kind of data separation needed at the speech end is that by which we identify speech patterns given conventional values for the language community as a whole, in contradistinction to aspects of the speech signal that are determined by properties of the individual speaker. Here I have in mind the size and shape of the speaker's vocal tract; the length of the speaker's vocal cords, or the speaker's articulatory skills, processing speed, changing mental and emotional states, and so on. Again, and again quite obviously, the reason we are willing to exclude such matters from the central task of describing a language is our belief that whatever orderliness there is to be found here is to be explained with reference to differences among individuals and their changing states, and has little direct bearing on the character of the language they speak.

Coughing and yawning, and the rest, usually occur independently of speech and can generally be left out of consideration altogether. But voice quality, pitch range, tempo and its changes, and so forth are with us always and can be removed from the speech signal only by processes of abstraction. The usual phrasing for this abstraction has it that the linguist observes patterns, contrasts, oppositions, features of articulation type, etc., rather than the phonetic events directly. I think my description is equivalent to the standard one, the difference being that in my account one speaks of recognizing an idealization rather than of selecting the data.

7.

Digression

The position I have taken is that differences in the bodies of the speakers affect language performance but not language structure—that they figure, in short, only when one is articulating the relation between an idealized phonetic and an absolute phonetic representation of the same utterance. While facts about human bodies might indeed figure in explanations about the character of language in general, *differences* between bodies of individuals, or set of individuals, cannot figure in explanations about differences between languages.

There is a conceivably different position we could take that bears on the way in which a language fits, and is employed by, the bodies of its users, something that ought to be mentioned because it raises another issue of external boundaries. If not just individuals but communities of individuals should have saliently different physical apparatuses for producing language, then it might be the case that different languages have been adapted to the different physical systems that their users make available to them. The claim might be made that certain languages differ from others precisely because of underlying physical differences between their users. Differing characteristics of human bodies could then be said to figure in the explanation of structural differences between languages. This would raise extremely interesting questions of whether language could be characterized independently of these bodily differences.

There are folk views that hold to a fairly direct explanatory connection between bodies and languages. There are views that particular languages have, or lack, certain properties because their native speakers have certain racially specific bodily features. One sometimes hears claims that the tongues of members of certain racial groups are inadequately shaped to deal with certain phonetic challenges. Such claims are invariably wrong, or at any rate inadequately defended; but if they were true, we would have a situation in which systematic physical differences between language users would partially explain systematic differences between languages.

There are in fact differences of the kind I have in mind, differences considerably greater than degrees of lingual agility. I am thinking of the differences between oral languages and manual-visual languages, such as the American Sign Language of the deaf. The physical apparatuses for these two types of communication system are different in obvious and striking ways, offering vastly different potentials for conventionalization. Whether a communication system like ASL, because of these extreme differences, is a 'real' language is a question that has troubled otherwise polite and fruitful conversations about the education and language rights of the deaf. Thus this issue clearly has a place in a discussion of the boundaries of linguistics. That is, if we are forced to decide that the physical characteristics of speakers of oral languages figure directly in the explanation of the characteristics of language in general, the manual-visual languages are not real languages. On the other hand, if it is important to us to include them in the set of genuine languages, we need to discover those quintessential properties of Language (with a capital 'L') that are independent of modality (yet certainly not general enough to encompass any semiotic system whatever) and then to explain how the modality differences make available different possibilities for conventionalization.

From here on I shall concern myself only with the familiar oral languages, but the serious issue raised about the character of manual-visual languages cannot be lost sight of in the larger picture.

8.

British and American traditions of phonemic representation have differed with respect to the size of the rank within which the criteria for linguistic-phonological representations were to be formulated. In the British tradition, it tended to be that of the simple word;[7] in the American tradition, it was the utterance, variously defined. In the general British view, phonetic phenomena observable at word boundaries had to be thought of as belonging to a separate realm, not to phonemic analysis as such; the relation of a phonemic representation to a (for the most part, unexplored) representation of sentence phonology had to be thought of as internal-regular. American phonetic theorists, by contrast, developed various notions of phonemic junctures, having the twin advantages of (1) making it unnecessary to define the rank-size concept 'word,' and (2) allowing a place for internal sandhi phenomena in units that were clearly of word size. In the American scheme, then, a level of representation of word phonology, if that could be defined, had to have a part-to-whole relation to a representation of sentence phonology.

The consequences of these differences extend further still, in particular to questions of the interdefinability of elements of different levels. In the British tradition, prior identification of words made up part of the criteria for the

---

[7] See. Firth (1935), but note also Trubetzkoy's (1958) claims concerning 'Wortphonologie'.

phonemic level. In the American tradition, by contrast, phonological conditions were briefly thought of as essential to the correct definition of words.

9.

A still different issue at the speech end has to do with the proper understanding of the relation between slow and fast speech. The question is: Should slow and fast speech each be described as variant phonological systems for the language? If so, are there just these two, or could there be more than two? If there can be more than two, is the number determinate? Or should we provide a single phonological system including all such variants? Or should we describe a kind of idealized maximally articulated speech style such that fast speech can be seen as derived from an idealized representation by means of a system of optional tempo rules?

There is an awkwardness in formulating these questions within my conceptual framework. Do we want to say that the record of the full set of representations of a fast-speech utterance contains a representation of a slow-speech version of that same utterance?

It is generally assumed that fast speech is derivable from (representations of) slow speech via processes of fusion, neutralization, and omission. Certainly nobody could propose a relationship in the opposite direction by which, for example, the maximally articulated version of 'Did you eat yet?' can be derived by regular rules from [ǰiče?]. But the linking rules cannot be completely regular. In particular, such rules must take into account that fixed expressions have been subject to more exuberant kinds of phonetic play than other expressions, so that the mapping process must take such separate conventionalizations into account. (The style that allows 'g'bye' for 'good-bye' does not allow 'g'boy' for 'good boy.')

10.

Among the various levels of phonic representations for given utterances, we have the problem of deciding on the nature of the relationship between word and sentence phonology, between phonological representations with and without prosodic features (in languages like English in which prosodic features do not have to be thought of as entering into the form of lexical items), and between representations of slow- and fast-speech versions of what is morphosyntactically the same text.

A different order of question arises when we consider possible explanatory links between phonological and nonphonological levels of representation. A clear problem exists with respect to the relative independence of phonology and morphology. We can recognize first of all a hierarchical relationship between phonemic and morpheme-alternant representations, and a taxonomic ('categorial') relationship between morpheme-alternant and morphemic representations. But, for English at least, it appears that there are more complicated relationships among these levels as well. For example, there are clear explanatory links between the phonotactic rules that constrain the possible structures of phonological representations, and the mapping between morphemic and morpheme-alternant representations—as is seen in the fact that many processes of allomorphy appear to be adaptations to English syllable structure. But there are also connections between morphotactic and phonotactic rules, as evidenced by the fact that some syllable-final sequences ending in /t/ or /d/, or /s/ or /z/, are possible only when that closing element represents a suffix of tense, number, or agreement.

11.

So far I have been talking mainly about the speech end of communication. I now turn to the non-speech end, the 'mental' end, if I can call it that, where we deal with meaning, conceptualization, expression, the transmission of messages.

The raw data at the speech end consisted of observations about physiological, acoustic, and perceptual events and experiences—observations from out of which various kinds of abstractions were required for sorting out the distinct levels of explanation. At the nonspeech end the raw data, if we can call them that, are observations about the course of specific communication acts—observations about the intentions of the speakers and the comprehension of the hearers. One way or another, most directly of course when we ourselves are speakers or hearers, we observe something about what people have in mind when they talk, what they actually say, and how what they say gets understood.

At this end, too, there are multiple sources of explanation for the data we observe. One dividing line, easy to state in principle but not always easy to find in real life, involves the familiar Chomskyan idealization of a language user not subject to failures of planning or execution; it is through this idealization that we have learned to recognize a difference between competence and performance. We can surely assume that whatever is orderly in communication, and that is to be accounted for by a science of language, should not include cases in which the speaker fails to express himself adequately because of interruption, memory failure, or planning failure, or cases in which the hearer fails to understand because of inattention, ignorance, or memory or process slippage. Here the difference between ideal and real-life communication is to be accounted for, at least partly, by considerations that fall outside the explanatory scope of a science of language.

I assume that, in principle, there is no room for controversy here as long as we acknowledge that your ability to understand me when I do not express myself well—and my tendency to misunderstand you even when you express your ideas perfectly—do not depend on principles that are not present when the process goes smoothly at both ends.

Not at all easy to exclude from the proper science of language are areas in which it looks as if what is going on should be explained by the assumptions of the communicating partners about what the world is like (including their assumptions of mutual rationality and cooperation among the communication participants), plus their informal knowledge of the principles of rhetoric or logic—or else it might be explained by what Schank and Abelson call informal psychology and informal physics (1977)—or by what some workers call perceptual strategies.[8] All of these play a role in explaining some parts of communication behavior, but the nature of their position in the layering of linguistic representations is often a matter of serious dispute.

As with questions in the phonology area, there are likewise continuing disagreements in the non-speech end about matters that everyone agrees are clearly within the linguistics proper:

♦ What kinds of information should be assigned to the lexicon, as distinguished from the grammar proper?
♦ Do word formation principles need to be stated independently of syntax?
♦ Are certain irregularities best stated as constraints on rules (hence, as information about those rules)—or as constraints on the behavior of specific lexical or phrasal items (hence, as information about those items)?

12.

A simple and familiar kind of example can be introduced to make the case that questions of internal and external boundaries are closely related. In early generativist work, two sources of explanation were introduced for native speaker judgments about the grammaticality and meaningfulness of sentences. These sources were taken to be the internalized rule systems called *syntax* and *semantics*. Roughly, syntax explained which linguistic products speakers were capable of constructing by virtue of their linguistic knowledge alone. This included, of course, infinitely many potential utterances that nobody would ever have the occasion or the patience to produce. Semantics

---

[8] For representative statements on the role of perceptive strategies in limiting the explanatory scope of linguistics proper, see Bever (1970), Langendoen (1976).

expressed, in some abstract way, what it was that these syntactically constructed objects could be used to communicate or express. The two systems were thought of as analogous to the sets of a formal mathematical system—one for forming well-formed formulas, the other for evaluating them. In roughly the same way that only well-formed algebraic equations could be evaluated as true or false, only grammatical—syntactically well-formed—sentences could be taken as candidates for objects to which semantic interpretations could be assigned.

In principle, this kind of fit between two levels of representation seemed reasonable enough; but the principle is hard to pin down when we are making decisions about borderline cases. A troublesome kind of example from the outset was a sentence like *Jimmy's stories amused the doorknob*.

There are two facts connected with this sentence that need to be assigned their separate places. One fact is that the sentence is in some way bizarre, and that this bizarreness has something to do with the wrongness of the fit between the verb *amuse* and its direct object *the doorknob*. The second is that the sentence can indeed be given some kind of interpretation; that is, it enjoys a kind of semantic coherence that the same string of words read backwards cannot enjoy. (Both of these facts are vague and intuitive in the extreme, but it is the purpose of a theory of language to make them less so.)

The first generativist interpretation given to sentences of this type was that they were not English sentences at all. The reason we perceived the sentence as bizarre, then, is that we know the syntactic rules of English, and we know that those rules are incapable of producing the sentence just encountered. If we want to account for the interpretability of that sentence in spite of its oddity, we need to appeal to some auxiliary theory or theories—in particular, a theory of semi-sentences, a theory of the ability to produce approximations to English, and a theory that can account for our ability to assign semantic interpretations to approximations of English sentences. That the proposed existence of such a theory was not altogether far-fetched, the argument went, is seen from the fact that such a theory is needed to account for metaphor anyway.[9]

On this first accounting, then, the *oddity* of the sentence was accounted for by a theory of syntax; its *interpretability* fell in the domain of some auxiliary theory.

The solution required a syntax that systematically excluded sentences exhibiting the kind of selectional mismatch we find here. Verbs of the kind represented by *amuse* must be syntactically marked as requiring for their direct

---

[9] For an early statement on the semantic interpretation of ill-formed sentences, see Katz (1964).

objects nouns taken from a syntactic class that does not include the noun *doorknob*.

The data, of course, do not in any way dictate that this is the correct solution. We could easily take the next step and say that the sentence is syntactically impeccable, and then offer a semantic explanation of its oddity, that explanation possibly taking the form that the verb *amuse* is semantically characterized as requiring a particular semantic class of direct objects, namely a noun phrase that can designate objects capable of certain cognitive experiences, and that the noun *doorknob* falls short of such conditions.

In this second solution, the *oddity* of the sentence is accounted for by the semantic component; the fact that it is not gibberish but has a form to which semantic rules can be applied is accounted for by the syntax. What is needed now is an account of its *interpretability*. One way of providing that would be to appeal to an auxiliary theory of language interpretation that used the semantic rules of a linguistic description for imposing an interpretation on sentences that were technically ill-formed. Another would be to construe a semantic theory in the first place in such a way that its role is to impose an interpretation rather than merely to accept or reject sentences according to their semantic well-formedness. In the former case, the *oddity* of the sentence is accounted for by the semantics, its *interpretability* by the auxiliary theory. In the latter case, both the *oddity* and *interpretability* of the sentence fall within the explanatory scope of a properly constructed semantic theory.

A third possible solution to the problem of the doorknob sentence is that it is both syntactically and semantically impeccable, and that its oddity consists entirely in our belief that anybody who could say this sentence in good faith must have a picture of the world that differs from our own in certain fairly interesting ways. In this third interpretation, a *linguistic* account of English contains no principles according to which the *oddity* judgment can be explained. The interpretability judgment, however, is straightforward. The sentence tells us that the doorknob in question got a certain kind of enjoyment out of hearing Jimmy's stories. In fact, we have to say that it is only by virtue of identifying precisely what the sentence could mean that its interpreter is able to figure out why what it says is so strange.

First we thought the bizarreness judgment was to be explained by the syntax. Then we turned it over to the semantics. In the end we took it away from the semantics too. Are we now ready to decide that it doesn't belong to linguistics at all?

Let us assume that we have two levels of representation for each meaningful utterance: *semantic* and *cognitive*. The semantic representation of our doorknob sentence is the one according to which it is seen as communicating something meaningful about a particular doorknob. The cognitive representation is the one that recognized that the utterance either is playful or assumes something unusual about the doorknob.

What, then, should be the nature of the relationships between the semantic and cognitive representations? Presumably we ought to be able to expect an external-regular relationship since the semantic representation is paired with both the context of situation and the background of beliefs, institutions, and practices shared by the speaker and the hearers.

We need to ask two crucial questions at this point. First, can the principles by which contextual information and semantic representations are integrated to construct cognitive representations be properly studied within a science of language? Second, does the final correct theory of language actually need a level of semantic representation distinct from the syntactic representations at one end and the cognitive representations at the other? My own suspicion is that there is probably no need for a level of semantic representation, but that if there is its role in determining the cognitive representation (of an ideal interpreter) should be regarded as studiable within linguistics, even if the external *facts* that contribute to that determination are not themselves facts that clearly belong to (that is, get explained by) the science of language.

No sensible person would claim that the fact about the deprived cognitive capacities of doorknobs needs to be incorporated into a theory of language — that is, to be explained by the principles of such a theory. But there may be a way of viewing the semantic end of a science of language as a system or apparatus that acknowledges facts, beliefs, models of the world, that are not themselves linguistic, and that provides interpretative principles that appeal to or build on such facts and beliefs. Workers in artificial intelligence, where this approach has been most explicitly developed, are not likely to claim that what they are doing is linguistics, but since some of them do claim that after they have done what they do there is nothing left that could be called linguistics, they are at least claiming that there is no line to be drawn between semantic and cognitive representations.[10] I wish to explore the value of that suggestion for linguistics.

13.

Two traditions of semantics have arisen within, or have impinged on, linguistics: *ethnographic* and *formal*. In ethnographic semantics, a distinction between semantic and cognitive representations could not naturally occur, since that discipline looks at the phenomena of the world, or the life and institutions of a particular cultural group, and asks how the stuff of that world gets labeled, classified, described, and talked about by linguistic means. It would

---

[10] This is certainly true of work using 'Conceptual Dependency,' as in Schank (1973).

not make sense to ask an anthropologist who has just told us that a particular genus of edible berries has been given a particular name by the group being studied what the word means in independence of its fit with this botanical domain. In the tradition of ethnographic, or 'lexical,' semantics, such a question could not occur.

It is my belief that many of the words we use are like the names of things we know and have meanings that cannot really be talked about independently of reference to that knowledge. Some ideas, from what is coming to be called 'frame semantics,' seem most compatible with the point of view I have in mind. The idea is that words are learned and understood against the background of a particular topic or context, and that any use of them necessarily brings in associations with those contexts. One can speak of such an association with reference to a framing of the situation, and the framing contributes to the interpreter's construction of the world of the text.

To know the meaning of a word is necessarily to have access to at least some of the details of the associated schematization. The noun *land* does not simply designate the dry part of the earth's surface (in one of its meanings); it designates that part from the point of view of a schematization that divides land from sea. The noun *ground*, by contrast, also designates the earth's dry surface (in one of its meanings), but this time as part of a schematization that separates the earth from the air above it. Thus *being on land* evokes a context in which it is relevant to contrast being on land with being at sea, and hence suggests a stage in a sea voyage, a moment in the life of an amphibious animal, or the like, whereas *being on the ground* suggests a contrast with being in the air, and thus evokes a scene of an interrupted air trip, or of an alighted bird, or the like. Each of these expressions is, and is perceived as, a member of a particular integrated set of expressions whose meaning can be correctly perceived only by those familiar with the larger schematization of which the element is a part. It is common in linguistic semantics to speak of the associated *words* as defining a language-internal structure of some kind, whose elements are said to be paradigmatically opposed to each other by means of a system of contrasts and relations that can be fully stated independently of contact with any world. But that, it seems to me, is misleading.

For words that can be thus described, we can say that a word designates a point in a field—a point that in principle cannot be separated from its field. Some extreme statements of the difference between the linguistic meaning of a word and encyclopedic information about what the word designates assume that this separation is an abstraction essential to the proper determination of the boundaries of linguistics.[11]

---

[11] For a recent statement about this distinction, see the beginners' semantics textbook by Hurford and Heasley (1983), where we find (p. 184) the following: "The linguistic semanticist

Some time ago I had occasion to realize that I didn't know how to use the word *steeplechase*. I didn't know whether it was

♦ the name of a kind of place where a certain kind of horse racing takes places;
♦ the name of a sport (so that I could say *I enjoy steeplechase*.);
♦ the name of a particular contest within this sport (so that one could say *The final steeplechase of the day is about to begin*.);
♦ the name of the kind of horse that is trained to race in the way we associate with the concept of steeplechase—with hedges, wall, and ditches as obstacles.

I think I completely understood the brute and institutional facts underlying the meaning of the word, but I didn't know how the word 'keyed' into the schema. I could allow myself to say that I knew the background against which the word was defined, but I didn't know what the word meant. I then wondered whether it would be possible to meet my counterpart, somebody who knew exactly what the word meant but was unfamiliar with the background of practices that motivated the existence of the word. It seems to me that such a person could not possibly exist.

14.

I have been trying to think of an example in which it would be particularly difficult to draw a distinction between meaning proper and context of use, and one that I suggest works is *The menfolk returned at sundown*. It seems to me that the word *menfolk* is used to isolate adult males as a group from females and children in a human setting involving the activities of whole families. A natural setting for the sentence, then, would be one in which the men in a village went off for the day's fishing in the morning and returned to their families at the day's end.

A question we need to ask is whether such a sentence can be used appropriately in settings that depart from the one suggested by the word's primary schematization, and another is whether, independently of judgments of appropriateness, the sentence can be said to have a truth value in such alien settings. Consider an all-male community of workers on the Alaskan pipeline

is interested in the meanings of words and not in non-linguistic facts about the world. Correspondingly, he attempts to make a strict demarcation between a dictionary and an encyclopedia....

A DICTIONARY describes the sense of predicates.

An ENCYCLOPEDIA contains factual information of a variety of types, but generally no information specifically on the meanings of words."

and a situation in which the workers returned to their dormitories at sundown. Clearly nobody would actually use the sentence in such a context, but what should you say if asked whether that sentence in that situation was *true*? A view of semantics that makes a sharp distinction between meaning and context of use would have to be able to answer that question one way or another, I believe. An ethnographic semantics view, by contrast, would simply allow us to say that the question of truth can't occur; the sentence has not been used in a situation in which it could directly convey anything that was either true or false.

Suppose, nevertheless, that we found somebody willing to say this sentence in the all-male community context described, and suppose too that people were able to interpret that sentence as meaning that the workers returned to their dormitories. We now have to deal with these facts: one, the sentence can be given an interpretation; two, the sentence is used inappropriately. A formal semantics view would have it that its interpretability is determined in a straightforward way by the theory of semantics for the language, but that judgments about its appropriateness are to be interpreted by a theory of usage, or register, or pragmatics. The ethnographic semantics account would see the bizarreness of the sentence in context as explained by a theory of semantics, since the background required by the meaning of *menfolk*, is wrong. It would account for the interpretability of the sentence in spite of the framing failure as involving either some kind of construal principles of the sort needed for a theory of metaphor, *or* the recognition of an artificial sublanguage derived from English whose semantic principles have been deliberately limited to those congenial to the formulation of certain logical relationships.

15.

Another important boundary issue for semantics centers on the contribution to linguistic semantics of the work of such scholars as Paul Grice and Oswald Ducrot.[12] In assessing and interpreting the data of speech comprehension, we have to keep in mind at least two sources of information: one the internally represented meanings of the lexical and grammatical forms at our disposal, the other a way of reasoning about why people say what they do. In Grice's case, this takes the form of principles of conversational cooperation plus a method for interpreting both adherence to and departure from these principles. In Ducrot's case, it takes the form of a series of laws of discourse.

Not many years ago, I kept at my fingertips a fine set of examples that I brought out for display whenever I wanted to impress people with the detail and richness of a native speaker's semantic competence. One of my favorites

---

[12] See Grice (1975), Ducrot (1975).

came from philosopher Stanley Cavell's discussion of the adverb *voluntarily*. (Cavell 1958:75–112) He suggested, and for many years I was only too willing to believe, that part of the meaning of *voluntarily* was that there was something fishy about what was being talked about in the predicate that the adverb modified. The adverb carried with it information about the type of event or situation that it could be used to qualify, and this quite independently of what the use of the adverb directly communicated. One of his examples was *Do you dress that way voluntarily?* Another example might be *English people drink warm beer voluntarily.*

Influenced by Grice and Ducrot, today's semanticist would be more likely to say that we should not be misled by an ability to distinguish stages in the comprehension process. Though we can indeed recognize an assumption of fishiness in these utterances, we are nowadays more likely to believe that it comes not from semantic information contained in the sentence but from our assumptions about why the speaker might question whether an action was performed voluntarily or under duress. If there wasn't something fishy about the action in the first place, such a question would be pointless. A fact once thought of as belonging to lexical semantics got taken over by a theory of rhetoric.

James McCawley has recently suggested applying Gricean principles to settle a long standing issue about the putative observation that no two expressions can mean exactly the same thing, in particular that a word cannot mean the same thing as any of its proposed definitions. On the face of it, it should seem reasonable to say that *kill* means nothing more or less than 'cause to die'; yet sentences in which these proposed equivalents are substituted for each other persist in giving different impressions. One possibility is that the proposed definition is simply wrong and that, with a little work, we should be able to come up with one that performs as a true definition ought to perform. A second possibility is that perfect defining paraphrases will never be found, simply because in principle no two expressions ever will or ever could mean the same thing. The doctrine expresses a kind of faith in the efficiency of language: a language would never allow itself to have different expressions unless it had different meanings to express with them.

The solution that McCawley favors is that a word and a phrase expressing its semantic analysis might indeed mean the same thing, but speakers can be assumed to have good reasons for choosing the more analytic expression when a simple and well-known word could have been used just as well. Such a choice can be taken as amounting to a violation of a Gricean obscurity-avoidance maxim and must therefore be seen as an attempt to convey some special impression. To put it intuitively, if a concept has been 'lexicalized,' that must be because it defines a category within a particular kind of framework; ignoring the lexicalization in favor of a paraphrase can be heard as a denial of the relevance of the categorizing framework. (McCawley 1978:245–259) ('I admit that what I did caused Smith's death.' – 'Are you then telling the court that you killed Smith?' – 'No, that's not what I said at all.')

Once again we have our familiar situation of looking at two facts and trying to figure out which part of the explanatory apparatus of our science can be called upon to explain each. One fact is our judgment that *kill* and *cause to die* mean essentially, if not exactly, the same thing. The second is that sentences in which the two are interchanged seem to convey slightly different messages. The two non-Gricean views agree in rejecting the first fact, attributing the judgment to a misperception of the sort that is not surprising in naive native speakers. The first of these views accepts the possibility that a more accurate defining paraphrase can eventually be found; the second insists that there is at best similarity, never identity, to be found between two expressions. The Gricean view was that the synonymy judgment was a matter of semantics, and therefore clearly a part of linguistics; and that the subtle-difference judgment is to be explained with respect to people's sensitivity to the effect of rhetorical choices.

The Gricean view I have just characterized is compatible with the assumption that there is a difference between a level of semantic representation (the level on which *kill* and *cause to die* mean the same thing) and a level on which belief structures, knowledge of context, and rhetorical selections have made their influence felt, a level that is (or is closely related to) the level of cognitive representation discussed earlier.

I think the 'convincingness' of the *kill* case needs to be countered with examples that are less abstract and general purpose. As I said earlier, in many cases a full description of lexical meaning requires some sort of schematic understanding of the background or frame of reference within which a particular cognitive category has been assigned a lexical form. The point can be made more strongly with *murder* than with *kill*. I believe there is no way to capture the meaning of the word *murder* without presenting (or taking for granted) the background of values and institutional knowledge within which it makes sense to categorize certain (but not all) actions of taking life as *murder*. In short, for some words it may indeed be impossible to provide a complete linguistic paraphrase with which the Gricean solution could even be tried out. I see a difference between *explaining* what something means and *presenting* what it means.

16.

Many of my points have been that, in opposition to the view that there is a separate representation of semantic structure that can be abstracted away from general features of context and topic, respect should be given to an alternative view that locates meaning fairly directly with potential context. Scholars who wish to maintain the separate abstract semantic level are also motivated to keep that level as pure and simple as possible—uncluttered, in particular, with such troublesome notions as *presuppositions*. I have only the shallowest understanding of all the issues connected with presuppositions, but there is one on which the use of our fact-parceling strategy can be demonstrated once again. I have in mind the arguments for and against reliance on the so-called 'negation test' for presuppositions—which I think fails to cover all cases of what one might want to call presuppositions, but I suspect that certain kinds of arguments against the test deserve critical examination.

The negation test, intended to distinguish logical entailment from presupposition, works like this. If P either entails or presupposes Q, then whenever P is true, Q is also true. But if P entails Q, not-P no longer commits one to the truth of Q. If P presupposes Q, not-P continues to commit one to the truth of Q.

Let me use the vague word 'impression' for what can be understood from a statement. From the sentence *Lucille made John read the letter*, we get two impressions: that John read some specified letter, and that Lucille somehow forced John to read it. From the sentence *John regretted reading the letter*, once again we get two impressions: that John read the letter, and that John felt bad about having read it.

Now consider putting each of these sentences under negation. With *Lucille didn't make John read the letter,* we form the impression that Lucille didn't force John to read the letter, but we are left opinionless about whether John read the letter or not. With *John didn't regret reading the letter*, the proposition about John's feeling bad after reading the letter is denied, but we are still left with the impression that he did read the letter.

Inferences that can be drawn from an affirmative sentence and that survive when that sentence is replaced by its negative counterpart, the argument goes, are the presuppositions of that sentence.

Ruth Kempson has questioned this distinction.[13] She instead bases a different kind of argument on judgments of contradiction and interpretability. Let us consider the results of appending the sentence *In fact, he didn't read the letter* to each of our four sentences.[14] First, the two affirmative sentences:

---

[13] On the elimination of presuppositions as special semantic rules, see Kempson (1975), Wilson (1975).

[14] See the discussion in Kempson (1975: 62–66).

Lucille made John read the letter. In fact, he didn't read the letter.

John regretted reading the letter. In fact, he didn't read the letter.

The first of these two-sentence texts contains a contradiction, since the second sentence denies what the first sentence asserts by entailment. The second text too presents a contradiction. A presuppositionist would characterize the contradiction by saying that what the first sentence presupposes, the second sentence denies. One who denies a distinction between entailment and presupposition could just as happily see both texts as presenting contradictions of the same type.

Next look at the two negative sentences with the appended sentence. In the first case, we get

Lucille didn't make John read the letter. In fact, John didn't read the letter.

There is nothing wrong with this text at all, just as you would expect if the relation we have been examining is one of entailment. But now the critical text:

John didn't regret reading the letter. In fact, he didn't read the letter.

This text can be read as communicating the information that John, who was innocent of having read the letter, did not—because he could not—feel bad about it.

When a sentence is negated, its entailments are neither affirmed nor denied. Thus, if we make both the *make* sentence and the *regret* sentence simple matters of entailment, everything we have seen is automatically explained, and no distinction remains between entailment and presupposition.

There is a problem with this last two-sentence text, however, and this is where Kempson and the presuppositionists assign facts to different theoretical domains. The little text,

John didn't regret reading the letter. In fact, he didn't read the letter.

elicits two judgments. First, it is interpretable in the way Kempson suggests. Second, it is definitely an odd thing to say. The theoretical dispute then concerns whether it is the oddity of the text or its interpretability that belongs to the realm of semantics. To Kempson, its *interpretability* is a matter of semantics, requiring nothing more than the well-established and independently-motivated theory of logical entailment; its *oddity* is to be accounted for by some auxiliary theory such as the theory of Gricean implicatures. (It is not relevant, nor informative, to deny feelings of regret for deeds one has not done.) For the presuppositionists, on the other hand, it is its *oddity* that is to be explained by semantic theory; its *interpretability* requires some presuppositions: the text is odd because the second sentence denies what the first sentence presupposes. Its interpretability makes it necessary to analyze the first sentence as a kind of metalinguistic statement, possibly a correction of what some previous speaker has said. Under that interpretation, the extra emphasis given to the word *regret* in the most natural rendering of the text would be explained. The sentence can be taken as a comment on the inappropriateness of the word *regret* in that context, something that could be signaled graphically by putting quotation marks around the word.[15]

Once again we have two facts such that putting either one in semantics requires putting the other somewhere else. One solution seems to make semantics simpler and better behaved than the other does. But it is no easy job to figure out which solution looks better for the whole theory. The presuppositionist view is more compatible with the position I have been taking: words have meanings and uses that can only be properly understood against some motivating background. The word *regret* 'names' a part of a particular kind of 'script' or 'scenario' involving deeds and feelings about one's own deeds. The presuppositionist view recognizes that its meaning cannot be divorced from its background.

17.

The problems I have looked at so far have been big and important ones, I think, but they pale before the ones I am going to turn to next.

It is commonly assumed in linguistics that, as a matter of methodological privilege, we can treat a speaker's competence in a language as a coherent, self-contained system with properties that can be considered, in principle, at a moment in time. This is the idealization of the *synchronic slice*. According to it, we sometimes allow ourselves to say that variation consists in a speaker's having access to more than one such complete and coherent system, and to say that language change consists in replacing one such system by another, either in the life history of an individual speaker or in the transmission of linguistic systems from one person to another in the changing generations.

---

[15] See the summarizing discussion of Kempson's rejection of 'speaker-based' presuppositions in Kempson (1975: 79–84). Wilson's rejection of the claim that 'external negation can be seen as denials of appropriateness' is given in Wilson (1975: 85).

A commitment to the methodological necessity of the synchronic slice may force us to take a completely unrealistic picture of linguistic knowledge. In a way, every idealization does that; but this idealization does not easily integrate with other idealizations or sources of explanation in a useful way.

A more realistic view might be one that sees the child's acquisition of linguistic competence as analogous to the work of historical comparative linguistics, working toward the elaboration of a system of representations and rules capable of accounting for the variety of related idiolects that have provided the child's data. Not only does the child's own internalized linguistic system have a time depth, but it must be seen as changing all the time.[16]

The living speaker's internalized 'reconstructed language' gives its users more things to say in more life-situations than any known reconstructed 'protolanguage' possibly could. But this reconstructed system is likely to have holes, leaks, vaguenesses, and pieces that don't fit together, just as the familiar historically reconstructed languages have.

While a cautious reconstructor of the child's input data would come up with an incomplete system, it is generally assumed that the child automatically imposes a closure or integration on the system it is developing, and that the nature of this integration can be discovered by careful elicitation or by noticing the forms of the child's novel utterances. But such assumptions are derived from the method, not from the facts. It could be that novel utterances are on-the-spot solutions to problems, that similarities of such solutions across speakers is evidence for the naturalness of some solutions as compared to others, and that the really considerable variations across speakers with respect to details of syntax and morphology are testimony to the independence of these solutions from speaker to speaker. We may also allow ourselves to question the assumption that each speaker has created or reconstructed a language system that exists as an integrated whole, and that many surprising properties of this whole can be revealed by subtle kinds of elicitation. We need to ask, at least in many cases, whether the native speaker judgments that come up through such interviews should be seen as existing before the interview and merely being pulled into the open air, or as decisions made on the spot as a result of the interviewing situation and the fact that each person's jerry-built grammar has a lot in common with every other person's jerry-built grammar.

18.

Related to the question of the coherence of a synchronic system is the problem of idioms. The central theoretical problem posed by idiomaticity is that

---

[16] See, for example, Bailey (1970).

of figuring out a way of describing certain forms as being *simultaneously analyzed and unanalyzed*—that is, as simultaneously having a structure and being learned and used as wholes. An internal grammar with time depth might offer a resolution by attributing to certain semantically unitary words or phrases assumptions, which in many cases will be historically accurate, about their word- or phrase-formational history. Wrong analyses of idioms give us some of the most interesting data on how this component works. There is pretty good evidence that speakers do assign morphosyntactic structure to idioms even if they have no reason to know anything about their component parts. Long idioms that are (from our point of view) misperceived and misanalyzed tend to be given morphological and syntactic structurings that account perfectly for their prosodic gestalts. That is, they are interpreted as lexical or phrasal structures capable of assigning correct stress patterns in just those cases in which no single lexical form could be given that prosodic rendering.

As William Safire has learned to his profit, it is often amusing to notice phrases that people have misperceived. Children often misperceive because they do not know what is meant by passages they have been asked to memorize. (Just who is the man Richard Stans that so many of us as children mentioned whenever we pledged our allegiance to the flag and to the republic for Richard Stans?) More interesting from a theoretical point of view are such adult misinterpretations as *for all intensive purposes* instead of *for all intents and purposes* or *it'll cost you a nominal egg* for *it'll cost you an arm and a leg*. These expressions are idiomatic; so the meaning of the whole is not a compositional product of the meanings of the parts. The problem is, why, when they are misperceived, they are not merely taken to be long, unanalyzed words.

The answer seems to be that it is only as constructs made up of morphemes and words that they can be pronounced—in particular, that they can be given the correct patternings of stressed and unstressed syllables found in these expressions that are characteristic of English phrases and complex words. A conjunction of two words with *and* generally assigns the phrase stress on the last lexically stressed syllable (*intents and PURposes, an arm and a LEG*). A structure consisting of an adjective followed by a noun, unless the adjective is used contrastively, generally requires that the phrase stress be assigned to the lexical stress on the noun (*intensive PURposes, a nominal EGG*). These expressions have been misperceived and mislearned, but in ways that assign the correct stress pattern. This phenomenon could exist only in a language in which it is perfectly normal for people to use expressions whose meanings did not have straightforward relations to their forms. The result of idiomatization is an inconvenient articulation between the morphosyntactic level and the semantic level, but a convenient and regular kind of relationship between the morphosyntactic level and the phonological level.

One way of viewing the functioning of set expressions and idioms in a language is to assume that one part of the theory-constructing activity in which a language learner engages while learning a language is constructing a history of word- and phrase-formation, something that could usefully be called 'folk etymology' were it not that that phrase is used only for etymologies known to be historically wrong. It's not just that speakers *do* this informal etymologizing but that the stress rules of English force them to.

Idiomaticity is a big question for the theory of language. It involves knowing the difference between what we have to know before we can use our language, and what we are able to figure out while we are using it. In particular, it involves questions of the nature of the articulation between morphosyntactic representations on the one hand and semantic or cognitive representations on the other. To be sure, speakers need to know the generative rules that characterize the morphosyntactic representations, and they need to know the compositional semantic rules that relate these to semantic representations. But they also need to know a large number of superimposed conventions governing the meaning, function, and popularity of certain expressions that cannot be sensibly accounted for by these general rules. One could, of course, accept a methodological *commitment* to a compositional or internal-regular relationship between morphosyntactic and semantic representations, mediated only by a lexicon of morphemes and morphemically simple words. Then, however, all the information that troubles scholars about idioms would have to be assigned to the selectional and collocational apparatus of a theory of the lexicon. The resulting analysis, even where it worked, would seem unnatural and unmotivated.

19.

All of this leads to another large question. The study of speech communication, or of language, is very different depending on whether, at the communication end, only the decoding direction is taken into consideration, or encoding also. Paul Kiparsky, some years ago, made what seemed to be a reasonable proposal for treating formulaic speech and other fixed expressions within transformational grammar. (Kiparsky 1976) It went something like this: Some formulaic expressions can be handled within the selectional apparatus of the lexicon, as long as we allow words with particular semantic features. Some will have to be listed in the lexicon as unanalyzed wholes, retried, and used as whole phrases rather than assembled from their constituents. The rest can be safely ignored: their literal meanings are accurately enough determined from the compositional principles of the semantic component, their folkloric base is sufficiently well-known, and their metaphoric base is transparent enough for hearers to be able to figure out what they mean.

It is the excluding third clause which, unlike the others, seems to favor the decoding point of view. Expressions like *bury the hatchet* can generally be understood without explanation, are freely translatable from language to language with their non-literal intentions preserved, and so on. They pose no problem for the decoder (let us say), but what about the encoder? If linguists had taken for granted from the start that the encoding operation also fell naturally within the scope of the linguist's responsibilities—that is, if it was thought that the linguist should have something to say about conventions governing what a speaker can say in particular situations to convey particular meanings—then an argument like Kiparsky's could not carry. There are many expressions whose meanings we can figure out when we encounter them, but which we could not know how to say on our own unless we were familiar with the particular conventions regarding their use. The standard answer is that this kind of knowledge belongs to folklore rather than linguistics, but one wonders how one can know in advance that this is the right attitude to take.

The fact is, not all linguists have made this assumption; so once again we are dealing with a boundary that is drawn in one way by some linguists and in another way by others. The stratificationalists in particular regard the encoding process as an essential part of the whole picture, and so do the large group of Soviet linguists who work on what they call *phraseologisms*.[17]

An attitude toward idioms that seemed reasonable fifteen years ago was that a semantic theory that fails to account for idioms has made the right choice. Idioms are by definition expressions that cannot be accounted for by compositional semantic principles or by the general principles of word formation and phrase formation that serve the language. A description of such a general system therefore has no responsibility to account for the form and meanings of idioms. If we could maintain that position about what we ordinarily think of as idioms, namely the *decoding idioms*, only then would it be self-consistent for us to maintain the same position with respect to *encoding idioms* (to use Adam Makkai's useful distinction (1972)).

In the framework of a system of representations and rules linking representations that we have adapted here, we obviously cannot begin by ignoring the encoding aspect. We can certainly assume that in many cases a part of the conveyed meaning of an utterance comes from the interpreter's awareness of whether the speaker chose or avoided the conventional expressions. Since

---

[17] A survey of the Soviet phraseological literature can be found in Jaksche, Sialm and Burger, eds. (1981).

judgments of this kind can be relevant even when the expression is completely semantically transparent, we can see that a full account of the encoder's knowledge is necessary to a full account of the decoder's abilities.

20.

It is common to propose a distinction between sentence meaning and utterance meaning. An implicit instrumental or internal-regular relation between the two levels is assumed to be capable of associating the semantic structure of a sentence to a particular instance of the sentence's use and of constructing its literal meaning out of that. We can speak of this as an anchoring operation by which, for example, indexical elements are assigned their referents. We can speak of sentence meaning as meaning in a zero context, as in the case of the famous Katz and Fodor anonymous letter (Katz & Fodor 1964:479–518), or of a neutral context in some more recent writings. The assumption here is that the sentence has a well-defined meaning that can be built on by using material taken from the context of its use.

But what if we find cases in which the context not only provides a disambiguating or an anchoring function, but also is capable of providing the information for achieving a primary semantic integration in the first place?

It is generally assumed that any interpretable sentence has a literal meaning on which its contexted meaning can be built. But maybe there are sentences that have *no* coherent literal meaning at all, that is, sentences requiring a context for their semantic interpretation even to get started? I have in mind the kind of expression that some people have called *contextuals*, as discussed in work by Geoffrey Nunberg, Herb and Eve Clark (1979:767–811), Paul Kay, Karl Zimmer (1971, 1972:3–20), and Pamela Downing (1977:810–842). If the customer who has ordered a ham sandwich is referred to by the waitress as the *ham sandwich* (Nunberg's example), if the one tour bus in a multi-bus tour that is scheduled to stop at a pumpkin farm is known briefly as the *pumpkin bus* (Zimmer's example), it might seem reasonable for us to say that these sentences do not have literal meanings outside of their context of use. In the one case, of course, we could *classify* what happens as pragmatic *metonymy* (Ruhl 1976:456–466), since it uses something associated with a person to refer to that person, and in the other case we could allow ourselves to appeal to the almost unrestricted ways in which elements in a noun compound can be related to each other. But somehow we need to bring into our account of language the fact that code-changing as well as code-exploiting creativity is an important part of linguistic competence, and that perhaps *ad hoc* name creating occurs in everyday language on a large scale. To understand a meaning, we have seen, requires understanding the contextual background within which that meaning has been codified. The difference between meanings that exist in advance and those that get created on the run is the difference between contexts known in advance and contexts presented to us as we go.

If the name-creating of the kinds just illustrated were made explicit—that is, if it were accompanied by announcements of the form *When I say 'ham sandwich'* (or *'pumpkin bus'*), *I will be referring to such–and–such*—then we would not think of informal name-creating as a part of semantic competence as such, but would include it in an auxiliary theory of metalinguistic competence. But in these and many other cases we are dealing with a class of expressions that, as I see it, have no literal meanings, are not being used metaphorically, and have no conventionalized meanings associated with them, but are nevertheless immediately and perfectly understood by everyone engaged in the situation in which they are produced. If we can recognize that the ability to produce and understand such expressions is a semantic skill, and if as I suspect contextuals play a very large role in everyday discourse, then it looks as if semantic theory will have to take into its scope the principles by which contexts figure in informal naming.

21.

In all of the cases we have looked at that touch on the meanings of utterances, it has been clear that a theory of language needs the means for relating either morphosyntactic or cognitive representations with the use of contextual information of one sort or another. On several occasions we found ourselves asking whether we need, in addition to these two, an intervening level of semantic representations. And with the last set of examples we were concerned not with whether we *need* semantic representations, but with whether we can *have* them.

It is my opinion that the final correct theory of the semantics of ordinary language will find no need for a level of semantic representation, that the everyday notion of meaning is more naturally associated with elements of cognitive representations, and that the concept of semantics can be limited to notions of the mapping between forms and meanings.

For a semantic-representation-free theory of language to work, we will have to recognize a level of representation that provides syntactically structured lexical material together with semantic information that can be associated with particular lexical items, phrasal items (where necessary), and particular syntactic forms (where necessary). This representation, together with information from the context of use, can be used to construct a cognitive representation. There may be no need, in other words, to require that compositional processes be applied to such a representation independently of the context in order to construct a mediating representation that could correspond to the context-free meaning of the sentence.

The position of formal semantics within such a theory is problematical, of course. I repeat my suggestion that formal semantics takes as its subject matter a language that is *derived from* a natural language like English; that its formal properties are selected for reasons very different from those which concern the ethnographic semanticist; and that by successive modifications and enrichments it can be made to look more and more like the source language.

I am by no means confident that the position I have taken is the correct one to take. But after hearing for so many years that those of us who have been concerned with the study of language as it is engaged in everyday acting and thinking are working in the periphery of linguistics rather than in its core, I wanted to hear what it would sound like to say it the other way around.

22.

Imagine with me that you and I have inherited a very large house and a great deal of furniture, paintings, carpets, appliances, etc., with which we can furnish it. We take the sheets off some of the furniture, unroll some of the carpets, and set to work. We begin by clearing out one room and finding furniture that seems to fit in it pretty well. Then we clear out another room, assemble some more furnishings, and decide to decorate it, too. We may find, while getting this second room ready, that one of the pieces we put in the original room looks better in this second room, and maybe we've found another piece or two that go well in the first room in its place.

As we continue decorating and furnishing the rooms of the house, we continue finding that, with each new room and each new collection of furnishings we uncover, the arrangements we made for the earlier rooms can be changed.

For a long time we live comfortably and conveniently in this house, and what's more, we feel fairly free to move things around now and then to suit our changing fancy, or to satisfy our differing tastes. We enjoy this flexibility because this is a very large house and we have managed to keep several rooms unused. Sometimes you take my two favorite chairs out of the parlor and put them into one of the storage rooms, and then move your favorite sofa from the living room into the parlor. When it's my turn to be satisfied with the decor, I drag the two chairs out of the storage room to bring to the parlor, put your sofa into storage, and ask you to find something else to take its place in the living room.

The main reason we enjoy this flexibility is that we don't care what we put into the storage rooms. But now suppose the day comes when we decide to put the whole house in order, including those hitherto unused rooms that we've only been using to get unwanted objects out of the way. It now makes a difference which paintings and chairs and rugs get put into those rooms, because they have to have a consistent and pleasing decor too. Now our decisions become more constrained. We can still have disagreements now and then, but we have by no means the same flexibility that we had when we had rooms we never used except to get things out of the way. We may even find that, in order to get the whole house furnished to our liking, we will have to remove a wall here and there, or subdivide some of the larger rooms, or even admit that some of the furniture we own doesn't fit in our house at all.

The parable isn't over yet. One day it occurs to us to draw the drapes! For the first time we notice the garden, the yard, and the mountains in the distance. Suddenly the decor in some of the outer rooms seems wrong. We now have to rearrange things to take into account the sunlight coming in the windows, we have to provide access to the garden, and so on. What our house looks like has to depend somewhat on what the surrounding world looks like.

I am talking about facts, not furniture, and about principles of explanation, not rooms and gardens. The house of language that we live in is a large house, with many rooms. We do not know yet how many rooms we have, or exactly what kinds of furnishings we will find. Until the house is completely explored and furnished, we need to be tolerant of competing plans for furnishing the small number of rooms we spend most of our time living in.

References

Bailey, C-J. N. 1970. The Integration of Linguistic Theory: Internal Reconstruction and the Comparative Method in Descriptive Analysis. *Working Papers in Linguistics, Vol. 2, No. 4*. Honolulu: The Department of Linguistics.

Bever, T. G. 1970. The Influence of Speech Performance on Linguistic Structures. *Advances in Psycholinguistics*, eds. G. B. Flores-d'Arcais and W. J. M. Levelt. Amsterdam: North Holland.

Bloch, B. and L. G. Trager. 1942.*Outline of Linguistic Analysis*. Baltimore: Linguistic Society of America, at the Waverly Press.

Bolinger, D. 1977. *Meaning and Form*. London: Longmans.

Cavell, S. 1958. Must We Mean What We Say? *Inquiry* 1; reprinted in *Ordinary Language*, ed. Y. C. Chappel, 75–112. Englewood Cliffs: Prentice-Hall.

Chomsky, N. 1982. *Lectures in Government and Binding: The Pisa Lectures*. Dordrecht: Foris.

Clark E. V. and H. H. Clark. 1979. When Nouns Surface as Verbs. *Language* 55: 767–811.

Downing, P. 1977. On the Creation and Use of English Compound Nouns. *Language* 53:810–842.

Ducrot, O. 1975. *Dire et Ne Pas Dire*. Paris.

Firth, J. R. 1935. The Technique of Semantics. *Transactions of the Philological Society*; reprinted in 1957, *Papers in Linguistics: 1934–1951*. London, 7-33.

Greene, J. 1972. *Psycholinguistics*. Harmondsworth: Penguin.

Grice, H. P. 1975. Logic and Conversation. *Syntax and Semantics 3: Speech Acts*, eds. P. Cole and J. L. Morgan. New York: Academic Press.

Halle, M. and Keyser, S. J. 1971. *English Stress: Its Form, its Growth, its Role in Verse*. New York: Harper and Row.

Halliday, M. A. K. 1961.Categories of the theory of grammar. *Word* 17: 241–292.

Hill, A. A. 1958. *Introduction to Linguistic Structures from Sound to Sentence in English*. New York: Harcourt, Brace and Co.

Hurford, J. R. and B. Heasley. 1983. *Semantics: A Coursebook*. Cambridge: Cambridge University Press.

Hymes, D. 1974. *Foundations in Sociolinguistics: An Ethnographic Approach*. Philadelphia: University of Pennsylvania Press.

Jaksche, H. J., Sialm, A., and Burger, H. eds. 1981. *Reader zur sowjetischen Phraseologie*. Berlin: Walter de Gruyter.

Katz, J. J. 1964. Semi-sentences. *The Structure of Language: Readings in the Philosophy of Language*, eds. J. J. Katz and J. A. Fodor, 400–416. Englewood Cliffs: Prentice-Hall.

Katz J. J. and J. A. Fodor. 1964. The Structure of a Semantic Theory. *The Structure of Language: Readings in the Philosophy of Language*, eds. J. J. Katz and J. A. Fodor, 479–518. Englewood Cliffs: Prentice-Hall.

Kempson, R. M. 1975. *Presupposition and the Delimitation of Semantics*. Cambridge: Cambridge University Press.

Kiparsky, P. 1976. Oral Poetry: Some Linguistic and Typological Considerations. *Oral Literature and the Formula*, eds. B. G. Scholz and R. S. Shannon. Ann Arbor.

Lakoff, G. P. and J. R. Ross. 1979. *The Imagination of Reality: Essays in Southeast Asian Coherence Systems*, eds. A. L. Becker and A. A. Yengoyan. Norwood: Ablex.

Langendoen, D. T. 1976. A Case of Apparent Ungrammaticality. *An Integrated Theory of Linguistic Ability*, eds. T. G. Bever, J. J. Katz and D. T. Langendoen, 183–193. New York: Thomas Y. Crowell.

Longacre. 1976. *Discourse Grammar*. Arlington, TX: Summer Institute of Linguistics.

Makkai, A. 1972. *Idiom Structure in English*. The Hague: Mouton.

McCawley, J. D. 1978. Conversational Implicature and the Lexicon. *Syntax and Semantics 9: Pragmatics*, ed. P. Cole, 245–259. New York: Academic Press.

Ruhl, C. 1976. Idioms and Data. *Sixth LACUS Forum*. Columbia, S.C.: Hornbeam Press, 456–466.

Schank, R. 1973. Identification of Conceptualizations Underlying Natural Language. *Computer Models of Thought and Language*, eds. R. Schank and K. M. Colby. San Francisco: W. H. Freeman.

Schank, R. 1975. *Conceptual Information Processing*. Amsterdam: North Holland.

Schank, R. and R. Abelson. 1977. *Scripts, Plans, Goals, and Understanding*. Hillsdale: Lawrence Erlbaum.

Trubetzkoy, N. S. 1958. *Anleitung zu phonologischen Beschreibungen*. Göttingen: Vandenhoeck & Ruprecht.

Wilson, D. 1975, *Presuppositions and Non-Truth-Conditional Semantics*. New York: Academic Press.

Zimmer, K. E. 1971. Some General Observations about Nominal Compounds. *Working Papers in Language Universals*, Stanford University 5: C l–21.

Zimmer, K. E. 1972. Appropriateness Conditions for Nominal Compounds. *Working Papers in Language Universals*, Stanford University 8: 3–20.

4

The Contribution of Linguistics to Language Understanding

1990
CHARLES J. FILLMORE

1. *The Problem*

In each of the several disciplines loosely collected under the heading 'cognitive science,' there are researchers hard at work trying to understand the mysterious process by which people communicate with each other in their languages. An open question in such efforts is whether linguistics has anything to contribute to this project. To put it differently, in studying language understanding, we find ourselves asking the paradoxical question of whether it helps to know anything about *language* itself. The question that gets asked is:

> in understanding a piece of language, to what extent do interpreters make use of what they know about language as such, in contrast with such things as their experiences with the physical and institutional world surrounding them, and common-sense reasoning founded on such experience?

In the opinion of some workers in language-oriented artificial intelligence, the actual linguistic material in a text does no more than pick out those facts or properties of the world on the basis of which language-independent inferencing processes do their work. The usual locution is that the word 'accesses' knowledge structures associated with things and event types in our experience. The 'labels' provided by the words in our language guide us to our memories of the 'things' in our world, and from there we rely on various sorts of inference strategies to figure out what people are trying to tell us when they talk.

In a famous debate with Ivan Sag, Roger Schank once estimated the role of syntax in language understanding to be roughly one percent of the whole. The syntactic structuring of the words in a sentence, a caricature of Schank would say, might reveal certain gross relationships among the words in the sentence—at the level of helping us figure out such things as who did what and to whom—but in a great many cases we could get along perfectly well without such information. By far the greatest part of understanding a sentence, this argument would go, consists of doing common sense reasoning based on our knowledge of the things and situations we have just been reminded of , and on our assumptions about why the creator of the message we have just encountered might want us to do or to believe.

One of my purposes today is to give evidence that the contribution of purely linguistic knowledge might be more than one percent.[1] I want to do this by displaying a range of language-interpretation phenomena which cannot be derived from anything other than the conventions of language, and which clearly participate in the activities of language understanding.

In taking this position, I am not merely being loyal to my guild. There are a great many professional linguists who would be quite content for linguistics as a pure science to have nothing at all to say about how language texts are understood by people. Whatever this latter inquiry is, it should probably be dealt with by the 'applied' branch of some stepchild of linguistics, such as pragmatics or discourse analysis, or by the natural-language division of artificial intelligence. It seems to me, however, that a great many of the lexical and grammatical resources in a language are best described in terms of the manner in which they shape, in expression and comprehension, the conceptual structures that organize linguistic messages.

2. *A Preliminary Example*

I would like to precede the presentation of my evidence by conceding that the linguistic structure of a sentence does indeed 'vastly underdetermine' (as the phrase goes) its creator's intended message. I will do this by following you through a normal interpretation of a single short sentence in English. As we work through this first example, it will become clear that, while the contribution of pure linguistics is surely more than one percent, it is certainly not close to 100 percent.

---

[1] Schank spoke only of syntax in the discussion just mentioned, but the tone of the argument could easily be taken as covering linguistic knowledge in general.

I ask you to imagine that you have overheard a particular English sentence, and that you have decided to treat this sentence as a kind of problem to be solved. The job you have taken on, as a linguistic detective, is to trace out the reasoning you go through in order to acquire an understanding of 1) the situation represented by the sentence and 2) the situation which gave rise to somebody producing the sentence. The sentence you overheard is this one:

> The defendant had indeed forged the will.

To give me the advantage of being able to refer to the speaker and the interpreter of the sentence as 'I' and 'you', and thus to avoid familiar and troublesome problems associated with English third-person pronouns, let us accept the conceit that I am the one who produced the sentence. Let us assume, furthermore, that you know nothing about the context in which my sentence was produced, and that you have forgotten anything you might have noticed about prosodic aspects of its delivery: your detective work has to depend entirely on what you know about these particular words and anything you can figure out about the grammatical structures in which they participate.

In carrying out this exercise, you will need to bring together several different kinds of knowledge. The results of your work will be a set of beliefs about what had to be true of the world represented by the text, along with certain suspicions about what *might have been true*, together with some assumptions about the setting within which I produced the sentence. Let us refer to the situation description that results from such an exercise as your 'envisionment' of the text—some coherent 'image' of, or set of possible descriptions of, some state of affairs which is compatible with the language of the text.

With a sentence as short as this, such an envisionment can be achieved without too much difficulty. With any normal long text, however, the appropriate envisionment would have to have a 'dynamic' or 'historical' aspect. That is, a complete interpretation of a large text cannot be simply a description of what has to exist in a world for which what the text says is true, but it has to include indicators of how an interpreter, experiencing the text in time, could be induced to engage particular expectations at particular points in the text, to have those expectations fulfilled or thwarted, to sense openings and closings of purposeful discourse activities represented by the text, and so on. Our sentence, however, is short and simple, and the task of constructing its envisionment will not present you with any such descriptive complexities.

You find in this sentence three content words: *defendant, forge,* and *will.* The envisionment that you ultimately derive from this sentence will depend a great deal on what you already know about the meanings and uses of these three words.

Defendant. The word *defendant* names a person who occupies a particular role in a criminal proceeding. He—or she—is the person who has been officially charged with a crime, and who can be referred to with this label only in connection with such a charge. To have a deep understanding of this word, you have to know about court trials, you have to be able to imagine the expectations and interests of a person accused of a crime in a court trial, and, more generally, you have to possess at some level an abstract schema of the workings of the criminal justice system in the culture of speakers of American English.

The defendant. As a general part of knowing English, you know that if a person is referred to by a definite noun phrase—notice the word *the*—whose head noun designates a 'role'—as does our word *defendant*—it must be the case that in the foreground of the envisioned 'world of the text' we have the kind of setting in which that role is defined, and we can assume that the person identified with the role name occupies that role within that setting. Thus you have the right to assume that when I spoke this sentence, my addressee and I were at that moment both thinking about a specific situation in which someone was officially accused of a crime.

By the time you reach the second word in our sentence you are already able to make a number of fairly detailed conclusions on the history of the situation which it depicts:

1. the person I referred to by the noun phrase *the defendant* was accused of a crime,
2. the accusation has led to a criminal trial,
3. the trial was 'a part of history' when I spoke the sentence: that is, it was in progress, or had at least been scheduled, or it may have already ended.

Will. The other noun in our sentence, *will*, belongs in a schema of estate inheritance, and that in turn links with what you know about death and about property ownership. A *will* is a document which specifies the conditions under which a person's possessions will be distributed after that person's death. When a living person wants to decide who is to own his or her property after he or she dies, a will is the legal instrument by which, within a wider system of the operation of the law, such decisions can be put on record.

Since a will is an important document, and since it is possible that persons named in a will can receive benefit from its provisions, it is important to know whether a document that appears to be a will is authentic—that it is the actual *will* which was created for and signed by the owner of the property to be distributed, and hence that it faithfully represents that person's intentions. These considerations lead you naturally to a consideration of the third content word, the verb *forge*.

Forge. This word, in the sense it must have in this context, fits into the notion of authenticity, just mentioned. To understand it, you need to know the difference between reality and appearance, especially in connection with certain crafted objects, including legal documents. Forging, in this context, is a process by which something which is not authentic is made to appear authentic. Forging differs from, say, artistic recreation, in the sense that the result of a forgery is intended to deceive.

A part of what you know about what the world is like is that false claims of authenticity often bring advantages to the person making such a claim. Forged currency can be spent, if the forgery is not detected; a successfully forged license allows privileges to accrue wrongly to its possessor. A forged will, if it is cleverly done, can bring undeserved wealth to its creator. A part of your understanding of *forging a will* is based on what you know about human nature: you can imagine the motives a person might have for attempting this kind of deception.

The sentence contains two noun phrases, identifying two objects, and it has a verb which represents a relation between them. You know, as a part of knowing English, that *forge* is a transitive verb with the *forger* (the *agent*) represented as its *subject* and the *artefact* (the *patient*) represented as its *object*. It may not have been necessary for you to know those facts, however, since you also know, about the activity of forging, that people do the forging and that documents are among the things that can be forged. If the grammatical organization of the words in the sentence had not told you which was which, you could have figured it out anyway—this is the Schankian argument—as long as you were given the information that all of these elements were part of a single clause.

So far, in the envisionment of the scene you have been able to construct from my sentence, you find a person accused of a crime described as having falsified a will. All of this is justified by a superficial interpretation of the words of the sentence, and it is supported by the nature of the grammatical relations they hold with each other. Some *natural*, but not *necessary*, intrusions into your envisionment of this text might be the assumptions: that the defendant forged the will in such a way as to benefit *himself*; that the person whose property is the subject of the will is now *dead*; and that the act of forging the will was in fact the *crime* for which the *defendant* was involved in a legal proceeding. (By using the word *himself*, in creating the conclusions I imagine you to have made, I have allowed you—based on folk knowledge of crime statistics—to assume that the person I had in mind in my sentence was male.)

These most recent embellishments are not necessary parts of the envisionment of that particular text: the sentence could be literally true of a situation in which those details did not appear. But since no communicator has the time to give you all of the details of what you are intended to understand, you have formed the habit of adding such details freely; and so has everybody else.

Indeed. Our sentence was 'The defendant had indeed forged the will.' It happens that there is nothing about the presence of the word *indeed* that has any effect on the envisionment you form of the situation represented by the sentence. But by the inclusion of that word my sentence has given you a reason to believe that at the point at which I spoke it there was some reason, on the part of my addressee, to doubt that the will in question had been forged by the defendant. One of my purposes in constructing the sentence in the way that I did was to impress upon my addressee that such doubts must be abandoned. The word *indeed* acknowledges, and proposes an end to, that assumed doubt.

This time you are not reasoning about the information that my sentence directly expressed, but about the function of a signal that I included in my sentence which made you wonder why I needed to be emphatic at this point in my discourse. The envisionment you are now constructing is that of a scene external to the text, a scene in which the text itself, and the individuals involved in its production, are among the elements.

The. Since both of the noun phrases in my sentence have definite articles, these facts about the text's form require you to believe that the person and the object known as the *defendant* and the *will* had to be a part of the conversation participants' current envisionment of the ongoing text, allowing each of the referents to be uniquely identified by this simple description. Their presence leads you to conclude that what we have here is a *mid-text sentence*. The discourse schema which provides for definiteness of noun phrases fits a text that is already in progress, and does not fit a situation in which the things being referred to are just now being introduced into the growing envisionment of the text.[2] The sentence you overheard, in other words, could not represent the beginning interaction between me and my addressee.

Had forged. There is more to say about the 'mid-text' character of my sentence. The verbal expression in it is the pluperfect form *had forged*, and that requires you to believe that my sentence was a part of a narrative in which a particular past time point had been established. At this point in the

---

[2] There are exceptions to the generalization given here about the definite article, e.g., the well-known cases of 'the sun', 'the president', 'the flag', etc.

conversation I was trying to introduce something in the 'history' of the narrative which preceded the 'current' narrative time point. Put differently, with this sentence I was not 'advancing the narrative': instead I was asking my addressee to hold in mind a recently established temporal reference point, while introducing an event or situation which is anterior to that point.

The interpretations you are building up by taking these things into account involve connection between aspects of the world represented by the text and the world containing the text. 'The world represented by the text' includes the defendant and the will and all the other people and props that had to be involved in the legal proceedings and their history. The people in 'the world containing the text' included me and whoever I was talking to, and that world also contains my intentions and motives, my knowledge of what my interlocutors already know or expect, and so on.

Now, how much of what you did involved knowledge of language? Once we agree that words are sometimes simply pointers to situation types, or to elements seen as figuring in situation types—that is, once we go along with the idea that words are names of frames with 'slots', or are the names of fillers of frame slots—we can minimize the 'linguistic' importance of such words. A very large part of the envisionment you achieved followed from very basic assumptions about how the named entities could coherently be part of a single scene. The purely linguistic elements were the functions of 1) the definite article and 2) the pluperfect tense—both of which are features of English discourse pragmatics; and 3) the rhetorical effect of the word *indeed*. These were all contributions made by the language, not derivable from knowledge about language-independent facts. But we might easily be made to agree that, while these discourse-structuring aspects of communication are important, an overwhelming case for the importance, in the process, of language knowledge has not yet been made. I have not yet given you many reasons for increasing language's contribution to language comprehension much above Roger Schank's one percent.

3. And Now, 'Language'

Workers in artificial intelligence who appear to favor the elimination of linguistic concerns in language-understanding research seem to have views that can be described in the following way.

> First, they assume 1) that the words in a language name concepts which are more or less directly linked to 'things' in the world—including objects and event types, and objects seen as playing roles in particular event types—and 2) that to a very large extent the process of understanding a text involves bringing into play what we know about those things that are indicated by

the words in the text. In our recent example, we had the three content words, and for lots of purposes that seemed to be enough.

Second, they assume 1) that syntactic rules, and the principles of compositional semantics based on structures built up on such rules, comprise the linguists' main independent contribution to theories of language understanding, and 2) that these contributions are of little value. In our case, we noted the transitivity of 'forge' and the compositional semantic instructions on how to match the grammatical elements in the sentence's syntactic structure with the 'slot-filling' elements of the underlying schemata. In this particular case, as was pointed out, we might indeed have solved our problem without that information.

A view which I hope to defend opposes these assumptions. Words are not just names of concepts, and syntax is not just a set of rules. Words and grammatical patterns represent combinations of syntactic, semantic, and pragmatic information, sometimes standing for conceptual categories of considerable complexity, whose contributions to the comprehension process is not a function of information we have about real-world objects.

I would now like to offer some examples of cases where knowledge about language, going beyond giving you the names of things, participates essentially in the interpretation process.

4. *Lexical Examples*

My first examples are lexical. I include these to make it obvious that words are not always names of things on the basis of knowledge about which reasoning can proceed. I will identify a number of words that bring along with them certain kinds of cognitive structuring or situating of the things that they 'name'. The examples are not new (cf. Fillmore 1982), but they present clearly the point I wish to make.

Coast, Shore. The English words *coast* and *shore* have in common the notion that they 'name' a sort of border between land and water, but they do so in slightly different ways. The word *coast* names the border of a major land mass, whereas the word *shore* names the border area of a water mass. These understandings are not based on knowledge that we have about what it is like for water to meet land, but on the schematizations just stated. On the basis of such schematizations, we know that a sentence like 'The trip took 3 hours from shore to shore' was a trip across water, and that a sentence like 'The trip took 3 hours from coast to coast' was a trip across land. The point is that the interpretation we give is not based on knowledge of the things, but on schematizations accompanying their names.[3]

Land, Ground, Earth. The next words—or rather phrases—come in pairs, each pair creating a paradigmatic opposition that is to be understood within a particular schematization of experience. The pairs are *on land / at sea, on the ground / in the air,* and *on earth / in heaven.* When any of these expressions is used, it communicates both the location designated and a denial of the paradigmatic opposite. Thus, a sentence like 'Pat spent only a short time on land' is generally taken as referring to a brief period in Pat's life which constituted an interruption of a sea journey; when we hear a sentence like 'Pat spent only a short time on the ground' we find it easy to believe that after this period Pat resumed flight, perhaps by re-boarding an airplane or balloon. And the sentence 'Pat spent only a short time on earth' means that Pat died young. The interpretations we are forced by these examples to construct are dictated by the schematic background motivating the contrasting oppositions, not at all by what we know about the 'facts' in question.

5. *A Little Bit of Grammar*

The linguist frequently notes relationships between meanings and the combinatorial properties of words. I can illustrate this by referring to two senses of the English verb *give* and the meaning of the verb *contribute.*

These two verbs have very similar predicate argument structures, in the sense that they both are three-argument predicates in which the arguments sort themselves out as the Giver (Agent), the Gift (Patient or Theme), and the Receiver (Goal). The verb *contribute,* however, differs from *give* both semantically and in subtle properties of its 'combinatorics.' Semantically, it adds to the simple notion of 'giving' the idea that there are multiple givers for a single recipient. Syntactically, unlike *give,* it allows its non-Agent arguments to be omitted, with specific interpretations assigned to their omissibility. (Cf. Fillmore 1985a.)

In describing a situation involving a gift between lovers, we could hear 'I gave a rose to my beloved', but neither '*I gave to my beloved' nor '*I gave a rose.' But in describing a situation involving a contribution to a social service agency, we could hear any of these: 'I contributed ten dollars to the Red Cross', 'I contributed ten dollars', 'I contributed to the Red Cross', or even 'I contributed' (more naturally, something like 'I already contributed'). For the contribute sentences, the omission of the Theme indicates only that the speaker has chosen to leave the nature or quantity of the gift unspecified;

---

[3] The facts are a bit more complicated than was suggested here, but the contrasting examples bear out the main point.

but omission of the Goal is possible only in a context in which the speaker takes it for granted that the addressee remembers, from the conversational context, what agency is the recipient of the gift.

The subtleties here include the fact that the mid-text character of a sentence with *contribute* is recognized by the *absence of one* (the Goal) of its two omissible arguments.

Now it happens that there is a metonymic use of *give*, i.e., a use where it can convey the meaning associated with *contribute*, and *in that use*, *give* shares the same omissibility properties of contribute. Thus we could hear 'I gave ten dollars to the Red Cross', 'I gave ten dollars', 'I gave to the Red Cross', and 'I gave' ('I already gave'), with exactly the same interpretations given to the omissions as before.

There is a generalization to notice here linking a semantic structure with a fairly subtle set of semantic notions, but it is not possible to see the interpreting native speakers automatically do, on hearing *give* with one or more of its arguments 'missing', as inferrable from what we know about *acts of giving*, but rather from the form/meaning associations just illustrated .

6. *The Semantics of Prepositions*

Sometimes we find that those paradigm cases of grammatical words called *prepositions* create particular image schemata which we have to co-interpret with the meanings of the words which accompany them, resulting in sometimes quite surprising combinations. A central meaning of *over* can be expressed as 'in a position, or on a path, perpendicular to a salient surface of the landmark,'[4] whereas *above* can be defined as 'vertically higher than the landmark.' The meanings do not create different images when 'the salient surface' is some portion of, or some object on, the earth's surface. 'The helicopter hovered over the playground' and 'The helicopter hovered above the playground' both express the same relationship between the helicopter and the playground. But in the following two sentences, we are asked to carry out quite different assignments: 'Hang the poster over the spot on the wall' and 'Hang the poster above the spot on the wall.' When we carry out the second instruction, we do not cover the spot; in carrying out the first instruction, we might believe, in fact, that our assignment is specifically to conceal the spot on the wall.

In a quite informal experiment I once did, I asked students to assume that a sheet of paper was a mask. In response to the instruction 'Hold the mask over your face' the mask was held vertically in front of the face. In response

---

[4] Following Ronald Langacker (1986), we refer to the object designated by the object of a locative preposition as 'the landmark'

to 'Hold the mask over your head' the mask was held flat on top of the head. In response to 'Hold the mask above your head' the mask was held vertically (presumably with the 'face' part facing forward) above the students' head. But students found the instructions 'Hold the mask above your face' puzzling, and those who knew what to do tilted their heads back and held the mask, parallel to the newly oriented 'face', above that face.

The activities on the part of the people carrying out these instructions were guided by the need to 'unify' the meaning of the preposition with the particular semantic organization of the world by which a particular surface on the human body is described as a face. There is obviously no way in which we can account for the different responses to these different instructions as involving reasoning from what people know about masks and faces!

7. *Tense and Time*

There is a great deal to say about the compatibility of the tense and aspect features signalled by a simple or complex verbal form and temporal or aspectual adverbs. It seems to me that all judgments about such compatibility possibilities represent styles of reasoning that go clearly beyond 'knowing about things.'

While the Reichenbach analysis of English tense and aspect (Reichenbach 1947: 287–298) has a number of flaws, for our purposes we can use the three analytic notions he proposed for describing certain basic tense/aspect forms. Reichenbach distinguishes 'E' as the time of an event ('Event Time'); 'S' as the time of the utterance containing the expression ('Speech Time'); and 'R' as a currently established temporal reference point ('Reference Time'). Using '=' to indicate that two of these time points are identical, and '<' to indicate that the former is anterior to the latter, we can define certain tense categories in English as follows:[5]

Present Tense $E = R = S$
Simple Past $E = R < S$
Pluperfect $E < R < S$
Present Perfect $E < R = S$

Now, by using these categories in our definitions of certain temporal adverbs, we can note the following:

---

[5] I am ignoring here some necessary qualifications about aktionsart differences and the interpretation of present tense, etc.

Today	E, R, and S are included in a single calendar day
Yesterday	E and R are included in one calendar day, S in the next calendar day
N units ago	E = R < S, and E and R are separated from S by N units
this morning	E and R are contained in the morning of the day which contains S

Given these specifications, we can note that expressions with *ago* are only possible (in nonliterary texts) with the simple past: 'He was here three days ago', but '*He has been here three days ago', etc.

Expressions with *yesterday* are possible with simple past and pluperfect, but not present or present perfect, since *yesterday* requires E = R and R < S, while the present perfect requires R = S. 'He was here yesterday', 'He had been here yesterday', but not '*He has been here yesterday', '*He is here yesterday'.

All tense possibilities are compatible with *today*. 'He is here today', 'He has been here today', 'He was here today', and 'He had been here today' (more naturally, 'He had been here earlier today').

In the case of *this morning*, we find an interesting interpretational twist. There is a difference in how we interpret 'He was here this morning' and 'He has been here this morning' that can be accounted for by computing the combinatory possibilities. Since this morning requires that R be included in the morning, and since the present perfect requires that R = S, the expression with the present perfect has to be *spoken* in the morning.

Again, we are dealing with interpretation phenomena that clearly depend on 'computations' based on linguistic knowledge, since there is no other way to argue for such relationships.

8. *The Negative Quantifier*

If you are told that I have no chairs in my house, you would know that the number of chairs in my house is zero. And if you are told that I have no kitchen in my house, you would know that the number of kitchens in my house is also zero. It can be seen from these examples that a claim about the emptiness of a set of objects can be expressed equally well with a singular or a plural noun (no chair, no kitchen). But there is an interpretation to be given to this choice. I used the plural with *chairs* because a house ordinarily has more than one chair; I used the singular with *kitchen* because a house ordinarily has only one kitchen. Or suppose I draw three smiling face figures, one with mouth, nose and eyes, one with just mouth and eyes, one with just mouth and nose. You would describe these figures by saying 'The first one is complete, the second one has no nose, the third one has no eyes.' You would not appropriately describe them by saying 'This one has no noses, and that one has no eye', even though each of these sentences should mean the same thing—namely, that the number of eyes, or the number of noses, is zero.

It appears that in these cases, the choice of singular or plural form of the noun depends on the number (one or more than one) of the members of the set that might be expected. If this is so, it should follow that if you hear me say, 'The thing that really surprised me about the wogil was that it had no blurk', you will know nothing about what a wogil or a blurk is , but you will at least know that I was expecting to find the wogil equipped with only one blurk. The truth-conditional meaning of the sentence does not convey this information, but the grammar of negative-quantifier noun phrases does.

9. *Grammatical Patterns and their Meanings*

Sometimes a grammatical pattern has a meaning of its own. It may be that this fact is not easily discovered, because usually the words that occupy the important positions in such a grammatical pattern themselves have meanings which fit the meaning of the grammatical pattern; but when we substitute a word from outside of that domain, we can discover the semantic contribution of the pattern itself. Much has been written about the Double Object Construction in English,[6] supporting the idea that it is dedicated to conveying a meaning of the sort suggested by the equation 'A verb B C' = 'A acts in such a way as to make C available to B'. ('A', 'B' and 'C' are all NPs.) Exactly fitting this pattern are such verbs as *give*, *send*, and *show*: 'I gave you my last dollar', 'She sent me a love letter', 'We showed them our passports.' But in a sentence like 'I slipped the officer a hundred-dollar bill' we construe the act of 'slipping something' as *part* of an act of 'giving something to someone', because of the occurrence of the verb *slip* in this context; and in a sentence like 'She killed me a frog' you will receive the impression that I was planning to do something with the dead frog—perhaps cook it.

English, along with a number of other European languages having articles, has what Knud Lambrecht has called the Bare Binomial Construction (Lambrecht 1984): a syntactic pattern in which two bare nouns (i.e., nouns which might ordinarily require an article appear alone) may be conjoined. A stereotyped example is *hat and coat*, as seen in the sentence 'He picked up hat and coat and headed for the door.' In this case the sentence is grammatical only because the two nouns are conjoined. With only one of them, the sentence could not exist ('*He picked up hat and headed for the door.').

---

[6] See especially the discussion in Adele Goldberg, 'The inherent semantics of argument structure: The case of the English ditransitive,' to appear in the journal *Cognitive Linguistics*.

The interpretation of such constructions seems to be something like this: that if 'A and B' is an instance of this construction, 'A' and 'B' designate objects that are joint participants in some culturally given or context-created scene. If we find bare noun conjunctions for which we are not already pre-pared with an interpretation, we find ourselves forced to create one. Thus, if we compare the following two sentences, we find that the first could merely describe a bit of bizarre behavior, whereas the second gives us the impression that the behavior is exactly appropriate. 'He removed his hat and his belt and entered the temple.' 'He removed hat and belt and entered the temple.'

10. *Conditional Sentences*

For my main example, I wish to show the tight connection between the mean-ings of English conditional sentences and features of its grammatical form. In the school of thought that I follow, a language is viewed as a repertory of lexical and grammatical resources for the expression and communication of thoughts, and the empirical study of a language is direct to the discovery of such resources.[7]

There are numerous ways of expressing conditional sentences in Eng-lish,[8] but I will limit my attention to expressions which use the introducer *if*, and in which the *if*-marked, or subordinate, clause (the *antecedent*) precedes the main clause (the *consequent*).

One descriptive problem that generative grammarians have had to face in dealing with English conditional sentences involves the complex system of compatibility relations between the two parts of a conditional sentence. That is, certain verbal forms occurring in the antecedent clause of a conditional sentence are compatible only with certain other verbal forms in the conse-quent clause. Some examples of compatible combinations are these:

---

[7] For some works in or near the construction grammar tradition, see Paul Kay 1984, Charles J. Fillmore 1985b, George Lakoff 1987, Charles J. Fillmore 1989 and Charles J. Fillmore, Paul Kay, and Catherine O'Connor 1988.

[8] For example: 'Do you like it? It's yours!' (If you like it, it's yours.); 'Come here and I'll give you a kiss.' (If you come here, I'll give you a kiss.); 'Criticize him the slightest bit and he starts crying.' (If you criticize him the slightest bit, he starts crying.); 'Get out of here or I'll call the police.' (If you don't get out of here, I'll call the police.); 'Anyone who does that deserves to be punished.' (If anyone does that, they deserve to be punished.); 'With his hat on he would look older.' (If he had his hat on, he would look older.); 'Otherwise, I wouldn't be here.' (If things were not the way they are, I wouldn't be here.); 'Unless you know Harry, you won't know what I mean.' (Only if you know Harry, will you know what I mean.).

If she opens it, they will escape.

If she opened it, they would escape.

If she had opened it, they would have escaped.

If she opened it, they escaped.

Some examples of incompatible (or at least difficult to contextualize) combinations are the following:

*If she'll open it, they had escaped.

*If she were here, I'll be happy.

*If she opens it, she had misunderstood my message.

What we need for this set of facts is some set of general principles according to which these acceptability judgments, and the accompanying interpretations, will be explained.

The concepts we need for stating these principles include the following: First, we need to have a vocabulary for describing the various verbal forms which enter into the compatibility relations just mentioned; second, we need to speak of something I will refer to as 'epistemic stance'—the speaker's stance on the reality of the proposition expressed in the antecedent clause; third, we will need to notice that some sentences give expression to what we can call the 'interlocutors' interest'—the speaker's view that of the alternatives recognized by a conditional sentence, one is looked on as matching the speaker's or the hearer's interest; and fourth, we will need to notice features of 'polarity'—the difference between positive polarity and negative polarity.

11. *Verbal Forms*

The treatment of verbal forms is made complex by the facts that 1) the relevant categories are not identifiable with particular morphemes or particular individual grammatical categories, but with complexes of these. What this means is that we will have to give different names to forms that have the same superficial appearance—or, as it happens, almost the same superficial appearance. Furthermore, in discussing the categories we need, it is necessary to keep in mind the difference between 'Time' (which we take as a semantic notion) and 'Tense' (a grammatical notion). Since we will want to use the same words for both of these categories, we shall distinguish them by using small caps for the true temporal notions (PAST, PRESENT, FUTURE).

The verbal-form categories I will use are these:

present	the form which, in the copula, results in *is, am, are* and in non-modals uses the sibilant suffix to express third–person–singular agreement.
past	the form which, in the copula, results in *was, were* and otherwise, in the 'regular' cases, the simple past–tense inflection.
future	the expression of future meaning with the modal *will* followed by the unmarked infinitive.
present subjunctive	this form is the same as the past–tense form, except that, in some dialects (perhaps especially in the U.S.) there is a single form for the copula: *were*
past sub-junctive	this form is the same as the pluperfect form (had gone, etc.), except that in colloquial English we also find a more complex form (*had've gone*, etc.), and in colloquial American English we find a form identical to what I will call 'conditional perfect': *would have gone*.
conditional	this form is constructed with *would* or *could* plus the unmarked infinitive (*would go*, etc.)
conditional perfect	this form is constructed with *would* or *could* plus the perfect infinitive (*would have gone*, etc.).

In general 'perfect aspect' and 'progressive aspect' can coexist with most of these forms and contribute their own meanings. In other words, in describing a conditional antecedent, the form 'if he has seen her' will be simply classified as 'present' for present purposes.

12. *Epistemic Stance*

For this discussion, I will be speaking of the two clauses found in certain complex sentences as 'P' (the subordinate clause) and 'Q' (the main clause). The immediately following discussion unites conditional sentences with sentences having a temporal subordinate clause.

I distinguish three sorts of epistemic stance—positive, neutral, and negative—which can be used when speaking of the speaker's commitment to the actuality of the proposition expressed in a subordinate clause.

In the case of 'positive epistemic stance', the speaker accepts the truth of the proposition expressed in the subordinate clause: Thus, in 'When Pat opened the door, the dog escaped', the speaker accepts the idea that Pat did indeed open the door and asserts that at that time the dog escaped.

In the case of 'neutral epistemic stance', the speaker takes no stand on the truth of the proposition expressed by the subordinate clause. Thus in, 'If Pat left the door open, the dog undoubtedly escaped', the speaker does not know whether or not Pat left the door open, but asserts an unfortunate consequence of such a state of affairs.

And in the case of 'negative epistemic stance', the speaker assumes that 'P' is not true, where 'P' is a proposition derivable from (and preserving the polarity of) the form of the antecedent clause. Thus, in 'If Pat had left the door open, the dog would have escaped', we hear the sentence as revealing the speaker's belief that Pat did not leave the door open.

In using the words 'positive' and 'negative' epistemic stance, rather than, say, 'believes true' and 'believes false', I have in mind the fact that we may be dealing with conceits rather than beliefs. And in the case of future-time expressions, such as the difference between 'If she invites them, they'll go' and 'If she invited them, they'd go', we will interpret the latter sentence not as expressing the speaker's *belief* that 'they' will not get invited, but that— say—'other things being equal', they are not likely to get invited.

It seems to me that there are three basic types of conditional sentences, from the point of view of Epistemic Stance. I can refer to these as Generic (in which the speaker accepts the existence of instances of P but is presenting the 'conditional' as a general principle), Neutral (in which the speaker makes no commitment about the actuality of P), and Negative (in which the speaker doubts the actuality of P). The following tables will show the relationships between Epistemic Stance, 'Time', and Verbal Form. Each cell in these tables names the form of the verbal expression that expresses the Epistemic Stance (the table), the Time (the column), and appearance as Antecedent or Consequence (the row). Any conditional sentence can be formed by choosing, from one of the tables, one cell from the upper column and one cell from the lower column. (There are some other constraints, to be noted below.)

	generic
'P'	present
'Q'	present

Neutral Epistemic Stance

	PAST	PRESENT	FUTURE
'P'	past	present	present
'Q'	past	present	future

Negative Epistemic Stance

	PAST	PRESENT	FUTURE
'P'	Past-subjunctive	Present-subjunctive	Present-subjunctive
'Q'	conditional perfect	conditional	conditional

Examples of Neutral-ES and Negative-ES conditionals, illustrating each formal possibility, follow:

Neutral Epistemic Stance

Neutral-ES: 1

o		
o		

If he went to Harvard, he *studied* Latin.

Neutral-ES: 2

	o	
	o	

If the rope is strong, I'm safe.

Neutral-ES: 3

		o
		o

If the rope *breaks*, we'*ll fall*.

Neutral-ES: 4

o		
	o	

If she *studied* Latin, she can *read* this sign.

Neutral-ES: 5

o		
		o

If I *bought* the winning ticket, I'*ll be* rich.

Neutral-ES: 6

	o	
		o

If you'*re* smart, you'*ll marry* Louise.

Neutral-ES: 7

	o	
o		

If the streets *are* wet, it *rained* last night.

Neutral-ES: 8

		o
o		

If he *dies* tomorrow, I *gave* him the wrong medicine.

Neutral-ES: 9

		o
	o	

If the light *goes* on, she's back home.

It should be noticed that there are different pragmatic purposes to conditional sentences, which we can think of as causative versus inferential.[9] Those in which the time of the antecedent follows the time of the consequent are necessarily of the inferential type.

Negative Epistemic Stance

Negative-ES: 1

o		
o		

If you *had eaten* it, you *would have died*.

Negative-ES: 2

	o	
	o	

If she *were* with me, I *would be* happy.

Negative-ES: 3

		o
		o

If she *invited* me, I *would accept*.

Negative-ES: 4

o		
	o	

If I *had bought* IBM then, I *would be* rich now.

Negative-ES: 5

o		
		o

If you *had joined* the club, you *would get invited* to the reception

Negative-ES: 6

	o	
		o

If I *were* you, I *would marry* Louise.

---

[9] For a more careful analysis of the relationships between the form and the pragmatic setting of conditional sentences, see Eve Sweetser 1990.

The upper left ('past subjunctive') corner of the Negative-ES diagram has a special status, in that there is a variety of forms that can express it. The standard form is identical to the pluperfect: 'If I hadn't opened it.' But there is a general colloquial form 'If I hadn't've opened it' and there is a special American colloquial form 'If I wouldn't have opened it.'[10] Thus:

> if I hadn't opened it
>
> if I hadn't've opened it
>
> if I wouldn't have opened it

A very important fact to notice about this collection of alternatives, and their evaluations, is that it characterizes not only the past Neg-ES forms of conditional antecedents, but also other contexts with Neg-ES meanings.

One such context is as the complement of the verb *wish*. *Wish* is the only verb in English which accepts these forms in its complement. We find (with the same acceptability judgments):

> I wish I hadn't said that.
>
> I wish I hadn't've said that.
>
> I wish I wouldn't've said that.

The verb *wish* is used not only for expressing past counterfactual wishes, but also for expressing present and future wishes. In the case of present-time wishes, we find the sentential complements of *wish* taking the same present-subjunctive form we found with present Neg-ES antecedents. Thus, in 'I wish you lived closer to Berkeley', the past-tense form is used to express a wish about a present-time situation, and in 'I wish she were here', the special form 'were' (rather than 'was') can be used.

There is one observation that keeps us from concluding that the complements of wish are simply identical, in their formal requirements, with Neg-ES antecedents, and that has to do with the FUTURE form. The future Neg-ES antecedent form is the same as the past tense, but in the case of *wish*, we do not get '*I wish you introduced me to Louise tomorrow', but 'I wish you would introduce me to Louise tomorrow', How are we going to account for the obligatory 'would' in this clause?

I would claim that clausal complements of *wish* and the antecedents of Neg-ES conditionals are indeed constructed in accordance with the same

---

[10] The examples are negative because it is my impression that dialects which welcome the 'had've' form are more likely to do so when the clause is negative.

principles, but so far we have left out one set of facts. When such a clause expresses the *Interlocutors' Interest* (or that of some other discourse-relevant individual), the future–time version is formed with the modal *would*. Since *wish* necessarily expresses the speaker's interests, the construction with *would* is obligatory in that case.

This means that we should be able to find cases of *would* in Neg-ES antecedents, and that such clauses should be taken as expressing one or both of the conversation participants' interests.

Consider first a comparison of cases where we learn from the consequent whether or not the speaker has a positive interest in the outcome.

If you spoke to my father about that, we'd get in serious trouble.

If you spoke to my father about that, I might get permission to go.

Both of these sentences are acceptable. We can infer from the first one that the speaker wants the addressee not to have this conversation, and from the second one that the conversation with the father is desired. But the *grammatical form* of the sentence does not express these judgments. But now let us look at the same sentences with *would*:

?If you would speak to my father about that, we'd get in serious trouble.

If you would speak to my father about that, I might get permission to go.

The oddity of the first of these sentences is that the consequent seems to contradict the assumption suggested by the verb form in the antecedent, assuming that the speaker of the sentence does not want trouble.

Having seen that there is a separate form for Neg-ES future antecedents revealing participant interests, we can now ask whether such a possibility also exists for Neutral-ES sentences. It appears there is, namely in the form of the modal *will*. We noted earlier that FUTURE Neutral-ES antecedents use the simple present tense form, instead of the expected *will*-future; but we can find *will* in sentences exhibiting the participants' positive interests. Compare:

If the sun'll shine, we'll be able to have our picnic.

?If it'll rain, we'll have to cancel the picnic.

If you break another dish, I'll give you a spanking.

?If you'll break another dish, I'll give you a spanking.

The questioned sentences in the preceding set are all odd, since they suggest that the speaker wants it to rain, or wants the addressee to break a dish.

In earlier work (Fillmore 1986) I suggested that the *will...will* form of a conditional sentence was dedicated to 'negotiations' or 'negotiated offers', supported by sentences like 'If you'll wash the dishes, I'll dry' and 'If it'll make you feel any better, I'll stay another day or two.' But I think now that the explanation of these forms is more general, and that the 'negotiation' aspect of the interpretation of these sentences is merely a by-product of the sentences' ability to express both participants' interests.

There is a generalization to be captured here. We are now free to say that in future–time antecedents, the modal *will* is used, and that this form has its present–tense form *will* in the Neutral-ES case, the past–tense form *would* in the Negative-ES case. Hence:

Neut		
		pres

Neg		
		past

In the cases where the future antecedent expresses the interlocutors' interests, the form *will* is used, in each case:

Neut		
		will

Neg		
		would

It is well known that the antecedents of conditional sentences are—or are capable of being—'negative polarity contexts', but this is only when the sentence does not express the interlocutors' interest. Some linguistic forms are generally welcome in only positive (or 'positive interest') sentences, e.g., *a little*. Other expressions, e.g., *any* (in the relevant meaning), are generally welcome only in sentences expressing uncertainty or negative interest. Compare the following.

If you come a little closer, you'll be able to see better.

If you come any closer, I'll call the police.

In the former case, I invite you to come closer, and propose a reason why you should be interested in doing so. In the latter case, I discourage you from coming closer, and propose a reason for you to want to do otherwise.

If we were to examine the compatibility problems for antecedent and consequent verbal forms in English conditional sentences, mentioned at the beginning of this section, we will find that the ones which are possible are those that 'fall out from' the combined principles governing tenses, epistemic stance, and interlocutor interests, and that the ones which are impossible cannot be derived from the patterns that such principles create. The contributions of these formal properties to sentence interpretation are considerable, and they are subtle, but in no case could we say that the reasoning we carry out in achieving the understandings we achieve are based on information that is available to us by anything other than pure linguistic means. Nor can we say that any of it has to do with 'natural' inferences related to 'conditionality'. A great deal of research has been done on conditional sentences in Japanese, and from this work it is clear that almost none of the semantic properties associated with English conditional sentences play a role in the structuring of the nearest equivalent in Japanese, and vice versa. Every aspect of this is based on language-specific linguistic conventions.

13. *Conclusions*

My purpose in this paper was a humble one—to suggest that the role of linguistics in, and the knowledge that linguistics can contribute to, a program of research dedicated to understanding the mysteries of human linguistic communication, should be seen as greater than one hundredth of the whole. That humility was insincere. Since, as I believe, almost every step of the process of understanding language texts must build on structures that exist by virtue of the lexical and grammatical resources of individual languages, and since whatever inferencing strategies get called on must produce conceptual structures that need to be integrated with those that are created by the linguistic properties of the text, I actually believe that the participation of linguistics in the final work is absolutely essential. Words, grammatical categories, and complex grammatical constructions, bring with them information needed for creating and packaging the conceptual structures that make up our understanding of language, and while much of this is motivated by or anchored in beliefs and institutions that exist independently of language, almost all of it is intimately tied to language itself as a system of conventions.

References

Fillmore, C. J. 1982. Frame semantics. The Linguistic Society of Korea (Ed.). *Linguistics in the Morning Calm*. Seoul: Hanshin, 111–137.

Fillmore, C. J. 1985a. Pragmatically controlled zero anaphora. *Proceedings of the Berkeley Linguistics Society* 12: 95–107.

Fillmore, C. J. 1985b. Syntactic intrusions and the notion of grammatical construction. *Proceedings of the Berkeley Linguistics Society* 11: 73–86.

Fillmore, C. J. 1986. Varieties of conditional sentences. ESCOL 3 (Eastern States Conference on Linguistics 3): 163–182.

Fillmore, C. J. 1989. Grammatical construction theory and the familiar dichotomies. *Language processing in social context*, ed. R. Dietrich and C. F. Graumann. North Holland: Elsevier.

Fillmore, C. J., P. Kay, and M. C. O'Connor. 1988. Regularity and idiomaticity in grammatical constructions: The case of *let alone*. *Language* 64: 501–538.

Goldberg, A. 1992. The inherent semantics of argument structure: The case of the English ditransitive. *Cognitive Linguistics* 3 (1): 37–74.

Kay, P. 1984. The *kind of/sort of* construction. *Proceedings of the Berkeley Linguistics Society* 10: 157–171.

Lakoff, G. P. 1987. *Women, fire and dangerous things*. Chicago: University of Chicago Press.

Lambrecht, K. 1984. Formulaicity, frame semantics and pragmatics in German binomial expressions. *Language* 60: 745–796.

Langacker, R. 1986. *Foundations of cognitive grammar*. Chicago: University of Chicago Press.

Reichenbach, H. 1947. *Elements of symbolic logic*. New York: MacMillan.

Sweetser, E. 1990. *From etymology to pragmatics*. Cambridge: Cambridge University Press.

Part 2

*The Foundations of Construction
Grammar*

Syntactic Intrusions and the Notion of Grammatical Construction[1]

1985
CHARLES J. FILLMORE

1. *Introduction*

It has always been assumed in the generativist tradition that *phrasal constituents* can be introduced into a sentence only by means of proper phrase structure rules (or their equivalents), and hence only at the initial level of a sentence's derivation. In the past two decades, in fact, it has seemed important to limit the introduction of individual *lexical elements*, even of the 'syntactic trappings' sort, to phrase structural means.[2] The phenomena that I'll be considering here, under the somewhat unhappy label of *syntactic intrusions*, will support the suggestion that the grammatical apparatus for introducing lexical and phrasal elements into a sentence sometimes requires a kind of context-sensitivity best expressed by reference to *host constructions* of a particular sort, such constructions often endowed with properties which are not independently determined by facts about their constituency or their derivation.

The phenomena to which I wish to direct your attention are, in both cases, instances of disapproved linguistic usages in English. I take the social status of my phenomena as a guarantee of the importance of what I have to say about them, rather than as evidence for its triviality. Whenever we find

---

[1] The author is grateful to Farrell Ackerman, Amy Dahlstrom, Georgia Green, Paul Kay, Tom Larsen, Mary Catherine O'Connor, and Peter Trudgill for comments on an earlier version of this paper. I first learned about Valerie Lambert's thesis from Peter Trudgill.

[2] Here I have in mind the lexical redundancy rule treatment of passivization, the phrase-structural introduction of COMP and its fillers, etc.

impressive regularities in language that we know we didn't learn either at mother's knee or in Miss Fidditch's classroom, we can be sure that we are in touch with structures seated deep in the language, and not inventions externally imposed upon it.

In defending a 'constructionist' point of view, I will need to point to situations in which semantic or pragmatic properties of linguistic structures can be seen as determinants of certain otherwise unexplained possibilities for introducing elements. And since some of the constructions which serve as hosts for phrase insertion have to be seen at what is, from a transformationalist point of view, a 'non-initial' stage of a derivation, I will also need to argue in favor of a single level representation of complex syntactic objects, as opposed to multi-level or derivational representations. (I claim originality for neither of these inclinations.)

2. *The Notation*

In representing constituent structure I use *container diagrams*, as in Figure 1: constituents are portions of text shown as contained in ovals or rectangles bearing category labels. Transparently, container diagrams have the same properties as *branching tree diagrams* or *bracketing representations* of constituent structures—the 'containers' constructed by closing off the brackets above and below. But since I intend to use lines and arrows for superimposing on pure constituent structure representations other sorts of information, the *branches* of branching tree diagrams would get in the way.

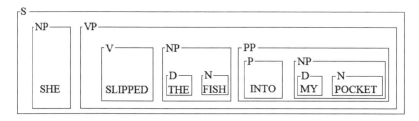

Figure 1

3. *Syntactic Intrusion Type I*

Consider, first, the mysterious extra syllable that occurs, in certain *past counterfactual clauses*, after the word *had* or *hadn't*. It can be heard in the second of the following two examples.

(1) If you had eaten it, you would have died.

(2) If you had *'ve* eaten it, you would have died.

Although there was a brief time when I thought this syllable was akin to the interloper syllable in expressions like *how big of a box*, it appears quite clearly to be a contracted form of *have*, sometimes given full pronunciation, but most typically realized as [əf] before a consonant and [əv] before a vowel. Using the name given it by the Oxford English Dictionary, I'll refer to the phenomenon as *redundant have*. The form is disapproved by normative grammarians, but it appears not to be subject to social class variation (Lambert 1983). As Lambert's research shows, speakers are not easily made aware of it.

It may be necessary to point out immediately that *redundant have* is not merely a colloquial variant of the pluperfect. That is, we do not find, at any level of informality, sentence (4) as a way of saying (3).

(3) At that time I hadn't opened your letter.

A 'redundant have' version:

(4) *At that time I hadn't *'ve* opened your letter.

The principal generalization to make about *redundant have* is that *it occurs in past counterfactual clauses*, that is in clauses pluperfect in form and with a polarity-reversing presupposition. We note that:

1. It occurs in the *if*-clause of a counterfactual conditional sentence:

    (5) If I hadn't *'ve* seen it, I would have stepped in it.

2. It occurs as the counterfactual complement of *wish*:

    (6) I wish I hadn't *'ve* said that.

3. It occurs in exclamatory sentences beginning with *what if* or *if only*.

    (7) what if I'd *'ve* opened it?[3]

    (8) if only I hadn't *'ve* said those things.

4. It occurs in certain expressions which invite the addressee to imagine a nonactual situation:

    (9) supposing you hadn't *'ve* caught the train.

5. It occurs in certain contexts in which the non-actuality or counterfactuality of the proposition is already assumed:

    (10) By the time you'd *'ve* noticed it, it'd 've been too late.

The reason redundant *have* is a problem is that its occurrence in these contexts is not supported by anything else we know about English. There is no other situation in English calling for an infinitive form to occur after the perfect auxiliary, certainly none that could be limited to the past tense of that auxiliary. It is limited, we have said, to clauses construed *counterfactually*, and these can occur in a wide variety of syntactic environments.

Occasionally you hear speculation on the origin of the phenomenon in terms of an analogically introduced rhythmic pattern which allows protasis and apodosis of a counterfactual conditional sentence to achieve a kind of metric balance, as in (11),

    (11) If Harry had've opened it, Lucy would've left.

where *had've* and *would've* are rhythmically paired. Such explanations are unsatisfying, not only because our *have* syllable occurs in counterfactual contexts not supported by a following clause—such as as a complement of

---

[3] Many American observers see examples like (7) and (10) as abbreviations of *would*, not *had*. The examples are drawn from or modeled after BrE attestations, where interpretation as *would* is ruled out. My assumption about the Americanism 'If she would have come' is that it is a reconstruction (or 'disabbreviation') of contracted 'had have.' Trudgill and Hannah speak of it as 'relatively recent' (1982:47) and limited to AmE. Victoria Liptack (U.C. Santa Cruz) has suggested in conversation that in *redundant have* it is not the *have* about which something special needs to be said, but the *had*: that, in fact, the word *had* comes to function, in past hypothetical clauses, as a modal. Looked at this way, the American 'disabbreviation' of *'d* as *would* would seem quite natural. I am not able to evaluate this proposal.

wish—but also because its *earliest* appearances seem to be, *not* in the *if*-form of a past counterfactual conditional sentence, but in the *fronted had*-form. In the O E D's section on *redundant 'have'*, there are two early citations. The first is from Sir Thomas Malory, fifteenth century,

(12) Had not he have be, we should never have retorned.

and the second from Owen Feltham, seventeenth century:

(13) Cleanthes might well have failed, had not accident have helped him.

Interestingly, the only instances of redundant *have* I find in Fowler (*Modern English Usage*), where he describes the phenomenon as 'illiterate blundering,' are of the *fronted had* form, that is, without *if*:

(14) Had I have been in England on Monday, I should certainly have been present at the first performance.

It is obvious from these examples that the intruded form is not simply cliticized onto *had*, since the word *had* can move away from it in *if*-less conditionals, as in (15).

(15) Had I *'ve* opened it.

Nor does it appear likely that it is cliticized to the following participle, as shown by examples such as (16).

(16) What if I hadn't *'ve* ever said that?

4. *On the Non-Existence of Counterfactual Conditionals*

Now since I have made such a point about the *redundant have* being limited to counterfactually understood clauses, and since the most common occurrences of it are in counterfactual conditional sentences, I am obviously obliged to say something about recent claims that conditional sentences with counterfactive presuppositions do not exist. Reinhart (1976) has suggested that conditional sentences said to introduce counterfactive presuppositions really only *implicate* the falsity of their propositional content. She describes two interestingly different possible contexts for the following sentence:

(17) If the Dean hadn't answered my letter, I would've resigned.

In one context we can imagine the speaker as someone who wrote to the dean, and who received an answer to her letter. The clause *If the Dean hadn't answered my letter* is construed counterfactually by implication: the Dean did answer the letter, and the speaker proposes that any world, distinct from the actual one, in which the Dean *fails* to answer the letter, is a world in which the speaker resigns. We know that this is a matter of implicature only, says Reinhart, from the fact that there are contexts in which a sentence with exactly the same lexicosyntactic form can be spoken with such an implicature absent. In this second context, the addressee, not the speaker, has written to the dean, and the dean did not answer the letter. The speaker, putting himself in the addressee's place, says

(18) If the Dean hadn't answered <u>my</u> letter <u>I</u> would have resigned.

This time there is no suggestion that the Dean answered the speaker's letter, or that the speaker ever wrote to the dean in the first place.

While it may be the case that the *sentential form* of a pluperfect clause in a conditional sentence does not always require a counterfactual interpretation, it happens that *redundant have* can appear only when such an interpretation is present. Thus, the person who stayed on the job as a result of the Dean's correspondence could say

(19) If the Dean hadn't *'ve* answered my letter, I would have resigned.

In the non-counterfactual context, however, you would not find anybody saying

(20) *If the Dean hadn't *'ve* answered <u>my</u> letter, <u>I</u> would have resigned.

The 'construction' at hand is a clause having the form and understood as counterfactual; and the intrusion is the intrusion of *have*, in unstressed contractable form, after the word *had*. See Figure 2.

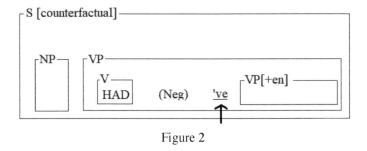

Figure 2

The very argument which I have just presented in favor of a view which recognizes grammatical constructions could, in an older framework, have been given in favor of a particular formulation of an insertion transformation, like *DO-Support*. If there is a difference, it is in my intuition that the phenomenon in question relates in a quite specific way to a structure which must be simultaneously formally and notionally defined, and my suspicion that grammatical theory will eventually provide the means of recognizing such structures. In the next example the inserted material is a class of phrases rather than a single morphological element, and so the feasibility of treating the phenomenon in terms of an insertion transformation is reduced.

5. *Interlude on Displacement Structures*

Since my second example involves *initial WH-phrases*, I need to digress on the 'constructional' nature of *displacement* structures, structures in which a constituent is *presented* for some grammatical or rhetorical purpose in one part of the sentence but *interpreted* in another. The constituent in question, displaced to the front of its clause, is linked to a gap at a specific site elsewhere in the clause, in such a way that at the place of the gap it satisfies the requirements of some predicational structure or provides some sort of adverbial modification of the clause.

In the exclamatory sentence represented by Figure 3,

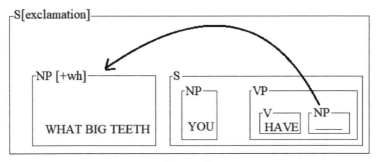

Figure 3

the phrase *what big teeth*, found at the sentence's beginning, is interpreted as the object of the verb *have*. To say that, of course, is not yet to have given the sentence an analysis. We could view a *displacement structure* of the sort just noticed simply and only as a *grammatical construction* of a particular kind: a *WH-word phrase* is in construction with a clause containing a *gap*, bearing with that gap the kind of interpretive link just described. Alternatively, we could say that the initial WH-phrase has been moved to the sentence's front by a transformation of WH-Movement, and regard the diagram showing the gap and the link as a record of the derivational history of the sentence's development from an abstract deep structure to the observed surface structure. As a kind of abbreviated 'T-Marker', in an older idiom.

The best sort of argument in favor of the 'constructionist' view is the inverse of the kind of argument we all learned in defending the transformationalist view. The standard case for the correctness of the movement treatment is a demonstration of the numerous ways in which 'fronted constituents' fit their assigned gap, in respect to phrasal category membership, case assignment, selection restriction, potential for theta-role bearing, and all the rest. If in their form they satisfied expectations contracted at the site of the gap perfectly, we had reason to believe they were generated there, suited the requirements of their environment at that site and must therefore have ended up where we see them by way of a movement rule. Arguments for a constructionist or nonmovement position, therefore, should concentrate on properties of initial constituents which do *not* agree with what is permitted or required at the site of the linked gap.

One such argument has been pointed out to me recently by Paul Kay, involving nominal constituents fronted before *that* and *though*, as in

(21) foolish child that he was, ...

(22) strong team member though she is, ...

(23) ridiculous suggestion that it at first seemed, ...

Said in X′ jargon, the nominal phrase in these expressions is an N′ rather than an N″; that is, it is something which could not be found, just like that, in the position from which it is alleged to have 'moved.' Semantically there is no doubt the fronted constituent fits and needs to be interpreted at the gap to which it is linked, but it couldn't have been generated at that place in that form. That is, we don't say

(24) *He was foolish child.

(25) *She was strong team member.

(26) *It was ridiculous suggestion.

6. *Syntactic Intrusion II*

But the phenomena that interest me just now are not things which are *left out* in particular positions in a construction but things which are *introduced* into a construction.

A favorite exercise in middle level syntax classes is to explore the conditions under which in English it's possible to pepper up one's speech with certain intruding interjections. I have in mind mainly *the*-phrases like *the hell*, *the devil*, *the heck*, *the deuce*, etc. (there may be others), but also certain formulaic prepositional phrases, usually with *in* or *on*, such as *on earth*, *in the world*, *in tarnation, in heaven's name*, etc. (The two types have slightly different distributional possibilities, but I will ignore those here.) A generalization that can be made about these phrases is that *they can occur immediately after any clause-initial interrogative WH-word, except which.*

1. The initial position requirement for our phrases predicts correctly that they do not occur in *echo questions*. Thus we get such judgments as the following:

(27) What did you see?

(28) What the heck did you see?

(29) You saw what?

(30) *You saw what the heck?

2.   The requirement that the WH-<u>word</u> welcoming our phrases be clause-initial predicts that insertion of *the heck*, etc., is only possible when all preceding parts of a WH-phrase are left stranded. Thus we get the following judgments:

(31) What did you fix it with?

(32) What the devil did you fix it with?

(33) With what did you fix it?

(34) *With what the devil did you fix it?

3.   The phenomenon occurs only in interrogative clauses, not in homophonous *free relatives*. In (35),

(35) I can't imagine what she cooked.

what she cooked is an interrogative clause. In (36),

(36) I couldn't eat what she cooked.

it is a free relative, meaning something like 'that which she cooked.' Notice that it is possible to say (37) but not (38).

(37) I can't imagine what in heaven's name she cooked.

(38) *I couldn't eat what in heaven's name she cooked.

4.   The phenomenon in question occurs only with *displaced* WH-words, hence not with the word *whether* in a subordinated interrogative clause. Thus we don't get

(39) *I don't know whether the heck they're coming.

5.   It doesn't occur with the word *which*, either as a determiner, as in (40),

(40) *Which the heck books do they recommend?

or as a full NP, as in (41).

(41) *Which the heck did you choose?

What, as well as *which*, can be used in 'determiner' position in interrogated noun phrases, but a number of informants who reject *which the heck* find (42) acceptable.

(42) What the heck books did they read?

6. Bolinger (1976) has suggested that the word *else* that occurs after indefinite prowords, plain and interrogative, really functions as a suffix rather than as a separate word. We can now see, however, that the mechanism that allows us to introduce *the heck* and its kin shows that to be not *quite* true. Notice examples (43) and (44):

(43) Who the hell else did you invite?

(44) Where the hell else do you want me to take you?

7. We are accustomed to thinking of the word *whose* as a single tightly bound word, but we are also aware of the modern English S-genitive as being sometimes called a *phrasal genitive*, as illustrated in such expressions as (45).

(45) The king of England's hat

Perhaps the suffix we see in *whose* is not as tightly associated with the *who* as the spelling would suggest, since we can, after all, say (46).

(46) Who the heck's fault do you think it is?

The observation that *the heck* follows the 'first word' exposes the true structure of the word *whose*.

It seems to me that the only way to account for the phenomenon of the intrusion of *the heck* into a question is to recognize a construction (see Figure 4) in which a WH-word, not *which*, is in initial position in a fronted WH-word phrase, and to introduce into the position after that word a special category—possibly unique to this construction—capable of being realized as one of our peppery interjections. It is not easy to imagine this category introduced merely parasitically on some constituent participating in WH-Movement: the clause in which it occurs has to be an interrogative clause, the WH-word has to be destined to become the first word in the sentence, and it can't be the word *which*.[4]

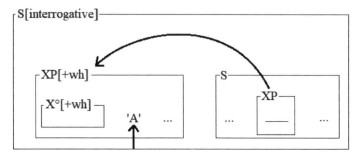

'A' = the heck, the hell, the devil, etc
X° ≠ which

Figure 4

7. Grammatical Constructions

It has been common, in recent work within the Transformationalist tradition (Chomsky 1981, Stowell 1981) to abandon the use of the phrase structural apparatus for providing the subcategorizational environment for lexical items, calling instead on structures linked to particular lexical items capable of serving as some such category as VP. The rejected batteries of phrase structure rules stand instead as a set of generalizations over the contents of subcategorization frames. Typically the pretense is maintained that such

---

[4] The full story has not been told. Our phrases may follow some instances of the *-ever* versions of free relatives: 'Do whatever the hell you want' (example from Georgia Green). Green and Morgan (1976) propose some pragmatic conditions for the choice of *the hell*, etc., and these have *something* to do with whether the speaker (or somebody whose interests the speaker cares about) is 'ignorant of' (to which one might add 'has no interest in') 'the answer to the question that corresponds to the *WH-the-hell* clause.' (Green and Morgan 1976:234). This explanation comes close, but counterexamples are disturbingly easy to construct.

structures are shallow, consisting solely of the lexical item in question and its co-constituents—its structural sisters. This pretense requires various technical tricks to take care of the instances in which a prepositional complement requires a particular preposition or a clausal complement requires a particular complementizer or a particular mood.

If new-style lexical entries for content words were to be seen instead as *constructions* capable of occupying particular higher-phrase positions in sentences and included both the needed semantic role and the needed specification of structural requirements (where sometimes nieces and grand-nieces are as important as sisters), we could see such structures as providing expansions of their containing categories. Structures of this sort with multiple occurrences of content-words would be the language's idioms. Structures of this sort lacking content words would be the language's major and minor grammatical constructions. Thus, it is possible to see Figure 2 as not merely the construction within which *redundant have* is introduced, but as the construction which provides the form of a past counterfactual clause in the first place, the 'intrusion' taken as optional. Figure 4, however, cannot be seen as the structure for WH-Movement, or for WH-Moved Questions, but only as the construction within which our family of interjections can be inserted.

The people who decide on such things would surely declare that the phenomena I have been describing belong to the 'periphery' of grammar and not its 'core', and they might be quick to tell us that within the 'core,' displacement structures are equivalently described constructionally or transformationally, the two being 'mere notational variants' of each other. I would like to suggest that since in the 'peripheral' cases the 'constructional' account has, as I see it, a number of advantages, perhaps a constructional treatment should be preferred throughout. This would at least make it less necessary to believe that there is a major discontinuity between Core Grammar and The Periphery.

References

Bolinger, D. 1976. Meaning and memory. *Forum Linguisticum* 1:1–14.

Chomsky, N. 1981. *Lectures on Government and Binding*. Dordrecht: Foris.

Fowler, H. W. 1926/1954. *A Dictionary of Modern English Usage*. Oxford: Oxford University Press.

Green, G. and Jerry L. Morgan. 1976. Notes toward an understanding of rule government. *Studies in the Linguistic Sciences* 6(1):228–248. University of Illinois Linguistics Department.

Lambert, V. 1983. *The Non-Standard Third Conditional in English: A Sociolinguistic Study*. M.A. thesis, University of Reading.

Reinhart, T. 1976. Polarity reversal: Logic or pragmatics? *Linguistic Inquiry* 7:697–705.

Stowell, T. 1981. *Origins of Phrase Structure*, Ph.D. Dissertation, MIT.

Trudgill, P. and J. Hannah. 1982. *International English: A Guide to Varieties of Standard English*. London: Edward Arnold.

6

The Mechanisms of 'Construction Grammar'

1988

CHARLES J. FILLMORE

1.

In this paper I will sketch out some of the working parts of a grammatical framework that gives central place to the notion of *grammatical construction*. Rejecting that view of grammar which prides itself in being able to get along without this concept, my colleagues and I have come to believe that, in a framework which takes grammatical constructions as its primary units, not only can we allow the individual constructions in the languages we study to be as complex as they need to be, but we are also able in its terms to recognize powerful generalizations of both language-specific and language-universal sorts.

Unfortunately, the framework I'll be speaking about is a moving target; in fact, it is one of a set of several moving targets with the same name. My goal in this paper is merely to lay out enough of the working assumptions on which I think most of the Berkeley constructionists are agreed, at least in the area of syntax, and to define and display some of the structures and notations which illustrate the application of these assumptions to a small selection of both central and noncentral phenomena in the syntax of English.

Not only is Construction Grammar a moving target; so are the theories with which one might compare it. Briefly, construction grammars differ from *transformational grammars* in not having transformations. That is to say, re-lationships that are presented in transformationalist theories as participating in the derivation of individual sentences, and hence in their structure, are treated instead as relationships defined in the grammar as a whole.[1] Construction grammars differ from *simple phrase-structure grammars* in that the categories that label the units of structure include complex bundles of information, rather than simple atomic categories. Construction grammars differ from phrase-structure grammars which use *complex symbols* and allow the *transmission of information* between lower and higher structural units, in that we allow the direct representation of the required properties of subordinate constituents. (Should it turn out that there are completely general principles for predicting the kinds of information that get transmitted upwards or downwards, this may not be a real difference.) And construction grammars differ from *phrase-structure grammars in general* in allowing an occurring linguistic expression to be seen as simultaneously instantiating more than one grammatical construction at the same level.

While construction *grammars* have similarities to a number of other approaches to grammar, meaning, and natural language understanding, construction *grammarians* differ from many other workers in the generativist tradition by their insistence on simultaneously describing grammatical patterns *and* the semantic and pragmatic purposes to which they are dedicated, and by their tendency to give attention to the fine and fussy details of what might be called the *noncentral constructions of a language*. This tendency shows itself, for example, in George Lakoff's detailed survey of constructions in English introduced by the words *here* and *there* (Lakoff 1987:462–585); in Knud Lambrecht's studies of the clause types of colloquial French that are used in structuring information (Lambrecht 1986), to which we should now add his contribution to this year's BLS collection; in Paul Kay's studies of scalar and metalinguistic qualifiers in English (Kay 1984, 1988); in the paper by Mary Catherine O'Connor, Paul Kay, and me, on the English *let alone* construction (Fillmore, Kay and O'Connor, 1988); and in a body of work currently in progress on the part of a number of graduate students.[2] Our reasons for concerning ourselves with otherwise neglected domains of grammar are not so that we can be left alone, by claiming territory that nobody else wants, but specifically because we believe that insights into the mechanics of the grammar as a whole can be brought out most clearly by the work of factoring out the constituent elements of the most complex constructions.

---

[1] This is a point which has been given particular emphasis by George Lakoff. At issue here is, for example, whether in the structure of a *sentence* one needs to represent simultaneously the position out of which a topicalized constituent has been 'extracted' or whether in the structure of the *grammar* one needs to show the relationship between topicalized sentences and sentences with all of their constituents 'in place'.

[2] There is, of course, a huge body of literature on the functions of specific grammatical constructions, especially in the Generative Semantics tradition, but also in numerous standard reference grammars and pedagogical grammars.

2.

By *grammatical construction* we mean any syntactic pattern which is assigned one or more conventional functions in a language, together with whatever is linguistically conventionalized about its contribution to the meaning or the use of structures containing it.

On the level of syntax, we distinguish for any construction in a language its *external* and its *internal* properties. In speaking of the *external syntax* of a construction we refer to the properties of the construction as a whole, that is to say, anything speakers know about the construction that is relevant to the larger syntactic contexts in which it is welcome. By the *internal syntax* of a construction we have in mind a description of the construction's make-up. The familiar *phrase-structure rules* can be read off as descriptions of (the syntactic portions of) constructions: the symbol to the left of the rewrite arrow, standing for the category of the whole construction, represents its external syntax, while the sequence of symbols to the right of the rewrite arrow indicates the construction's internal syntax, and it does this by specifying the external categories of the constructions which can serve in given positions within it. The constructions that most hold *our* interest, however, are of greater complexity than that of simple phrase-structure sub-trees of depth one.

There are various interchangeable notations for representing linguistic structures in construction grammar. One that I will use is a boxes–within–boxes notation in which information about the external syntactic, semantic and pragmatic requirements of a construction is written in the perimeter of the box, with smaller boxes drawn inside to display the construction's internal syntax. In Figure 1, a category with the *xxx* value of the attribute *aaa* has as its two constituents one with the *yyy* value of attribute *bbb* and, to its right, one with the *zzz* value of attribute *ccc*.

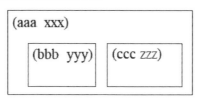

Figure 1

Formally, diagrams of this sort are exactly equivalent to constituent structure diagrams with fancily decorated node labels.

An advantage in using the box notation is that in a step–by–step demonstration of the parsing of a sentence, we can draw boxes around the elements of surface linguistic expressions, allowing us to build up a complex description of a complex expression by showing how it exemplifies the superimposition of construction upon construction.

The grammar of a language can be seen as a repertory of constructions, plus a set of principles which govern the nesting and superimposition of constructions into or upon one another. The generation or analysis of linguistic expressions involves fitting grammatical constructions together in as many ways as possible, allowing them to come together only when they match each other's requirements (or when there's something interesting to say about what happens when they don't), and stopping when every lexical category is occupied by a phonological form, and when every obligatory attribute has been provided with a value. In ways made familiar in all versions of generative grammar, whenever we can find more than one way of assembling constructions to yield the same expression form, that form is shown to be ambiguous in ways explained by the differences in the contributing constructions.[3]

3.

At least some of the grammatical properties of a construction can be given as feature structure representations, that is, as sets of attribute–value pairs, and can be seen as generally satisfying the requirements of a unification-based system. Since the basic phrasal categories will be selected from a set of fixed and mutually exclusive types, we can represent these by the attribute *category*, abbreviated *cat*, paired with one of the values it accepts, such as *N*oun, *V*erb, *A*djective, etc.; they will thus be introduced with such formulas as (cat N) or (cat V). We are currently representing the ranks or levels of headed constructions in terms of *maximal* and *minimal categories*, where maximal categories fill major structural positions in constructions, and minimal categories are the stored or derived units of the lexicon. We believe that these distinctions give us a way of achieving successfully what is aimed at by the so-called 'X-bar theory'. Major category units will be expressed as pairs of features of the category and level types. Thus, a maximal nounphrase will be represented as

(cat N) (max+)

whereas a lexical adjective will be represented as

(cat A) (min +)

---

[3] While I will be speaking mostly of constructions on the level of phrases and clauses, we assume that similar principles are at work in word-formation and in the conventionalized patterns that structure discourse.

Maximal categories which are phrases are (max +)(min –); structures which are phrasal but nonmaximal are (max –) (min –). There are no incompatibility relations between the level features of maximality and minimality. The abandonment of the notations of X-bar syntax in favor of the separation of features of phrasal maximality and minimality creates the possibility that lexical items which may but need not serve as maximal phrases can be listed as having unspecified maximality, and lexical items which necessarily serve as maximal phrases, such as proper names (when used as proper proper names) and personal pronouns, can be listed as having their maximality feature marked '+'. We therefore avoid the need to recognize a name like *Joe* or a pronoun like *she* as simultaneously an N-zero, an N-bar, and an N-double-bar. Instead of a columnar representation of the categorial nature of the name *Joe*, as in Figure 2, we will prefer a representation in which *Joe* is given simultaneously as a word and as a maximal phrase, as seen in Figure 3.

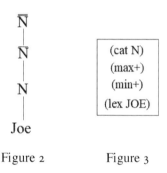

Figure 2   Figure 3

Here JOE is recognized as a lexical item (hence as *min+*) but one whose external syntax is that of a maximal phrase. With names and personal pronouns there are obvious reasons why they are lexical items, and reasons of grammatical behavior why they are maximal nominals; but there is no reason to assign to such words an additional intermediate structural level of the so-called N-bar.

4.

Considerations of maximality in nominal expressions lead in a natural way to our first example of a construction: the English *determination construction*, which consists of a maximal noun phrase containing a determiner and a non-maximal nominal head.

Since the 'determiner' in a 'determiner plus nominal' construction can be any of a variety of categories (that is, it can be an article, a possessive nominal, or a demonstrative), I introduce the term 'determiner' as a *role* name rather than as a *category* name. The category of its fillers can be left unmentioned. Articles will be marked in the lexicon as necessarily having the determiner role, demonstratives and instances of the possessive construction will be described in a way that shows them capable of filling the determiner slot. The construction will look something like what is shown in Figure 4:

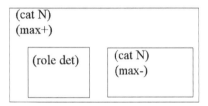

Figure 4

This diagram states that the combination of a determiner with, to its right, a nonmaximal nominal, counts as a maximal noun phrase. A pronoun or a proper name will not fit the second slot in this construction because it would be marked with maximality value '+', and what is required here is maximality value '−'; a mass noun will fit it because with a mass noun the maximality value is left unspecified; a singular count noun will fit it because a count noun is marked with maximality value '−'. Thus:

proper noun:	**(cat N)(max +)**
mass noun:	**(cat N)(max　　)**
singular count noun:	**(cat N)(max −)**

(We will naturally need to include a mechanism in the morphology for demarking count nouns when they are made plural, as well as mechanisms for recognizing that both mass nouns and proper nouns have special uses in which they exhibit the syntax of count nouns.)

It is now necessary to modify my earlier statement that maximal phrases fill major structural positions in sentences. English has various constructions requiring nonmaximal nominals, that is, lexical or phrasal nominals that would need a determiner in order to appear in true argument position in a clause. One of these is the *Unique-Role Nominal Predicate Construction*, exemplified by sentences like *I was chairman of the committee, She is chief surgeon to the royal family, You are now president of the club*, and so on. (The semantics of 'unique role' is suggested by the unacceptability of **she is member of the club*; the inability of a non-maximal phrase to occur in 'argument' position is shown by the unacceptability of **president of the club resigned*.) Another construction allowing a nonmaximal nominal is *Fronting to That*, as in subordinate clauses like *foolish child that I was* (Compare **I was foolish child*.) These are both cases in which a nominal predicate is a count–noun, or a modified count–noun-headed phrase, in which the 'obligatory' determiner is missing.

5.

The *Determination Construction* just exemplified can be used to illustrate the *unification* process, and the manner in which entities can not only satisfy the requirements of structural positions in a construction but can bring to a construction properties and requirements of their own.

It may be useful to think of the positions within a construction as *offices* (for example, political offices). The obligatory features associated with positions in the description of the construction can be thought of as the *qualifications* for the office, and the role indicator identifies the *function* of the office. This much involves the *institution* within which the office has a role, independently of any specific *candidate* or *incumbent*. A candidate which does not satisfy the qualifications of the office cannot fill the office. When a particular *incumbent* occupies the office, that incumbent has properties of its own, not only the properties which allowed it to occupy the office, but also properties which cause it to make its own demands. The way in which an obligatorily transitive verb brings into the office of verbal predicate the requirement of finding room for a direct object can be compared with the way in which a married male incumbent in the office of President of the United States brings with it the not always welcome additional role and office of the First Lady.

If the determiner brought into the determination construction is the plural demonstrative *these*, and the head noun is the mass noun *butter*, the combination, **these butter*, will not work, because the features of number, singular and plural, as well as the features of configuration, count and mass, will clash. *These* requires that the office next door be occupied by a plural noun. This means that we need devices which provide for the contribution of each constituent element to the description of the external syntax of the whole: such a device will identify those properties of incumbents which become properties of the office as occupied by that incumbent. It is obviously important for a maximal nominal to be recognized as singular or plural, for reasons of verb agreement, and as definite or indefinite, establishing its qualification for inclusion in certain of the existential sentence constructions. Thus, number and definiteness, whether brought in as the requirements of determiners or of nouns, will become properties of the maximal noun phrase as well. (The recognition of the need to do this is in no way a unique feature of Construction Grammar.)

6.

The lexicon, which in important ways is not distinct from the repertory of constructions, associates with each lexical item, explicitly or implicitly, information about the grammatical constructions in which the item can participate. To the extent that a given lexical item is closely tied to one or more specific grammatical constructions, describing that item is equivalent to describing the constructions in which it participates. Thus, in Paul Kay's (unpublished) construction grammar treatment of complex English kin-terms, the word *removed*, as it appears in such phraseological units as *second cousin once removed,* is included as a lexically specified part of the construction itself. This is in contrast to an absurd view according to which the active verb *remove* would have to be described in such a way that, when it occurs as a postnominal modifier of the word *cousin*, in a past-participial form qualified by an ordinal number, it just happens to contribute the right meaning to the complex phrase.

In those cases in which generalizations about lexical items can be made without reference to particular constructions, the combinatorial properties of lexical items can be stated as their *valence descriptions*. The valence description of a complement taking predicator can be thought of as the staffing demands which a particular incumbent brings to an office. The valence description of a word identifies its grammatical and semantic complements (including the subject), showing, for each of these, wherever full specification is called for, its grammatical function, its semantic role, and its morphosyntactic marking. There are numerous redundancy relations among these, suggesting that much of the information displayed in Figure 5 (offered as a partial lexical description of the English verb *give*) is predictable from other information; the figure shows the structure when all the predictable features are filled in. (The labels on the rows distinguish Grammatical Function (GF), Semantic Role (SR), and Morphosyntax (MS) of the predicator's complements.

(cat V)		
(min +)		
(lexeme GIVE)		
valence		
GF: SR: MS:	subject agent N	object patient N	complement recipient P[*to*]

Figure 5

The semantic information associated with a lexical item, about which I unfortunately have nothing to say in this paper, does its work in part by providing an indicator of the *semantic frame* with which the item is associated. The *semantic role array* in the valence description (what I used to call the *case frame*), identifies the elements which are foregrounded ('profiled', to use Ron Langacker's term) within such a frame. We will often find that information about the syntactic requirements of a lexical item can be read off from, or at least motivated by, the associated semantic frame. The semantic interpretation of the sentence will be accomplished by unifying, or otherwise integrating, semantic information from the semantic frames activated by the predicator with those introduced by the obligatory and optional companions (the complements and adjuncts) of the predicators.

7.

I introduced the word *subject* as the name of a grammatical function or role specified in a predicator's valence description. We need to distinguish two notions of 'subject' in this discussion: (1) the subject argument of a predicator, typically the argument associated with the highest-ranking semantic role, and (2) the subject of a finite sentence. I shall refer to these as the *P-subject* and the *S-subject*, respectively. In simple sentences, the P-subject and the S-subject are the same.

The *subject predicate construction*, of English and many other languages, is, in common with the determination construction already discussed, a construction which deals with the maximality value of a category, at least in the treatment that is being proposed here. I treat a clause or sentence as a maximal verb-headed phrase. Figure 6, displaying one of the constructions for defining the S-subject in English, shows that something capable of filling the role 'subject', united with a nonmaximal verbal, yields a maximal verb phrase, on

condition that the unit as a whole (and hence its head verb) is *finite* (hence
the '(infl tense)').

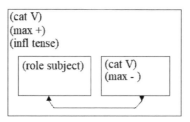

Figure 6

The arrow connecting the two boxes indicates that the constituent in the left
box is available as an instantiation of the P-subject requirement of the head
verb of the verb phrase in the second box. Whatever other requirements the
verb has must be satisfied elsewhere, for example, inside the verb–phrase
box. In those cases in which no P-subject is assigned to the verb which heads
the verb–phrase, either directly or by a process to be described shortly, the
language provides a way of filling this first slot anyway—for example, with
the word *it*.

It should be noticed that the S-subject is not given a category specification, in the same way that the determiner in the determination construction
lacks a category specification. It will have whatever category is required of
the P-subject of the head verb in the verb phrase. This means, of course, that
we do not need to treat infinitives, *that*-clauses, interrogative clauses, preposition phrases, etc., as NPs just when they appear as the subjects of sentences.

The construction just observed is not the only means of introducing an S-
subject. An *inversion* variant of a maximal V-phrase, has a finite auxiliary
verb in initial position, the subject following and the complements of the auxiliary appearing after that, as suggested by Figure 7. The example here is simplified, covering the case where the auxiliary requires only one non-subject
complement. (I am here making the common assumption that auxiliaries are
raising verbs, and that the copula *be* for these purposes is a member of the
class of auxiliaries.)

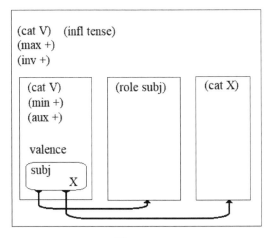

Figure 7

The feature 'inversion' is a part of the external syntax of the construction. What we have here, by the way, is a variety of *polarity item*. This construction can be selected when the clause as a whole has the feature of interrogation (as in yes–no questions), or when it is in the scope of negation (as when it follows a negative word like *never* and *seldom*), or when it is, as a whole, the antecedent of a counterfactual conditional sentence (as in *were she here, had I known*, etc.).

8.

A V– ('V minus') phrase, a phrase of the type *(cat V)(max –)*, consists of a lexical verb together with some or all of its non-subject complements or augments. I say 'some or all' because some of them may be present at some distance from the V-constituent, just in case it is in topic or WH-phrase position. A non-maximal verb phrase built around the verb *remove*, and incorporating all of its local, i.e., non-subject complements, is illustrated in Figure 8.

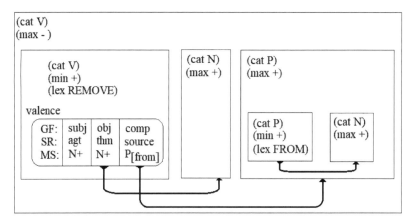

Figure 8

Again, the arrows are instantiation links, showing that certain of the 'staffing needs' of the verb have been met inside the verb phrase. In addition to the obligatory complements of a predicator, other phrasal elements may be introduced into a verb–phrase as long as they contribute meanings which integrate into the semantic frame built up around the predicator, or can fit the semantic frame of the predicator into their own semantic frames. They differ from complements in not being syntactically required.

Under certain conditions, complements may be missing. In languages in which there are lexically specifiable conditions on the omissibility or optionality of complements, information about such omissibility will be included with some system of diacritics on particular complement descriptions, as suggested in Figure 9, something along the lines of Fillmore 1969 and Fillmore 1985. Here, parentheses represent omissibility under conditions allowing an 'indefinite interpretation', square brackets representing omissibility under conditions of conversational givenness. (In this notation, I follow Allerton 1975.) That this is not a simple matter of lexical marking was forcefully argued in Sally Rice's paper elsewhere in this volume[4].

---

[4] [Editors' note: Rice, Sally.1998. Unlikely Lexical Entries. *Proceedings of the Fourteenth Annual Meeting of the Berkeley Linguistics Society*, pp. 202–212.]

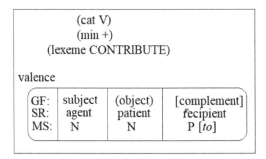

Figure 9

9.

The subject argument of a verbal predicate can be instantiated in the subject position in the subject–predicate construction; non-subject arguments can be instantiated inside the verb phrase, as we have seen. There are additional means of cashing out the argument requirements of a predicate, among them various sorts of left isolate constructions. A *left-isolate* which is an interrogative word occurs in the construction suggested by Figure 10, where the arrow is interpreted as meaning that the left-isolated constituent complements or augments the semantic structure in the predication to its right. The result of the union of the WH-element with its partner to the right is a complete clause, that is, a maximal verb-headed constituent.

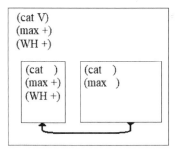

Figure 10

Notice that the maximality of the verbal constituent is not indicated; what this means is that if the interrogated element is the subject, then the structure fits the structure of the subject predicate construction as well, and the sister constituent is a 'verb phrase' ('V–') rather than a 'sentence' ('V+'). If, however, the verbal category is maximal, then the instantiation link is to some non-subject inside the sister constituent. The link will mean that the fronted element must be unified with the valence description of some predicate inside the sister constituent.[5] When the second constituent is V+, it will have the feature 'inversion' (and the structure shown in Figure 7) just in case the sentence is a main–clause question.

10.

Control relationships are coded into valence descriptions, and represented in diagrams with links that we call *co-instantiation* links. These link an argument requirement in one predicate with an argument requirement in a 'higher' or 'commanding' predicate, and assert that in whatever way the argument of the higher predicate gets realized, it simultaneously satisfies the argument requirement of the predicate with which it is linked. Omitting the details here, suffice it to say that the difference between co-instantiation of the type usually called *Raising* and that usually called *Equi* has to do with whether or not the co-instantiating argument has a semantic role assigned to it. Co-instantiation indices are of the familiar types: $S(S)$ means that the subject role of the commanding predicate co-instantiates the subject role of the complement; $O(S)$ means that the direct object of the commanding predicate co-instantiates the subject role of the complement; $S(X)$ means that the subject of the commanding predicate co-instantiates a non-subject; and $S(\ )$ means that the subject of the commanding predicate co-instantiates either the subject or a non-subject of the complement. A simple example, using the adjective *worth*, is presented in Figure 11. *Worth* is here described in that usage by which it requires a gerundial local complement, and by which it co-instantiates with its subject a non-subject of that gerund. To get a sentence like *She seems worth knowing*, we have to notice that the subject of *know* is taken as generic; the object of *know* is co-instantiated with the subject of *worth*; and the subject of *worth* is co-instantiated with the subject of the copula. (Instantiation links are marked 'I', co-instantiation links as 'CI'.)

---

[5] The familiar 'Ross constraints' are handled in this theory by characterizing particular constructions as insulated, that is, as having impenetrable boundaries with respect to the relations indicated with instantiation arrows; many of the determinants of such insulation appear to be semantic in nature (on which see Lakoff 1986); but that's another story.

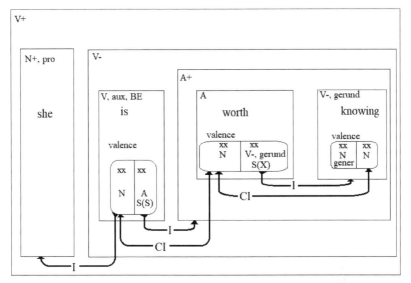

Figure 11

11.

In addition to links of instantiation and co-instantiation, there are also links of necessary coreference which characterize certain constructions. A simple example, shown in Figure 12, is the phraseological unit *do one's best*. Here the requirement is that the possessive nominal prefixed to the word *best* must be coreferential to the subject of the verb. That means that the pronominal form must match that of the P-subject of *do one's best* (*I did my best, she did her best*, etc.). That is to say, however the P-subject of *do one's best* in this construction gets realized—by being directly instantiated in a subject–predicate construction, by being co-instantiated by the subject of the verb *try*, the object of the verb *persuade*, or whatever, that entity must unify with the possessive pronoun inside this construction. (Just in case this element is inside a construction which causes its subject to be given the generic or 'arbitrary' interpretation, the possessive form will be the word *one's*.)

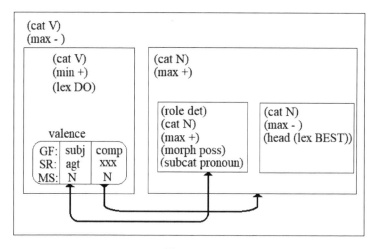

Figure 12

12.

Because of the nature of the English inflectional system, the fitting together of lexical verbs with the subject–predicate construction forces us to recognize another necessary property of English grammar. We need to distinguish inflectional forms from lexemes, and we need to associate with inflectional forms whatever special requirements they impose. To show the difference, we might compare a valence description of the verb *have* in what we will pretend to be its simple 'possession' sense, with the inflected form /has/.

The verb *have* occurs in a large number of constructions: it functions, for example, as an auxiliary, as a simple transitive verb, and as a complement–taking verb in a number of different contexts. Figure 13 shows its use in indicating simple possession. In each of these constructions, the inflected form *has* can stand in as its representative, as long as certain requirements which it itself imposes are satisfied. Notice the three boxes in Figures 13, 14 and 15.

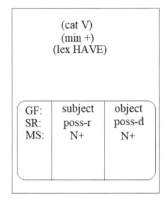

Figure 13

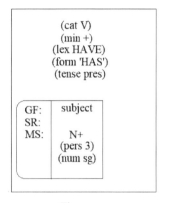

Figure 14

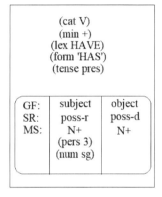

Figure 15

The phonological form *has*, interpreted in Figure 14, is a representation of this verb associated with the present tense, but its standing for any of the instances of the abstract verb *have* brings with it the requirement that the subject be third person and singular. The lexicon of forms creates or contains entities which must unify with grammatical elements and provide them with phonological forms. The product of this unification can be shown in Figure 15, a superimposition of the information in Figures 13 and 14.

A verb inflected for tense can only occur as the head verb in the subject–predicate construction, and, as we see, it imposes restrictions on the grammatical nature of its subject. In languages in which there is both subject agreement and object agreement, we must be able to describe the morphology as creating forms with associated requirements on their subjects and arguments.

The phenomena of 'agreement' will thus be merely matters of unification involving the selection of word forms.

In addition to simple unification, we need to have a notion of *obligatorily evaluated attributes*. The attribute given in Figures 14 and 15 as 'form' is one of these: every lexical item must have this attribute filled in (possibly, in certain cases, with zero). Morphemes which have allomorphs (and lexemes which have allo-lexes) will generally leave the 'form' slot unfilled. The item which brings information filling such a slot will typically bring grammatical requirements of its own, as we have seen with the word *has*.

13.

Our grammar needs a way of dealing with the subtle character of contexts which are created or defined by particular grammatical constructions. Positions in the grammatical templates we manipulate are contexts within which special principles obtain determining what can occur in it and how what occurs in it gets construed.

In every grammatical theory much is made of the fact that particular complement-taking lexical items create contexts which welcome or require particular features: the indicative-clause complement of *hope* defines a context for the futurate present, the verb *doubt* assigns negative polarity to its complement, the verb *wish* assigns subjunctivity to its complement, etc.

Many grammatical constructions can be shown to have this same context-characterizing property. As a simple example, the syntactic idiom which has the introducers *it's time*, *it's about time*, and *it's high time*, generally requires that the following indicative clause be past tense in form. (*it's time you brushed your teeth*; *it's high time you started thinking about your future*; *it's about time you did that*.)

Mention was already made of a copular sentence in which a non-maximal nounphrase appeared as the nominal predicate, as in *Sally is president of the club*. There we saw that the position after *be* allowed, atypically, a nonmaximal nominal. Another and quite distinct copular sentence is the one used for pointing out referents in the common perceptual world of speaker and hearer, as in such sentences as *this is my teacher*, *those are my new friends*, *that's my old car*. An interesting property of this construction is that the demonstrative pronouns occurring as subjects have a clearly different function and meaning-range here than they have in contexts in which they are the arguments of predicates, and it's an interesting job to try to characterize such contexts. Outside of this *Deictic Presentative* context, *this* or *that* requires construal as a non-human entity. Thus if I ask you, *Are you planning to eat that?*, I have said something perfectly ordinary, but if I ask you, *Are you planning to marry that?* I am being insulting. In *that's my uncle*, *this is my mother*, and the like, no such insult is implied.

The conditions on this construction seem to be these: the word *that* appears as the subject of a tensed verb and while it may be the immediate subject of a verb other than *be*, it must be the ultimate subject of the verb *be*. That is, it must instantiate or co-instantiate the P-subject of *be* (as well as that of the predicate nominal), but no other semantic-role bearing position. Thus, *That seems to be my son-in-law* is all right, but *That seems to like you* isn't. *He's my best friend* and *That's my best friend* are both normal things to say, but while *I regard him as my best friend* is okay, *I regard that as my best friend* is not. An embedded identificational clause is all right if it's indicative: *I think that's my friend* is okay, but *I consider that to be my friend* is not. A striking contrast can be seen in the two otherwise semantically identical sentences: *That's my son-in-law* and *That married my daughter*.

In this construction, the predicate nominal has to be a referring expression. In the one we saw earlier, it had to be instead a name of a unique role. Hence, although it's possible to say *That's the chairman of the club*, it's not possible to say *That's chairman of the club*. The construction which allows *that* to refer to a human is not the one which allows the predicate nominal to be non-maximal.

14.

A more complex instance of obligatorily assigned values, corresponding to the technical notion of *feature inheritance*, on which I have had something to say in Fillmore 1986, and which McCawley has further discussed during these meetings, is that of what I call the *correlative conditional construction*.[6]

This construction has a number of properties, suggested by Figure 16, which are uniquely linked with it, but many others which are not. Our concern here is in factoring out the numerous other constructions which contribute to the whole package. Some of its properties can be imported into the description of this construction from the fact that it is a conditional sentence; others from the fact that in two places it is an example of the category comparative; by being a conditional sentence, it is also in the class of subordination constructions (including temporal and conditional clauses) which provide very special ways of treating tense and auxiliary categories. In short, a complex set of qualifications for the 'offices' defined for this construction come from numerous sources, yielding a marvelously complex package.

---

[6] I use the term 'correlative conditional' rather than my own earlier term 'comparative conditional' for language–comparative purposes: some languages have constructions with essentially the same function as the English one without making use of a 'comparative' construction.

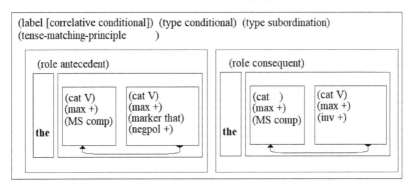

Figure 16

(Certain of the properties of this construction will be 'inherited' from others of its properties: that it is an instance of a conditional sentence, that it involves a subordinate–clause/main–clause construction, that the first element of each major piece is of the type 'comparative' (indicated with MS comp in the diagram), and so on. We note that the antecedent clause is optionally a negative polarity context, suggested by expressions like *the more you do any of that*; that the antecedent clause is optionally introduced by *that*, as in *the longer that you stay here*, and that the consequence clause is an optional 'inversion' structure, as in *The sooner you learn how to pronounce her name, the more likely is she to go out with you*. Many of these properties are unique to the correlative conditional construction; many are predicted by, while others are 'motivated' by, the membership of this construction in other construction types.)

15.

Summarizing, we treat grammatical constructions as syntactic patterns which can fit into each other, impose conditions on each other, and inherit properties from each other. Grammatical constructions define positions which require or welcome fillers with certain properties, and fillers of those positions can introduce constructions of their own and can impose requirements of their own on positions within the constructions which contain them. At least some aspects of the grammar operate on simple principles of unification, augmented by principles of inheritance and principles for checking for the presence of obligatory elements. Since lexical items can be treated as the heads or markers of the grammatical constructions in which they participate, a grammatical formalism can be constructed, we believe, which is built exclusively on grammatical constructions.

References

Allerton, D. J. 1975. Deletion and pro-form reduction. *Journal of Linguistics* 11:213–238.

Fillmore, C. J. 1969. Types of lexical information. *Studies in Syntax and Semantics* (Foundations of Language Supplementary Series Vol. 10), ed. F. Kiefer, 109–137.

Fillmore, C. J. 1985. Pragmatically controlled zero anaphora. *BLS* 12:95–107.

Fillmore, C. J. 1986. Varieties of conditional sentences. *ESCOL (Eastern States Conference on Linguistics)* 3:163–182.

Fillmore, C. J., P. Kay, and M. C. O'Connor (to appear in *Language*). Idiomaticity and regularity in grammar: The case of *let alone*. (Available as *Berkeley Cognitive Science Report* 51.)

Kay, P. 1984. The *kind of/sort of* construction. *BLS* 10:157–171.

Kay, P. 1988. Even. *Berkeley Cognitive Science Report* 50.

Lakoff, G. 1986. Frame semantics and the coordinate structure constraint. *CLS* 22.

Lakoff, G. 1987. *Women, Fire, and Dangerous Things: What Categories Reveal about the Mind.* University of Chicago Press.

Lambrecht, K. 1986. Pragmatically motivated syntax: Presentational cleft constructions in spoken French. *CLS* 22.

7

Grammatical Construction Theory and the Familiar Dichotomies

1989
CHARLES J. FILLMORE

1. *Introduction*

Every modern linguistic theory can be thought of as a complicated machine with a very large number of moving parts; in no case, unfortunately, has anybody yet been able to connect all the parts together so that we can see if any of these machines can run. This fact makes decision making on the part of potential investors and customers extremely difficult; it's impossible to see clearly what some of the machines can do that the others cannot. So if I want you to invest in my particular design, the best I can do is to give you an idea of what I want my machine to be able to do when it's finished, to show you some of its parts, and to try to convince you that it can do some things that you ought to be interested in.

The design I want to draw to your attention is a framework currently being developed by some of us in Berkeley—me, Paul Kay, George Lakoff, and a number of our students—called Construction Grammar or Grammatical Construction Theory. Our reason for entering a new product on the market is our conviction that there are many important aspects of knowing a language which the competition has preferred to ignore or to postpone, and we are interested in seeing what happens when such phenomena are made a major focus of inquiry.

Not too many years ago, the standard sales pitch for generative grammar was a demonstration of how it could account for the main *grammatical constructions* in a language and the nature of their interaction. In such demonstrations, complex sentences were taken apart to show what constructions went into their composition, and a system of rules—both the phrase–structure rules and the transformational rules—was put on display, to show how they succeeded in characterizing these constructions: identifying their components, guaranteeing that the constructions had the properties they needed, and showing how some of them were related to others. A phrase structure rule created the Subject/Predicate construction; a transformational rule created the structure for the Topic/Comment construction; a collection of phrase structure rules established the material for verbal government in transitive predicates, and in general for complementation structures; transformational rules created the structures for passive sentences, questions, commands, negations, and so on.

In sharp contrast to this tradition, recent developments within mainstream syntactic theories have the putative 'advantage' of *eliminating* the intuitive notion of 'construction' from the theoretical base, in favor of a set of highly abstract independent principles. In studies guided by syntactic theories since the emergence and later elaborations of the Extended Standard Theory, a typical argument form has been that of examining the data of some (pretheoretically identified) grammatical construction, and arguing that each of the linguistically significant properties exhibited in this body of data is independently explainable by an appeal to one or more of a small number of subtle and abstract, but simple principles, and being proud of the fact that in the formulation of these principles there was no need to mention specific grammatical constructions. An important aspect of such demonstrations was the suggestion that whenever one finds phenomena which do not fit this mode of explanation, we can count on finding some independently needed auxiliary theories to account for them, such as, for example, a rich theory of lexical entries, theories of language use and common-sense reasoning, context effects, and so on.

The fact that these highly valued explanatory principles are *abstract*—including no mention of specific grammatical constructions—and the fact that they are *formal* in character—including no mention of communicative purposes—goes along perfectly with the idea that the syntactic principles of a language can be fully described in isolation from everything else there is to know about languages and their users.

Possession of these principles constitutes the most important part of what might be considered *linguistic competence* at the syntactic level. There is merely the matter of deciding which aspects of linguistic competence belong to the local language and which belong to the innate principles of universal grammar.

Except for the shared assumption of a richly structured lexicon, the view which I wish to offer is different in many ways from the one I have just caricatured; it is the view that a grammar of a language is in large part a repertory of holistic patterns, the language's *grammatical constructions*. Each such construction is dedicated to a particular function in the creation of meaningful utterances in the language, and each has associated with it instructions on its role in the interpretation of the phrase or sentence containing it. These instructions are free to refer to the speaker's purposes, the cultural and conversational background, the speaker's estimate of the hearer's understanding of what is going on, and so on.

Grammatical Construction Theory differs from a number of other frameworks, first in its insistence that syntactic patterns are often tightly associated with interpretation instructions, but secondly, in that it takes as a major part of its assignment the task of accounting for the workings of complex grammatical constructions as well as simple ones. I am not speaking here about the complexity of sentences, but the complexity, or rather the *richness*, of individual constructions. We have all seen demonstrations of grammatical frameworks which do superbly well in the treatment of sentences whose complexity consists of a multi-layered assembly of *simple* elements. But my colleagues and I are interested not only in structures which can be fully understood in terms of their constituent elements, but also in constructions which are complex to begin with. This means that we give serious and careful attention to what is idiomatic and phraseological in language.

There is both a friendly and an unfriendly way of describing such a focus. The *unfriendly* way is to say that the facts of grammar can be neatly divided into the *core* and the *periphery*, and to scold us for concentrating on the periphery, that is, on what is irregular and idiomatic. This way of talking is to characterize our focus as both trivial and postponable. Trivial because the core is more important, being the locus of what is innate and universal in language; postponable because serious scholarship needs to understand the nature of the core first. The friendly way is to divide grammatical patterns into those which are *easy to describe* and those which are *hard to describe*, and to say that we are working on the hard ones. As it happens, however, we are not only working on the hard ones. My own recent work has been devoted to creating a mechanism for dealing with the 'easy' structures which is consistent in its form and operation with the mechanisms needed for the 'hard' structures.

In Grammatical Construction Theory, constructions are taken as *structured* but not strictly *decomposable*, that is, they are taken as having properties in the manner of the properties of a 'gestalt' in Gestalt Psychology. The properties of a construction may often be seen as 'motivated by', but they do not necessarily 'follow from' any facts about their composition. Each grammatical construction can be identified with a certain set of components, a collection of constraints on the syntax or semantics of the components, a statement of the use of the construct as a whole, together with a set of instructions for incorporating information linked with its parts into an interpretation of the whole. The constraints will include conditions on the thematic or categorial identity of the components, requirements on the morphological or lexical tagging or heading of specific components, and the linear order of elements where this is relevant. In some ways Grammatical Construction Theory resembles the grammatical theory to which I was first exposed, namely Kenneth Pike's Tagmemic Theory (Pike 1967), with its slots, fillers, conditions, and roles, and its inherent engagement in the behavior and purposes of human beings. Grammatical Construction Theory, incidentally, is nontransformational. That is, interpretation principles take the place of *deletions*; lexical rules, principles of linear order, and principles of construal take the place of *movements*.

Within Grammatical Construction Theory, there is a continuity between the most general principles of grammar and the most specific, and our goal is to be able to describe all of these in a uniform formalism. Patterns of the sort familiarly treated in terms of phrase structure principles are merely treated as constructions with simple and shallow structural requirements. Lexical items, in their turn, are described in terms of the constructions they take part in. Idioms and speech formulas are described in terms of their form, their areas of flexibility, their meanings, and the conditions of their use.

One way of contrasting the methods of theorists of constructionist and non-constructionist bents is to see them as starting their work from the opposite ends of a continuum of relative idiomaticity. Those starting out at one end devise rules and constraints to account for the most general, productive and 'compositional' processes in a language. Such theorists wait until they are convinced that they have secure knowledge of the simple structures before they have a reason to approach areas of irregularity and noncompositionality; and when they do move toward the other end, their aims are to discover whatever hidden regularities they can find in such phenomena, allowing the phenomena to be taken in as instances of the general principles, or, where that is impossible, to consign the phenomena either to the lexicon or to conventions operating outside of grammar proper. From the other end of the continuum, theorists are devising ways of accounting for all of the details of phraseological entities, generalizing these accounts in such a way as to become able to take care of the simpler constructions.

I should point out that I do not assign moral values to the two ends of this continuum. It's only by having linguists paired off in these ways that we can expect them to keep each other honest.

2. *A Sample of Construction Types*

There are, I claim, vast worlds of syntactic phenomena which require treatment in terms of grammatical constructions, holistic grammatical patterns characterizing structures whose properties do not, in any obvious or familiar way, 'follow from' what can be independently known about their constituent elements. The existence of such phenomena is relevant to a conference devoted to Natural Language Processing in a Social Context in two ways. First, because it emphasizes those richnesses of language which clearly require more than mere exposure to the data (to set the parameters and let the innate mechanisms automatically fill in the details), but secondly because the connectedness of many grammatical construction types to human interactions makes it impossible to accept certain views of the separability of the inner structure of language from a study of it use.

A quick example of a 'clear case' construction is the one noted in such expressions as *Me, get married?*; *Fred, write poetry?*

♦ A part of the description of a construction is the identification of its components and a statement of the structural relations which they hold relative to each other. In this case, the components are (1) an oblique NP in 'topic' position, and (2) an infinitive phrase holding a predication relation to the preceding NP. (The 'obliqueness' of the first element is only apparent when it's a personal pronoun, like the *me* of *Me get married?*) The fact that the first component has to have 'topic' status explains why one does not find as instantiations of this pattern expressions whose first elements are capable of being subjects but not capable of being topics: Thus we don't find sentences like: **It, rain?*; **There, be a revolution?*; **It be obvious that she loves me?*.

♦ An account of the construction must specify the 'external syntax' of the construct as a whole. In our case, any instantiation of the construction is necessarily a complete utterance, that is, it is not 'embeddable'. These expressions cannot, for example, be embedded as *that*-clauses to verbs of thinking, speaking, perceiving, etc.

♦ A description of a construction must indicate the construction's contribution to the interpretation of the whole. In this case, it is to attach to the proposition whose parts it presents the judgment that it is surprising or incredible.

♦ I have said that in many cases information about usage is a part of the description of given constructions. In this case, we find that it is uttered in reaction to a conversation partner's suggestion that the expressed predication is true.

(Notice that the just-mentioned aspects of the interpretations of the sentences are only the ones contributed by this particular construction. The other constructions which the sentences instantiate will fill in other details, these other constructions including Predication, Topicalization, and the constructions headed by each of the lexical items.)

The 'conventional' character of the construction can be made apparent by comparing it with the corresponding German construction, which has three components: (1) a nominative NP in topic function (e.g., *ich*); (2) the word *und*, and (3) an infinitive phrase holding a predication relation to component number 1 (e.g., *Fußball spielen*). The whole has question intonation. (*Ich und Fußball spielen?*) Thus, alongside of an English sentence like *Me, go to church?* we have the German *Ich und in die Kirche gehen?*.

Now I've claimed that these are examples of a syntactic pattern with very special pragmatic purposes, purposes that need to be described along with a statement of the details of its syntactic structure. When I've given examples like these before, I often have people tell me how 'natural' the form/meaning relationships are in these cases, my critics' point being that there is no need to regard these structures as anything special. It may be necessary, therefore, to point out the difference between 'explanation' and 'motivation'. Wherever we claim that something is a separate construction, what we mean is that somebody could know everything else that there is to know about the language except how to produce and interpret instantiations of the construction at hand. I'm sure that a convincing story could be told with respect to the German formula about how 'natural' it is that *conjunction* with *und* and *rising intonation* should figure in a construction which has the meaning that this one does. But the fact remains, it is a construction which needs to be described as something on its own. Though its meaning could probably be guessed, in context, it remains true that the conventionality of the connection between its form and its interpretation could not have been predicted by someone who knew everything else about the German language except this one pattern.

2.1 Figurative vs. Literal Interpretation

One area in which the 'independently needed auxiliary theories' are often called to do service is in explaining the occurrence of 'figurative' language, the language of metaphors, metonymies, similes, and exaggerations. Everyone agrees that there exist 'frozen metaphors', idioms whose metaphoric base can be reconstructed but for which no separate act of metaphoric construal is necessary on the part of an interpreter each time they are heard. Setting these examples aside, it is common to say that 'figurative' language is derivative of (and in a sense 'superimposed on') 'literal' language. This means that what triggers a figurative interpretation is the detection of an expression in discourse in which the literal interpretation is judged not to fit.

Surely, for novel creations of figurative language, something of the sort must take place, but the process is not independent of grammatical form. There are also certain grammatical structures in English which either require or forbid such secondary interpretations.

The first of these that I will discuss involves comparative structures: in illustrating it I will use *comparisons of equality* based on copular sentences. The full form of such expressions is seen in a sentence like *Joe is as tall as Bill is.* Everyone who learns English knows that the copula (or auxiliary element) at the end of comparative sentences can be omitted, so we know that the *is* at the end is optional. Thus we can say *Joe is as tall as Bill is* and *Joe is as tall as Bill* and mean the same thing.

However, as Jerry Morgan (1975) and Michael Brame (1984) have independently pointed out, just in case the final *is* is not omitted, the expression can only be given a literal interpretation. Thus, *Miami is as hot as Hell* is a perfectly good sentence, but someone who says *Miami is as hot as Hell is* is claiming to have information not yet available to the rest of us, since we see this as a comparison of the actual temperatures of two separate locations.

The phenomenon just observed is broader than I've suggested: it actually concerns the presence or absence of the finite auxiliary or copula in the truncated second element of a comparative sentence in which the comparands are subjects. It is not limited to 'comparison of equality'. Thus if I say *Joe is more stubborn than the rock of Gibraltar*, you will allow me to be exaggerating; but if I say *Joe is more stubborn than the rock of Gibraltar is*, you have to judge me as downright incoherent.

But there is another construction related to the difference between literal and figurative interpretations in comparative sentences. This one is limited to comparison of equality, and has to do with the optionality of the first *as*. It is possible to say both *Miami is as hot as Hell* and *Miami is hot as Hell*. Both of these—with the *as* present or with the *as* absent—can be interpreted figuratively. But when the word *as* is omitted, the utterance is necessarily *figurative*. Thus, *Joe is as tall as Bill* is a normal sentence, **Joe is tall as Bill* is not, since it is difficult to imagine anyone intending such a sentence to be given a figurative interpretation. *Joe is fat as a cow*, on the other hand, if we don't really mean it, is okay.

Since a comparison of equality *with as absent* is necessarily figurative, and one *with is present* is necessarily literal, it follows that a sentence like

*Joe is fat as a cow is should be utterly impossible; and that seems to be true. The missing *as* requires the sentence to be figurative, the presence of *is* requires it to be literal, and it cannot be both. Such a sentence would represent a superimposition of two mutually incompatible constructions, and it is ruled out for that reason.

There are other constructional devices associated with figurative language. In particular, there is a superimpositional construction by which matched modifiers of the terms of a metaphor serve to explain the metaphor's interpretation. Both English and German use a metaphoric expression of the form *He threw out the baby with the bathwater*; but it is possible to modify each of the terms of the metaphor with an expression which provides the metaphor's interpretation. Consider, in this regard, a sentence like *He threw out the baby of personal morality with the bathwater of traditional religion.* ('When he gave up his religion, he stopped being a moral person.') This is a case where there is no possibility at all of building the interpretation of the sentence out of the interpretation of its major constituents, since the phrases *the baby of personal morality* and *the bathwater of traditional religion* have no sensible interpretations at all. These are cases where the construction immediately invites the metaphoric interpretation, with no intervening literal interpretation being possible. The traditional account of figurative interpretation has it as the result of some sort of implicit negotiation between speaker and hearer. But that is incomplete. There appear to be devices of grammar which determine the operation or non-operation of such processes from the start.

2.2 The More the Merrier

There is a construction in English (and there are parallel constructions in most languages, I would guess) which states a correlation between values on two connected scales. Examples of the construction I am thinking of are *The more you drink, the more disgusting you get*; *The faster we drive, the sooner we'll get home*. Analogous structures in German make use of the function words *je* and *desto*.

The description of the components of this construction is not as simple and straightforward as some of our earlier examples, because the special requirements go fairly deeply into the tree structure. I can build the structure this time from the bottom up.

These constructions contain the word *the* used as a kind of *degree modifier,* prefixed to a comparative expression of any of the categories permitting grammatical comparison: *the better, the more slowly, the happier, the less.* Historically this *the* appears to go back to a demonstrative in the instrumental case; it appears in a number of other contexts in modern English too. (*What big eyes you have, Grandmother! – The better to see you with, my dear.*)

Such comparison phrases can be preposed to clauses with a gap which is satisfiable by an instance of the category represented by the comparative phrase. *The bigger he is*, where the *he is* could be supplemented with an adjective phrase giving us something like *he is so big*. *The more we eat*, where the *we eat* can have an object provided, giving us *we eat so much*. *The faster we drive*, where the *we drive* can have an adverb added to it, giving us *we drive so fast*.

Exactly two phrases built up in this way can be juxtaposed to create the construction at hand. There are certain properties which distinguish these two juxtaposed phrases from each other syntactically. In the first half of the expression, the truncated clause following the comparative phrase may optionally begin with the complementizer *that*, as in *the more that you eat*; but this option does not exist for the second clause.

The second special property is that the tense and auxiliary elements of the two clauses must be compatible with each other in ways that match certain such requirements in conditional sentences. Thus, we seem to have three possibilities:

1. Simple present and simple present, expressing a general principle. *If you eat you get fat. The more you eat, the fatter you get.*

2. Simple present in the first clause and the *will* future in the second, expressing a prediction. *If you eat this you will get sick. The more of this that you eat, the sicker you'll get.*

3. Simple past and simple past, expressing a past correlation. *If she came early, I came early. The harder we worked, the easier it became.*

Semantically, the resulting construct expresses a particular kind of correlation: as the value specified in the first half of the expression increases, the value specified in the second half increases correspondingly. The construction is *used* in special ways more or less connected with the fact that conditional sentences in general tend to be comments or to serve as the instruments of indirect speech acts of one sort or another. I have some ideas about how this story might be told, but nothing very coherent just now.

2.3 *Topic and Focus in Colloquial French*

In a recent Berkeley doctoral dissertation, Knud Lambrecht has given a detailed study of grammatical constructions in colloquial French which serve highly specific topic indicating and focus indicating functions. Lambrecht observes that in spoken French, lexical NPs hardly ever occur in subject position, that in fact it hardly ever happens in colloquial French that a single clause will contain more than one lexical NP. He proposes for spoken French a *Preferred Clause Type*, consisting of an initial verb with clitic or incorporated pronominal subject. He claims that the preference for this clause type in the spoken language is so strong that the language contains special devices just to make it possible to introduce a NP in a non-subject position so that it can be available for pronominal reference in subject position in the next clause.

In this regard, French and English are markedly different. While Wallace Chafe and Andrew Pawley have shown that it is also rare in English conversational texts to find lexically specified subjects, English nevertheless is quite free to announce new information in the form of sentences containing lexical subjects bearing focal stress, as in *My brother showed up this morning, A baby crocodile lives in his bathtub, My eyes hurt, The phone's ringing, My car broke down*, etc. In French, according to Lambrecht, such 'canonical sentences' are characteristic of the written language only. Main clause sentences containing information in which nothing is topically linked to the ongoing discourse have to distribute their contents into two clauses. The NP-introducing clause uses the verbs *avoir* or *être* in one of the so-called 'clefting' constructions, or a verb of perception. These constructions introduce nominals whose referents are destined to be picked up by a 'relative pronoun' *qui* in the next clause. (Since *qui* does not count as a lexical subject, its presence does not constitute a departure from the preferred clause type.)

For entities not marked as related in any special way to the speaker or hearer, the so-called *ya-cleft* is used (*il y a* ...); in cases where there is relevance to a speech act participant, the verb *avoir* is used with a pronominal subject.

Thus, for 'The telephone's ringing' one could not say *Le téléphone sonne*, but only *Ya le téléphone qui sonne*; for 'My eyes hurt' one could not say *Mes yeux me font mal* but only *J'ai les yeux qui m'font mal*, and for 'My car broke down' one could not say *Ma voiture est en panne* but only *J'ai ma voiture qui est en panne*. (An important part of Lambrecht's treatment is his demonstration that these structures are distinct in numerous ways from the relative clause constructions which they superficially resemble.)

2.4 There Constructions

In *Woman, Fire and Dangerous Things* (Lakoff 1987: 462–585), my colleague George Lakoff has given an analysis of a number of constructions in English which make use of the word *there*, or the words *there* and *here*, in initial position. His analysis covers a dozen or so distinct there-constructions, out of which I will select just one. The construction I will discuss can be called Deictic Presentative, and can be used in two related contexts. When it is used in the present tense, it has the function of announcing the presence or appearence of something. Consider:

> Here I am.
>
> There it goes.
>
> Here comes Joe.
>
> There he stands, big as you please.
>
> Here lies Joe Jones.

But when it is used in the past tense, it represents a point of view in a narrative. Examples:

> There it was, in the middle of the road.
>
> There it hung, over his front door.
>
> There it went, right before her eyes.

Careful examination of these constructions shows that they must satisfy a large number of conditions:

1. Instantiations of this construction contain a simple verbal element, that is, a verb in simple present or simple past tense. The only verbs that regularly appear in this construction are *be*, *come* and *go*, *sit*, *stand* and *lie*, and occasionally *hang*. That is, the elementary verbs of existence, movement, and posture.

2. In the present-tense usage, the first word in the construction is either *here* or *there*; in the narrative use it is *there*. The word satisfies a locative complement requirement of the verb. Other locative adverbs will not do.

3. The order of elements after the deictic introducer is Subject followed by Verb just in case the subject is a pronoun, Verb followed by Subject in case the subject is a lexical noun phrase. Thus:

> Here's Joe.
>
> Here he is.
>
> There goes Joe.
>
> There he goes.
>
> There stood my brother.
>
> There he stood

4. The part described so far can be optionally followed by a comment, in the form of a predicate phrase of the adjectival, participial or nominal kinds:

> Adjectival: There he sat, stark naked.
>
> Present Participial: Here he comes, running as fast as he can.
>
> Predicate Nominal: There he is, our leader.

The function of the construction is to allow the speaker to draw the hearer's attention to something in their current shared perceptual field, or, in the narrative usage, to represent the perceptual experience of the individual (character or narrator) whose point of view is being exhibited in the narrative. There are many ways in which one could argue that the collection of properties that goes into the description of this construction is quite natural and motivated, but it remains true, in my opinion, that it is the grammarian's responsibility to describe the construction in its own terms, rather than to expect this particular assembly of properties to be, one by one, independently accounted for in terms of other facts about the grammar of English.

2.5 Let Alone

There is a construction which Paul Kay, Mary Catherine O'Connor and I have called *the let alone construction* (Fillmore, Kay and O'Connor 1988). It is responsible for sentences like

> He wouldn't give me ten cents, let alone ten dollars.

Similar, but, I think, slightly different possibilities are open to German using the expression *geschweige denn*. This construction, the details of which I won't have time to go into, has a large number of syntactic peculiarities, that is, syntactic properties which we have not found elsewhere in the language. It has a special semantic structure, requiring a deep analysis of *scalar* notions in semantics. And it has a special set of pragmatic requirements. That is, sentences of this sort only occur in contexts in which something has been said which the producer of the *let alone* sentence needs to deny or correct, and the utterance has the effect of separating out into two pieces the satisfaction of a Gricean *relevance* condition and the *quantity* condition.

Kay, O'Connor and I are using this construction as a test case for our position on grammatical constructions. It appears to us to be a clear instance of a grammatical form which cannot be sensibly described without listing, all at once, its syntactic, semantic and pragmatic features.

2.6 Bare Noun Binomials

Another contribution of Knud Lambrecht (1984) within the constructionist tradition is his study of German 'bare binomial' expressions. It is possible in German (as well as in English and in many other languages having determiners) to conjoin two bare nouns, creating a special semantic effect and limited to special pragmatic conditions. Lambrecht calls these *bare noun binomials*. In English the process can be formally distinguished from ordinary coordinate conjunction only when the nouns figuring in the construction are singular count nouns, because mass nouns and plural nouns can occur without articles anyway. In German the requirement is that the nouns so conjoined lack determiners and case endings.

The requirements for these expressions seem to be (1) that the context is one in which the referents of the nouns have the status 'given' in the discourse, and (2) that the nouns so conjoined have a unity which is provided by the culture—in that they both figure in some established cultural schema— or that they have a unity provided by the immediately preceding text. In all of the languages in which the construction has been observed, it provides the structure for a large number of fixed expressions, of the type *knife and fork*, *hat and coat*, *Haus und Hof*, *Mann und Frau*, etc.

The particular 'frame' or 'knowledge structure' which provides the unity between the objects united with this construction is not merely something which makes it possible to link the two words together, but it must figure in the way in which the piece of text containing the expression is understood. Thus, it is the two sides of a coin which provide a reason for uniting the two elements of *Kopf* and *Zahl* in the expression *Kopf oder Zahl*; and that framing must be present in any utterance in which the expression is meaningfully used.

Similarly, in a sentence like *He picked up hat and coat and headed for the front door*, the frame which unites a hat and a coat is one in which someone wears these items for going outdoors. A sentence like *I'm going shopping for hat and coat* does not sound so natural, since a shopping excursion gives no special unity to the pair of objects consisting of one hat and one coat.

The special character of the 'bare noun' conjunction, that is, the property which shows it to be something other than ordinary coordinate conjunction is evident in the fact that the phrase can be used in many contexts in which a single bare noun could not occur. These are cases where elements fit their context grammatically only if they are conjoined. You can't say *He picked up coat and headed for the door*. A German example borrowed from Lambrecht is *Er zog sich Schuhe und Strümpfe aus*. A sentence like *Er zog sich Schuhe aus* is ungrammatical.

When the culture provides the unifying frame independently of the ongoing context, we can say the unity is preschematized. It is also, however, possible to create a context which provides the unity on the run, so to speak. In such a case, a first instance of a conjunction of the two nouns does not allow them to be 'bare', but the next one does. Lambrecht's example, taken from his *Language* article, is:

> Er ging in den Laden, um ein Hemd und ein Messer zu kaufen. Er fand, was er brauchte, und nachdem er Hemd und Messer bezahlt hatte, verließ er zufrieden den Laden.

The study of bare noun binomials obscures the fact that the phenomenon in question is somewhat more general than what is seen in this particular pattern. There are a great many other syntagmata in which a unity between two objects is presupposed by the use of pairs or multiples of bare nouns. One can talk about a situation in which *boy meets girl*; the act of saluting can be spoken of as *raising hand to hat*; the situation of begging for money can be expressed by describing someone as *with hat in hand*; and so on. We seem to be dealing in general with situations in which the pre-established unity of the elements of a linguistically described situation can be indicated by using bare nouns instead of full noun phrases in the constituent which identifies the schematized situation.

I have argued that the formula itself is associated with the principle that the speaker assumes that the hearer knows the classificatory basis uniting the two things. This can be seen by realizing what we do cognitively when we confront a bare noun binomial whose motivating frame we do not know in advance. If we were to read the statement that *The worshipper removed belt and neckties and entered the temple*, we would feel that there is probably some ritualistic reason unknown to us why belts and neckties are connected in this setting.

2.7 Negotiating Conditionals

I am currently engaged in a study of conditional sentences in English and other languages. I am convinced that conditionals make up a family of constructions distinguished from each other in respect both to the pairings of tense and aspect features of the two clauses and to the kinds of purposes to which they are put. Of the eight or nine that I think can be distinguished from each other in English, I shall mention only one, what I will refer to as the *negotiating conditional*. Characteristic of this variety of conditional sentences is the existence of the modal *will* in each of the two clauses.

The grammar books frequently tell us that the future tense is unmarked in the protasis of a conditional sentence. Thus, in a sentence like *If he takes the bus, he'll be late*, the time intended with the verb of the first clause might well be future time. In the kind of conditional sentence which has a simple present in the protasis and a *will* in the apodosis, what gets communicated is a contingent prediction of some future event. But in a conditional sentence with two *will*s, the interpretation is that the speaker assumes that the hearer has an interest in the event named in the *apodosis* occurring, and the sentence is presented as a kind of negotiation or compromise. In the clearest cases, one person's part of the proposed bargain is expressed in the first clause, the speaker's offer is expressed in the second clause.

A way of describing this which minimizes the 'constructional' character of these sentences is to point out that, since the *will* of futurity is not welcome in the protasis of a conditional sentence, the *will* that shows up there is the *will* of intention. The construction itself, the argument goes, does not have anything to do with 'negotiation': it's just that if a conditional sentence is produced in which the condition proper identifies someone's willingness to do something, there is a natural *implicature* connecting such a situation with a 'negotiation', that is, with the speaker trying to negotiate some kind of behavior on the interlocutor's part.

Evidence for this interpretation takes the form of pointing out that the subject of the *if*-clause in double-*will* conditionals must be something capable of having intentions. The meaning of *will* in conditional clauses is thus supposed to account for the fact that it's not possible to say, **If it'll rain I'll bring my umbrella*. The oddity of this sentence is explained by noting that the subject of the *will* of intention has to be an Agent, and the *it* of *it rains* is not an Agent.

My own interpretation of such sentences is that a negotiation has to involve something presented on both sides, and it just happens that the possibility of rain falling can't count as an 'offer' on the part of one of the negotiators. The subject of the first *will* in a double-*will* conditional sentence does not have to be something capable of intending. It is possible to say things like, *If it'll be of any comfort to you, I'll stay another week.* Here I am saying that if you assure me that my presence will be comforting to you, I will agree to stay around. Bernard Comrie has offered as a counter-example to the claim that future *will* doesn't occur in *if*-clauses the sentence *If it'll definitely rain, I'll take my umbrella* (Comrie 1986). I think, however, that he has missed an important point here. I interpret the sentence as meaning that if you assure me right now that it will definitely rain, then I will make the decision right now to take my umbrella.

In a typical use of this construction, the second clause expresses the speaker's part of the bargain. Interestingly, when this is reversed, the utterance is heard as a 'review' of the other person's negotiating position. *If I'll do this, you'll do that, right?*. When both clauses have third-person subjects, as in *If he'll do this, she'll do that*, the utterance is heard as a conversation between negotiators, or as a report of a negotiating position.

3. *Some Consequences*

One of my purposes with this paper is to suggest that working with the constructionist framework forces us to rethink a number of the familiar 'dichotomies' in linguistics, dichotomies motivated by idealizations and abstractions which are absent from the constructionist approach. In particular, it is common in certain brands of linguistics, but alien to construction grammar to identify the inner structure of language, or to circumscribe some of its subdomains, by 'abstracting' them away from a number of corrupting and interfering forces.

The dichotomies that concern me are the distinctions often made between competence and performance, the social and the individual aspects of linguistic structure, lexicon and grammar, syntax and semantics, grammar and pragmatics, meaning and understanding, diachrony and synchrony. In some cases I will ask whether the dichotomy is intelligible at all; in some cases I will ask whether theories which do not recognize particular versions of them are theories worth taking into account.

3.1 *Competence and Performance*

The best known and most disputed of the dichotomies is the division between *competence* and *performance*. Competence, as expressed in Chomsky (1965:

4), is 'the speaker-hearer's knowledge of his language', performance is 'the actual use of language in concrete situations.'

The numerous unclarities associated with these paired notions have been spelled out by Dell Hymes (1974: 92–97), John Lyons (1977: 25–30) and others. It is simply not always clear what it is that 'purely linguistic knowledge' is being 'abstracted away from.'

1. The first notion, supported by the kinds of examples that accompanied the dichotomy's first introduction, treats linguistic performance as a matter of the success with which language users achieve their intentions. In this case, purely linguistic knowledge is abstracted away from limitations in time, motor capacity, or mental capacity, with respect to speakers' abilities to plan what they want to say or to execute their plans, and from hearers' abilities to perceive or attend to what others say. What motivates the distinction is the view of human organism as impediments to the full realization of linguistic abilities. Expressed this way, there can hardly be any serious disagreement about the existence of such a distinction; though there have been linguists who would prefer to think of human beings as 'achievers' of language-producing goals rather than as 'impediments' to the achievement of some goals; and Labov has convincingly argued against the common assumption, in discussions about this version of the distinction, on the error-rampant character of ordinary talk.

2. A second aspect of some early versions of the distinction had to do with the idealization of a *homogeneous speech community*. Lyons speaks of this notion of competence as a species of language standardization. The description of a language is abstracted away from speakers' awareness of dialectal or idiolectal variation. The methodological decision to consider language one variety at a time is obviously quite independent of the various other versions of our distinction. A concern with a *homogeneous* speech community is probably motivated by a belief that single-variety grammars are complete and coherent, all of them being *système otout se tient*. But I don't think we can have that anyway.

3. A third notion, first introduced by Jerrold Katz and Jerry Foder (Katz and Fodor 1963:176–181), is one which sees linguistic knowledge as abstracted away from the *situated use of language*. This is the interpretation of the distinction which has caused the greatest amount of confusion, because it obscures the distinction between the use of language and the existence of principles governing the use of language. One way of speaking of this is to say that it involves a confusion between *use*

and *usage*, that is, between what people do and how what they do is governed and evaluated by cultural institutions and community practices. The study of usage is itself an area in which a distinction between the possession of knowledge and the practice of that knowledge needs to be drawn. Since in Construction Grammar, numerous grammatical constructions are described as instruments of interaction, this version of the distinction is necessarily to be rejected.

4. A fourth interpretation of the distinction treats linguistic knowledge as *impersonalized*, that is, as independent of the speaking individual's communicative needs and decisions. A grammar can characterize what is in the language, but the study of what people choose to mean is quite separate: and the information that nobody would ever choose to say certain things ought not to be a part of the description of a language. On this too, there is little room for dispute.

There are still other distinctions hidden in this dichotomy: for example, from time to time it has been proposed that stylistic word order variations, or certain kinds of ellipsis, are matters of performance, and that therefore, in languages where they operate, their description need not be seen as part of the grammar.

Some of these distinctions are sensible, to be sure, but a constructionist account of grammar might line things up differently. In treating constructions as among the resources of a language, we can discuss those which are possessed (known and used) by every member of the community and those which are found in the repertories of some speakers but not others; we can describe those in individual speakers' repertories with respect to the degree of their mastery, we can examine the readiness and completeness with which they become employed, the manner and sequence in which their details get mastered by learners, and the difference between their roles in recognition and in production of language in individual learners.

However, the abstraction of linguistic knowledge away from context is rejected outright in the constructionist view, since a part of the understanding of grammatical constructions is knowing, one at a time, what they are for and what principles guide their choice. This requires a notion of context *type* in contrast to context *token*, of course, and that in turn presupposes the possibility of discovering a descriptive framework for context types. To us this is a necessary part of the full description of a grammar.

3.2 *Social and Individual*

A constructionist view of the difference between the social and the individual in language can be treated in terms of individual versus community-wide 'possession' of given constructions in repertories. The disputes that one hears about in discussing these two aspects have to do with such notions as Labov's 'Saussurean paradox' that one studies the community-wide possessions by examining the speech of a single individual, and one studies the individual aspects of language by studying groups, and knowing where variation occurs.

The question of the distribution of linguistic resources among individuals throughout a community is a particularly important one in the case of second language learning. A second language learner has no way of knowing which of the patterns he encounters in the data he uses for language learning belong to the community as a whole and which belong to the individuals surrounding him. Individual styles, it would seem, consist in the particular set of constructions that get selected and ranked in the expressive tool kit of individual speakers, which remain as part of the learner's receptive abilities, which become part of the learner's production.

3.3 *Lexicon and Grammar*

A constructionist view of the boundary between syntax and lexicon is that such a boundary is hard to find. It is not always possible to give an account of the syntactic structure of a sentence without referring to the particular lexical items whose combinability requirements or whose 'construction-tagging' roles determine the form of the given piece of text. It appears to me, in fact, that there are relatively few grammatical patterns which can be described entirely in terms of the patterning of phrasal categories. Predication and modification, in general, seem to be among these; but in by far the majority of construction types, either the implementation is strongly limited by lexical choices or the structure itself is dictated by the properties of given contained lexical items. A linguistic description of a lexical item is a (perhaps abbreviated) description of the grammatical constructions in which the item is empowered to play a role.

Not only do constructionists see as a continuum the proper ties of syntactic, phraseological, and lexical structures, but they also are convinced that phraseological patterns make up the vast majority of structures that enter into everyday discourse.

3.4 *Syntax and Semantics*

The constructionist rejects the view that semantics is merely a system of rules which, applied to syntactically organized linguistic objects, yield their interpretations. Rather, the view is (1) that semantic structures are tightly

integrated into the character of grammatical constructions, and (2) that semantic purposes can frequently be seen as part of what motivates given kinds
of syntactic constructions.

The argument that syntactic structure is independent of semantics comes
from some such notions as these: (1) that the range of relationships that can
exist between subject and predicate is very great, (2) that the kinds of 'modification' relations that can hold between an adjectival modifier and its nominal head can be great, more clearly associated with the meanings of individual lexical items than with the 'construction' and its meaning. In my opinion,
even the subject/predicate construction has semantic conditions that need to
be imposed on it; we might point out the significant differences between subject selection in English and German, as outlined recently by Jack Hawkins
(Hawkins 1981). Yoshiko Matsumoto (Matsumoto 1988) has discovered a
large number of ways in which modification has different possibilities in
English and Japanese. Set intersection cannot stand at all as the basic model
for the semantics of modification.

The verb/object construction appears to be merely a grammatical realization of a particular predicate–to–argument relationship; but many scholars
have noticed the special function of the direct object role that becomes apparent in a study of the various valence-changing operations in a number of
languages. Here, too, a grammatical construction is a necessary contributor
to the interpretation of the relation between a verb and its arguments, inter-
acting in significant ways with the predication relationships themselves.

3.5 Grammar and Pragmatics

There is undoubtedly an important distinction to be made between knowledge
of the grammar of a language and knowledge of what one can do with the
products of that grammar, but such a distinction must take into account the
fact that many constructions in a language have well-understood pragmatic
functions. Any aspect of the study of usage which requires mention of particular linguistic forms—as opposed to merely mentioning meanings—belongs
properly to the study of grammar.

In listing evidence of the connection between linguistic forms and matters
of rhetoric and usage, one could include the existence of topic and focus constructions of the kind reviewed by Lambrecht, the connections between
speech act force and variations of *mood*, the structure of politeness formulas
and expressions of deference and arrogance, etc. These are, in Levinson's
words (Levinson 1983: 8) 'aspects of linguistic structure (which) directly encode (or otherwise interact with) features of the context,' and it would surely
be a mistake to omit such encodings and interactions in a description of such
structures.

3.6 Meaning and Understanding

Related to the difference between grammar and pragmatics is the difference between *meaning* and *understanding*. This is taken to be the difference between what something conventionally means, on the one hand, and the process of figuring out why somebody might mean that in a given context, on the other hand. The constructionist view, informed by a 'frame semantics,' is compatible with the idea that in many cases a sentence has no coherent semantic structure of its own, but is provided, rather, by its lexicogrammatical structure, with 'recipes' or 'sets of instructions' on how an interpretation can be provided, such recipes frequently calling for ingredients not contained in the sentence's components. In very many cases, it is the act of applying such instructions *to the context* which is responsible for creating an interpretation. In contrast with the conceptually complete sentences which scholars tend to examine when putting on display the communicative capacity of human language, most sentences people actually produce do not have everything in them needed to construct a semantically complete and pragmatically grounded proposition. That this is not necessarily a 'failing' of language, but one of its valued properties, is emphasized by Dell Hymes, who, paraphrasing Habermas, tells us (Hymes 1974: 205) that 'human life needs areas of symbolic interaction and communication in which much can be taken for granted.'

3.7 Diachrony and Synchrony

The study of phraseological structures suggests in many ways that the learning of such structures constitutes a kind of historical reconstruction, by which I mean that the learner creates 'by abduction' a theory of how in the history of the language the particular construction got formed, and acts on that assumption. The evidence supporting this point of view is the evidence of mislearned phraseologisms. Complex phraseologisms are hardly ever mislearned as simply long unanalyzed words, but are given, in their mislearned forms, a lexicogrammatical structure. (*By in large* is a common version of *by and large*; *to all intensive purposes* is a common rendering of *to all intents and purposes*. This suggests that speakers, as language learners, are constantly assigning linguistic structure to what they learn, even if the structures they assign clearly do not assist them in understanding the expressions.)

I relate the question of diachrony–in–synchrony to the linguistic process of *analogy*, because that process involves the learner's assigning an analysis to some linguistic form (i.e., assuming that the form was constructed in such–and–such a way) and that other forms can be built on the same pattern. There is much more to be said about this, but on another occasion.

4. *Conclusion*

There is a kind of interest in meaning and context which relies on linguistics to achieve a complete decontamination of its field in order for the serious study of usage to be carried out. It is as if linguists were told by ethnographers and psychologists, 'Look, we want you to tell us as clearly as you can just what language is, and please leave it to us to figure out all of the cognitive, social and cultural things that hang around language. If you talk about all of those things yourself, I can't use your descriptions in doing what I need to do.'

The success, or perhaps the 'apparent' success, of the Gricean turn in semantics and pragmatics in the last decade has reinforced belief in the wisdom of these assumptions, since a number of features of understanding that some people used to attribute to semantics can now quite justifiably be assigned instead to usage effects. The clean picture we get of the workings of language has an autonomous syntax generating morphosyntactic objects, a theory of semantics building coherent semantic structures on those morphosyntactic objects, and a theory of pragmatics confronting semantic structures with contexts. As you have heard, I don't think things are quite that simple, or, as I would really like to say it, I don't think things are quite that difficult.

References

Brame, M. 1984. Universal Word Induction vs. Move alpha. *Linguistic Analysis* 14:313–352.

Chomsky, N. 1965. *Aspects of the Theory of Syntax*. MIT Press.

Comrie, B. 1986. Conditionals: A Typology. *On Conditionals*, ed. E. Traugott. Cambridge: University Press.

Fillmore, C. J., Kay, P. and O'Connor, M. C. in press. Regularity and Idiomaticity in Grammatical Constructions: The Case of 'Let Alone'. *Language*.

Hawkins, J. A. 1981. The Semantic Diversity of Basic Grammatical Relations in English and German. *Linguistische Berichte* 75:1–25.

Hymes, D. 1974. *Foundations in Sociolinguistics: An Ethnographic Approach*. Philadelphia: University of Pennsylvania Press.

Katz, J. J. and Fodor, J. A. 1963. The Structure of a Semantic Theory. *Language* 39:170–210.

Labov, W. 1975. *The Grammaticality of Everyday Speech*. Paper delivered at the Linguistic Society of America winter meeting. New York City.

Lakoff, G. P. 1987. *Women, Fire and Dangerous Things*. Chicago.

Lambrecht, K. 1984. Formulaicity, Frame Semantics, and Pragmatics in German Binomial Expressions. *Language* 60:753–796.

Lambrecht, K. 1986. Topic, Focus, and the Grammar of Spoken French. Ph.D. Dissertation. University of California. Berkeley.

Levinson, S. C. 1983. *Pragmatics*. Cambridge.

Lyons, J. 1977. *Semantics*, Vol. I and II. Cambridge.

Matsumoto, Y. in progress. Noun Modification in Japanese. Ph.D. Dissertation. University of California. Berkeley.

Morgan, J. L. 1975. Some Interactions of Syntax and Pragmatics. *Syntax and Semantics: Speech Acts 3*, eds. Cole, P. and Morgan, J. L., 289–303.

Pike, K. L. 1967. *Language in Relation to a Unified Theory of the Structure of Human Behavior*. The Hague.

8

Inversion and Constructional Inheritance

1999
CHARLES J. FILLMORE

Within a unification based grammar having grammatical constructions as its basic building blocks,[1] the formal device of *constructional inheritance* makes it possible to represent the grammar of a language as a 'mere' repertory of constructions while at the same time acknowledging and representing significant grammatical generalizations. In this paper I will take the English SAI (Subject-Auxiliary Inversion) construction as the focus of an exploration of constructional inheritance, both in reference to the higher-level constructions which are the source of SAI, and a sample of the lower-level constructions which inherit it.

1. *Construction Grammar*

In the version of Construction Grammar that Paul Kay and I and our associates have been shaping over the last ten years, a grammar is viewed as a repertory of constructions. A construction is a set of formal conditions on morphosyntax, semantic interpretation, pragmatic function, and phonology that jointly characterize or license certain classes of linguistic objects. A complete grammar of constructions that did everything it needed to do for a given

This paper was written for the Grammatical Constructions panel at the 1997 HPSG conference at Cornell University. Since I am not fluent in HPSG, I have not attempted to recast my comments in its terms. I am indebted to Paul Kay, Andreas Kathol, and two anonymous reviewers for advice on a preliminary version of this paper.

[1] See Fillmore and Kay 1993, Goldberg 1995, Kay 1995, Kay and Fillmore 1994, Michaelis and Lambrecht 1996a, b.

language would provide for any well-formed linguistic object in that language at least one ensemble of grammatical constructions whose interactions account for the pairing of form and meaning which that linguistic object represents: and for any linguistic object that was *n*-ways ambiguous it would allow *n* ensembles of constructions, each of which could assign it a different pairing of meaning and structure.

Any phrasal and many lexical constructions will have an internal part and an external part. The external part describes the kind of object instances of the construction are; getting the description right means showing what role the whole phrase can play in the rest of the grammar. The internal part describes the kinds of objects instances of the construction contain; getting the facts right means identifying the kinds of constituents that can participate in the construction.

The set of constructions in a grammar includes *Phrasal Constructions*, those whose internal descriptions identify the separate parts and the nature of their mutual dependencies of government (valence) and/or agreement. An example of a phrasal construction is the·SAI construction: for SAI we need to state that the first constituent is a finite auxiliary, the second constituent is something capable of being the subject of that auxiliary, and the remainder, if there is anything else, will be its non-subject complement(s).[2]

Utterances that are instances of the SAI construction can thus have two constituents, as in (1a), three constituents, as in (1b), or four constituents, as in (1c).

(1)   a.   [Did] [you]?

       b.   [Has] [anybody] [seen them]?

       c.   [Was] [she] [here] [this morning]?

In addition to phrasal constructions there are various kinds of *Lexical Constructions*. Among them we have 'simple' lexical constructions consisting of a lexical form with specification of its syntactic and semantic properties and (where relevant) its valence. For these there is no contrast between internal and external properties. There can be other lexical constructions which specify as their internal structure a particular set of lexical features, and as their outer structure a different set of lexical features, where both the

---

[2] Auxiliaries are treated as complement-taking verbs. In the usual case an auxiliary verb will 'take' a subject and a VP complement (*we have written the letter; she can reach the top shelf*); but in the case of the verb BE we sometimes need to assume more than one complement, as in example (1c). (We follow the practice of incorporating circumstantial adjuncts among the complements in a VP.)

'mother' constituent and the 'daughter' constituent are single lexical items. This is a construction-grammatic way of representing 'lexical rules' (and is in general the only occasion in construction grammar for anything corresponding to 'unary branching'). Familiar examples are items which are mass nouns internally and count nouns externally (*a beer*), or vice versa (*some chicken*), or those which are proper names internally and common nouns externally (*another Jane*).

There are also *Linking Constructions* which license particular mappings between semantic functions (thematic roles) and grammatical functions. Some predicates, when taken 'off the shelf', might have only the semantic part of their combinatorial options lexically specified (e.g. agent, theme, recipient); linking constructions, then serve to assign grammatical functions, in a context-sensitive way, to constituents that can instantiate these semantically specified elements.

Lastly we can have constructions which specify dependencies between phrasal entities, independently of how they enter into phrasal constructions. This is characteristic of (lexical and syntactic) idioms.

A grammar is a repertory of constructions; but instead of being just an unstructured collection, the grammatical constructions in a language form a network connected by links of *inheritance*. We recognize grammatical generalizations by showing the ways in which some constructions contain or are elaborations of other constructions (see Sag 1997 on relative clauses, Zwicky 1994 on constructions 'invoking' other constructions). If construction C inherits construction D, then C shares all of the conditions of D while adding some of its own. We will say, for example, that a construction for Yes–No Questions inherits the SAI construction but imposes certain limitations and adds features of interpretation.[3]

2. Ancestors of SAI

I will first describe the inheritance path of constructions that leads to SAI; and then I will turn to a sampling of the constructions which inherit SAI.

All of the constructions we will be examining here are phrasal constructions. The external properties of the phrase will be represented as feature structures written in an outer box, the internal properties will be written in the constituent boxes. Constituent order in the diagrams is represented by juxtaposition of boxes.[4]

---

[3] We see no need for the inheritance process to incorporate defaults and overrides in the manner of Lakoff 1987 and Goldberg 1995. The equivalent of 'default' values is provided by constructions that assign values to attributes whose values are otherwise unspecified.

[4] Some constructions, not described here, have constituents with unspecified order, requiring a slight modification of the representations.

A central typological fact about English is that in phrasal constructions for which one constituent is obligatorily lexical (i.e., is a single word), that constituent precedes the others in the phrase.[5] The construction which captures this fact is the *Lexically Tagged Phrase* construction, LTP.

Figure 1: LTP (Lexically Tagged Phrase).

This diagram tells us that the LTP construction has a lexical (not phrasal) member on the left and one or more constituents following it. Since it is a primary construction, it does not inherit any other construction. The plus sign after the second box is a 'Kleene plus', indicating one or more repetitions of the type of entity preceding the plus.[6] The feature structure 'level [lexical+]' indicates that this element is obligatorily a single lexical item. The feature structure 'level [max+]' means that the constituent so-marked is a 'maximal' phrase, in the traditional sense.

There are two slightly less general constructions that directly inherit LTP: one of these is what can be called the *Lexically Marked Phrase*, in which the first element is a 'marker' and what follows is the head; and the other is the *Lexically Headed Phrase*, in which the first element is a head and what follows consists of (some of) the complements of that head.

---

[5] There are phrases containing lexical items that are not themselves expandable as phrases, but which do not constitute instances of the description of LTP. A constituent filled with the word *ago*, for example, does not require lexical membership: *ago* occupies the position that can also be filled with a prepositional phrase such as *before today*, etc.

[6] A 'Kleene star'—an asterisk in the same position—would allow any number, that is, zero or more repetitions. However, we are dealing here with phrasal constructions, and for that we need at least two constituents.

Lexically marked phrases include

(2)   a.   that she liked it

      b.   if you have any

      c.   to leave home

The 'markers' are the clausal subordinators *that* and *if*, and the verbal subordinator *to*. The construction:

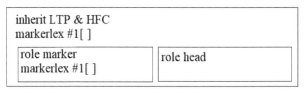

Figure 2: LMP (Lexically Marked Phrase).

In the description of the LMP we notice that the second element lacks the Kleene plus, since the 'head' constituent is either a single clause or a single verb-phrase. Another thing to notice is that the construction specifies the projection of the lexical identity of the marker onto the parent node. This is because we need to be able to identify the phrase as a whole as a 'that-clause', an 'if-clause', a 'to-marked infinitive', etc. The two instances of '#1[ ]' are unification indices, guaranteeing that whatever marker shows up in the marker position is registered with the entire constituent. The third property to notice is the inheritance of an as-yet undescribed construction called HFC, which stands for *Head Feature Construction*. That, and the attribute 'role', will be described shortly.

2.3

The *Lexically Headed Phrases* have valence-bearing lexical heads in phrase-initial position, the remainder constituting some (or all) of its complements. This construction requires an appeal to two other constructions, in addition to the LTP, namely the Head Feature Construction already mentioned, and the *Valence Raising construction* (VR).

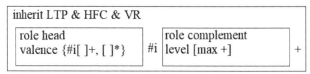

Figure 3: LHP (Lexically Headed phrase).

One of the attributes introduced in the last two constructions is 'role'. The role attribute figures only in the structure of phrases, where individual constituents are marked according to their role in the phrase. The possible values of this attribute include *marker*, *head*, *complement*, *modifier*, *specifier* and *conjunct*.

The valence of a valence-bearing word is a specification of the set of elements which the presence of the valence-bearer calls for in order for the semantic and syntactic structure that is built up around it to be completed. The elements of this set are described in terms of two kinds of *relational* features, their *grammatical function* (gf) and their *semantic ('thematic') function* (sf), together with their phrase type (NP, PP, etc.).

The valence value in the first constituent refers to the set (enclosed in wavy braces) of valence members. Some of these (one or more, as shown by the Kleene plus) are prefixed by a unification index '# i'. What follows the unification index is an empty pair of square brackets standing for the feature structure which identifies a valence member. The variable 'i' is understood as running through an unspecified number of elements in the valence description, and its occurrence twice in the formula means that each of the so–identified elements in the valence formula is matched by one of the constituents on the right. The remaining valence members (those represented by '[ ]*'), if there are any, are either not syntactically realized ('licensed omissions'), or are realized in a position external to the LHP. A syntactically unrealized constituent is the understood complement of *I tried*; examples of non-locally realized valence members are subjects of indicative sentences, or WH–fronted constituents.

2.4

It was said that the LMP and the LTP constructions both inherit HFC, the *Head Feature Construction*. This is the construction which specifies that certain features of a phrasal head[7] are projected onto the mother. In positing this construction we are required to distinguish *head features* from other kinds of features, and that requires us to say something about the architecture of the feature system we are using. Let it suffice for present purposes to say that the features we need to identify as head features are those which specify categorial and inflectional features. In particular, the set of head features does not include *role features* (the head of a phrase is notated with the feature 'role head') because the role of the mother in its own phrase is not necessarily that of 'head'. The set of head features does not include *level features*. *Lexicality* is a level feature; a phrase containing a lexical element, however, is

---

[7] The reader should be alerted that the word 'head' occurs as a value of the attribute 'role' but also as an attribute of a feature structure containing the 'head' features.

necessarily not lexical. *Maximality* is a level feature; a mother and head daughter may of course differ in maximality. We also posit a level feature *srs*, standing for 'subject requirement satisfied'. A predicate phrase in an indicative sentence is [srs –] but the clause which contains it and provides it with a subject is, of course, [srs +].

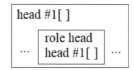

Figure 4: HFC (Head Feature Construction).

This construction does not inherit LMP: the constituent providing the features projected onto the mother is identified by the role label 'head' and not by position. The head in a 'marker + head' construction is to the right; the head in a 'head + complement' construction is to the left. Other constructions (e.g., modification), not discussed here, can have phrasal heads, and these can be leftmost or rightmost, depending on the construction.

2.5

In construction grammar, the valence of a valence-bearing head is projected onto the mother node, and that is shown in the *Valence Raising* construction.[8] This makes our use of the word 'valence' a bit awkward, since that word was originally introduced for naming the combinatorial privileges of individual words. Instead of abandoning the word 'valence', we will extend its use to include the kind of syntactic/semantic structure that can be built around a word. The valence that comes with a verb, then, is interpretable as identifying (part of) the structural potential of any clause that it heads. Similarly, the valences of non-verbs determine the syntactic/semantic structure of their phrasal projections.

The Valence Raising Construction looks like this:

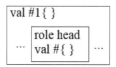

Figure 5: VR (Valence Raising).

---

[8] Actually, for reasons connected with our treatment of adjuncts, a more accurate version of this rule shows a subset relation between the valence of a head daughter and the valence of the mother constituent.

Again, the projecting constituent is identified by its role, not its position. The valence of a verb (the leftmost constituent in its phrase) is projected to a verb phrase; the valence of a verb phrase (the rightmost constituent in its phrase) is projected to the sentence as a whole.[9]

2.6

There are four major kinds of Lexically Headed Phrases, separated according to the category of the lexical head. These we will refer to as VHP (Verb-Headed Phrase), AHP, NHP, and PHP. These (perhaps awkward) names are intended to keep them distinct from the familiar and informally used VP, AP, NP and PP, since the latter are conventionally used for constituents which might be smaller than the corresponding LHP (they might not be phrasal) or they might be larger than the corresponding LHP (they might contain 'specifiers' and/or 'modifiers'). In our representation, a word which itself serves as a maximal constituent simultaneously bears the level features [lexical +] and [maximal +]. Here we exhibit only the VHP construction; the others will be identical in form but will differ in the value of the cat ('category') attribute.

Figure 6: VHP Verb-Headed Phrase.

2.7

The VHP construction can be elaborated in two ways: it underlies both the predicational VHP (as in *ate his lunch*) and the inverted clause as in *did they see us?*). The constructions specifying these elaborations are named VPC (*Verbal Predicate Construction*) and, following general practice, SAI (*Subject–Auxiliary Inversion*).[10]

The VPC specifies that all of the complements of the lexical head are nonsubjects; the mother has the level feature [srs –]—'subject requirement not (internally) satisfied'.

---

[9] We ignore here the problem of valence projection in cases where the head constituent contains a conjunction of valence-bearing elements.

[10] In Kay & Fillmore 1994, this was called Inversion, abbreviated INV.

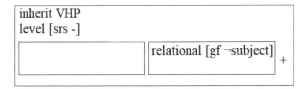

Figure 7: VPC (Verbal Predicate Construction.

2.8

The SAI construction identifies three positions. The occupant of the first has to be a finite auxiliary. The second has grammatical function subject. It is important that the constituent is not just 'a subject' but is in fact the subject of the auxiliary in the first constituent, but that doesn't have to be separately specified, since the phrase as a whole is [srs +] and all other complements are specified as [gf ¬subject]. It should be noticed that the third constituent bears the Kleene star, meaning that this part of the construction might be missing, or might be multiple. Recall the examples in (1) above.

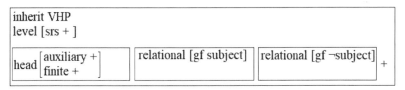

Figure 8: SAI (Subject-Auxiliary Inversion).

The full inheritance structure of SAI is displayed below:

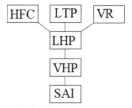

Figure 9: Inheritance structure of SAI.

A complete description of SAI will have all of the properties of each of the ancestor constructions.[11]

---

[11] The reader will have noticed that neither SAI nor any of its ancestors is provided with semantic or pragmatic information. This appears to be a major feature by which Construction Grammar and HPSG formalisms are not mutually intertranslatable: the basic 'typologically relevant' constructions are not *signs* in the sense of Pollard and Sag. Whether SAI itself has a

3. *Non-Interrogative Constructions Inheriting SAI*

The English SAI construction is host to a large number of constructions most famously a family of question constructions that use the SAI order. In this paper I will survey those which are not, or are not mainly, questions.[12]

3.1

One heir of SAI can be called the *Blessings, Wishes, and Curses Construction*, BWC. In these sentences the auxiliary is limited to the modal *may* and the sentence expresses the speaker's (real or pretended) act of calling on divine or magical forces to bring about something the speaker desires.

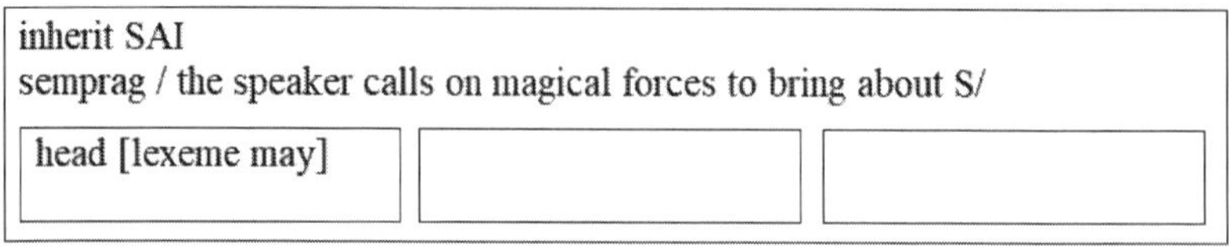

inherit SAI		
semprag / the speaker calls on magical forces to bring about S/		
head [lexeme may]		

Figure 10: BWC (Blessings-Wishes-Curses).

Examples in (3):

(3) a. May she live forever!

b. May I live long enough to see the end of this job!

c. May your teeth fall out on your wedding night!

It is important to recognize that there is no independent semantic force of SAI syntax, or any independently discoverable meaning of the modal *may*, that could explain the semantic/pragmatic force we recognize with these sentences, either compositionally or by providing the basis for a context-based interpretation. This has to be described as a separate construction.

---

pragmatic or functional component shared by all of its inheritors is something on which I do not take a stand. (But see Michaelis & Lambrecht 1996b.)

[12] The original version of this paper concentrated on questions, but their treatment will be dealt with in later work.

3.2

A construction that we might call *SAI-exclamation* underlies a class of utterances which express the speakers' judgements or evaluations of events in the speaker's personal experience. Such utterances (explored in N. A. McCawley 1973) are clearly not questions, because (i) they can be used to express experiences that addressees did not share (and therefore could not answer questions about), (ii) they do not get rendered with rising intonation, and (iii) they do not invite a response from the addressee.

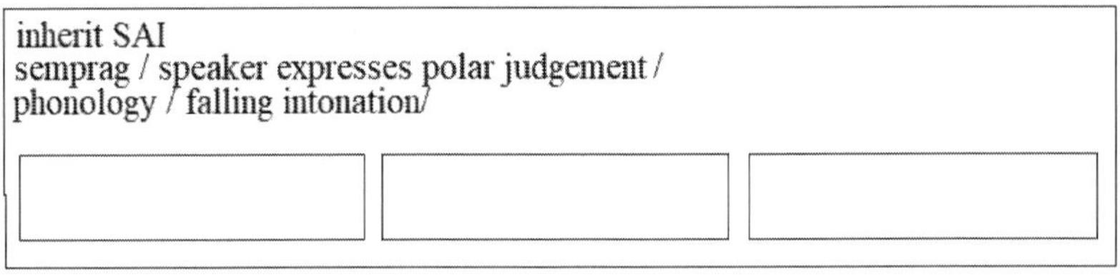

inherit SAI semprag / speaker expresses polar judgement / phonology / falling intonation/		

Figure 11: SAI Exclam (Sai Exclamation).

These utterances can be preceded by any of a number of conventional ejaculations, such as *Man!*, *Boy!*, *Wow!*, etc. Examples in (4):

(4) a.   Boy, was I stupid!

b.   Wow, can she sing!

c.   Man, am I hot!

Since instances of this construction are exclamations, they typically express judgements about situations that are beyond the norm on some scale. Example (4b) (even without the 'Wow!') suggests that it is the construction itself, not the semantics of the contained predicates, which determine the 'beyond norm' interpretation. This sentence has to be interpreted as suggesting that she can sing unusually well.

3.3

There is a purely morphological construction that 'uses' SAI, in the sense that it specifies SAI as the context in which it applies. This is the construction which creates the phrase *aren't I?*. The form *aren't I* as the contracted form of *am not* occurs only in SAI structures. The usage specifications associated with *aren't I?* have to do with register, and are compatible with any of the various varieties of constructions in which its conditions (negative copula, present tense, occurring with first person singular subject) are met. Thus we find *aren't I?* occurring in what can be described as different sub-constructions of interrogative SAI.

(5) a. I'm getting closer, aren't I?

    b. Aren't I the clever one!

    c. Aren't I a little too old for you, honey?

    d. Aren't I gonna get anything out of this for myself?

I offer no suggestion on how the registral information should be presented. To some speakers the form is absolutely natural, with no registral value whatever; to others it sounds cautious or pretentious; to still others it is simply bad English.

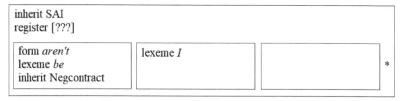

Figure 12: 'Aren't I?'.

The first constituent is an instance of the morphological construction *Negative Contraction* (negcontract), the construction which produces *won't, can't, didn't*, etc. and which I will not describe.

3.4

There is a class of *emphatic negative imperatives*, accepting only the subject pronoun *you* and the negative form *don't*, illustrated in (6a) and (6b),

(6) a. Don't you even touch that!

    a'. Don't even touch that!

    b. Don't you dare talk to me like that!

    b'. *Don't dare talk to me like that!

Obviously these are not questions. It appears that these are not merely Negative Imperatives (*Don't do that!*) which happen to include an overt second-person subject: sentence (6b') strikes me as ungrammatical.

inherit SAI mood imperative		
form *don't* lexeme *do* inherit Negcontract	lexeme *you*	

Figure 13: ENI (Emphatic Negative Imperative).

3.5

As an alternative to versions of conditional clauses prefixed by such markers as *if* and *unless*, there is an SAI version, limited to the auxiliary forms *were*, *had* and *should* (and, obsolete or obsolescent, *did*).

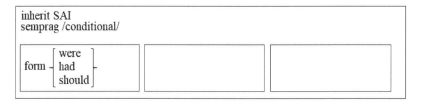

Figure 14: Aux Cond (Auxiliary Conditional).

Examples of present counterfactual, past counterfactual, and non-past contingent Aux-Cond sentences are given in (7).

(7) a.   Were they here now, we wouldn't have this problem.

b.   Had we known what was in it, we wouldn't have opened it.

c.   Should there be a need, we can always call for help.

In characterizing the construction in Figures 12 and 13, we needed to specify not just that the sentence was negative, but that the auxiliary had the neg-contracted form. By specifying the actual forms of the auxiliary in the Aux-Cond construction in Figure 14, we rule out the possibility of neg-contraction. The clause itself can be negative, however, as can be seen by comparing the affirmative sentences in (7) with the negative sentences in (8).

(8) a.   Were it not/*Weren't it for your help, we'd be in trouble   now.

    b.   Had you not/*Hadn't you invited me, I wouldn't have known about this.

    c.   Should you not/*Shouldn't you comply with this request,   your permit will be taken away.

When the words inserted into the first position of Aux-Cond are *were* or *had*, an additional feature accompanies them: [mood counterfactual]; with *should*, however, it is [mood contingent]. An instance of the Aux-Cond construction can occur as a subordinate clause to a full two-part conditional sentence, as in any of the grammatical sentences in (6) or (7), or, in the case where the subjunctive is counterfactual, it also lends itself to use in a *Wishing* construction (not described), which, among others of its features, welcomes the word *only*.

(9)   Had I only known!

3.6

An example of a construction in which SAI can characterize one constituent of a multiple-constituent construction is the *Correlative Conditional* construction (not described here, but see Fillmore 1987), in which the second element is optionally of the SAI type. Sentence (10a) shows the presence of SAI; sentence (10b) shows the more usual form in this construction.

(10) a.   The faster you finish eating those hot dogs, the sooner [will] [we] [be able to claim the prize].

    b.   The faster you finish eating those hot dogs, the sooner we'll be able to claim the prize.

4. *Pointing to the Treatment of SAI Questions*

It seems to me there are four sorts of phenomena that join with SAI to create the kinds of questions we find: two flavors of polarity, intonation, and (for some questions) participation in a new family of constructions with its own inheritance hierarchy.[13] Polarity occurs on two levels: the polarity of a

---

[13] Briefly, that new family of constructions begins with what we call the *Left Isolate* (LI) construction, by which a maximal phrase is found to the left of its valence-bearing phrasal head. From this beginning are formed the Subject/Predicate construction, and a large group of constructions involving the potential of 'long-distance dependency' between the left-isolated constituent and the predicator whose valence requirements it satisfies. *WH-MainClauseNon-*

sentence as a whole has to do with whether the sentence is affirmative or negative; polarity can also color a context in respect to the welcoming of polarity items. I will distinguish 'polarity' as an attribute having the values 'affirmative' and 'negative', from 'polarity context' as having the values 'pospol' (positive polarity) and 'negpol' (negative polarity) or 'neutral'. The reason for requiring this range of distinctions is because positive and negative polarity *contexts* can occur distinctively in either affirmative or negative *questions*. For example:

(11) a.   Do you want a little?   [pol aff, polcon pos]

b.   Do you want any?   [pol aff, polcon neg]

c.   Don't you want a little? [pol neg, polcon pos]

d.   Don't you want any?   [pol neg, polcon neg]

4.1

Underlying both real questions and a new variety of exclamatory construction, there is a general *appellative SAI* construction which specifies only appellation, a 'pragmatic' feature indicating that the speaker appeals to an addressee for a reaction. The uninformative 'semprag appellation' in the diagram below will have to be cashed out as a scenario involving speaker intentions and certain features of illocutionary force.

Figure 15: Appellative (Appellative SAI Construction).

I will make (but leave undefended) the claim that there is a constructional contrast between *negative SAI questions* and *affirmative SAI questions*, and, furthermore, that each of these is host to still more elaborated question types. The first of these divisions should not be surprising: grammar does not need two ways of formulating Yes/No questions, so if affirmative SAI sentences can serve that purpose, SAI questions, with negative syntax are free to serve other purposes. Being precise about the difference between the plain question

---

SubjectQuestions, for example, inherit LI at the top and SAI in the right sister, for questions like 'What did you see?', or *WH-MainClauseSubjectQuestions* inherit LI at the top and Subject/Predicate in the right sister, as in 'Who said that?'.

in (12a) and the biased question in (12b) is difficult, but there is no doubt that an important difference exists.

(12) a.   Did you understand what I said?

b.   Didn't you understand what I said?

I believe that there are only partly predictable interpretations of positive and polarity contexts as they occur independently in positive and affirmative SAI questions, and that the whole range of issues includes at least the impressive collection of insights in Ann Borkin's paper of twenty-some years ago (Borkin 1977). I believe that Borkin's observations, explained in terms of the kinds of speaker intentions or attitudes expressed with the selection of positive or negative polarity items, can instead be described as conditions on constructions which create positive or negative polarity contexts within which positive or negative polarity items are welcome. A full account requires subtle and careful specification of features of intonation, mood, register, and discourse functions, as well as precise accounts of the semantics of polarity. But all of that is for another occasion.

4.2

There is at least one noninterrogative construction which inherits the feature 'appellative' from the preceding construction. This is the *Negative SAI exclamation construction*. Sentences based on this construction are negative in form but express *affirmative* judgments about some experience which speaker and addressee have shared or are sharing.

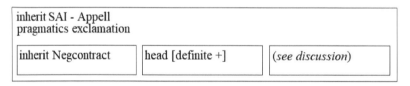

Figure 16: NegSAI Exclam ('Negative' SAI Exclamation).

Instances of this construction are compatible with falling or rising intonation, but in either case they assume addressee assent, or seek addressee validation, on the *affirmative* version of the proposition underlying the sentence. Unlike the positive SAI Exclam construction of Figure 11, this one isn't used with completely private judgments: if I exclaim *Wasn't I hot!*—as opposed to *Was I hot!*—the chances are I'm asking for confirmation of my fine performance on the basketball court rather than seeking confirmation of my degree of discomfort from the heat.

Sentences of the type in question include those in (13).

(13) a. Isn't she amazing!

   b. Wasn't that awful!

   c. Aren't they beautiful.

The description of this construction will clearly have to include semantic constraints on the predicate phrases. A corpus search[14] for sentences which began with neg-contracted auxiliaries and did not end in question marks yielded predicates that tended to have a clear end–of–scale character. A sampling of the adjectivals: *amazing, brilliant, disgusting, extraordinary, fabulous, fantastic, glorious, hopeless, horrible, huge, incredible, ludicrous, magnificent, marvellous, splendid, stupendous, terrific,* and *wonderful.* With predicate nominals one finds *a grand girl, a hideous thought, a scream,* etc., and the exclamatory *something* (as in *Isn't that something!*).

5. *Closing*

A major intellectual challenge in writing a construction grammar of a language is found in the problem of figuring out whether newly encountered phenomena can be accounted for by the constructions already posited for the grammar, in standard unificational and compositional ways, or by exploiting the possibilities of contextual interpretations, or whether the newly considered phenomena require the positing of a new construction. At times researchers will discover ways in which certain postulated constructions can be dissolved by showing that all of their properties 'fall out from' constructions or principles that can be independently called on to analyze the phenomena. But at the same time researchers will continue discovering layers of conventionalization in linguistic forms that superficially appear to be plainly derivable by familiar means, and therefore will find themselves positing new constructions. It seems to me that a theory of grammar which uses grammatical constructions and posits a rich network of inheritance relations among them gives a point to such reformulations, in that the before and after stages of such recastings will show a clear difference between two important kinds of linguistic discoveries—finding generalizations where previous scholars wrongly posited idiosyncrasy, and finding new levels of conventionalization where previous scholars wrongly posited generality.

---

[14] Using the British National Corpus, made available to me at the International Computer Science Institute through the courtesy of Oxford University Press.

References

Borkin, A. 1976. Polarity in Questions. *Chicago Linguistic Society* 7:53–62.

Fillmore, C. J. 1987. Varieties of Conditional Sentences. *Proceedings of the Third Eastern States Conference on Linguistics*, Columbus: Ohio State University. 163–182.

Fillmore, C. J., and P. Kay. 1993. Construction Grammar (ms). UC Berkeley.

Goldberg, A. 1995. *Constructions: A Construction Grammar Approach to Argument Structure*. Chicago: University of Chicago Press.

Kay, P. 1995. Construction Grammar. *Handbook of Pragmatics*, eds. J. Verschueren, J-O. Östman, and J. Blommaert. John Benjamins.

Kay, P., and C. J. Fillmore. 1993. Grammatical Constructions and Linguistic Generalizations: The *what's X doing Y?* Construction (ms), UC Berkeley.

Lakoff, G. 1987. *Women, Fire and Dangerous Things*. University of Chicago Press.

McCawley, N. A. 1973. Boy, is Syntax Easy! *Chicago Linguistics Society* 9:369–377.

Michaelis, L., and K. Lambrecht. 1996a. Toward a Construction-Based Theory of Language Function: The Case of Nominal Extraposition. *Language* 72:215–247.

Michaelis, L., and K. Lambrecht. 1996b. The Exclamative Sentence Type in English. *Conceptual Structure, Discourse and Language*, ed. A. Goldberg. CSLI: Stanford.

Sag, I. A. 1996. English Relative Clause Constructions, *Journal of Linguistics* 33(2):431–484.

Zwicky, A. 1994. Dealing out Meaning: Fundamentals of Syntactic Constructions. *Proceedings of the Twentieth Annual Meeting of the Berkeley Linguistics Society*. 611–625.

Part 3

Constructional Analyses

9

Varieties of Conditional Sentences

1987
CHARLES J. FILLMORE

1. *The Grammatical Construction Model*

There is a large family of related grammatical structures, which I shall refer to as conditional sentences, the description of whose properties, it seems to me, requires an appeal to theoretical apparatus which is missing from, or does not have a position of prominence in, most current grammatical theories. My plan in this paper is to lay out a number of facts about these various structures, and to present them as offering support for a theory of grammar which assigns a central role to the concept of grammatical construction. The facts that I'll be surveying are for the most part not new facts, from the point of view of descriptive grammars of modern English, but they may be unfamiliar to people who want grammars to be constrained in particular ways.

A simplest example of the kind of sentence I'll be looking at is

(1) If she sits here she'll be able to see the parade.

My discussion will be limited to questions of linguistic structure, and will touch hardly at all on the vast world of logical, psychological, and philosophical issues in the treatment of the meanings and functions of such sentences. In fact, I will also be ignoring a number of syntactic issues about these sentences, since I will be dealing mainly with sentences in which the antecedent clause comes first.

Because of the particular theoretical axe I am grinding, the basic questions I will be asking are these:

(a)   To what extent are facts about the form and interpretation of a conditional sentence predictable from knowledge about its constituent elements (words such as IF and WOULD, grammatical features such as PAST, etc.)?

(b)   To what extent are such facts predictable from knowledge about elemental grammatical relations (such as predication, subordination, etc.)?

(c)   To what extent must an account of the meaning and function of a conditional sentence of a given type be sensitive to subtle structural patterns whose total effects cannot be seen as the *compositional product* of its parts but must be described in terms of separate *grammatical constructions*?

Whenever we get non-zero answers to this last question, we are dealing with results that encourage those of us who are working within a grammatical mode (such as the Berkeley Grammatical Construction Theory[1]) in which holistic structural patterns are included among the basic units of grammatical description. In examining the properties of individual grammatical constructions within the family of conditional sentence constructions, we will be concerned with describing simultaneously constraints on their syntactic form, generalizations about the semantic interpretations, and principles governing their use.

As an example of what I take to be a syntactic pattern which must be described in its own terms, and which has properties that do not simply 'fall out from' what is known about its constituent parts and its constituent relations, we can take a construction that is in some ways simpler, and in some ways more complex, than the main types of conditional sentences we'll be examining later on. I will refer to the construction (facetiously) as the BCHF construction (standing for 'The bigger they come, the harder they fall,' a stereotyped instance of it). Examples of BCHF can be seen in (2a)–(2c):

---

[1] Work representative of early formulations of Grammatical Construction Theory is represented in Fillmore (1985), Fillmore, Kay and O'Connor (ms.), Kay (1984), Lakoff (in press), and Lambrecht (1986a, 1986b, and in press.)

(2a) The more you eat, the fatter you get.

(2b) The longer we stay here, the more bored we're going to be.

(2c) The more harshly I scold him, the worse he behaves.

The structural pattern in accordance with which these sentences are constructed has a combination of properties which make it unique in type, though perhaps none of these properties are complete strangers to the language as a whole.

First of all, its main structure is bipartite, the two elements being constituents of *essentially* the same type. There is no established category name for the combination (except, of course, 'Sentence'), and there is no established category name for the individual paired immediate constituents. Let us call the two constituents of such sentences 'L' and 'R' (standing for Left and Right). At the grossest level, then, the structure is as shown in Figure 1.

$$\frac{\text{BCHF}}{\text{L} \mid \text{R}}$$

Figure 1

Each of these parts ('L' and 'R') has itself two segments (or can be so analyzed), a segment containing a compared expression and a clause with a gap of the type which welcomes the category represented by the compared expression. We can call these the 'X' segment and the 'Y' segment. A representation of such subdivisions is given in Figure 2.

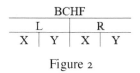

Figure 2

The 'X' segment, in each case, consists of two parts, the word *the* followed by a comparative expression in any category allowing the grammatical process of comparison. We shall refer to this as CompPhrase in each case, allowing it to be a compared nominal phrase, as in (*the*) *more husbands* (*she has*), a compared adjectival phrase, as in (*the*) *bigger* (*it gets*), or an adverbial phrase, as in (*the*) *more carefully* (*you hold it*). In Figure 3, 'A' and 'B' are variables standing for whatever grammatical categories are selected as the 'X' segment of the 'L' and the 'R' constituents respectively.

The 'Y' segment is a clause with, as noted, the potential for housing a phrase of the type represented by the 'X' segment. Thus, the missing element

in *you get* in (2a) might be *fat*; the missing element in *we're going to be* in
(2b) might be *bored*; the missing element in *he behaves* in (2c) might be
badly. Using the *slash category* notation developed in Generalized Phrase
Structure Grammar (Gazdar 1981), we may describe such a clause as 'S/A'
for the clause in the 'L' segment, 'S/B' for the clause in the 'R' segment.
These observations are summarized in Figure 3.

BCHF						
L			R			
X		Y	X		Y	
Degree *the*	Comp. Phr. A-Phrase	S/A-Phrase	Degree *the*	Comp. Phr. N-Phrase	S/B-Phrase	

Figure 3

The relationship between the 'X' segment and the 'Y' segment is a relationship of long-distance dependency, and thus exhibits those properties of
long-distance dependencies which allow such phrasings as

(2)   The more carefully you assume he's going to behave, ...

where *more carefully* modifies *behave* and not *assume*; but never a thing like

(3)   *The more stupidly the guy who worded it liked cheese, ...

with *more stupidly* construed as modifying *worded it*.

The relationship between the 'X' segment and the 'Y' segment is not like
the familiar comparative construction, which requires a THAN-phrase or a
THAN-clause (*bigger than Harry, bigger than we expected*); but we note that
in the 'L' part but not the 'R' part (in my dialect at least), the subordinated
clause can be marked with the opener *that*.

(5)   The bigger that it gets, the heavier it becomes.

(6)   ?The bigger it gets, the heavier that it becomes.

The clause in the 'L' segment, but not that in the 'R' segment, is a potential *negative polarity context*.

(7)   The more you do any of that, the easier it gets.

The clause in the 'R' segment has the (obsolescent) potential of being in inverted form.

(8) The older she got, the less likely was she to agree with me on this question.

Summarizing, we can sketch out the main syntactic characteristics of this construction as shown in Figure 4:

BCHF					
L			R		
X		Y		X	Y
Degree *the*	Comp. Phr A-Phrase	S/A-Phrase (polarity context) (THAT-Comp possible)	Degree *the*	Comp. Phr. B-Phrase	S/B-Phrase (inversion possible)

Figure 4

Semantically, the 'L' part and the 'R' part establish two scales (or perhaps two ranges on the same scale), and the utterance as a whole is seen as asserting a correlation or dependency relationship between values on these two scales, the 'A' half determining the independent variable, the 'C' half determining the dependent variable. (For (2c), 'Changes in the degree of harshness in my scolding yields corresponding changes in the degree to which he behaves badly.')

The point of an assertion of the correlation is in part revealed by the pairing of tense and modality in the two halves. Thus, if the 'L' and 'R' halves both have the simple present tense, the utterance as a whole stands as a general principle.

(9) The more he drinks, the sillier he gets.

If the 'L' half has a simple present tense and the 'R' half has a WILL–future, the sentence stands as a contingent prediction.

(10) The faster we drive, the sooner we'll get there.

And when the 'L' half and the 'R' half both have the simple past tense, the sentence represents a past correlation.

(11) The more he drank, the sillier he got.

It seems clear from the above that any successful description of these phenomena requires us to assemble *for this single construction* an organized body of facts which cannot simply be taken for granted as following from other facts independently knowable about the grammar of English.

The construction we have just examined (about which there is still more to be said) illustrates the method of description that will be pursued in what follows; it is also arguably one of the varieties of conditional sentences. In the final description we would characterize the sentence as a whole as a variety of conditional sentence (on the grounds that some of its formal and semantic properties can be predicted from that fact), and we would relabel 'L' and 'R' as 'Antecedent' and 'Consequent.'

2. *Conditionals as Constructions*

As in the case of the BCHF construction just examined, conditional sentences in general can be seen as having a topmost bipartite structure, and, once again, we can profit by looking for constraints on the composition of these two major segments, and by showing how matched conditions on the two parts join to define particular kinds of grammatical constructs.

2.1 *Features on Verbal Heads*

In those cases in which both parts are finite clauses, we shall be interested in the pairings of the tense, aspect and modality features of the two parts. Evidence that speakers of English have immediate knowledge of grammatical features of the parts of conditional sentences can be seen in the immediacy with which speakers can interpret sentences that have superficial lexical ambiguities. Let us consider the potential ambiguities in the forms HIT and 'D (apostrophe + D) in some simple sentences.

The word-form HIT in English has four different possible grammatical descriptions: it can stand for the (non-third-person-subject) present tense form, the simple past tense form, the past participle, and the bare infinitive. The contraction written *'d* abbreviates either HAD or WOULD; and WOULD itself has at least two possible interpretations in these contexts: as the past tense form of one of the several uses of the modal WILL, or as a conditional modal.

These word-forms are disambiguated in specific ways in the interpretations native speakers give to the sentences in (12) and (13) below. Consider first (12 a) and (12b).

(12a) If you hit him, he'll cry.

(12b) If you hit him, he'd cry.

The HIT of *if you hit him* can be either a present tense verb or a past tense verb. (The local context does not allow either of the two non-finite possibilities.) The first sentence allows two interpretations, one an event-contingent prediction, going along with the Present Antecedent : WILL–Future Consequent pattern ('I accept the possibility that in the near future you might hit him; if that happens your act of hitting him will be followed by his crying'); the second interpretation is a fact-contingent prediction which fits the Unrestricted Antecedent : WILL Consequent ('You are wondering if he will cry; should it be true that you hit [past] him, then I can assure you that he will cry'). We know that in (12b), the word HIT has to have the past tense interpretation, because, of the two conditional patterns which fit this sentence, each one assigns past tense to the first element. The first possibility is that the sentence fits the pairing Past Antecedent : Past Consequent corresponding to a meaning something like, 'In those days, every time someone hit him he cried.' The second possibility is that the sentence fits the pattern Hypothetical Antecedent : Conditional Consequent, where the meaning is something like: 'He is in such a state right now, that an event of someone hitting him would be followed by a burst of tears on his part.' In both of these interpretations, the contraction 'D stands for WOULD, but in the former case it is the past form of the modal WILL, and in the second case it is the conditional modal.[2]

We now consider the examples in (13):

(13a) If you'd hit him, he'd cry.

(13b) If you'd hit him, he'd've cried.

This time we will notice that the combination 'D HIT in the two sentences permits two different interpretations: WOULD HIT and HAD HIT. In (13a) both contractions represent WOULD, and in each clause, the verb following WOULD is in its bare stem form. The meaning of (13a) is something like, 'In those days, whenever anyone hit him he cried.' Both WOULDs are the past tense of the modal WILL in its *dispositional* meaning. The second sentence we can accept as fitting the pattern by which we have Past Perfect Antecedent Conditional (Perfect) Consequent—the pattern for the *past counterfactual conditional*. And here the meaning is, 'At the time in question you did not hit him; but an act of your hitting him at that time would have been followed by a crying event.'

---

[2] I know that I am supposed to be embarrassed at the fact that I am glossing conditional sentences with conditional sentences. In these glosses I am not attempting to capture the meaning of the sentence's *conditionality*, but the difference in meaning of the sentences by which a single sentence form is taken to be ambiguous.

2.2. *Antecedents as Polarity Contexts*

The antecedents of conditional sentences are potential sites for negative polarity items. Words in the ANY series—*anything, anybody*, etc.—have two almost contradictory senses, one in which they are something like the *universal quantifier*, and one in which they are something like the *existential quantifier*. The latter is limited to *polarity contexts*. The selection between the two is recognized instantaneously, as can be seen in native speakers' ability to make such judgments as the following. In (14) the most natural interpretation is that the speaker is insulting John. This is because, in the consequent clause, which is not a polarity context, *anyone* can only have the *universal quantifier sense*. The sentence tells us that the world in which John can do 'it' is a world in which everyone can do it. However, in (15) we have the opposite reaction. Here, John is being praised, because *anyone* in the antecedent has (or can readily have) the *existential quantifier* sense, and the meaning of the sentence is: if there is someone who can do it, that someone is John.

(14)   If John can do it, anyone can do it.

(15)   If anyone can do it, John can do it.

Given these two interpretations of *anyone*, there is a potential paradox in sentence (16):

(16)   If anyone can do it, anyone can do it.

This sentence looks like a simple tautology, but on one interpretation it is simply a case of bad reasoning.[3]

Again, the point has been that the recognition of the difference between the antecedent and the consequent of a conditional sentence allows immediate discernment of a distinction that is in fact quite difficult to be precise about analytically.

---

[3] Actually, sentences (15) and (16) both permit interpretations in which the proposition equivalent to that of the self-standing sentence *anyone can do it* is taken as the content of the apodosis. In this case (15) is not praise and (16) is a tautology.

3. *Preliminaries*

Before we begin trying to put the details together, we will need to make some preliminary observations and terminological decisions.

3.1. *Varieties of Antecedents and Consequents in Conditional Sentences*

An antecedent may or may not constitute a clause. A clausal antecedent can be declarative, interrogative, or imperative in form. In sentence (1), repeated here, it is declarative:

    (1)   If she sits here, she'll be able to see the parade.

The interrogative type, shown in (17), is rare in English, but it is common in a number of other languages.

    (17)   You want it? It's yours.

Imperative antecedents sort themselves out into three subtypes, to be distinguished later; at this point, I merely offer examples, one of each type:

    (18)   Eat your spinach and you can have dessert.

    (19)   Break it and you've bought it.

    (20)   Pick it up and your hands get all sticky.

It will be noticed that in all three cases, the pattern which accepts an imperative form in the antecedent requires an AND introducing a declarative consequent.

Nonclausal antecedents appear in two contexts. In the first of these, the consequent is introduced by a conjunction, usually AND, where the antecedent can be a quantified expression indicating the extent by which some unnamed change would have a certain result, as in (21).

    (21a)   One more stupid mistake like that and you'll be fired.

    (21b)   Another hour and we'd have made it.

    (21c)   A little bit closer and we're dead.

The second type of nonclausal antecedent is a *circumstantial adverb*, possibly anaphoric, followed by an ordinary finite clause of the kind that could appear in a consequent clause.

(22a)   In my place, what would you have done?

(22b)   With more help we could have finished in time.

(22c)   In that case, I wouldn't go.

(22d)   Otherwise I won't recognize you.

(22e)   Then I'd do it.

As we had clausal antecedents of three types, we can have clausal consequents of the same three types: *declarative*, as in (23); *interrogative*, as in (24); and *imperative*, as in (25).

(23)   If I like it, I'll buy it.

(24)   If you don't like your new job, what will you do?

(25)   If you can't take the heat, get out of the kitchen.

True nonclausal consequents are hard to find, but just for the sake of symmetry, we might slip into our collection such telegraphic conditionals as (26):

(26)   No shirt, no shoes, no service.

which gets disabbreviated as 'If you're not wearing a shirt and shoes, you will not be served here.'

Lastly, we can make mention of conditional sentences which have only one part, the content of the missing partner being inferrable (in principle, at least, from the context. There are self-standing antecedents, as in (27), and there are self-standing consequents, as, for example, the second sentence in (28).

(27)   If I had only met her first.

(28)   Thank goodness the cable arrived when it did. I'd be dead now.

3.2. *Tense and Modality*

I have suggested features of verb grammar figure in the description of the parts of a conditional sentence. In particular, tense forms and the perfect and modal auxiliaries have roles in conditional sentences which differ in important ways from what can be said about them when they occur in self-standing sentences.

Notice first the range of uses open to present tense forms in main clauses. With a point–event verb, like DIE or ARRIVE, the present tense is out of place as the expression of real present time, but it can be used in *scripting*, as in stage directions (see 29); in expressing the scheduling of future events, as in (30); or in expressing the generic, habitual, or repeated occurrences of an event type, as in (31).

(29)   Gilda dies.

(30)   They arrive tomorrow.

(31)   He always shows up at noon.

For the simple future, however, the auxiliary WILL is necessary, as in (32):

(32)   He will arrive on time.

It has often been remarked that in a temporal or conditional subordinate clause, the future WILL does not occur, and that in these contexts the simple present tense can also have a future meaning. Consider the way we would understand sentences (33) and (34):

(33)   If he dies within the next two years, we'll be rich.

(34)   If they arrive early, we won't be ready for them.

In addition to the antecedents of true conditional sentences, we find clauses introduced by IF which are not parts of conditional sentences. In these cases, the generalizations about the difference between present tense forms and WILL forms do not hold. Compare (35a) and (35b):

(35a)   I wonder if he will arrive early.

(35b)   I wonder if he arrives early.

In the second of these, the present tense can only be given one of the meanings it could bear in a main clause usage. That is, it cannot have the simple future meaning in this IF–clause that it could have in the IF–clause of a true conditional sentence.

It will be important for our discussion to notice the ways in which the modals WILL and WOULD figure in the description of conditional sentences.

There is a *true future* WILL, in sentences like (36):

(36)   She will be here tomorrow morning.

and there is a *back-shifted* (past tense form) version of that modal, which shows up in indirect discourse, as in (37):

(37)   She said that she would be here tomorrow.

There is a *disposition* WILL, in sentences like (38) and (39):

(38)   He'll go on and on about his bowling.

(39)   He'll cry at the least provocation.

With this modal, the past tense form has a true past–tense meaning, which can be seen by substituting WOULD ('D) for WILL ('LL) in (38) and (39):

(38')   He'd go on and on about his bowling (in those days).

(39')   He'd cry at the least provocation (in those days).

And there is a set of what we will be calling *conditional modals*, among them WOULD, SHOULD and COULD, which characterize the consequent clauses of hypothetical conditional sentences, and do not count as the 'past tense' form of anything.

With respect to past tense forms, we can distinguish a *temporal* past tense indicating merely that some event or situation obtained in the past, from *hypothetical* past tense form, which indicates that the situation being depicted is hypothetical. This is the form we see in conditional sentences of the type (40):

(40)   If he invited me, I would go.

If a conditional sentence concerns the hypothetical past, each of these portions must have the 'perfect' form, where it is the 'perfect' form which contributes the past–tense meaning. Notice (41):

(41)   If he had invited me, I would have gone.

Various combinations of these possibilities account for the formal ambiguities in certain conditional sentences. Thus, sentence (42) is ambiguous in ways that can be accounted for by distinguishing uses of the past tense form in *spoke* from the antecedent and uses of the modal *would* in the consequent.

(42)   If he spoke to me, she would get jealous.

Where *spoke* and *would* are both taken as instances of the *temporal* past tense, then the latter is the past tense of the dispositional WILL, and the meaning is that she was disposed to get jealous whenever he spoke to me during the period of time referenced by the past tense. On the other hand, if *spoke* is taken as the hypothetical form, and *would* as the conditional modal, the meaning is one which points to her present state of mind.

3.3. *Kinds of Relationships between Antecedents and Consequents*

A number of writers (my main source here will be Sweetser 1984) have pointed out that there are crucial differences among conditional sentences depending on the illocutionary and epistemic points of the utterance.

For some conditional sentences, we can speak of their two parts as *integrated* and as defining a single situation. In these cases, there is a clear *contingency* relationship between the contents of the two clauses: the antecedent identifies a contingency for the situation in the consequent to come about. An example is (43):

(43)   If you say that again, I'll scream.

Here, an event of you-saying-that-again will be the occasion of an event of me screaming. Following Eve Sweetser, we can refer to these as *content conditionals*.

A second type may be thought of as expressing *abductive inference*. Sweetser refers to these as epistemic conditionals. An example is (44):

(44)   If the lights are out, they're not home.

Such sentences have an argumental force, they are used in reasoning. Here the information given in the antecedent is taken as support for a belief in the proposition given in the consequent. A paraphrase for such a conditional sentence might be something like, 'If the lights are out, that gives us a reason to believe that they're not home.'

The third type has been given the name *performative conditional*, or *speech act conditional*. Examples are (45) and (46):

(45)   If you're looking for a typist, I can do twenty words a minute.

(46)   If I don't see you before you leave, have a good time.

In all of these cases, the antecedent indicates a condition of *relevance* to the hearer of the information about to be imparted.

A famous paradox attributed to Chisholm involves introducing a speech act conditional into a reasoning chain:

(47)   If you need money, there's a poundnote in your wallet. If there's a poundnote in your wallet, you don't need money. Therefore, if you need money, you don't need money.

What's wrong, of course, is that the first sentence is performative in character, and a performative utterance, not evaluatable on its own as true or false, cannot be taken as a step in a process of reasoning.

In addition to the types just surveyed, there are two others that ought to be included in our list. The first is the *concessive conditional*, that is, a conditional sentence in which the antecedent is uttered in a context in which the truth of its clause is taken for granted. We find it in (48) and (49):

(48)   If you've lived in Tokyo for fourteen years, how come you don't know a word of Japanese?

(49)   If California is a viable place for investment, it's because the basic business climate is solid.

And the last type I'll mention is what I'll call, oxymoronically, *unconditional conditionals*. In these cases, the word IF could be replaced by EVEN IF. Examples are (50)–(52).

(50)   I wouldn't eat that stuff if you paid me to.

(51)   Will we have a picnic if it rains?

(52)   If you push the off button it keeps running. If you *unplug it* it keeps running!

3.4. *Independent Evaluation of the Two Clauses*

Although to a linguist and semanticist the integrated conditionals are perhaps the most important ones, the others being 'marked' and somewhat irregular, we find that in philosophical and psychological studies of conditional sentences, the examples considered are almost always those involving clauses which appear capable of standing alone and whose integration, therefore, is not made obvious. Typical philosophers' examples involve such conditionals as (53) and (54):

(53)   If the match is struck, it will light.

(54)   If John comes, Mary will be happy.

Subjunctive conditionals figure heavily in these works, too, but in constructing examples of subjunctive conditionals, clauses with essentially the same kinds of relationships between them are most common, cf. examples such as the following:

(55)   If the match had been struck, it would have lighted.

(56)   If John had come, Mary would have been happy.

Conditional sentences in psychological research appear in studies of reasoning, more than as genuine studies of the comprehension of conditional sentences. Martin Braine (Cognitive Science Lecture. 1986. University of California at Berkeley) has described a series of studies in which children are asked to make judgments about the contents of boxes containing certain kinds of toys, and about the truth of conditional sentences concerning the contents of such boxes. The sentences he uses in his experiments are of the following sort:

(57)   If there's a cow, there's an apple.

(58)   If there's no horse, there's a chicken.

In all of these cases, the two clauses joined in a conditional sentence have independently determinable truth values, and the reasoning being measured by the children's abilities to deal with the sentences involves the use of such sentences as expressions of truth-functional relationships. Similarly, a number of researchers have examined subjects' reasoning abilities with sentences about cards having one kind of figure on one side and another kind of figure on the other side, the sentences used in such experiments being of the form seen in the following:

(59)   If there's a circle on one side, there's a vowel on the other side.

(60)   If there's a consonant on one side, there isn't a square on the other side.

At the grammatical level, it is easy to find instances of antecedent and consequent clauses that cannot stand alone and be evaluated. Consider sentence (61):

(61)   If anyone touched his bicycle, he would cry.

The clause *anyone touched his bicycle* cannot stand alone as an English sentence, and *he would cry* cannot stand as an English sentence without there being a context in which the contingent circumstance is understood. The sentence has two interpretations, depending on whether a past repeated contingency is being reported, or a present hypothetical contingency. In both cases, the principal understanding we have of the consequent clause is that he would cry *because* his bicycle got touched.

In other cases the meaning of the conditional involves a complex integration of the semantic elements of the two constituent clauses which *could* receive interpretations if they appeared as self-standing sentences. To see this, consider sentence (62):

(62)   If it rains in California, everybody always gets gloomy.

The sequence *it rains in California* makes a perfectly good sentence, and what it says is, in fact, true. *Everybody always gets gloomy* is another perfectly well-formed sentence, and the proposition it expresses is undoubtedly false. Were this sentence to be found in a beginning logic exercise, and if the constituent clauses were assigned the truth values I have just assigned to them, the sentence would simply have to be declared false: the antecedent is true and the consequent is false.

But that does not capture the 'ordinary' meaning of our sentence. Somehow we need to be able to say that the phrase *in California* in the antecedent has the whole sentence in its scope: a particular contingency relation is said to hold *in California*. The word *always* in the consequent has the whole sentence in its scope: the relationship expressed by the whole sentence is claimed to be uniform across time. And the quantified expression *everybody* is understood as including just those people in California who are subjected to rainfall: the linguistic material identifying its domain of application cannot be found exclusively in its own clause. As an ordinary sentence of English, our sentence has a meaning that could be paraphrased as follows: 'Each person in California when subjected to rainfall gets gloomy as a result of being subjected to rainfall on those occasions.' It is important to see that the antecedent clause and the consequent clause *combine* to create a *single scene*, and that it would be thoroughly misleading to express this in terms of a function from the independently determined evaluations of the separate clauses.

4. *Some Types of Clausal–Antecedent Clausal–Consequent Conditional*

At this time I would like to present a superficial survey the properties of those conditional sentences in English which have clausal antecedents and clausal consequents. Our general mode of description will be that of characterizing structural features of the clauses and requirements on their pairings. Many features of the description have been alluded to above.

4.1. *Antecedents Having Imperative Form*

There are types of conditional sentences in which the antecedent is expressed *in the form of* an imperative sentence, with the consequent introduced after a coordinating conjunction. In the first kind, the antecedent does in fact represent a command, that is, it represents something the speaker wishes the hearer to do:

(63a)   Wash the dishes and I'll give you a penny.

(63b)   Buy me a drink and I'll tell you the whole story.

If the consequent is something the speaker thinks the hearer desires, the consequent is introduced with AND, as above; if it is something undesirable, it is introduced with OR, as with examples (64):

(64a)   Wash the dishes or I'll give you a whack.

(64b)   Buy me a drink or I'll tell Sue how you spend your evenings.

In the second kind, the command represents something the speaker wishes the hearer not to do:

(65a)   Do that again and you're fired.

(65b)   Step one inch closer and you're in trouble.

For these there is no alternative version with OR.

A third kind of conditional sentence with the antecedent in imperative form is the so-called *pseudo–imperative* conditional, a kind of conditional sentence used, as Dwight Bolinger expresses it, mainly to comment on the foibles of life or the dispositions of the people in one's environment (1977: 162). The structure seems to be Imperative Antecedent : Present Consequent. A sentence like (66):

> (66)   Just look at Harry and he breaks out in tears.

is not either an expression of the speaker's desire to have the addressee look at, or not look at, Harry. The force of the antecedent clause is something like, 'If you look at him' or 'whenever you look at him'. Another example is (67):

> (67)   Have one bad day and they say your career is over.

Bolinger has pointed out that pseudo–imperative conditionals do not permit speech-act conditional interpretations. He notices that both of the following conditionals are acceptable:

> (68a)   If you write any letters, people think you're homesick.

> (69a)   If you write any letters, I'll be glad to mail them for you.

It appears, however, that only in the case in which a true contingency is expressed between the two clauses (as with 68a) and not in the case of the speech act connection (as with 69a) can there be an equivalent pseudo–imperative version. Compare the (b) forms of these sentences:

> (68b)   Write any letters and people think you're homesick.

> (69b)   *Write any letters and I'll be glad to mail them for you.

Other examples, borrowed or adapted from Bolinger (1977), are these:

> (70a)   If you get the least bit sick around here, they put you to bed.

> (70b)   Get the least bit sick around here and they put you to bed.

> (71a)   If you get sick, I'll bring you some chicken soup.

> (71b)   *Get sick and I'll bring you some chicken soup.

(72a) If you own a nice piece of property, they tax you dry.

(72b) Own a nice piece of property and they tax you dry.

(73a) If you own a nice piece of property, I'll buy it from you.

(73b) *Own a nice piece of property and I'll buy it from you.

In these cases, the starred sentences can only be construed as positive command imperatives. It would appear that the pseudo–imperative has only an integrative meaning, and does not allow a speech–act use.

4.2. *General Principle*

There is a variety of conditional sentence which expresses a kind of *general principle*, a contingency relation between two events or states of affairs, one being the occasion of the other. These have the form Present Antecedent : Present Consequent, or Past Antecedent : Past Consequent. Examples:

(74) If he gets up early, she gets up early.

(75) If you push this button, the machine starts.

(76) If it rains, it pours.

(77) If he wanted chocolate, she wanted chocolate.

(78) If it rained, we were miserable.

This pattern, with its interpretation, is not exclusively a feature of conditional sentences, but appears in other varieties of subordinate clause constructions, too. Consider examples (79) through (82):

(79) When it rains it pours.

(80) After it rains the air smells fresh.

(81) Before he starts reading he clears his throat.

(82) The more he knows, the less he speaks.

4.3. *Future Contingency*

There is another tense and aspect pattern characteristic of subordination constructions, and that is the pattern by which the subordinate clause has the simple present tense, in future meaning, and the consequent clause has the WILL–future. The pattern is Present [Zero Future] Antecedent : WILL Consequent. Examples are:

(83)   If he does that, I'll never speak to him again.

(84)   If he likes it, he'll buy it.

Examples of the same pattern, with the same interpretation, can also be found in temporal clauses and in the BCHF construction, as in examples (85)–(87).

(85)   When she comes back, we'll have a party.

(86)   After he takes them home, he'll go out for a drink.

(87)   The sooner he finds out, the sooner he'll leave home.

4.4. Open Conditionals

There is also a variety of conditional sentence in which the relationships between the tense forms of the two clauses is much more flexible, since the meaning is something like 'If it turns out that P is so, then it will follow that Q is so.'

Notice the variety in the following

(88)   If she knows what time I got home, I'm in trouble.

(89)   If she noticed what time I got home, I'm in trouble.

(90)   If she finds out what time I got home, I'm in trouble.

Many of the instances of epistemic or abductive inference conditionals might also fit into this type. Consider:

(91)   If he shows up tomorrow, he understood what we told him.

(92)   If he told you that, he's a liar.

4.5. Negotiating Conditionals

In this section I describe a class of conditional sentences which seemed to me to form a natural type when this paper was first drawn up, but for which I now have doubts. The doubts are due to counterexamples contributed by Paul Kay, David Dowty, and several questioners at the ESCOL meeting. I will give the general outline of my proposal here, and then mention the problems at the end of this section.

There is a type of conditional sentence which has WILL in each clause and which (as I saw it) is dedicated to a conversational activity that could be described as that of *negotiation*. I spoke of these as *negotiating conditionals*. Examples:

(93)   If you'll do this, I'll do that.

(94)   If you'll do problems one through six, I'll do the rest.

The ordinary predictive conditionals can also be used in negotiation utterances but the double–WILL form seemed to be limited to a negotiation context.

It is frequently said about such sentences that the interpretation I give them is not *conventionally* associated with this structure, but follows from certain independent facts. In English (as in a number of other languages) the 'future' tense is not welcome in certain kinds of subordinate clauses (conditional and temporal in particular), so when we *do* find WILL in such a clause, it is not the temporal WILL but the WILL of *intention*, the WILL of WILLING, so to speak. Thus, the negotiation interpretation follows from the mere fact that when one person's willingness to do something is presented as a precondition to someone else's intention to do something, that state of affairs is itself definitional of negotiation. The double–WILL pattern, in other words, is *usable* in negotiation, but it is not conventionally *dedicated* to such a pragmatic function, the argument goes.

Evidence given in the discussion of such sentences seems to be compatible with each position. The main item of evidence that the WILL in the antecedent is the WILL of intention is the oddity of sentences whose IF–clause subjects designate things which cannot possess intentions, such as what we see in (95),

(95)   *If it'll rain, I'll bring my umbrella.

as well as sentences whose verbs indicate events over which people generally do not have control, such as

(96)   *If you'll win, you'll get a nice prize.

The 'negotiationist' account would be that the oddity of these sentences has to do with the reality that whether or not it will rain cannot be a bargaining chip in any realistic negotiation, and that winning is not something one agrees to do—it is just something that happens.

But it seems to me that there are some arguments which the volitionist position cannot easily deal with. Thus, in a context in which I produce a sentence like (97),

(97)   If it'll make you feel any better, I'll stay another week.

I am asking you to assure me that another week's stay on my part would be agreeable to you. If you give me that assurance, I'll stay. Bernard Comrie is quoted as having come up with an example which has convinced him that the English clause is not hostile to the future–WILL. His example is (98):

(98)   If it'll definitely rain, I'll bring my umbrella.

In my judgment, this sentence allows the paraphrase *if you assure me* that it's going to rain, then I'll plan now to bring my umbrella. This sentence can still be absorbed into the negotiation interpretation. A sentence like (99), by contrast

(99)   If it rains, I'll bring my umbrella.

can be taken as a contingent commitment: a future situation in which it rains will be followed by my bringing my umbrella. The sentence with WILL in the antecedent, however, means something like 'If you can assure me right now that it's going to rain at time t, I'll commit myself right now to bringing my umbrella at time t.'

Negotiation sentences are clearest to come by when the subject of the antecedent is second person and the subject of the consequent is first person. It is possible to produce double–WILL conditional sentences which do not meet these conditions, but the negotiation interpretation takes over in these cases too. Thus, if I were to overhear somebody saying (100),

(100)   If I'll bring them there, you'll pay for them.

I would imagine that a party to the negotiation is reviewing the conditions with his or her negotiating partner. ('Okay, let's see if I've got it right. I'll bring them there, you'll pay for them. Is that it?') If I were to hear somebody say (101),

(101)   If she'll do the first one, he'll do the rest.

I would be inclined to assume that this is the negotiator speaking, or that somebody is reporting a negotiating stance on the part of some third–person participants. I could not think of these sentences as *merely* reporting a contingency relation between one person's actions and another person's willingness to do some specified thing.

The damaging counter-examples include (102), a self-illustrating objection to my proposal, offered by an ESCOL discussant:

(102)   If you'll buy that, you'll buy anything.

and several by Paul Kay which indicate resolve rather than negotiation, namely (103)–(106):

(103)   If it'll help me succeed, I'll turn my mother in to the narcs.

(104)   If you'll look in your pocket, you'll find your missing keys.

(105)   If he'll just put out some effort, he'll do well.

In the counterexamples directed to my attention by David Dowty (from Wekker 1976), future time seems to be clearly expressed in the antecedent-clause WILL, and I have nothing to say about that. Two of his examples were (106) and (107):

(106)   If the play will be cancelled, let's not go.

(107)   If he will be left destitute, I'll change my will.

My decision not to eliminate this section from the paper altogether was a decision made in the fine tradition of continuing to find satisfaction in a hypothesis long after the destroying counterexamples are in.

4.6. Hypothetical Conditionals

The hypothetical conditional has Past [Hypothetical] Antecedent : Conditional–Modal Consequent. The form I refer to here as Past [Hypothetical] is identical with the past tense form in all cases except with the copula, in which case, in some dialects, the form is *were* for all subjects. The hypothetical conditional does not necessarily presuppose the falsity of the proposition presented in the antecedent, but it is incompatible with its accepted truth. In this way the hypothetical conditional is different from the open conditional, for which both possibilities are left open.

Examples of the hypothetical condition are:

(108)   If he fell down like that again, he'd break his neck.

(109)   If you lived here, you'd be home now.

(110)   If I did that, I'd be fired.

(111)   If she practiced more, she'd be quite good.

(112)   If we wanted to, we could get married today.

4.7. Counterfactual Conditionals

Counterfactual conditionals are perhaps the most widely discussed variety of conditional sentences. There are *present counterfactuals* represented by the Past [Hypothetical] form of a *stative* verb. Consider examples (113) and (114).

(113)   If he were here, he could help us.

(114)   If I were you, I wouldn't have brought that stuff.

Another type of counterfactual conditional is the *past counterfactual*, marked by the pattern Pluperfect [Hypothetical] Antecedent : Conditional (Perfect) Consequent. Examples follow:

(115)   If he had opened it, we'd be dead.

(116)   If he hadn't shown it to me, I wouldn't have believed it.

In both of these types, the antecedent can be formed with an inverted auxiliary or copula. Thus:

(117)   Had I opened it, we'd be dead.

(118)   Were he still here, we would not be alive.

A number of scholars have suggested that there is no such thing as a conditional sentence which genuinely has a counterfactual presupposition; that all putative counterfactual conditionals are really hypothetical conditionals and are compatible with the falsity of the antecedent proposition.

Tanya Reinhart (1976) supports this claim with a sentence which, she says, allows either the truth or the falsity of the antecedent proposition. Her example is sentence (119):

(119)   If the Dean hadn't answered my letter, I would have resigned.

This sentence is described as being appropriate in either of two situations. First, the situation in which the speaker wrote a letter to the dean, the dean answered the letter, and, as a result, the speaker decided not to resign. In the second situation, the speaker is addressing someone who wrote a letter to the dean and who received no response but who nevertheless did not resign. In this second sentence the speaker says (119) with heavy stress on *my* and *I*.

I believe that evidence can be found that there is nevertheless a genuine separate counterfactual clause type in English, and that evidence is a little-studied phenomenon of colloquial English. I have in mind the nonstandard complex auxiliary *had've*, found in (120) and (121):

(120)   If you had've opened it, we'd be dead.

(121)   If you hadn't've married her, where would you be now?

It is my opinion (supported by informally elicited grammaticality judgments of my friends) that this auxiliary element is limited to occurrence in counter-factual clauses.

First of all, we know that this auxiliary element is not merely a colloquial version of the simple pluperfect. Whenever the true pluperfect is intended, this extra element is not welcome. Compare (122a) and (122b).

(122a)   At that time I hadn't known Harry.

(122b)   *At that time I hadn't've known Harry.

It is usable in other clauses which are counterfactual, outside of the system of conditional sentences. Examples:

(123)   I wish I hadn't've said that.

(124)   Supposed you hadn't've met me.

(This section repeats observations from Fillmore 1985.)

4.8. Counteridenticals

There is an interesting variety of counterfactual conditional sentences which Nelson Goodman refers to as *counteridenticals*. This is the kind of conditional sentence in which we are asked to imagine that one object takes the place of another object, or one person takes the place of another person. At issue is which properties of which object, in this exchange, will show up in the imagined world. I once speculated that such sentences, when dealing with people, always had the effect of putting the 'soul' of the being designated by the subject into the body and circumstances of the being introduced in the predicate. In other words; it seemed to me that the grammar of counteridenticals would allow me to express certain possibilities with (125) but not (126):

> (125)   If I were Larry Holmes, I would beat you up.

> (126)   If I were Larry Holmes, I would have to give up boxing because of my asthma.

Sentence (125) would mean that somebody with my intentions and the body of Larry Holmes would be able to do impressive damage to you. The intentions would stay, but the body would change. Sentence (126), with the body changing, seemed to me impossible.

A similar understanding seems to have been shared by Goodman. He suggests, using unnatural-sounding sentences, that the (a) sentences below are all right, but that the (b) sentences created by exchanging antecedents and consequents between them would not be (1983:6).

> (127a)   If I were Julius Caesar, I would not be living in the twentieth century.

> (127b)   *If Julius Caesar were I, I would not be living in the twentieth century.

> (128a)   If Julius Caesar were I, he would be living in the twentieth century.

> (128b)   *If I were Julius Caesar, he would be living in the twentieth century.

I think now that this speculation was wrong, though I do not have an account of the oddity of the (b) sentences above. A sentence which allows the exchange to go in either direction is (129),

> (129)   If I were your father, I would spank you.

This sentence could be uttered in two kinds of situations: first, by someone who would like to be in the father role, so that he could effect a punishment which the real father is apparently unwilling to do; and second, by a temporary caretaker who wants the child to be grateful for his lenient tendencies, since the real father in this situation would be more punitive. It will be noticed that prosodic salience would go with the constituent (*I* or *your father*) which designates the individual to be hypothetically introduced into the other individual's circumstances.[4]

5. *Conclusion*

I have convinced myself that in order to be clear about the grammar of language, it is necessary to sort out the constructional devices which it puts at its speakers' disposal, and to explain their form, their meaning, and their conditions of application, with extreme care and thoroughness. I believe that these constructions live in a language as packages of conventional knowledge, as assemblies of properties held in place by principles of mutual compatibility and incompatibility. In perhaps all cases, the assembled properties defining a single construction are never unique to this construction, but are properties available for the definition of other constructions too.

---

[4] Gilles Fauconnier's treatment of conditional sentences in terms of his theory of *mental spaces* introduces a great many more subtleties than those I have mentioned here. Several of his examples take the situation of a painter who misrepresented the color of the eyes of a subject. A sentence like (i) is one in which the individual represented by the phrase *the girl with green eyes* is the depicted individual in the painting; but the speaker could also have referred to the real girl and said (ii). In this case the phrase *the girl with blue eyes* refers to the real blue-eyed girl, the *blue eyes* in the predicate phrase refers to a painting which does not exist but which might have existed.

(i)   If you were a more careful painter, the girl with green eyes would have had blue eyes.

(ii)   If you were a more careful painter, the girl with blue eyes would have had blue eyes.

These examples suggest the expressibility of complex relationships between entities in real and hypothetical 'spaces' in conditional sentences.

References

Bolinger, D. L. 1977. *Meaning and Form*. London: Longman.

Fauconnier, G. 1985. *Mental Spaces*. Cambridge: MIT Press.

Fillmore, C. 1985. Syntactic intrusions and the notion of grammatical construction. *Proceedings of the Berkeley Linguistics Society #11*. 73–86.

Fillmore, C. J., P. Kay, and M. C. O'Connor. ms. Idiomaticity and regularity in grammar: The case of *let alone*.

Gazdar, G. 1981. Unbounded dependencies and coordinate structure. *Linguistic Inquiry* 12:155–184.

Goodman, N. 1983. The problem of counterfactual conditionals. *Fact, Fiction and Forecast*. Cambridge: Harvard University Press, 3–17.

Kay, P. 1984. The *kind of/sort of construction*. *Proceedings of the Berkeley Linguistics Society #10*:157–171.

Lakoff, G. P. to appear in 1987. *Women, Fire and Dangerous Things* (esp. Case Study #3, *THERE* constructions). Chicago: University of Chicago Press.

Lambrecht, K. 1986a. Formulaicity, frame semantics, and pragmatics in German binomial expressions. *Language* 60:753–798.

Lambrecht, K. 1986b. Pragmatically motivated syntax: presentational cleft constructions in spoken French. *Papers from the Twenty-Second Annual Meeting of the Chicago Linguistics Society*.

Lambrecht, K. forthcoming. Presentational cleft constructions in spoken French. *Clause Combining in Grammar and Discourse*, eds. J. Haiman and S. A. Thompson. Amsterdam: Benjamins.

Reinhart, T. 1976. Polarity reversal: Logic or pragmatics?. *Linguistic Inquiry* 7:697–705.

Sweetser, E. E. 1984. *Semantic Structure and Semantic Change: A Cognitive Linguistic Study of Modality, Perception, Speech Acts, and Logical Relations*. U.C. Berkeley Linguistics Dissertation.

Wekker, H. Chr. 1976. *The Expression of Future Time in Contemporary British English*. North Holland. [not consulted]

10

Epistemic Stance and Verbal Form in English Conditional Sentences[1]

1992
CHARLES J. FILLMORE

1. *Introduction*

Sometimes we hear about people who can see, or know, the future. We might at first think it would be useful, or fun, to have such an ability, but we'd be wrong. Anybody who thinks about it will realize that an ability simply to see *the future* would be utterly terrifying, and that a person who possessed such powers could be of no use to anyone.

By contrast, an ability to see *alternative futures* could be handy indeed. Our former First Lady's former astrological consultant is said to have such an ability. She was able to know, for example, that if the President were to schedule a cabinet meeting for a day when the configuration of the heavens was unfavorable, exceedingly bad things were certain to follow. She gave this information to Mrs. Reagan, and Mrs. Reagan shared it with our President. We will never know what our country owes to this woman's generosity.

Anybody possessing reliable knowledge of alternative futures is also in a position to know alternative presents, since when the once-future moment comes, such a person will know how things might otherwise be. Anybody who knows alternative futures and presents also knows alternative pasts, since after the critical moment has passed, this person knows something about what might have been. We can speak of such a person as knowing about

---

[1] For reactions to earlier versions of this paper, the author is indebted to David Dowty, Gilles Fauconnier, Paul Kay, George Lakoff, Kiki Nikiforidou, Ivan Sag, and Seiko Yamaguchi.

alternative worlds. If at one time I knew that having a cabinet meeting on a particular Tuesday would result in such–and–such happening on the following Thursday, then—supposing the cabinet meeting got cancelled—when the Wednesday of that week came, I could be said to know about a particular alternative world that its past has certain properties and that its future has certain properties.

The discourse of persons with knowledge of alternative worlds could provide valuable data for linguists interested in the structure and meaning of conditional sentences. Alternative worlds don't have names or identification numbers, but fortunately, the grammar of our language makes it possible to identify one (or more) of the alternative worlds by mentioning one of its (or their) properties in the protasis clause of a conditional sentence, and then to say something about that world (or those worlds) in the apodosis clause.

Even though most of us lack such special abilities, we still freely and confidently produce conditional sentences. Sometimes contingencies that we attribute to alternative worlds follow from regularities that we expect to hold in all reasonable nearby worlds. This is so for sentence [1].

[1] If you remove three nickels from a pile of five, there will be two left.

Sometimes we feel that we understand ourselves well enough to be able to predict our behavior in particular worlds. This we can see in sentence [2].

[2] If I win the lottery, I'll hire a secretary.

And sometimes we're simply guessing. Sentence [3] is something that some of us were heard to say, a quarter of a century ago, and we were just guessing.

[3] If Goldwater gets elected, the country will go to war.

I'm interested in becoming clear about certain surface-grammatical properties of English conditional sentences. None of the philosophical, logical, pragmatic, or psychological issues connected with conditional sentences will be touched on in what I have to say, and actually only a few of the linguistic issues. My objective is to come up with as simple an account as I can of the verbal clusters heading clauses functioning as protasis and apodosis in English conditional sentences, and to relate these to particular features of the meanings of their sentences. The verbal-expression categories that concern me are named and illustrated in Table 1:

simple present	go, goes	see, sees	is, am, are
simple past	went	saw	was, were
WILL future	will go	will see	will be
pres SBJ-1	went	saw	were
past SBJ-1	had('ve) gone	had('ve) seen	had('ve) been
conditional	would go could go	would see could see	would have been could have been
conditional perfect	would have gone could have gone	would have seen could have seen	would have been could have been

Table 1

The category given here as 'Subjunctive-1' is what Jespersen calls the 'Imaginative' forms: my Present Subjunctive-1 is his Preterit of Imagination, and my Past Subjunctive-1 is his Pluperfect of Imagination (Jespersen 1933:254–259). I use Subjunctive-2 to refer to the use of the Baseform in sentences like 'I require that he *speak* to her immediately' or 'If this *be* treason...'. Since Subjunctive-2 has no tense associated with it, for the forms that interest me here, I will simply speak of Present Subjunctive and Past Subjunctive without the '1'. My discussion will not cover the phraseologically limited use of Subjunctive-2 in conditional sentences.

Instances of true Perfect aspect are also found in conditional sentences, but only in contexts where the aspectual meaning is independently justified. The same is true of instances of Progressive aspect. There is nothing special to say about these. There *is* something special to say about modal auxiliaries and their use in conditional sentences, but I must unfortunately ignore these.

There are numerous discrepancies between surface form and grammatical category in the data we will be examining. Formations with HAD plus the Past Participle will sometimes simply be instances of the plain Pluperfect, but at other times they will be functioning as the Past Subjunctive. This difference, usually invisible, will nevertheless be detectable to speakers who control the nonstandard variant with HAD'VE, as in 'had've eaten', 'hadn't've known', etc.: that extra morpheme is welcome in sentence [4], where the IF–clause gives us an example of the Past Subjunctive

[4] If we hadn't('ve) met Harry, where would we be now?

but it is not welcome in sentence [5], where we are dealing with a simple past perfect.[2]

---

[2] A number of scholars have argued against the validity of the category 'counterfactual' (Comrie 1986, Reinhart 1976, Dudman 1984:151). I have argued, however, that the existence of past

[5] At that time we still hadn't(*'ve) met Harry.

Other forms capable of realizing more than one category are WILL, WOULD, COULD, and WERE. WILL is sometimes a simple future marker, sometimes an expression of propensity or intention (or of any of several other uses). WOULD and COULD sometimes function as Conditional Modals, and sometimes as Past Tense forms of the modals WILL and CAN respectively. WERE is sometimes a past–tense form of BE; at other times it is the Present Subjunctive form of BE. For all verbs other than BE, and for BE in some dialects, the two categories of Past and Present-Subjunctive are not formally distinct.[3]

In some cases the generalizations I need to make will require reference to specific word forms. This is true, for example, of SHOULD, WERE and HAD in fronted–auxiliary conditionals as in sentences [6b, 7b, 8b]. SHOULD, WERE and HAD are the only auxiliaries participating in this construction in my speech.

[6a] If you should happen to meet Harry, don't mention my name.

[6b] Should you happen to meet Harry, don't mention my name.

[7a] If Harry were here, we wouldn't be having such a good time.

[7b] Were Harry here, we wouldn't be having such a good time.

[8a] If Harry had known about this party, he would be here.

[8b] Had Harry known about this party, he would be here.

The phenomena which I hope to be able to explain are the permitted verbal clusters in the protasis and apodosis clauses of conditional sentences, the compatible and incompatible combinations of verbal forms across the two clauses, and the semantic interpretations that accompany each permitted pairing—as these figure in my speech, and in that of some but not all of my friends.[4] Some permitted combinations are given in sentences [9a–9d].

---

counterfactuals could be supported by the occurrence of the 'had've' form identified here. See Fillmore 1985.

[3] Examples of ambiguity due to different sources of identical surface forms can be seen in the following sentences: (i) If they weren't busy they would play with the children. (ii) If it broke they would make us pay for it. (Dudman 1984:145)

Each is interpretable as a generalization over iterating past situations or as a speculation about the present (i) or the future (ii).

[4] There are forms accepted by some scholars which I am quite sure do not occur in my speech and which I do not propose to deal with. Jespersen could apparently say 'If he were to call, I will give him the message,' and Dudman (1984:152) assigns a future interpretation to 'If Grannie had

[9a] If she opens it, they'll escape.

[9b] If she opened it, they'd escape.

[9c] If she had opened it, they would have escaped.

[9c] If she opened it, they escaped.

Some impossible combinations are given in sentences [10a–10b].

[10a] *If she'll open it, they had've escaped.

[10b] *If she were here, they'll be happy.

The examples prefixed with question marks in [11] require some cognitive acrobatics, namely whatever it takes to imagine independent reasons for the verbal expression forms.

[11a] ? If she'd opened it, they've escaped.

[11b] ? If she opens it, she had misunderstood our note.

These will all be of the type that my colleague Eve Sweetser refers to as 'epistemic conditionals'—conditional sentences in which the contingency relation holds between assuming a fact and drawing an inference from that fact, rather than between two states of affairs.[5] My account of the selection and interpretation of verbal expression forms and their pairings in protases and apodoses of conditional sentences will critically involve a notion of 'concord': in particular, it will be argued that the choice from among four categories of epistemic stance must be identical in the two linked clauses of a conditional sentence. While the surface-form consequences of the choice of one or another epistemic stance are different for protasis and apodosis, the category itself must match in the two clauses.[6]

---

attended the rally she would have insulted the President' [said of a dead Grannie and a future rally].

[5] See Eve Sweetser (1990), p. 116. The contrast can be illustrated by normal interpretations of the following pair of sentences: (i) *If it rained last night, the streets are wet*, (ii) *If the streets are wet, it rained last night*. The first sentence is an example of what Sweetser calls a 'content conditional', the second is what she calls an 'epistemic conditional.' Sweetser is the only person I know who can readily contextualize the question-mark-marked sentences in [11].

[6] John Haiman, in Haiman 1986:219–220, in the service of an argument that conditional sentences have much in common with coordination structures, offers a brief survey of the manner in which languages can differ from each other in respect to the differences or commonalities of structural properties of the two parts of a conditional sentence.

2. *Characterizing Conditional Sentences*

Sentences that belong in the family of constructions including the conditionals are those which express some sort of coexistence relation between two states of affairs, let me call them P and Q, where Q is said to hold in that alternative world (or set of alternative worlds) which is identified by the presence of P. (A more general definition would recognize the variety of speech acts possible with such constructions, but to make things easy I'll limit myself mainly to conditionals in which the apodosis poses some sort of state of affairs.) The set of Constructions I've characterized in this way includes causal and temporal modification, with which conditional sentences have much in common, and with which I will be comparing them.

The grammar of English provides, in addition to conditional constructions, numerous other ways of identifying alternative worlds, among them the following:

Questions:
[12]   Do you like it? It's yours.

Commands:
[13]   Come here and I'll give you a kiss.

Pseudo-Commands:
[14]   Criticize him the slightest bit and he starts crying.

Certain Relative–Clause Constructions:
[15]   Anyone who does that gets what he deserves.

Situation–Creating Adverbials:
[16]   With his hat on he would look older.

Anaphoric Devices:

[17]   Then/In that case/Otherwise (etc.), I wouldn't be here.

And several others.

My main examples will be conditional sentences with a preposed *if*–clause and with an immediately following main clause. Complexities introduced by the presence of 'bridging' predicates in the main clause will not be explored. Thus, for a sentence like [18], the morphosyntactic relationship that concerns me is obviously that between *had said* and *would have done*, and not that between *had said* and the simple present-tense form *wonder*,

[18]   If he <u>had said</u> that, I *wonder* what she <u>would have done</u>.

and for sentence [19], I'll be interested in the connection between *ask* and *will marry*, and not that between *ask* and *am*.

[19]   If you <u>ask</u> her politely, I *am* sure she<u>'ll marry you.</u>

I will limit myself to examples which lack this complexity.

3. *Explanatory Concepts*

The semantic concepts that figure in determining the phenomena in question are:

(1)   *relative time*: the relative positions in time of states of affairs P, and Q, and the time of speaking,

(2)   *epistemic stance*: the speaker's assumption about the actuality of P, and in some cases, of Q

(3)   *interest*: whether or not the speaker puts a positive valuation on the alternative situation in which P holds

The relative temporal position of P or Q and the time of speaking determines the tense associated with the P or the Q clause, and the simultaneity of P and Q, or the simultaneity of P or Q with the time of speaking, determines the choice of static rather than dynamic predicates.

The epistemic stance, which will be one of four types, expresses the kind of commitment the speaker has to the proposition expressing P. The labels I use for these will be 'A' for 'Actual' or 'Assumed', 'H' for 'Hypothetical', 'C' for 'Counter–factual' or 'Counter to Expectation', and 'G' for 'Generic'. (The last is different in a number of ways from the first three and will not be emphasized in this paper.)

The speaker's positive or negative valuation of the posed P situation will be associated with the 'polarity' of the P-clause: a positively evaluated P requires positive polarity, others take negative polarity.[7]

---

[7] Well-known examples of the difference in interest and polarity are due to Robin Lakoff 1969: In the pair: (i) *If you take some candy, I'll whip you* and (ii) *If you take any candy, I'll whip you* the positive polarity clause represents something that the speaker wants to happen (and could

4. *A Proposed Notation*

In order to think about these relationships in a perspicuous way, I have found it useful to work with diagrams that allow me to keep track of two elementary kinds of relationships that figure in the production and understanding of conditional sentences, *relative time* and *epistemic stance*. A simple diacritic will be used to identify speaker interest. By *epistemic stance* I mean the epistemic relationship which the speaker has to the world represented by the conditional sentence: the speaker might regard it as the actual world, might regard it as distinct from the actual world, or might not know whether the alternative world represented in the conditional sentence is the actual world or not. (As many scholars have pointed out, the notion 'actual' requires some accommodation in the case of the future, in recognition of the fact that we cannot really be sure of what the future will bring.)

I use a simple matrix notation involving columns and rows, in which the columns represent ordered time periods, and in which the rows have the following interpretations. The top row represents the world in which the P expressed by the protasis is a part and the bottom row represents the world in which the P expressed by the protasis is absent. (Here we make the pretense that there are just two alternative worlds to concern ourselves with.) The middle row does not represent a world, but will be used to indicate a state of the speech event in which the speaker does not know whether or not P holds.

Figure 1

Since the top row represents the world that the sentence is about, independently of the speaker's epistemic stance, we need a separate device for indicating the speaker's presumptions about this world. One of the cells in the diagrams will be shaded as a way of indicating simultaneously the speaker's epistemic stance *and* the time of the speech event relative to the P and Q situations. Since the top row represents the world in which P holds, a shaded cell in a top row indicates that the speaker accepts the world of P as the actual world. The letter 'A' will stand for 'Actual' or—in dealing with

---

only meaningfully be addressed to a masochist); the negative polarity clause represents something the speaker does not want to happen.

the future—'Assumed', meaning that the state of affairs expressed by the P clause is taken for granted. See Figure 2

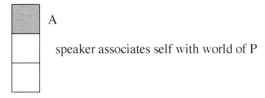

A

speaker associates self with world of P

Figure 2

Since the bottom row represents a world in which P does not hold, a shaded cell in a bottom row indicates that the speaker accepts as actual a world in which P does not hold. The letter 'C' will mean that the P clause is taken as 'Counterfactual' or—in the case of the future—'Counter to Expectation.' See Figure 3.

C

speaker associates self with world of not-P

Figure 3

And since the middle row represents a situation in which the speaker does not know whether P holds or not, a shaded cell in a middle row indicates just that fact. The letter 'H' represents the presentation of P as 'Hypothetical'. See Figure 4.

H

Speaker uncertain about P

Figure 4

The equivocal interpretations of the labels 'A' and 'C' are necessary because of some important realities concerning our relation to the future. The difference between sentences [20] and [21]

[20]   (A) When Mom comes home we'll have dinner.

[21]   (H) If Mom comes home we'll have dinner.

is that with [20] the speaker assumes, but does not know, that Mom will indeed come home. In [21] the speaker simply does not know. Some languages do not mark this difference. The difference is slight, but the kids are nevertheless likely to find sentence [20] more comforting than sentence [21]. In talking about the future, 'A' will be read 'Assumed'. And the difference between sentences [22] and [23]

[22]   (H) If you try it you'll like it

[23]   (C) If you tried it you'd like it.

is that in [23], the speaker's beliefs are biased toward an assumption you are at present unlikely to be willing to try it. The current expectation is that you're not going to try it. Here the 'C' will be read 'Counter to Expectation.'

The columns in my diagrams represent succession in time. If the column containing P is to the left of the column containing Q, P is to be interpreted as occurring before Q. If P and Q are together in a single column, then they are taken as two states of affairs existing simultaneously. If the shaded cell representing the speaker's epistemic stance is to the right of P, then P is in the past. And so on. The shaded cell represents, by its row, the speaker's epistemic stance, and by its column the time of speaking relative to the states of affairs P and Q.

5. *Illustrations*

The easiest illustrations of the notation have the two elements P and Q of a conditional assertion, both in the past, with Q following P. In Figures 5 through 7, we represent situation-types. exemplified by the three sentences [24–26].[8]

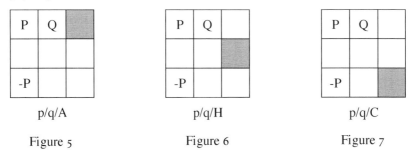

	p/q/A		p/q/H		p/q/C
Figure 5		Figure 6		Figure 7	

[24]   (A) Because he left the door open, the dog escaped.

[25]   (H) If he left the door open, the dog escaped.

[26]   (C) If he had left the door open, the dog would have escaped.

Sentences of the 'A' type can express cause or explanation, as in example [24], or temporal relations, as in sentence [27].

[27]   (A) When he opened the door, the dog escaped.

For the most part, the sentences which concern me will be those represented by the Hypothetical and Counterfactual stances; but, as Akatsuka has made us aware (1985, 1986:339), there are some contexts for conditional sentences in which the situation identified by P is assumed to be true of the actual world.

Digression 1: The Value of 'Q'. All of the schemas I will be presenting will have the bottom row marked for P-being-absent (i.e., for the proposition expressing P being false), but I will leave the value of Q unspecified, even though in many situations the falsehood of Q will be taken for granted. Even in temporal 'A' sentences different assumptions about the value of Q may be assumed. Sometimes temporal 'A' sentences are understood with an intended

---

[8] The symbols at the bottoms of the diagram are linear representations of the same information as is provided in the diagram. A sheer juxtaposition of two symbols represents simultaneity, separation by a slash represents temporal order. The symbols A, H, C represent epistemic stances, and their position in the sequence represents the temporal relation.

or understood causal or enabling relation holding between the two elements of the clause, as in the case of our sentence [27] above. The simplest way to understand the sentence is to believe that if he *hadn't* opened the door, the dog *wouldn't* have escaped. However, a sentence like [28]

[28]   (A) When he opened the door, it started raining.

is more clearly a 'temporal' clause, the subordinate element only giving a time specification for the main clause event. These two situations can be represented by the two schemata of Figures 8 and 9. (The outlined fonts given to 'Q' in the bottom row are to remind us that these determinations are not part of the literal meanings of the sentences.)

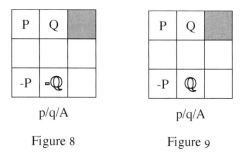

p/q/A

Figure 8   Figure 9

In the most natural interpretation we are likely to give to sentence [28], it is likely that in that alternative world which differed at that point from the actual one only by his not having opened the door, it started raining at precisely that time anyway.

In some sentences that look like conditional sentences, the independence of the Q event on the P event can be made explicit, as in the concessive conditional sentence [29], introduced by the word 'even'.[9]

---

[9] A characteristic of concessive conditionals that needs to be added to this story is that there is a contextually given expectation that 'P' would ordinarily result in 'not-Q'.

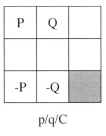

p/q/C

Figure 10

[29] Even if he had left the door shut, the dog (still) would have escaped.

(This time P stands for a situation of his leaving the door closed.) But the same understanding about the unconditional nature of the Q assertion is also possible with the word 'even' missing, as long as there is high pitch and extra-heavy stress on the auxiliary, everything else said in a low monotone, as suggested by sentence [30], or with the word *still* (stressed and with high pitch) introduced in the apodosis. [10]

[30]   If he *had* left the door shut, the dog (still) would have escaped!

Digression 2: Static and Dynamic Predicates. In talking about the present moment and its alternatives we become quickly aware of the need for distinguishing static from dynamic predicates. In a sentence like [31], I am concerned about whether at the present moment she lives in my neighborhood.

[31]   (H) If she lives here I'll get a chance to meet her.

But in sentence [32] I'm talking about a future possibility.

[32]   (H) If she moves here I'll get a chance to meet her.

---

[10] Without the *still* in the apodosis, it cannot be said that an *even if* conditional necessarily requires Q in the not-P world. The test case is one in which the protasis expresses a point within a scalar model (see Fillmore, Kay & O'Connor 1988) for which the 'not-P' situation could be either a lower or a higher value on the scale. The relevant sentences are of the sort *Even if he had taken just a little, he would have died*. The claim that he took just a little can be falsified by a situation in which he took none at all (in which case he did not die) or by a situation in which he took a great deal (in which case he died). On this point I am indebted to Seiko Yamaguchi, Kiki Nikiforidou, and Paul Kay.

The same present-vs.-future contrast is seen in the subjunctive conditionals, as seen in sentences [33–34]:

[33]   (C) If she lived here I'd get a chance to meet her.

[34]   (C) If she moved here I'd get a chance to meet her.

The one is counter-factual (since I can know for sure, in the relevant sense, that she does not live here), the other is counter-to-expectation (since, though I don't expect her to move here, I cannot be absolutely sure that she won't). **End of Digressions.**

With P in the past and Q in the future, we have the situations schematized in Figures 11–13 and exemplified by sentences [36–38].

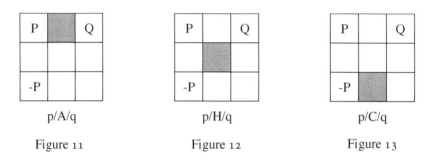

p/A/q   p/H/q   p/C/q

Figure 11   Figure 12   Figure 13

[35]   (A) Because you studied hard, you will pass the test.

[36]   (H) If you studied hard, you will pass the test.

[37]   (C) If you had studied hard, you would pass the test.

With both P and Q in the future, matters become slightly complicated. We cannot know for sure what the future will bring, so the 'Actuality' stance involves an assumption about which one cannot be absolutely sure, and the 'Counterfactuality' stance does as well. For these examples a temporal rather than a causal connection is easier to construct for the 'Actuality' stance. Notice Figures 14–16, illustrated by sentences [38–40].

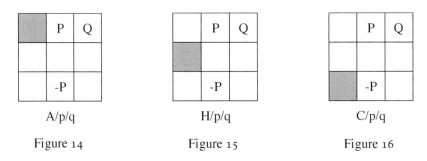

A/p/q

H/p/q

C/p/q

Figure 14

Figure 15

Figure 16

[38] (A) When you try it you'll like it.

[39] (H) If you try it you'll like it.

[40] (C) If you tried it you'd like it.

Sentences [38–39] show the commonality of temporal clauses and conditional protases with respect to the possible expression of the future. The signalling of future meaning with the present-tense form characterizes P but not Q.

In schemata in which P precedes Q, a causal relationship is easy to assume between the two, and some languages apparently require such an understanding to be part of the meaning of conditional sentences. But, given the Hypothetical stance, it is possible for P to follow, rather than precede, Q. The meaning is that in that world in which P comes to hold in the future, Q held in the past. See Figure 17 and sentence [41].

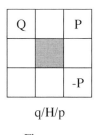

q/H/p

Figure 17

[41] (H) If he gets better by tomorrow, we gave him the right medicine.

For this sentence a 'causal' relation holds from Q to P rather than the other way around. In some languages this relationship would have to be expressed in some such way as 'If he gets better by tomorrow, we will then know that we gave him the right medicine.' But English does allow a sentence like [41]. In general, for conditional sentences which have what Eve Sweetser has referred to as 'epistemic conditional' meanings—where the relationship is not one of causation but of reasoning—the verbal expression forms are determined on independent grounds, not by virtue of being a conditional sentence.

It is possible for the speech time to coincide with either the Q or the P, especially in cases in which P precedes Q. Examples [42–44] are based on Figures 18–20.

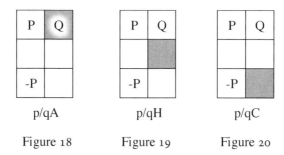

p/qA   p/qH   p/qC

Figure 18   Figure 19   Figure 20

[42](A) Because he moved to Berkeley he's happy.

[43]   (H) If he ate that stuff he's dead.

[44]   (C) If you had listened to me you'd be rich.

Examples [45–47] represent the structures shown in Figures 21–23.

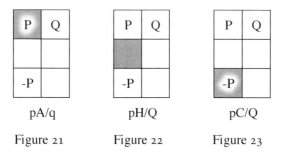

pA/q   pH/Q   pC/Q

Figure 21   Figure 22   Figure 23

[45]   (A) Since you're a member of our club you'll be invited to the dance.

[46]   (H) If you're a member of the club you'll be invited to the dance

[47]   (C) If you were a member of the club you'd be invited to the dance

And we find that it's possible for both P and Q to concern the present, as shown in Figures 24–26, illustrated by sentences [48–50].

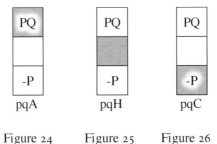

Figure 24   Figure 25   Figure 26

[48] (A) Since he's Harry's friend, he's my friend.

[49] (H) If he's Harry's friend, he's my friend.

[50] (C) If he were Harry's friend, he'd be my friend.

The remaining figures and examples are merely to fill out the possibilities.

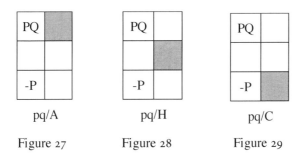

Figure 27   Figure 28   Figure 29

[51] (A) Since he lived in Twin Pines he knew David.

[52] (H) If he lived in Twin Pines he knew David.

[53] (C) If he had lived in Twin Pines he would have known David.

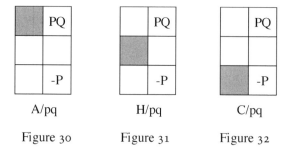

A/pq   H/pq   C/pq

Figure 30   Figure 31   Figure 32

[54] (A) When you understand what happened, you'll appreciate me.

[55] (H) If you enjoy the concert, you'll remember me.

[56] (C)?? If you were to enjoy the concert, you'd remember me.

There is a fourth class of conditional sentence, which we can refer to as 'generic', in which the specific temporal position of the speaking moment is not relevant. We can refer to this as 'G', for Generic, illustrated with sentences [57–58].

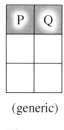

(generic)

Figure 33

[57] (G) If he says yes, she says no.

[58] (G) If he said yes, she said no.

The fact that we have both present-tense and past-tense versions of 'G' shows that there is some connection between the temporal location of the speech event relative to the events of P and Q, but this relationship is not, let us say, measurable. We are describing laws, tendencies or propensities with these sentences. The dirtying of the top row in the diagram is merely to indicate that the speaker does assume the world in which P and Q co-occur to be actual; but I do not wish to pretend that this is a part of a consistent notation. It should be noticed that *if* can be replaced by *when* or *whenever* in generically understood conditionals.

6. *WOULD'VE*

There is a made-in-America version of the past Subjunctive which is identical to the conditional perfect. For much of the time during which I've concerned myself with conditional sentences I've been unwilling to believe that this was common enough to deserve my attention, but in the meantime I've come to believe that it might actually be the dominant form in this country. I've recently heard it used by a Senator, a Presidential Press Secretary, several university professors, and a number of my dearest friends. That is the form shown in examples [59–60].

[59] If he would have opened it we would have died.

[60] If I would've met you earlier I wouldn't have married Louise.

The existence of this form gives the grammarian an interesting dilemma. I've already spoken of the colloquial form 'had have'. The coexistence of 'had have' and 'would have' means that versions in which the first word is contracted are structurally homonymous. Thus with sentences [61–62] we don't know how they are to be uncontracted—as WOULD HAVE or as HAD HAVE. The situation is particularly troubling since some of my informants insist they have *only* the contracted forms.

[61] If he'd've opened it we'd've died.

[62] If I'd've met you earlier I wouldn't've married Louise

7. *Hoping and Wishing*

The connection between conditional sentences and expressions of wishing has long been noted for English (see Palmer 1968:136), and students of Japanese are struck by the fact that expressions of hoping and wishing in that language have the form of conditional sentences in which the apodosis is the judgment that the presence of P is, or would be, good. Thus:

[63] Hayaku kaette kitara ii ne.
early returning if-come good-PRES. NE
('I hope he comes back soon')

[64] Hayaku kaette kureba yokatta noni.[11]
early returning if-come good-PAST NONI
('I wish he had come back sooner')

The 'H' and 'C' conditionals have much in common, in form and meaning, with the complements of the verbs HOPE and WISH respectively. In the case of HOPE, we express the fact that a past, present, or future hypothetical state of affairs is positively valued.

[65] I hope he had a parachute.

(admitting ignorance about the past)

[66] I hope she knows the answer.

(admitting ignorance about the present)

[67] I hope it rains soon.

(admitting ignorance about the future)

The Subjunctive forms found in the protases of 'C' conditionals also appear as complements of WISH, and with *almost* the same form selections. Thus, we find

[68] I wish she lived closer.

[69] (I wish she would live closer.)

[70] I wish she hadn't said those things.

[71] I wish she hadn't've said those things.

[72] (I wish she wouldn't have said those things.)

We notice in [71–72] that the nonstandard forms found in past subjunctive conditionals are also found in complements of WISH.

The special case is with the future 'C' form, which requires the auxiliary WOULD.

---

[11] The preferences for the *-tara* and the *-reba* forms of the Japanese conditional, different in [63] and [64], requires another story.

[73] I wish she would try harder.

[74] I wish you wouldn't say that.

What HOPE and WISH have in common is the speaker's positive interest in the state of affairs expressed as the complement clause. We can express this in our familiar diagrams, this time using 'P' to represent the verb's complement, by marking this P with a 'plus' diacritic to represent the speaker's interest.

We might characterize HOPE as involving epistemic stance H plus a positive attitude toward P, and WISH as involving epistemic stance C plus a positive attitude toward P. The future form expressing this positive attitude is expressed with the modal WOULD rather than the simple Subjunctive form. The relevance of this fact to the understanding of conditional sentences is that precisely the same form is used in the case of 'C' protases for which the speaker has a positive interest. Thus, in the context C/P+, the WOULD form can be selected in conditional sentences as well as in wishes. This can be shown by recognizing that sentences [75] and [77], for which the context makes it clear that the P in question is desired, are semantically well-formed, but sentence [76] and [78], in which the speaker's positive interest is denied, are not.

[75] If you would help Harvey a little, I'd really be happy.

[76] * If you would help Harvey a little, I'd kill you.

[77] If he would talk a little louder we could hear him better.

Compare: *If he would only talk a little louder.*

[78] If he would talk any louder I'd go crazy.

8. *Some Generalizations*

There were a number of generalizations to notice in constructing the sentences that illustrated the various schemata presented above. Among them:

(1) [H/p including H/p+]   The present tense form marks future H protases (*when she comes back, if she comes back*) and complements of HOPE (*I hope she comes back*)[12]

---

[12] I am avoiding here the troublesome question of the conditions under which WILL in future meaning can occur in a conditional protasis. For discussion see Comrie 1982, Palmer 1986:195, Haegeman & Wekker 1984.

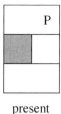

present

Figure 34 [H/p]

(2) [H/p]   The modal SHOULD can appear as the marker of future H protases in conditional sentences (*if you <u>should meet</u> Harry, greet him from me*).

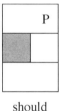

should

Figure 35 [H/p]

(This form is limited to conditional sentences; it does not occur in complements of HOPE.)

(3) [Cp, C/p in protases, Cp+ in WISH-complement]   Present Subjunctive characterizes present and future C protases, the difference between present and future interpretation depending on the difference between static and dynamic predicates (*if you <u>knew</u> him you'd love him, if you <u>met</u> him you'd love him*). We also get *I wish you <u>liked</u> him* but not **I wish she <u>came</u> back soon*. For WISH the positive-polarity form is required (next section).

pres-subj-1

Figure 36 [Cp, C/p]

(4) [C/p+] The modal WOULD marks future C wishes (*I wish you would try to be more cooperative*) and positively evaluated future C protases.

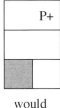

would

Figure 37 [C/p+]

(5) [p/C including p+/C]   Past Subjunctive characterizes past C protases (*if you had known him, you would have loved him, if you had met him you would have loved him*) and the complements of WISH (*I wish you had been more cooperative*).

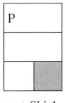

past-Sbj-1

Figure 38 [p/C]

(6) [p/C]   The conditional perfect is used, in American English, in past counterfactuals (*if you would have fixed it, it would have worked*).

cond-perf

Figure 39 [p/C]

(7) [Cq and C/q]   Plain conditional forms characterize present and future C apodoses, the difference between present and future depending on the difference between static and dynamic predicates (*if you teased him, he'd love it; if you teased him, he'd kick you*).

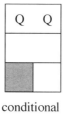

conditional

Figure 40 [qC, q/C]

(8) [q/C]   Conditional perfect forms characterize past C apodoses (*if you had said that, I would have liked it*)

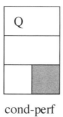

cond-perf

Figure 41 [q/C]

(9) In all other cases forms are selected that would be selected independently of their appearance in a conditional sentence. What that means is that in all other cases, the meaning of the verb cluster in a conditional protasis or apodosis is the same meaning it would have in a simple independent clause.

9. Applications

If we return now to sentences [9–11], it is easy to show that the sentences which are perfectly straightforward have verbal expression properties that are predictable by the form-assignment diagrams we have just examined, those which are ungrammatical cannot be generated by our principles, and the questioned ones require special means of motivating aspectual forms within the individual clauses.

Thus, for *If she opens it, they'll escape*, we note that the present tense of *opens* in the P-clause is appropriate for the configuration H/p, and the WILL-future form in the Q-clause fits the configuration H/q, and H/p/q is a possible diagram.

For the sentence *If she opened it, they'd escape* we find that the simple past tense in *opened* fits the model for C/p and the conditional form *would escape* fits the model for C/q, and the result is C/p/q, a possible configuration.

For the sentence *If she had opened it, they would have escaped*, we find the *had opened* compatible with p/C and the *would have escaped* compatible with q/C, and the result is p/q/C, a possible configuration.

For the sentence *If she opened it, they escaped*, we find the past tense form *opened* compatible with p/H and the past tense form of *escaped* compatible with q/H, resulting in the well-formed configuration p/q/H.

However, for the ungrammatical sentence **If she'll open it, they had've escaped*, what we notice is that the form *will open* requires H/p while the form *had've escaped* requires p/H, and there is no way to build these into a well-formed conditional sentence.

And for **If she were here, they'll be happy*, we find the form *were* in the P-clause requiring pC, and the form *will be* in the Q-clause requiring H/q, and once again, there is no way of building these into a conditional sentence.

For the first of the questionable sentences *?If she'd opened it, they've escaped*, we have a past perfect (hence past) in the P-clause, and a present perfect (hence present) in the Q-clause, hence p/qH, a well-formed configuration. However, this requires us to construct a context for which it makes sense to have the kind of temporal reference point justifying the pluperfect in the dependent clause and the present perfect in the main clause. And that takes some work.

Similarly, with *?If she opens it, she had misunderstood our note* we have q/H/p, requiring an epistemic inference from the future event of her opening to the conclusion that, in respect to some previously established past-time reference point, she had misunderstood our note. And motivating such a context is not easy.

10. *Conclusion*

The diagrams used in this paper have only been to help the reader—or at least the writer—keep track easily of the distinctions being explored and contrasted. What I have tried to show in this paper is that the semantic/pragmatic feature of epistemic stance plays an important role in the determination of grammatical and ungrammatical (or interpretable and uninterpretable) conditional sentences, and that some sort of 'unification' mechanism is required in a grammar to guarantee that these features are identical in the related two clauses of a conditional sentence. Conditional sentences, thus, are special grammatical constructions with two parts whose properties must be established in parallel. Though this matching requirement is disguised by (1) surface-form differences across the two clauses, in the case of H and C constructions, (2) dialect variation (as with the two colloquial English 'past subjunctive' varieties), and (3) the homonymy of construction-specific forms (of the types 'conditional' and 'subjunctive' as named here) with independently compositionally derived verbal clusters, we find that once all these other facts and influences are sorted out, the grammar of conditional sentences in English is shown to be subject to precise constraints on the matching of these clearly definable but quite abstract epistemic stance variables, the functioning of which is necessary simultaneously to the syntactic and the semantic descriptions of conditional sentences.

References

Akatsuka, N. 1983. Conditionals. *Papers in Japanese Linguistics* 9:1–33.

Akatsuka, N. 1985. Conditionals and epistemic scales. *Language* 61:625–639.

Akatsuka, N. 1986. Conditionals are discourse bound. In Traugott et al., 333–351.

Comrie, B. 1982. Future time reference in conditional protases. *Australian Journal of Linguistics* 2:143–152.

Comrie, B. 1986. Conditionals: A typology. Traugott, et al. 1986: 77–99.

Dancygier, B. and E. Mioduszewska. 1984. Semanto-Pragmatic Classification of Conditionals. *Studia Anglica Posnaniensia* 17:121–133.

Dudman, V. H. 1984. Conditional interpretations of if-sentences. *Australian Journal of Linguistics* 4.2:143–204.

Fillmore, C. J. 1985. Syntactic intrusions and the notion of grammatical construction. *BLS* 11:73–86.

Fillmore, C. J., P. Kay, and M. C. O'Connor. 1988. Regularity and idiomaticity in English grammar: The case of *let alone*. *Language* 64:501–538.

Funk, W.-P. On a semantic typology of conditional sentences. *Folia Linguistica* 19(3/4):365–414.

Haegeman, L. and H. Wekker. 1984. The syntax and interpretation of futurate conditionals in English. *Journal of Linguistics* 20:46–55.

Haiman, J. 1986. Constraints on the form and meaning of the protasis. In E. C. Traugott, et al., 215–227.

Jespersen, J. O. 1933/1964. *Essentials of English Grammar*. University of Alabama Press.

Lakoff, R. T. 1969. Some reasons why there can't be any *some–any* rule. *Language* 45:608–615.

Lambert, V. 1983. The Non-Standard Third Conditional in English: A Sociolinguistic Study. M. A. Thesis, University of Reading.

Palmer, F. R. 1968. *A Linguistic Study of the English Verb*, University of Miami Press.

Palmer, F. R. 1986. *Mood and Modality*. Cambridge University Press.

Reinhart, T. 1976. Polarity reversal: Logic or pragmatics. *Linguistic Inquiry* 7:697–705.

Shopen, T., ed. 1985. *Language Typology and Syntactic Description: Volume II: Complex Constructions*. Cambridge University Press.

Sweetser, E. 1990. *From Etymology to Pragmatics: Metaphorical and Cultural Aspects of Semantic Structure*. Cambridge University Press.

Thompson, S. A. and R. E. Longacre 1985. Adverbial clauses. In Shopen 1985. 171–234.

Traugott, E. C., A. ter Meulen, J. Snitzer Reilly, and C. A. Ferguson, eds. 1986. *On Conditionals*. Cambridge University Press.

11

Under the Circumstances
(Place, Time, Manner, etc.)

1994
CHARLES J. FILLMORE

1.

The effort to produce (with Paul Kay) a coherent and complete statement of the construction grammar model has brought me back to many of the same issues that troubled me some thirty years ago.[1] One of these has to do with the proper treatment of adverbial elements, especially of the kind sometimes referred to as circumstantials.

The category of expressions showing up in some linguistic traditions under such names as circumstant, circumstantial, circumstance, goes back, terminologically at least, to a distinction made by the French Slavist, generalist, and typologist, and the founder of formalized dependency grammar, Lucien Tesnière, in his posthumously published *Eléments de Syntaxe Structurale* (1959). Tesnière distinguished what he called actants and circonstants, which I will render in English as actants and circumstantials. (1959:102) Actants are the parts of a sentence that designate the people and props that are necessarily present in the 'little drama' (*petit drame*) that a verb represents; and the circumstantials are those expressions that correspond to stage directions, specifications of the time and place of the action, etc., for such little dramas.

---

[1] Given the occasion at which this paper was read, I hope I can be forgiven for its personal and old-man's-reminiscences tone.

Tesnière identifies the circumstantials as those expressions in a sentence that designate *temps, lieu, manière, etc.* (1959:103). This phrase 'time, place, manner, etc.' has been repeated countless times since then, to characterize what might or might not be seen as a natural class of adverbial notions. The 'etc.' in the phrase covers a great deal, making the search for coherence difficult, but adverbs of time, place and manner (and maybe one or two other types) do indeed seem to have special properties that invite us to think of them together.

The difference between actants and circumstantials is related, in Tesnière's view, to the notion valence (1959:238). The valence of a verb was taken to include just the actants, of which there could be at most three, corresponding more or less to subject, direct object, and indirect object (1959: 111–115). Of the actants there could be only three, but of the circumstantials there could be unlimitedly many.

In John Lyons' book *Semantics*, there is a section dealing with this same contrast where we read the following:

> 'the syntactic distinction between nominals and adverbials correlates, though only imperfectly, with the syntactic distinction between the subject or complements of a verb and its various adjuncts. This latter distinction also correlates, though again imperfectly, with a further distinction that is commonly drawn between the valency-roles or participant-roles, and the circumstantial roles associated with a situation. [...] If we are describing an action in English, we may tell our interlocutor not only who did what to whom (or what), but also when, where, how or why he did it. [...] These circumstances are normally referred to by means of syntactically optional adverbs or adverbials, whereas valency roles are associated, in what we may take to be the kernel sentences of English, with nominals (and, in certain instances, place-referring adverbials) functioning as the subjects or complements of the verb.' (Lyons 1977:496–7)

In this passage Lyons identifies a number of important partially correlated distinctions: the grammatical category distinction between nominals and adverbials; the grammatical role distinction between subject-&-complements on the one hand and adjuncts on the other; and the distinction between valence roles and circumstantial roles, illustrated as the semantically based difference between the who and the what on the one hand, and the when, where, how and why, on the other hand. And lastly, there is the distinction between the obligatory and the optional companions of given verbs.

We can add three more to this list of oppositions. First, there is a traditional distinction between *direct* and *oblique cases* for the familiar case languages; anciently the *casus rectus* was the nominative case and the term *casus obliquus* covered everything else, but there are also traditions in which

nominative and accusative are the direct cases, everything else being classified as oblique. Secondly, there is an idea of the structural *core* or *nucleus* of
a clause, comprising subject, direct object, indirect object, and directional
complements, everything else constituting the *periphery*. And thirdly, in
'frame semantics' it has been useful to have a distinction between adverbial
elements that provide *frame-internal* information—information that fills in
details of the internal structure of an event or process associated with the
meaning of the predicator—as opposed to information about the setting or
incidental attending circumstances of that event or process, the *frame-external* information. These latter elements have also been referred to as *extrathematic*.

If we sense that, in spite of a great deal of non-correspondences, there is
in some sense a single underlying distinction here, what we have is clearly a
kind of *prototype* concept. In this prototype, or idealization, we find that certain components of sentences designate people and things, get expressed as
nominals, show up as subjects and objects, get marked by nominative and
accusative case in languages that do things like that, express meanings that
fit directly into the semantic frame expressed by the verb, and are obligatory
accompaniments to the verbs that govern them. The remainder are those parts
of sentences that designate 'time, place, manner, etc.', that show up as optional adjuncts, and are expressed obliquely, perhaps with the help of such
subordinating and role-marking devices as prepositions and postpositions.

But that is the prototype: reality, as noted by Lyons, departs from this
prototype in numerous ways. The non-correspondence between the expression of circumstantial meanings and optionality can be illustrated with verbs
having obligatory place specifications, such as *live* in the sense 'reside' (1);
verbs that require time specifications, such as *last* (2); and verbs that require
manner specifications, such as *phrase* (3).

(1) We live in Berlin.

(2) The meeting lasted two hours.

(3) He phrased his question clumsily.

Circumstantial meanings can stand in core grammatical relations to their
verbs, as in (4), with *yesterday* as direct object; (5), with *three days* as subject,
and (6) with *the room*, marking the origin of a movement, as direct object.

(4) I spent yesterday trying to fix the pump.

(5) Three days elapsed before the package arrived.

(6) She left the room hastily.

In fact, for each pairing of the distinctions we are considering—grammatical category, grammatical function, semantic role, optionality etc.—we could readily find examples, across a wide variety of languages, that show that they are not interdefinable.

2.

My topic is not circumstance concepts in general, but circumstantial adverbs in languages that express such notions phrasally.[2] In the early days of generative grammar, students looking for research topics were wisely advised, 'Whatever you do, stay away from adverbs!'. The so-called 'UCLA Air Force' grammar (Stockwell, Schachter and Partee 1973), dedicated to collecting all of the most significant results in transformational grammar of the preceding ten years, apologizes for having very little to say about adverbs, for having only one slot for adverbs in their phrase-structure rules, and for pretty much limiting their discussion of adverbs to positive and negative preverbal adverbs like *often, sometimes, seldom, hardly, never*, and the like.

In addition to a vast non-formalist literature on the functions, meanings and distribution of adverbs and adverbials in English[3], there is now also a considerable body of technical literature on the semantics and grammar of adverbials within the various formal grammar traditions.[4]

A basic sorting of adverbs emerging from all such discussions divides them into classes according to whether they modify verbs, verb-phrases, or sentences: McCawley's parade examples are *completely*, as a verb-modifier, *reluctantly*, as a VP modifier, and *probably*, as a sentence modifier. This appears to be identical to the three-way distinction presented by Bally (1950:124) where he presents three types of adverbial modification: *intrinsic*, referring to adverbs which qualify and quantify the meanings of the verbs or adjectives and *extrinsic*, referring to those which provide indications of *place*, *time, cause, condition, end, means*, etc. To these he opposes a third type, referred to as *modal*, including *certainly, perhaps*, and *not*.

It would appear that the V-modifiers might correspond to manner adverbs, and the VP-modifiers correspond to the others. The modal adverbs don't belong under the circumstances. There is a special class of adverbs discussed by Adrienne Lehrer (Lehrer 1975) that includes *stupidly, foolishly*,

---

[2] There is a class of head-marking languages that express notions of manner, location, destination, etc., morphologically, inside the verb-sentence. On the nature of one such language, and on the typology of means of expressing circumstantial notions, see Talmy 1972, 1985.

[3] Representative studies of adverbs (single-word adverbials) are Jacobson (1964) and Greenbaum (1969); perhaps the most complete description of the semantic varieties of adverbials is found in chapter 8, 'The semantics and grammar of adverbials', of Quirk et al., (1985: 475–653).

[4] Representative studies are Lakoff and Ross (1976), McCawley (1983, 1991), McConnell-Ginet (1982), Thomason and Stalnaker (1982).

cleverly, etc. With these, the speaker assesses an actor's actions, sometimes as modal or sentential adverbs and sometimes as manner adverbs. Thus, in the intended meaning of sentence (7) what is judged to be stupid is merely the fact that the speaker answered the letter at all; but in sentence (8), the adverb is taken as characterizing a way of behaving, a manner.

(7) I stupidly answered his letter

(thus complicating my legal position).

(8) You behaved stupidly at the party.

My own first concern with types of adverbs came as a reaction to Chomsky's 1965 *Aspects of the Theory of Syntax*, where we find a tentative phrase-structural base for a transformational grammar of English (1965:102), reproduced as Figure 1.

(i) S → NP Predicate-Phrase

(ii) Predicate-Phrase → Aux VP (Place)(Time)

$$\text{(iii)}\quad \text{VP} \rightarrow \left[\begin{array}{l} \textit{be}\ \text{Predicate} \\ \text{V} \left[\begin{array}{l} \text{(NP)(Prep-Phrase)(Prep-Phrase)(Manner)} \\ \text{Adj} \\ \text{S'} \\ (\textit{like})\ \text{Predicate-Nominal} \end{array}\right] \end{array}\right]$$

$$\text{(iv)}\quad \text{Prep-Phrase} \rightarrow \left[\begin{array}{l} \text{Direction} \\ \text{Duration} \\ \text{Place} \\ \text{Frequency} \\ \text{etc.} \end{array}\right]$$

(v) V → CS

Figure 1

Problems with this particular set of rules with respect to the claims they make about how particular adverbs get introduced were carefully examined in a famous semi-published paper by Lakoff and Ross, around 1967, one of whose titles was 'Why you can't do so into the sink.'[5] Lakoff and Ross argued that direct objects, indirect objects, and directionals were properly inside the VP, and that everything else had to be handled with a very different mechanism.

[5] The paper is reprinted under that title in McCawley (1976). It was printed in Report NSF-17 of the Aiken Computation Laboratory of Harvard University, under its polite title 'A criterion for verb phrase constituency'.

In Chomsky's case it was the notion of subcategorization that put certain kinds of adverbs inside the VP. Adverbs of different types were introduced in different positions—inside and outside the VP node—depending on whether or not they participated in strict subcategorization. By examining the phenomenon of VP-replacement by 'do-so', Lakoff and Ross came up with a completely different basis for making such a decision. In the case of manner adverbs in particular, it was from Chomsky's wish to show that certain English verbs were incapable of occurring with manner adverbs that this class of adverbs had to be introduced as structural sisters to the verb; but from the fact that manner adverbs may be external to 'do-so' substitution (*and I did so deliberately*), Lakoff and Ross had to provide a means by which they could be external to a VP constituent (at some level).

My own concern with this set of rules was a bit different. I was puzzled by the role, in the formalism, of labels like Place, Time, Manner, Frequency, and the like. An important principle of Chomskyan linguistics from the start was that the grammatical functions of sentence components are secondary, derivative of configurational properties. According to this principle, there is no need to include in the theory of grammar, as theoretical primitives, such notions as *subject* or *object*, since the subject of a sentence is simply that single NP which is an immediate constituent of the sentence, and the direct object is that single NP which is an immediate constituent of the VP. The use of the non-categorial node labels we see in Figure 1 was a recognition, it appeared, that it isn't possible to create enough structural configurations to define all of the structural relations that are needed.

The practice of using semantically motivated labels in rewritings of the category Prep-Phrase brought with it a number of problems. First, it is not the node labeled 'Prep-Phrase' which immediately dominates a phrase headed by a preposition, but one of these semantic-function labels; and those prepositional phrases that occurred outside of the immediate environment of the verb (i.e., those introduced by rule (ii)) would not be dominated by a 'Prep-Phrase' node at all. One could rewrite the grammatical category Prep-Phrase as any of several distinct semantically motivated labels, and then allow each of these to be further expanded as a preposition followed by a nominal. Thus, the category symbol Prep-Phrase could be rewritten as Directional, and that in turn could be rewritten as Preposition plus NP, yielding ultimately such expressions as *through its nostrils* or *into the ashtray*.

The text surrounding and justifying these rules introduces the role of the *complex symbol* (the CS of rule (v)) and the notion of *strict subcategorization*, relating a verb (or any lexical head) to its partners within a verb phrase. An intransitive verb was simply a verb that could get along all by itself inside its VP; a transitive verb needed the company of a NP; and so on. Since some circumstantial notions do, and some do not, participate in verb subcategorization, this made it necessary to provide two positions for circumstantial adverbs: (i) those which participated in the subcategorization of a verb, the verb's *complements*, and (ii) those which served as *adjuncts* outside of the system of strict subcategorization. If you have doubts about whether some element of a particular sentence is a complement or an adjunct, you simply ask yourself whether it does or doesn't participate in the subcategorization of the verb it's somehow associated with. The reason we find the label Place twice in the formulas, once inside and once outside the VP, is because it is an obligatory associate of some verbs (e.g., *live* as in 'Joe lived in London') but it is merely an optionally licensed adjunct with others (e.g., *die* as in 'Joe died in Paris').

Such talk gives the impression that the notion of subcategorization is itself uncontested. I will raise some questions about that later on.

3.

Discussions of the various dependents and companions of verbs involve grammatical functions, structural configurations, morphosyntactic marking, and semantic roles. Linguists have disagreed about which of these sorts of notions should be taken as the starting point for making meaningful generalizations about the structure of sentences in languages. I played around in those days with the idea that the semantic roles should give us the place to start. What we needed to do, I thought, was to understand verbs according to the semantic roles that could be, or had to be, expressed around them, and that we should see an important part of the workings of a grammar as providing the means for giving expression to those entities.

For Chomsky's rules it appeared that we needed semantic labels for everything surrounding a V or a VP except subjects and objects. Since verbs even had to be subcategorized according to their compatibility with particular semantically-typed complements—in particular, place, time, and manner—it was obvious that at some level at least it was necessary to regulate the operation of a grammar by referring to such notional categories. Since, furthermore, everybody knew that subjects and objects could have interestingly different kinds of relations to their verbs as well—some sentences expressed what some actor did, some expressed what some undergoer underwent, or what some experiencer experienced, while others expressed simple states or happenings—I came to the conclusion that it might be possible to construct a grammar in which we started out with semantic role specifications of all of the arguments of valence bearing words, not just the adverbial constituents, and then looked for rules that determined how one built up the kinds of structures that had subjects and objects. This, some of you will know, and a few of you will remember, was the origin of *case grammar*, so-called. A central idea of case grammar was that there was a separate mechanism for providing syntactic realization for semantic role notions.[6]

Superficially[7], the differences separating Chomsky 1965 from the emerging *generative semantics* model and the case grammar model can be summarized as follows. The generative semanticists limited themselves to primitive phrase structural configurations, expressing a wide range of argument relations with abstract predicates like DO, BECOME, CAUSE, etc., and less abstract predicates like IN, UNDER, DURING, etc. They had no need to give semantically motivated labels to nodes in a constituent structure representation since all such relations were provided lexically, in deep structure.[8]

Case grammar used a large inventory of role names for the semantic roles, dealing with the primary grammatical functions in terms of a level–to–level mapping that arranged for the selection and structuring of subjects and objects. The 'cases', in the form of a partially ordered list, and the ways in which given clusters of them were tied to specific predicators, took the place of selection restrictions, strict subcategorization, as well as devices for licensing of potential circumstantial elements. An undeveloped structural distinction between sentence parts called *proposition* and *modality* were available for one level of scope asymmetry, but in general little thought was given to such problems.

But the Aspects model used a mixed notation, with grammatical category names for some sentence constituents and semantically motivated labels for others, as seen in the rules copied in Figure 1.

As we have seen, the Aspects grammar introduced adverbs at two different levels; the generative semantics model made it necessary to introduce adverbs one at a time, so to speak, since each one needed a sentence level constituent as its only argument, in the case of Place and Time adverbials, or as one of its arguments, in the case of Manner adverbials; and the case grammar model distinguished the case inventory, which provided a list of possible semantic role names, from the case frames of individual verbs, thus separating the necessary from the optional complements of the verb. (It was assumed that incompatibilities could be ruled out by semantic considerations.) An embarrassment for generative semantics was that multiple adverbs in a single

---

[6] See, e.g., Fillmore (1968, 1969, 1971). Related notions, unknown to me at the time, appear in Gruber (1965). Some scholars believe that current work in theta theory and associated principles of linking show an influence from case grammar.

[7] The hedge 'superficially' is in recognition of the fact that while the generative semanticists used (at first, anyway) phrase-structural representations of familiar sorts, their motivation was, of course, to start out with what they believed represented the semantic structure of a sentence.

[8] Most of the generative semantics work that I paid attention to, when it was all happening, was unpublished. Rather than try to identify the major publications, I refer the reader to the discussions and references in McCawley (1976) and R. Harris (1993).

sentence had to be located in a way that showed asymmetric scope relationships, whether these were semantically justified or not.[9] An embarrassment for case grammar was that there was no obvious structural way to show scope relations between sentence elements when the semantics of the sentence required such relations.

4.

Another embarrassment for case grammar was the inability of its practitioners to answer the question of how many such semantically motivated sentence elements there were, how their differences could be justified, and so on. In considering circumstantials in particular, from a cross-linguistic point of view, there are various questions we need to ask. One is whether it makes sense to look for a universal language-independent set of circumstantial notions. It would be convenient if we could, because that would justify and make respectable certain ways of comparing the expression of circumstantial notions across languages. In Foley's study of the case systems of Papuan languages (New Guinea) he begins by identifying a particular set of notions and then lays out the ways in which these notions are reflected in case marking differences among these languages (Foley 1986:96–99). Foley recognizes the notions *instrumental, cause, location, ablative*, and *allative*, and sorts the languages in the Papuan group according to the ways in which these notions are encoded: one language encodes all of them with a single case ending, one provides separate case endings for each one, and the others group them morphologically in various combinations. The result of such a survey offers nontrivial suggestions for understanding the nature of certain kinds of linguistic change among these languages.

In creating our list of universal circumstantial categories, we can probably assume that whenever we find one language displaying a particular distinction, we can consider the notions thus distinguished as belonging to our collection. Thus we will wish to make a distinction between frame-internal location and event-setting location from the fact that Korean uses different case postpositions for marking them: the distinction between the location expressions for cooking a chicken in a pot and cooking a chicken on the patio.[10]

On the principle that whenever types of sentence constituents are distinct from each other, you get at most one instance of each type per clause, we might conclude that when we find more than one type in a given sentence, the two should be separate entries in our list rather than being variants of the

---

[9] That is, if a sentence had adverbs specifying both spatial and temporal locations, one of them would have to have the other in its scope.

[10] Personal communication, Jeong-Woon Park.

same type. Thus, with respect to time, we need to distinguish temporal extent from temporal location, as seen in (9).

(9)   I worked [for three hours] [yesterday].

Such considerations lead to the discrimination of a wide range of adverbial notions connected with space (simple location, origin, destination or path of movement, distribution, distance, etc.) and time (extent, location, starting point, ending point, frequency, etc.).

If we can demonstrate a clear ambiguity in the interpretation of some circumstantial expression, we conclude that we are dealing with two separate notions, and we might expect them to be realized in distinct ways in some languages. A rule of thumb for understanding the circumstantial concept of Manner is that it is something which answers the question 'How?'. But actually the word 'how' incorporates Means as well as Manner. I like to illustrate the difference between means and manner by referring to a question/answer joke form that was current ten or fifteen years ago, in which the question was something like (10a) and the answer was always (10b).

(10a)   How should you lift a python out of a trashbin?

(10b)   Very carefully.

The joke turns on hearing the question as asking about the *means* by which one can accomplish this task, and hearing the answer as saying something about the *manner* in which this action should be carried out.

I am convinced that at some level we do indeed need to make all the distinctions that have been discussed, and many more. These distinctions are needed because they figure separately in giving semantic descriptions of verb meanings, because there are frequently clear ordering relations that hold among them, and because they enter into incompatibility relations with each other that are going to require formulation in terms of failed unification.

5.

I suggested a while ago that the notion of strict subcategorization is in need of some clarification. Here is an example of a potential problem. Some verbs that speak of something moving, or being moved, into a place, can be modified by adverbs that give information about the amount of time the thing remains (or is to remain) in that place. Notice the effect of the temporal adverbs in sentences (11) and (12):

(11)   She went to Estonia for a year.

(12)   We put the wine in the freezer for 30 minutes.

The phrases 'for a year' in (11) and 'for 30 minutes' in (12) do not give information about the time of the going or the putting, but about the time of remaining at the destination of the going and the putting. What shall we say about these examples? Shall we say that *go* and *put* (and countless other verbs of simple and caused translocational motion) have different senses according to whether or not they welcome a time–extent phrase? Or shall we say that there is a grammar-independent interpretation principle that derives, say, a 'storage' meaning of *put* from a context in which it is modified by a temporal extent adverbial? Is such a permanent or context extended sense to be seen as resulting from a kind of event–metonymy, whereby going somewhere is a part of an act of going there to stay, putting something somewhere is a part of an act of keeping it there for a period of time? How does our initial under-standing of strict subcategorization help us make these decisions?

With respect to event metonymy, we could consider the (perhaps clearer) case of the verb *write*. Compare sentences (13) and (14).

(13)   I've written the final chapter.

(14)   I've written a letter to the chancellor.[11]

Writing involves producing written text of some sort, in both of these examples, but in (14) we find a directional adverbial, *to the chancellor*. What business does a directional adverbial have modifying a verb that means 'to write'? Is this an optional adjunct, or do we have here a separate entry for *write* that is specialized for letter-writing. The reason this case is clearer, I think, is that we can call on a sort of 'ambiguity test' to resolve the question. Ordinarily one doesn't simultaneously affirm and negate the same verb in the same sense, but it's easy to imagine a harried dissertation writer who has been rep-rimanded for neglecting the family back home producing a sentence like (15).

(15)   I don't write because I'm too busy writing.

---

[11] The structure I have in mind is equivalent to what one would find in 'I've written one to the chancellor'. In other words, I do not intend 'a letter to the chancellor' to be read as a single constituent.

In many cases we can find clear differences of syntactic behavior and semantic scope evidencing clearly different functions for the same adverbial phrase. Consider the following sentences:

(16)   They sent people to Siberia for twenty years.

(17)   For how many years did they send people to Siberia?

(18)   For twenty years they sent people to Siberia.

(19)   How many years did they send people to Siberia for?

We can imagine sending someone to Siberia as a form of punishment, the length of the banishment corresponding to the severity of the crime. Sentence (16) is ambiguous in being able to express either that the punishments in the case being reported involved twenty-year sentences, or that the practice of exiling people to Siberia continued for a twenty-year period. In one of these cases the temporal expression is frame–internal; in the other case it is frame–external. We might wish to say that in the former interpretation, 'for twenty years' is a complement (belonging to a class of expressions that might include 'for life'), and that in the latter interpretation it is an adjunct. There are certain (imperfect) distributional traits that parallel the difference in status between complement and adjunct.

Sentence (17) is also ambiguous, corresponding to the fact that sentence-initial position for full phrases is available for both complements and adjuncts if the phrases are interrogative.

Sentences (18) and (19), however, are not ambiguous (according to the majority of my informants), and each invites a different interpretation. Sentence (18) is an instance of a topicalized adjunct and hence refers to the length of time during which the practice of sending people to Siberia continued; sentence (19) is an instance of 'WH-Extraction', has only the interpretation that the speaker is asking about the terms of the exile, and fits the (imperfect) generalization that while extraction from complements is possible, extraction from adjuncts is not.

Now these observations seem to support these principles, but our question is whether we need to speak of the difference in terms of those principles. After all, sentences (20) and (21) are both acceptable, and considering what was noted earlier about their two verbs, one of them looks like extraction from a complement and the other extraction from an adjunct.

(20)   What town did he live in?

(21)   What town did he die in?

In any case, the simple question of whether a time-span phrase is 'optional' for a verb like *send* involves us quickly in a complex net of reasoning. A brute-force way of dealing with such phenomena in my own work just now is to assign the grammatical function *oblique* to the frame–internal circumstantials and *adjunct* to the frame–setting circumstantials and to expect the syntactic consequences to be sensitive to such a distinction, rather than a distinction in structural form.

6.

In the Construction Grammar model[12] we have made certain assumptions about the proper way to treat certain classes of adverbs. We assign to each verb (or verb sense) in a language a *valence description*, offered as a set of the argument types that are most tightly associated with the verb's meaning. This set is projected into a similar bit of information structure tied to the verb-phrase, and ultimately to a clause as a whole, which covers all of the licensed elements of the clause, including those required by the head verb, but also including other optional, adverbial elements which are introduced as augments to the valence set that comes prepackaged with the verb. Since some adverbs appear to modify parts of the structures of semantically complex verbs, anyway, we don't have to assume from the start that the compositional properties of expressions with multiple scopal adverbs have to be accounted for in purely structural terms.

We are in general proposing an essentially flat structure for a verb and almost all of the (non-subject) phrases that can go with it, and that means that we have to do some serious worrying about the arguments others have given in favor of highly structured configurations for adverbs, configurations in which at some level each adverb takes an entire verb–phrase, or perhaps an entire clause, as one of its arguments. This includes both the 'higher predicate' analyses of the generative semanticists, and the unlimitedly nested V-bars of certain other systems.

Those who propose complex structures for positioning adverbs have two kinds of motivations. One of these is to be able to account for certain facts of syntactic mobility: for example, if certain kinds of adverbial phrases are seen as positioned outside of the VP, that makes it easy to understand why they can appear in front of the VP as well as sentence-finally. They have the same structural relation to the rest of the VP in either case. A second motive is to provide for compositional means of interpreting sentences containing more than one adverb, especially for cases in which the two adverbs can have

---

[12] Information about the model will eventually become available in Fillmore and Kay (forthcoming) and Kay and Fillmore (forthcoming).

different semantic relations to each other in terms of scope. It's my impression that some such arguments are valid and others are not.

Much of the evidence in arguments about scope is evidence about constituent order, or with the positions in which adverbs can be inserted into a sentence. In considering questions of constituent order, there appear to be certain arbitrary ordering principles, such as the kind which dictates a general preference in English for place indications to precede time indications. Compare (22a) with (22b).

> (22a)   She worked in the office this morning.

> (22b)   ?She worked this morning in the office.

The difference here appears to be one of preference rather than grammaticality.

Some problems of the positioning of adverbs appear to be specific to certain words or certain phrase types. In reading through various accounts of adverb positions recently, I was struck by the frequency with which words meaning 'yesterday' figure in such discussions for French, German and English.

In comparing such sentences as (23)–(26),

> (23)   John soon will leave for Detroit.

> (24)   *John tomorrow will leave for Detroit

> (25)   John recently left for Detroit

> (26)   *John yesterday left for Detroit.

McCawley (1983:280) observes an apparently arbitrary positional requirement on the words *tomorrow* and *yesterday*. McCawley relates this to a principle according to which PPs do not occur in front of verbs in English (Jackendoff 1977:73). He proposes to fit these facts into that same generalization by declaring *tomorrow* and *yesterday* to be honorary PPs. I think this may not be the best explanation. We noticed that (22b) seemed to be merely dispreferred over (22a); but if the time adverb were *yesterday* our rejection would be stronger, I believe. Notice (27).

> (27)   *She worked yesterday in the office.

There are no constraints on placing preposition phrases *after* a verb.

Charles Bally (1950:74) finds pragmatic reasons for ordering sentence elements in French based on the special communicational effect of putting something in the accent-bearing sentence-final position. To illustrate this point, he compares (28) with (29).

(28)   Je suis allé a Paris *par avion.*

(29)   Je suis allé par avion *à Paris.*

In (28) going to Paris is taken for granted and information about the means of travel is being introduced; in (29) the means of transportation is taken for granted and it's the destination that's being emphasized. But then Bally adds that there appears to be a constraint against positioning certain words in accented position, however much you might want to. This is true, for example, of *hier*, 'yesterday':

(30)   *Je suis allé a Paris *hier.*

In this case, a decision to classify *hier* as a preposition phrase won't help us: preposition phrases are not blocked in clause-final position.

The Helbig/Buscha grammar of German has a large section on how the negating adverb *nicht* gets positioned in a German sentence relative to various other parts of a VP (1980:459–467). We learn, for example, that if a temporal adverb is expressed as a preposition phrase, either order is possible.

(31)   Er besucht mich am Abend nicht.

(32)   Er besucht mich nicht am Abend.

In the case of *gestern*, 'yesterday', however, *nicht* precedes: we get (33) but not (34). Here, too, classifying the trouble-maker a preposition phrase won't help.

(33)   Er besuchte uns gestern nicht.

(34)   *Er besuchte uns nicht gestern.

If we were merely concerned with the positioning of circumstantials, one at a time, within other structures, we would have to recognize both that there are certain generalizations that each language offers, but also that there appear to be numerous arbitrary constraints. But more serious questions arise when we see what happens when we try to put two or more circumstantials in the same sentence and the interpretation varies depending on which comes first.

Semantic scope differences are sometimes claimed to accompany different orderings for adverbs, but to understand the significance of these discussions we have to be clear about the difference between (i) the logical structure of the sentence and (ii) matters of accent and emphasis of the sort suggested a moment ago for French. McCawley sees the following two sentences as justifying stacked or nested structures for English, structures in which the final adverb modifies the entire remainder of the sentence:

> (35)   I can do it on a typewriter in 10 minutes.
>
> (36)   I can do it in ten minutes on a typewriter.

The first version is supposed to suggest that as far as doing it on a typewriter is concerned, all I need is ten minutes; the other is supposed to suggest that as far as doing it in ten minutes is concerned, I'd need a typewriter. But are these differences truly scopal? Clearly both sentences end up claiming that I can do this work within a ten-minute period using a typewriter. We could easily justify a claim about the pragmatics of English sentences that the end of a sentence can serve as focus position whenever the speaker says something for which the remainder of the sentence alludes to some context proposition.[13]

But the same function can be satisfied by other means, not involving order, as well. Thus, an appropriate answer to question (37a) could be (37b), and an appropriate answer to (38a) could be (38b).

> (37a)   How long will it take if you do it on a typewriter?
>
> (37b)   I can do it in TEN MINutes on a TYPEwriter.
>
> (38a)   Could you do it in ten minutes?
>
> (38b)   I could do it on a TYPEwriter in ten minutes.

What these observations are taken to mean is that here we are not strictly dealing with questions of adverb scope, but of relating, pragmatically, a present utterance to a spoken or understood context proposition. There happen to be these two ways of identifying focused information in English: in

---

[13] On context proposition see Fillmore, Kay and O'Connor (1988).

sentence-final position, as with McCawley's examples, or internally, with heavy accent, as with my examples.

Some linguists speak of an intuitive notion of relative scope of modification. Zellig Harris issues the principle: 'When a verb has two or more adverbs ... on it, each modifies the verb as already modified by the nearer adverbs.' (Z. Harris 1982:308) He uses the example shown in (39a), noting that the order can be reversed if interrupted by a comma, as in (39b).

    (39a)   He spoke quietly later.

    (39b)   He spoke later, very quietly.

In both cases, of course, his speaking, which took place later than some contextually given reference time, was in a low voice. But voice volume is clearly frame–internal for speaking, and temporal location is frame–external, and it is common to have frame–internal elements follow more closely on the verb than frame–external elements. A similar point can be made regarding preverbal and postverbal adverbs, for which Harris offers the examples (40a) and (40b). (1982:310)

    (40a)   He frequently drives slowly.

    (40b)   *He slowly drives frequently.

I am not convinced that the difference between frame–internal and frame–external elements should be thought of in terms of logical scope. In a sentence like (41), it is not even clear that the more distant element is less integrated into the 'talking' frame.

    (41)   He spoke quietly about his childhood.

The Avery Andrews examples (1983), designed to justify the need for 'nested VPs', are more convincing.

    (42a)   John knocked on the door twice intentionally.

    (42b)   John knocked on the door intentionally twice.

For these sentences too we could still say that there were in fact two intentional door-knocking events, but that would miss out on an important interpretational difference. The first tells us that John had the intention to perform two door-knocking acts; in the second case, the meaning is that two of the possibly numerous door-knocking events that John took part in were deliberate.

My interpretation of these observations is that we are not merely dealing with a general problem of adverb ordering, or even with any requirement that adverbs in general need to be introduced as modifiers of (potentially nested) V-bars, but rather, that in some cases we have a special construction. It is my impression that the adverb orderings we see in the (42) examples are not merely instances of the left–to–right ordering of elements in a flat structure, but are instead evidence of a special construction allowing further adverbial information to be added at the end of a VP, supported by my feeling (I hope there is more to it than that) that in both cases 'comma intonation' is natural between the two adverbs. (Somewhat in the manner of (39b).)

The 'special construction' I have just suggested might have exactly the same form as the kind of V-bar modification Andrews has in mind; but the difference is that in the Andrews view, all instances of adverbial modification require such a device; in my view, there are sister-ordering possibilities within a VP for the ordinary cases.

7.

I do not find in the behavior of circumstantial adverbs convincing reasons for abandoning a theory in which their appearance in a VP is essentially 'flat'. For such a theory we need valence sets for verbs, reflecting the core elements of the verbs' frames, and we need mechanisms for augmenting valence sets 'in the lexicon' for a large number of regular and perhaps a small number of grammaticized irregular cases, sometimes incorporating circumstantial information as complements.

We need mechanisms for projecting the valence set of a verb into the complement set of a VP, and we need context-sensitive ways of allowing any of a large number of circumstantial adjuncts to be added to sentences. Circumstantial adverbs that directly fit the semantic frame evoked by a verb (the 'obliques') will in general precede those that are frame-external (the 'adjuncts').

And we need, I think, at least one construction which provides a place for an adverb as a left sister of a VP which will have scope over all of the adverbs in that VP, and possibly one construction which does the same at the end of a VP.

Some ordering principles will recognize the difference between complements and adjuncts, and some will relate to features of discourse.

It seems to me, now at least, that the features that Arnold Zwicky (in his contribution to this volume[14]) has outlined for a properly defined construction grammar are compatible with a theory that allows relatively flat structures for adverbs, at least for the circumstantials. [15]

---

[14] [Editors' note: Zwicky; Arnold. 1994. Dealing Out Meaning: Fundamentals of Syntactic Constructions. *BLS* 20: 611–625.]

[15] There is no doubt that the semantics of grammar will need to provide clear logical scope asymmetries for interactions between negation, quantifiers, and circumstantials. I do not have a ready-made proposal for how such matters are to be handled in a monotonic non-derivational theory.

References

Bally, C. 1950. *Linguistique Générale et Linguistique Française*. 3rd ed., Berne: A Franke S.A.

Fillmore, C. J. 1968. The case for case. *Universals in Linguistic Theory*, eds. Emmon Bach and Robert Harms, 1–90. New York: Holt-Rinehart-Winston.

Fillmore, C. J. 1969. Toward a modern theory of case. *Modern Studies in English*, eds. David A. Reibel and Sanford A. Schane, 361–75. Englewood Cliffs: Prentice Hall.

Fillmore, C. J. 1970. The grammar of hitting and breaking. *Readings in English Transformational Grammar*, eds. Roderick A. Jacobs and Peter S. Rosenbaum, 120–133. Waltham, Mass.: Ginn.

Fillmore, C. J. 1970. Subjects, speakers, and roles. *Synthese* 21:251–274.

Fillmore, C. J. 1971. Some problems for case grammar. *Monograph Series on Languages and Linguistics* 22:35–56. Georgetown University.

Fillmore, C. J., and P. Kay. (forthcoming). *Construction Grammar Coursebook*.

Foley, W. A. 1986. *The Papuan Languages of New Guinea*. Cambridge: Cambridge University Press

Greenbaum, S. 1969. *Studies in English Adverbial Usage*. London: Longmans.

Harris, R. A. 1993. *The Linguistic Wars*. Oxford: Oxford University Press.

Harris, Z. 1982. *A Grammar of English on Mathematical Principles*. New York: John Wiley & Sons.

Helbig, Gerhard, and Joachim Buscha. 1980. *Deutsche Grammatik: Ein Handbuch für den Ausländerunterricht*. Leipzig: VEB Verlag Enzyklopädie.

Jacobson, S. 1964. *Adverbial Positions in English*. Stockholm: AB Studentbok

Kay, P., and C. J. Fillmore. (forthcoming). Grammatical Constructions and Linguistic Generalizations: The What's X doing Y? Construction.

Lakoff, G., and J. R. Ross. 1976. Why You Can't *Do So* Into the Sink. *Syntax and Semantics 7. Notes from the Linguistic Underground*, ed. James D. McCawley, 101–112. New York: Academic Press.

Lehrer, A. 1975. Interpreting certain adverbs: Semantics or pragmatics? *Journal of Linguistics* 11: 239–248.

Lyons, J. 1977. *Semantics, vols. I and 2*. Cambridge: Cambridge University Press.

McCawley, J. D. (ed.) 1976. Notes from the Linguistic Underground. *Syntax and Semantics 7*. New York: Academic Press

McCawley, J. D. 1983. The syntax of some English adverbs. *CLS* 19:263–282.

McCawley, J. D. 1991. Remarks on adverbial constituent structure. *Interdisciplinary approaches to language*, eds. Carol Georgopoulos and Roberta Ishihara, 415–433. Dordrecht: Kluwer Academic Publishers.

McConnell-Ginet, S. 1982. Adverbs and logical form. *Language* 58:144–184.

Quirk, R., S. Greenbaum, G. Leech, and J. Svartvik. 1985. *A Comprehensive Grammar of the English Language*. London: Longman.

Shopen, T. (ed.) 1985. *Language Typology and Syntactic Description III: Grammatical Categories and the Lexicon.* Cambridge: Cambridge University Press.

Stockwell, R. P., P. Schachter and B. Partee. 1973. *The Major Syntactic Structures of English.* New York: Holt-Rinehart-Winston.

Talmy, L. 1972. Semantic Structures in English and Atsugewi. Doctoral Dissertation, University of California at Berkeley.

Talmy, L. 1985. Lexicalization patterns: Semantic structure in lexical form. *Language Typology and Syntactic Description III: Grammatical Categories and the Lexicon*, ed. Timothy Shopen, 57–149. Cambridge: Cambridge University Press.

Tesnière, L. 1959. *Eléments de syntaxe structurale.* Paris: Klincksieck.

Thomason, R. H. and R. Stalnaker. 1973. A semantic theory of adverbs. *Linguistic Inquiry* 4:195–220.

12

Mini-Grammars of Some Time-When Expressions in English

2002
CHARLES J. FILLMORE

1. *Introduction*

In this paper I propose construction grammatical analyses of two semantically defined types of adverbial expressions in English, expressions that indicate —sometimes vaguely, sometimes precisely—the time at which or within which some event occurs or some state of affairs obtains. I will use the term (temporal) TARGET to refer to that time. The expressions in questions occur as, or are the semantically significant parts of, adjuncts modifying clauses, and give information about the time coordinates of the eventualities designated by those clauses.

In the first of the constructions I will examine, the TARGET is understood as situated at a particular DISTANCE earlier than or later than some explicit or implicit temporal LANDMARK. It will become clear that this construction is an elaboration of a more abstract pattern that is not limited to expressions about time and that the syntactic patterns it exploits fit large-scale generalizations about English. After that I will examine a construction, or more accurately, a family of constructions, which appear to have structural properties quite limited to the temporal domain; expressions of this second type have to do with locating a temporal TARGET in respect to segmentations of the time flow of the kind provided by diaries and calendars.

The general framework within which the description will be couched is what could be called Construction Grammar Lite, i.e., construction grammar without the technical niceties—in particular, a version that is satisfied with informal representation of the semantics, which ignores the hierarchical structures that hold the grammar together, and which expects the reader to fill in much of the syntactic detail. (See Kay & Fillmore, 1999 for a version with the technical niceties.) I will proceed by developing relevant features of the external properties of the word-types or phrase types we examine, those properties that are relevant to the syntactic and semantic functions they serve in the sentences where they occur, and the most important of the constraints of form and meaning on the constituents that combine to make them up.

The grammar of temporal adverbials in English houses numerous mysteries and complexities. In some cases, special grammatical constructions have to be posited that do not appear elsewhere in the language, while in the cases that can more or less be accommodated by the 'regular' grammatical principles of the language, lexical idiosyncrasies abound. The existence of such irregularities appears to be characteristic of this semantic domain cross-linguistically; the fact that areas of idiomaticity in time expressions exist in the grammars of other languages can be seen by examining the relevant sections of tourist phrase books.

Many temporal idioms show fine semantic distinctions, not obviously motivated by their form. For example, *some day* differs from *one day* in that the former occurs only in irrealis contexts. (See Exx. 1.)

(1)   a.   One day a wonderful person will come into your life.

      b.   One day a wonderful person came into my life.

      c.   Some day a wonderful person will come into your life.

      d.   *Some day a wonderful person came into my life.

This collocation of *some* with *day* is clearly idiomatic: the word does not combine naturally with singular forms of other calendar units; there is no *some week*, *some month*, *some year*. Occurrence of *some* with plural calendar units—*some days*, *some weeks*—gives an iterative meaning, based on the ordinary meaning of *some* with plurals and mass nouns, and the same is true of *sometimes*. But *some time*, like *some day*, also has the irrealis interpretation. (See Exx. 2.)

(2)   a.   I'd like to see you some time.

     b.   I'd like to see you sometimes.

     c.   *I do things like that some time.

     d.   I do things like that sometimes.

There are differences among time expressions in their external distribution. For some reason, *yesterday* and *tomorrow* do not occur in contexts that welcome *recently* and *soon*. McCawley (1983) pointed out that the distributional restrictions of *yesterday* and *tomorrow* match those of prepositional phrases, like *in the morning*, and proposed that therefore *yesterday* and *tomorrow* should be treated as honorary prepositional phrases.[1]

The distributional differences in question are related to the adjunct position differences discussed in Quirk et al. (1985), distinguishing I ('initial') positions, M ('middle') positions and E ('end') positions in a clause.[2] The words *yesterday* and *tomorrow* do not occur in the 'M' positions, but *recently* and *soon* are not so restricted. (See Exx. 3, 4.)

(3)   a.   She was in town recently. (E)

     b.   She was recently in town. (M)

     c.   She was in town yesterday. (E)

     d.   *She was yesterday in town. (M)

     e.   She was in town in October. (E)

     f.   *She was in October in town. (M)

(4)   a.   You'll be married soon. (E)

     b.   You'll soon be married. (M)

     C.   You'll be married tomorrow. (E)

     d.   *You'll tomorrow be married. (M)

And there are baffling irregularities and subregularities in the phrasal constitution of some time expressions, for example those concerning the selection

---

[1] McCawley 1983:280; that there is more to it than that is suggested in Fillmore 1994:167–168.

[2] Quirk et al. (1985: 190–200). We ignore the subtypes described by Quirk et al. and consider only positions 'M' for between the subject and the verb or after an auxiliary, and 'E' for postverbal positions (but not in front of direct objects) in non-prosodically-interrupted VPs.

of the prepositions *in* and *on*. These differences go beyond the simple difference usually described in treatments of the time semantics of English prepositions, such as the generalization about selecting the preposition *on* in the
context of a unit meaning 'day'.[3] Compare the grammaticality judgments in
the following lists, contrasting *in* with *on*. (See Exx. 5, 6.)

(5) a. He was here in the morning.

    b. *He was here in that morning.

    c. *He was here in Christmas morning.

    d. *He was here in Christmas day.

    e. ?He was here in the morning of Christmas day.

    f. He was here in the morning on Christmas day.

(6) a. *He was here on the morning.

    b. He was here on that morning.

    c. He was here on Christmas morning.

    d. He was here on Christmas day.

    e. He was here on the morning of Christmas day.

    f. *He was here on the morning on Christmas day.

We will be examining the make-up of phrases that designate time points or
time periods, as well as the ways these can appear in temporal adjuncts.

2. *Terminological Warm-up*

In order to characterize the object of our investigation, it is necessary to equip
ourselves with some special terminology. The first group of terms concerns
the referential properties of temporal expressions.

Some time phrases are *Deictic*, meaning that the TARGET is identified by
means of implicit or explicit reference to the moment of speaking ('now'). In
the simplest case there is of course the word *now* which directly refers to
'now'. The word *today* refers to the calendar day that contains 'now'; *this
month* is the month containing 'now'; *next year* is the calendar year following
the year that contains 'now'; *yesterday morning* is the first part of the calendar day that precedes the day containing 'now', and so on.

---

[3] The essential phenomena are reviewed in Section 7 below.

Some temporal expressions are *Anaphoric*, meaning that the TARGET is anchored to a temporal reference point recoverable in the ongoing discourse. Thus a phrase like *during the preceding week* places the target within the calendar week that precedes the week containing a temporal landmark implicit or explicit in the discourse context; *afterwards* requires an understanding of a time point already introduced in the discourse and presents the TARGET as later than that.

In some cases the referent of a temporal expression is *Absolute*, in the sense that it identifies a time point or time period within some institutionally standardized time scale. For example, where the institution is the one maintained by the calendar keepers of the western civilized world, we have dates like *July 6, 1941*.

Some time expressions are *Existential*; they are indefinite, not anchored in deictic, anaphoric, or absolute time. Examples are *once upon a time, one day, some day, one fine morning*, and the like.[4]

And lastly, some are *Generic* or *Iterative*, fitting repeated or habitual event types; in some cases the time specification is quite general (7a), as with *sometimes*, and in other cases the generalization is stated with respect to some cyclically recurring temporal unit (7b-d).

(7) a. I see her sometimes.

b. I work nights.

c. I visit Mother on weekends.

d. On cold mornings I don't take a shower.

The next group of terms we need includes temporal units that we know about from clocks and calendars, or from our experience of cyclic changes in the environment.

Measurement units (MUs) designate temporal spans measurable by certain time-keeping means (clocks and celestial regularities), as with the nouns *minute, year*, and *month* in the following examples. (See Exx. 8.)

(8) a. We waited more than ten minutes.

b. The project took two years.

c. It's due two months from today.

---

[4] There are deictic aspects to some of these: *once upon a time* requires past tense narrative context, and, as noted, *some day* is not welcome with past tense reference.

Examples are *millennium, century, decade, pentad, year, month, week, day, hour, minute, centisecond,* and *millisecond.* We will allow the term to cover some units that are not actually measurable but that in many respects follow the grammar of the standard measurement units; at the large end of these vague measurement units we find *eon* and *age* (usually *ages*), at the small end, *moment* and *jiffy.*

Calendar units (CUs) are cyclically recurring temporal units fitted into a scale of absolute time such that when one ends the next one begins. Thus a period that begins on January 1 and ends on the next December 31 is a calendar year; the day that follows December 31 is in a new calendar year. Many of the words that have measurement uses also occur as calendar units. As examples of such double use, note that the phrase *within a year* evokes the measurement sense, *within the year* evokes the calendar unit sense. A notification) announced in October, that a project needs to be completed *within a year* is more generous than one declaring that it needs to be completed *within the year.*

Calendar units generally have well-defined beginnings and ends, but in a few cases there are different traditions, or different standards—or there exists a state of native-speaker uncertainty—for determining what these are. This is true, for example, of *day* and *week*: communities have made different decisions about whether the day begins at midnight, at dawn or at sundown, or whether the week begins on Sunday or on Monday. (Or, as we have all recently learned, whether a new century or millennium begins in 00 or 01.) The collection of calendar units includes *millennium, century,* etc., more or less matching the list of the true measurement units, but calendric uses of *hour* or *minute,* or anything smaller, require very special contexts.

Calendar Subunits (CSUs) are cyclically recurring time points, such as *Halloween, weekend,* or *summer solstice,* or are members of repeatedly cycling ordered series. Some of these cycles begin and end with calendar units (such as the months of the year or the days of the week), while others do not have coterminous boundaries with the larger cycle, such as the seasons of the year (in the northern hemisphere, *winter* extends across the last part of one year and the first part of the next), and the parts of the day (*night,* on one reckoning, stretches across the last part of one day into the first part of the next). If a time unit of type X contains exactly one occurrence of a time unit of type x, then x is a Calendar Subunit (CSU) and X is its corresponding Calendar Unit (CU). Thus, CSUs *January, February,* etc., belong with CU *year*; CSUs *spring, summer, fall* etc., also with CU *year*; CSUs *Monday, Tuesday,* etc., belong with CU *week*; and CSUs *morning, afternoon,* etc., with CU *day.*

3. *The Descriptive Framework: Construction Grammar Lite*

A grammatical construction is a syntactic pattern dedicated to some particular semantic or pragmatic purpose. It consists of a syntactic pattern with associated semantic information and is to be described in terms of information relevant to what the words or phrases that instantiate it can 'do' in the sentences of the language, as well as information about what its constituent parts can be.

In Construction Grammar—a grammar whose main structural units are grammatical constructions—any coherent linguistic entity is to be understood as instantiating one or more grammatical constructions. A sentence or phrase can be accepted as well-formed and given an interpretation if a set of constructions can be found which it is an instance of: thus, slightly simplified, *green apple* can be parsed because *green* is an adjective and *apple* is a noun and we know of a construction in English which juxtaposes an adjective with a noun, in that order, to build a larger phrase and which offers it an interpretation. A sentence or phrase is judged ungrammatical and cannot be parsed if no constructions can be found in the grammar that motivate its form and meaning. A phrase like *the only* cannot be parsed because there is no construction in the language that allows the juxtaposition of a determiner with the word *only* to form a whole phrase. A sentence or phrase is ambiguous if the grammar's constructions allow two or more ways of assembling its parts and giving it an interpretation.

That is the way we talk when 'the grammar' is 'finished': that is, when the grammarian has reason to believe nothing can come up that has not already been prepared for. While engaged in the process of *writing* a grammar, however, the situation is turned around. We need to discover what the combining and interpreting principles of the language are, and this requires looking for relevant properties of an expression and its components, checking its external or distributional properties, and looking for other expressions that share those properties. In particular, this involves discovering higher-level patterns of which the ones we are observing can be seen as instances or elaborations.

In stating the necessary properties of a construction, we use *feature-structures*, systems of *attribute-value matrices*, in which each consists of sets of pairings of attributes with their *values*. In our representation, an attribute and its value will be connected with an equals sign. If some element of a construction has associated with it a formula 'X=A', that will mean that the value needed (or observed) for the attribute 'X' is 'A'. For example, the notation 'Number=Plural' will mean that in the relevant position, the Plural value of the category Number is required. We will also use 'X=[ ]' (the value of 'X' is unspecified) to mean that some value for the variable X is needed (even if it is unexpressed) but is not specified by the given construction; we will use 'X=null' if no expression of a value for the attribute is called for.

Unification indices, written with hatch-marked numbers (e.g., '#7[ ]') stand for values of an attribute which have to be matched, elsewhere in the same construction-description, with another token of the same value if it has the same index. Thus in a NP construction that licenses the juxtaposition of a determiner and a following nominal, the feature specification 'Number=#1[]' will occur three times: in the constituent that accepts the determiner, in the constituent that constitutes the nominal head, and in the highest level of the phrase as a whole. This will guarantee not only that the grammar accepts *this cat* and *those cats*, and does not accept **that cats* or **these cat*, but also that the whole phrase will be given the same number specification for purposes of number-agreement on a predicating verb.[5]

In some cases, the grammar of the language provides a limited set of possible values for an attribute. This is of course true in the case of 'closed class' categories, like tense, number, etc. In other cases, where for example a family name is called for, there is no theoretical limit to the set of possible fillers for that slot (as in the description of the phrases used with military, clerical, governmental, or academic titles).

4. *Vector Construction*

The first construction we will examine supports phrases that identify a temporal TARGET as being at a particular DISTANCE from, and in a particular DIRECTION from, an implicit or explicit temporal LANDMARK. A temporal LANDMARK is a moment or period in time, or an event seen as taking place in a particular time period, with respect to which the location of some other time point is calculated; since we are dealing with time, the DIRECTION attribute permits only two possible values, 'before' or 'after'; and DISTANCE is distance in time.

Since all instances of this construction involve a point of origin (the LANDMARK), a direction, and a magnitude (DISTANCE), we can refer to it with some poetic license as a Vector Construction, the elements of which are symbolized in Figure 1.

---

[5] The pretense that number agreement is this simple is just for the sake of introducing the notation.

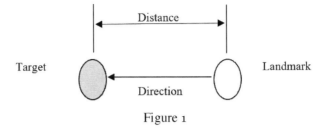

Figure 1

In the diagram, the conventional association with a left-pointing arrow might suggest that the TARGET time is earlier than the LANDMARK — the 'before' case — but the DIRECTION from the LANDMARK can stand for either of the two possibilities. In other domains the arrow pointing away from a LANDMARK will be able to stand for 'above' (space), 'older' (age), and so on.

The semantic information common to all such expressions can be seen in that part of Figure 2 which is below the Name and above the line reading 'Text = [ ]'. The semantic features identified here include the domain in which the pattern holds (in our case, time), plus a LANDMARK, a DIRECTION, and a DISTANCE. The meaning of the whole (in the second line) is represented in a very informal way intending merely to show that the TARGET (T) is described as located at a DISTANCE (Dis), in a particular DIRECTION (Dir) from the LANDMARK (Lm).

This construction as it stands can support an actual expression if there is a lexical entry with a graphic or phonological form filling the Text attribute and which brings with it values for the Domain, Landmark, Direction, and Distance attributes.

The brute force meaning description ('Dis Dir Lm') is instanced by such expressions as *three years before the war*, where *three years* is the DISTANCE, *before* is the DIRECTION, and *the war* is the LANDMARK. The diagram in Figure 2, however, has no internal structure, and so as it stands it is suited only to single lexical items capable of expressing the full configuration of such features by themselves. An appropriate lexical entry must show a linguistic form as a value for the Text attribute and values for each of the semantic attributes unspecified in Figure 2.

```
Name = Location_wrt_Landmark
Meaning = T is Dis Dir Lm
Domain = [ ]
Landmark = [ ]
Direction = [ ]
Distance [ ]

Text = [ ]
```

Figure 2

One such possibility is the adverb *recently* (Figure 3); another is the adverb *soon* (Figure 4). In both cases the LANDMARK is identified as 'prag', the DISTANCE from it is 'slight'. In one case the DIRECTION is 'before', in the other case it is 'after'.

```
Name = Location_wrt_Landmark
Meaning = T is Dis Dir Lm
Domain = [time]
Landmark = [prag]
Direction = [before]
Distance [short]

Text = [recently]
```

Figure 3

```
Name = Location_wrt_Landmark
Meaning = T is Dis Dir Lm
Domain = [time]
Landmark = [prag]
Direction = [after]
Distance [short]

Text = [soon]
```

Figure 4

The attribute *Domain* will in our main examples be specified as time. Once the domain is specified, other properties of constituents that instantiate the construction must be compatible with the idea of time. That is, the LANDMARK has to be a time expression, or reference to an event occurring in time; the DISTANCE has to be measurable in temporal units; and the DIRECTION has to be one of the two temporal directions, 'before' ('earlier than') or 'after' ('later than').

In the two single-word constructions in Figures 3 and 4, the words *recently* and *soon* are described as designating a temporal target at a slight distance from the landmark: 'earlier' in the case of *recently*, 'later' in the case of *soon*. That the landmark is represented with the symbol 'prag' means that the identity of the landmark is 'pragmatically' determined. If the discourse context does not provide a temporal reference point, then it will be interpreted as 'now'. Thus, *recently*, without such contextual support, will be interpreted as a short time before 'now', and *soon* interpreted as a short time after 'now'. (See Exx. 9.)

(9)   a. I recently received some good news. (LANDMARK is 'now'.)

        b. She had recently had a bad experience. (LANDMARK is 'prag'.)

        c. They'll be here soon. (LANDMARK is 'now'.)

        d. He would soon learn what she meant. (LANDMARK is 'prag'.)

In a more complete description we would need to add syntactically interpretable features reflecting the positional possibilities for these two adverbs: they are both capable of occurring in initial, middle and end positions in their clauses. Since almost all of the other constructions dealt with in this paper do not allow the middle positions, we will not bother to introduce formal devices for specifying positional information in our diagrams.

A two-part phrasal expansion of this same configuration of information given in Figure 2 permits the same information to be parceled out between two major syntactic constituents, as in Figure 5. Here the first constituent expresses the DISTANCE, while the second expresses the DIRECTION and the LANDMARK. The internal structure of a phrasal construction can be specified by representing the constituents in separate boxes below the feature structure that identifies the external properties of the phrase as a whole. Constituent structure is thus represented in terms of boxes inside boxes. Unification of the constrained attributes makes it possible to compose the meaning of the whole from the semantic contribution of the parts.

The collection of feature structures at the top of the diagram is identical to what was seen earlier except that the values of the critical features are marked with unification indices.

```
Name = Location_wrt_Landmark
Meaning = T is Dis Dir Lm
Domain = #1[ ]
Landmark = #2[ ]
Direction = #3[ ]
Distance #4[ ]

    ┌─────────────────────┐  ┌──────────────────────────┐
    │ Name = Distance     │  │ Name = Dir. from Landmark │
    │ Domain = #1[ ]      │  │ Domain = #1[ ]            │
    │ Distance = #4[ ]    │  │ Direction = #3[ ]         │
    │                     │  │ Landmark = #2[ ]          │
    │                     │  │                           │
    │ Text = [ ]          │  │ Text = [ ]                │
    └─────────────────────┘  └──────────────────────────┘
```

Figure 5

This time the subordinate constituents separately provide the information needed in the phrase's external properties: the properties that these constituents bring with them must be copies of—or to express it procedurally, must be copied into—the values marked with the same unification indices in the enclosing structure.

Perhaps the simplest phrase that satisfies the structure given in Figure 5 is *long ago*, where the single word *long* indicates the DISTANCE —vaguely— as 'great', and the single word *ago* simultaneously provides 'now' as the LANDMARK and 'before' as the DIRECTION.[6] The structure of the expression *long ago* is given in Figure 6.

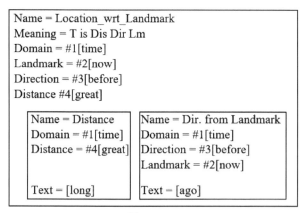

```
Name = Location_wrt_Landmark
Meaning = T is Dis Dir Lm
Domain = #1[time]
Landmark = #2[now]
Direction = #3[before]
Distance #4[great]

    ┌──────────────────────────┐  ┌────────────────────────────┐
    │ Name = Distance          │  │ Name = Dir. from Landmark   │
    │ Domain = #1[time]        │  │ Domain = #1[time]           │
    │ Distance = #4[great]]    │  │ Direction = #3[before]      │
    │                          │  │ Landmark = #2[now]          │
    │                          │  │                             │
    │ Text = [long]            │  │ Text = [ago]                │
    └──────────────────────────┘  └────────────────────────────┘
```

Figure 6

---

[6] The difference between 'now' and 'prag' is that 'now' as a semantic constraint is intended to show a limitation (in nonliterary texts) to actual speech time.

In trying to characterize the construction these phrases instantiate, we need to look for the paradigmatic alternatives—preserving the basic semantic structure of the whole—of each of these constituents. Some of these paradigmatic alternatives can, like *ago*, be single words; others will be phrases. Since *ago* takes 'now' as the LANDMARK and 'before' as the DIRECTION, by making one minimal change we can see that *hence* is a paradigmatic alternative to *ago*. With something like *two years hence* we have a temporal target two years later than 'now': *hence* assigns the temporal deictic center as the LANDMARK and 'after' as the DIRECTION.

In noticing this, we have encountered a lexical idiosyncrasy: it seems not possible to say **long hence*. The time-qualifying word *long* seems to be welcome with the one, not with the other, and this is one of the construction-specific irregularities spoken of earlier. But actually, the occurrence of *long* with *ago* is already an irregularity. As a temporal measurement term, in most contexts *long* is a *negative polarity item*. *I won't stay long* is grammatical, but **I'll stay long* isn't. As the DISTANCE indicator in the temporal Vector Construction, it is not so limited, since we have both *long ago* and *not long ago*.

The example with *hence* was *two years hence*, showing a phrasal expansion of the temporal DISTANCE constituent. In other instances of the same construction we have phrasal components in both positions. For example, in *three weeks after you were born* we see the occasion of your birth as the LANDMARK, forward in time, or 'later', as the DIRECTION, and the DISTANCE is expressed as a quantity (*three*) of units of temporal measurement (*weeks*).

A phrasal version of the DISTANCE constituent can house an expression of Quantity followed by the name of one of the Measurement Units discussed earlier. (See Figure 7.) The fact that there is a feature 'Domain = time' in the MUnits constituent but not in the Quantity constituent reflects the fact that the quantity expressions are not sensitive to features of temporality, but the units needed are indeed units of time measurement. The construction can be satisfied by phrases like *three days, several centuries*, *seven minutes*, and so on. Figure 8 shows the structure of *three days*.

Instantiations of the DISTANCE component of Figure 5 can be plural nouns indicating precise or vague measurement units (*years ago*, *eons ago*), or, following the pattern in Figure 7, quantified expressions with precise measurement units (*three months ago*, *twenty seconds ago*). In addition there can be indefinitely quantified vague temporal measures (*some time ago*, *a short while ago*, *a few moments ago*, etc.).

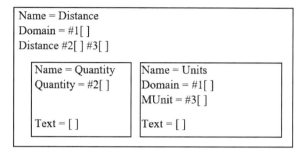

Figure 7

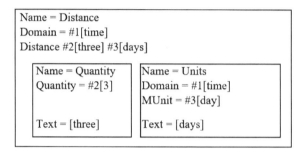

Figure 8

Vague temporal measures at the high end—representing very long periods—do not seem to welcome even informal quantification: *?several eons ago*, *?a number of ages ago* and certainly not **four eons ago*. Other possibilities, not provided for by the Units constituent in Figure 7, include quantified expressions with recurring calendar subunits (*three Fridays ago*, *three summers ago*) or nouns designating event types (*three weddings ago*, *three hangings ago*) or even metonyms of event type (*three husbands ago*, *three beers ago*).

Except for the last three subtypes, the phrases that appear as left sisters of the Vector Construction indicating temporal spans are not limited to their function in the temporal vector construction. They can represent time spans in many other contexts as well: expressions with the preposition *for* can indicate the duration of some activity (10a), those using the preposition *in* can indicate the period before the end of which some eventuality is completed (10b). There are also verbs like *spend*, *waste*, *take*, and *last* that select these phrases for directly associating temporal spans with events (loc–d).

(10) a. We lived in Vienna for three years.

    b. We expect to finish in three months.

    c. They spent four years building the bridge.

    d. She wasted twenty years on that project.

    e. It took three centuries to finish the cathedral.

    f. The war lasted 100 hours.

The second part of the vector construction can also be expanded into a two-part phrase, the first constituent indicating the DIRECTION, and the second indicating the LANDMARK. The structure can be seen in Figure 9.

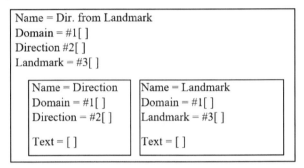

```
┌─────────────────────────────────────────────────────┐
│ Name = Dir. from Landmark                           │
│ Domain = #1[ ]                                      │
│ Direction #2[ ]                                     │
│ Landmark = #3[ ]                                    │
│                                                     │
│  ┌──────────────────────┐ ┌──────────────────────┐ │
│  │ Name = Direction     │ │ Name = Landmark      │ │
│  │ Domain = #1[ ]       │ │ Domain = #1[ ]       │ │
│  │ Direction = #2[ ]    │ │ Landmark = #3[ ]     │ │
│  │                      │ │                      │ │
│  │ Text = [ ]           │ │ Text = [ ]           │ │
│  └──────────────────────┘ └──────────────────────┘ │
└─────────────────────────────────────────────────────┘
```

Figure 9

By selecting the preposition *before* and the LANDMARK name *Christmas*, we can create the phrase *before Christmas*, as shown in Figure 10. (It should be clear that by embedding Figures 8 and 10 into Figure 5 we would get *three days before Christmas*.)

```
┌─────────────────────────────────────────────────────────┐
│ Name = Dir. from Landmark                               │
│ Domain = #1[time]                                       │
│ Direction #2[before]                                    │
│ Landmark = #3[Christmas]                                │
│                                                         │
│  ┌──────────────────────┐ ┌──────────────────────────┐ │
│  │ Name = Direction     │ │ Name = Landmark          │ │
│  │ Domain = #1[time]    │ │ Domain = #1[time]        │ │
│  │ Direction = #2[before]│ │ Landmark = #3[Christmas] │ │
│  │                      │ │                          │ │
│  │ Text = [before]      │ │ Text = [Christmas]       │ │
│  └──────────────────────┘ └──────────────────────────┘ │
└─────────────────────────────────────────────────────────┘
```

Figure 10

With the SMALLCAPS DIRECTION in Figure 9 indicated with the prepositions *before* or *after*, the LANDMARK can be expressed as a time-word, as a NP indicating an event, or as a verbal or clausal expression indicating an event. (See Exx. 11.)

(11) a. before/after today

b. before/after the birth of my first child

c. before/after entering first grade

d. before/after my first child was born

There is another preposition that does not in other contexts convey a temporal direction, but does in this particular construction: *from*. Thus, *two years from today* refers to a period two years in the future from today. This preposition is future-oriented like *hence* but unlike *hence* it can identify a LANDMARK that is close to but not necessarily identified with the moment of speech. *From* in this context appears to be limited to accepting only actual time expressions as its complements. (See Exx. 12.)

(12) a. from today

b. from next Monday

c. from that day

d. *from the birth of my first child

(cf. from the time of the birth of my first child)

e. *from my first child was born

(cf. from the day my first child was born)

It should be noted that we recognize two major constituents to the Vector Construction, not three: we do not segment these expressions into DISTANCE + DIRECTION + LANDMARK. This is because there are single-word variants of the combination DIRECTION + LANDMARK (and there are no single-word variants of the combination DISTANCE + DIRECTION), but also because the organization we have established fits the so-called 'X-bar' generalization about the structure of phrases, where a specifier is in construction with a phrase that has the basic structure of head plus complement. This allows us to use a generally accepted principle of phrase structure for explaining the properties of the construction as a whole. Expressions that do not provide a DISTANCE specification lack the specifier; expressions that lack explicit mention of the complement either have the LANDMARK information incorporated in the head (as with *ago* and *hence*) or have the LANDMARK information interpreted anaphorically. The syntactic category of the whole is determined by the lexical head, and that is *before* and *after* (and *from*) in the case of the phrasal expressions and *ago* and *hence* in the case of the lexical right sisters. If we think of preposition phrases and particles as being functionally identical, in respect to their external distribution, we can say that the right sister in each case is a PP, the left sister is a specifier, and *ago* and *hence* function as intransitive prepositions.

We regard the temporal vector expressions as instances of a more abstract vectorial pattern; there are other scales or coordinate systems in which LANDMARK, DIRECTION and DISTANCE play similar semantic functions. This can be realized in spatial relations, as with these examples in 13,

(13) a. thirty miles east of here

b. 30,000 feet above the stadium

c. two centimeters below your left eye

where something is located in space at a DISTANCE (*thirty miles, 30,000 feet, two centimeters*) from a LANDMARK (*here, the stadium, your left eye*) in a DIRECTION (*east, above, below*).

Past and future are so salient in our experience of time that it would not be particularly useful to be able to refer to one thing separated in time from some other specific thing while expressing no interest in the DIRECTION. In the spatial domain, however, it is possible to speak of the distance between two things without indicating DIRECTION. For example, with *away* and *from* the DIRECTION is unspecified. *Far away* is in many ways analogous to *long ago*, but in the spatial phrase, the LANDMARK is 'prag' and the DIRECTION is unspecified, whereas in the temporal phrase, the LANDMARK is 'now' and the DIRECTION is 'before'. *Many miles from here* does not have DIRECTION specified, though in the time domain the same preposition is directionally oriented, as in *two years from today*.

There are, of course, unlimitedly many domains in which things can be separated from other things within a scale; the possibilities are unrestricted with comparative adjectives. Temporal examples with *earlier* and *later* were not treated in the earlier discussion, since they are included in the more general picture. (See Exx. 14.)

(14) a.   three inches taller than her father

   b.   several years older than her step-mother

   c.   ten degrees warmer than today

   d.   much heavier than you

   e.   20 IQ points smarter than Charlie

   f.   several hours earlier than we expected

In these last cases, the compared adjective provides the DIRECTION (*taller*, *older*, *warmer*), the *than*-phrase introduces the LANDMARK, and the quantity phrase gives the DISTANCE.

The abstract construction inherited by all of these phrase types is governed by the lexical head. Given some instances of polysemy (as what we saw with *from*), we can say that it is the lexical head of the second constituent that determines the semantic domain of the relevant scale (time, space, intelligence, temperature, age, etc.), requiring, thus, that the LANDMARK be a potential landmark within such a scale, and that the measurement phrase (and the corresponding measuring units) be units of the given scale (IQ points for intelligence, meters or miles for space, degrees Fahrenheit or Celsius for temperature, and so on). This of course is why the domain feature must unify in all positions where it is indicated in the formulas. And the lexical head either incorporates information about the LANDMARK (i.e., *ago* and *hence*), or requires that the LANDMARK be indicated in an explicit complement, or allows omission of the complement under anaphoric conditions.

Lexical entries for the items that can appear as PP heads in temporal version of this construction have properties suggested in the following list, using the abbreviations Lm, Dir, and Dis.

(15) a.   AGO:

        Lm is incorporated ('now')

        Dir is incorporated ('before')

        Dis is obligatory

        Special: can occur with specification of 'close-to-now' Lm (as in *three years ago today*)

b. HENCE:

    Lm is incorporated ('now')

    Dir is incorporated ('after')

    Dis is obligatory

    Special: registral limitations (literary?)

c. BEFORE:

    Lm is omissible with 'prag' interpretation

    Dir is 'before'

    Dis is omissible with unspecified interpretation

d. AFTER:

    Lm is omissible with 'prag' interpretation

    Dir is 'after'

    Dis is omissible with unspecified interpretation

    Special: for Lm-omission case, *afterwards* is preferred?

e. FROM:

    Lm is obligatory (with 'close to now' implied)

    Dir is 'after'

    Dis is obligatory

5. *Temporal Location in Calendar Units and Calendar Subunits*

The second topic is a family of temporal expressions that locate the TARGET by way of a simple or complex reference to a calendar unit, like month, year, day, or morning, e.g., *yesterday morning*, *next month*, *last night*, *the preceding week* and the like. These expressions too require an anchoring LANDMARK: the Lm is 'contained in' a calendar unit identified in the semantics of the construction (possibly the one that includes the Target) and is generally going to be either 'now' or 'prag'. In most of the discussion that follows, the LANDMARK will be 'now'; we will concentrate on deictically centered phrases.

Within this class of constructions there are a number of separate subconstructions, with surprising interfering subregularities. Figure 11 gives the semantic structure of the first group of expressions that concern us.

```
Name = Location_in_Calendar_Unit
Meaning = T is in #2[ ] which #3[ ] (a relation)
           the #2[ ] which includes #4[ ]
Domain = time
CU Type =  #2[ ]
Relation = #3[ ]
Landmark = #4[ ]

Text =[ ]
```

Figure 11

For purposes of generalization, the concept Relation stands for a relation between the temporal unit containing the TARGET and that containing the LANDMARK. The simplest case, where the unit with the TARGET *is* the unit with the LANDMARK, *is* expressed indirectly, by the relation 'identical to'. Thus, *today* locates the TARGET within the calendar day that also includes the LANDMARK (and the LANDMARK is 'now'). In *yesterday* and *tomorrow*, then, the Relation is specified as 'precedes' and 'follows', respectively. (See Figures 12–14.)

```
Name = Location_in_Calendar_Unit
Meaning = T is in #2[day] which #3[equals]
           the #2[day] which includes #4[now]
Domain = time
CU Type =  #2[day]
Relation = #3[equals]
Landmark = #4[now]

Text =[today]
```

Figure 12

```
Name = Location_in_Calendar_Unit
Meaning = T is in #2[day] which #3[precedes]
              the #2[day] which includes #4[now]
Domain = time
CU Type =  #2[day]
Relation = #3[precedes]
Landmark = #4[now]

Text =[yesterday]
```

Figure 13

```
Name = Location_in_Calendar_Unit
Meaning = T is in #2[day] which #3[follows]
              the #2[day] which includes #4[now]
Domain = time
CU Type =  #2[day]
Relation = #3[follows]
Landmark = #4[now]

Text =[tomorrow]
```

Figure 14

These deictic day names are lexical instances of deictic period names. The most general pattern is phrasal, using the words *this*, *next*, and *last* followed by calendar units other than those at the level of day. The name invented here for the class of words occurring in first position is LTN (for *last–this–next*). These words have no function but to introduce the three values of the Relation attribute. Figure 15 gives the structure of the LTN+CU construction.

```
Name = Location_in_Calendar_Unit
Meaning = T is in #2[ ] which #3[ ] (a relation)
            the #2[ ] which includes #4[now]
Domain = time
CU Type =  #2[ ]
Relation = #3[ ]
Landmark = #4[now]
```

```
Name = LTN                  Name = Calendar Unit
Domain = time               Domain = time
Relation = #3[ ]            CU Type = #2[ ]


Text =[ ]                    Text = [ ]
```

Figure 15

With both constituents filled in, we have expressions like *this week*, *last month*, *next year*) and so on. The filled-in sample in Figure 16, for *next year*, describes it as referring to the year that follows the year that contains 'now'.

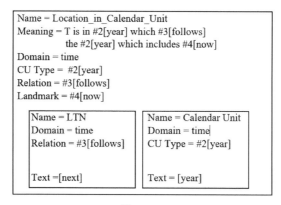

```
Name = Location_in_Calendar_Unit
Meaning = T is in #2[year] which #3[follows]
            the #2[year] which includes #4[now]
Domain = time
CU Type =  #2[year]
Relation = #3[follows]
Landmark = #4[now]
```

```
Name = LTN                  Name = Calendar Unit
Domain = time               Domain = time
Relation = #3[follows]      CU Type = #2[year]


Text =[next]                 Text = [year]
```

Figure 16

The lexical entries that can occur in the LTN construction are just these:

```
Name = LTN
Domain = time
Relation = [precedes]


Text =[last]
```

Figure 17

```
Name = LTN
Domain = time
Relation = [follows]


Text =[next]
```

Figure 18

```
Name = LTN
Domain = time
Relation = [equals]


Text =[this]
```

Figure 19

Figure 20 shows the semantic structure of a new family of expressions, this time locating the Target within a Calendar Subunit of a Calendar Unit that has a particular relation to the calendar unit containing 'now'. This configuration has only one purely lexical realization in English, namely the word *tonight* (Figure 21). *Tonight* is the 'night' part of the day that contains 'now'.

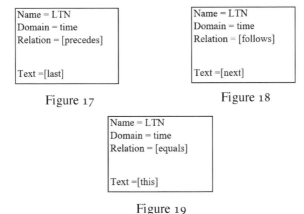

```
Name = Location_in_Calendar_Subunit
Meaning = T is in #5[ ]
            which is a part of the #2[ ]
            which #3[ ] the #2[ ]
            which includes #4[now]
Domain = time
Relation = #3[ ]
CSU-type = #5[ ]
CU-type = #2[ ]
Landmark = #4[now]

Text = [ ]
```

Figure 20

```
Name = Location_in_Calendar_Subunit
Meaning = T is in #5[night]
            which is a part of the #2[day]
            which #3[equals] the #2[day]
            which includes #4[now]
Domain = time
Relation = #3[equals]
CSU-type = #5[night]
CU-type =  #2[day]
Landmark = #4[now]

Text = [tonight]
```

Figure 21

There is a more general phrasal version, again using the 'LTN' vocabulary for showing the relation to the deictic center. The Target is in a CSU that is contained in a CU that holds a particular relation to the CU that contains the LANDMARK, the LANDMARK being 'now'. The LTN+CSU construction is shown in Figure 22; one realization of it is shown in Figure 23. This is the construction that supports *last spring* (the spring of the year that precedes the present year), *next Friday* (the Friday of the week that follows the present week), *last night* (the night of the day that precedes the present day), *this October* (the October of the present year), and so on.

```
Name = Location_in_Calendar_Subunit
Meaning = T is in #5[ ]
            which is a part of the #2[ ]
            which #3[ ] the #2[ ]
            which includes #4[now]
Domain = time
Relation = #3[ ]
CSU-type = #5[ ]
CU-type =  #2[ ]
Landmark = #4[now]

    Name = LTN              Name = Cal_Sub_Unit
    Relation = #3[ ]        CSU-type = #5[ ]
                            CU-type = #2[ ]
    Text = [ ]              Text = [ ]
```

Figure 22

```
Name = Location_in_Calendar_Subunit
Meaning = T is in #5[spring]
            which is a part of the #2[year]
            which #3[precedes] the #2[year]
            which includes #4[now]
Domain = time
Relation = #3[precedes]
CSU-type = #5[spring]
CU-type =  #2[year]
Landmark = #4[now]

    ┌────────────────────────────┬──────────────────────────┐
    │ Name = LTN                 │ Name = Cal_Sub_Unit      │
    │ Relation = #3[precedes]    │ CSU-type = #5[spring]    │
    │                            │ CU-type = #2[year]       │
    │ Text = [last]              │ Text = [spring]          │
    └────────────────────────────┴──────────────────────────┘
```

Figure 23

We saw earlier that the basic LTN+CU structure did not apply to the 'day' level, but the LTN+CSU structure does—at least partly: we can say *this morning*, *this afternoon*, *this evening*, and *last night*. *Tonight*, we have seen, is a special case; and for the rest there is a separate construction. But for all of the others we must turn to a third construction.

The new construction, devoted to identifying parts of days, can be referred to as the DN+DPN (Day Name plus Day Part Name) construction; it is for locating a temporal Target within a day part associated with some particular day. The DN in question is not limited to the deictic day names, but includes weekday names; but it is limited to lexical rather than phrasal day names. This time there is no LANDMARK other than the day name itself—which requires its own pragmatic interpretation. The structure is what we see in Figure 24. Since this applies only to calendar terms at the level of days and parts of days, there is no need to add a specification of the temporal domain.

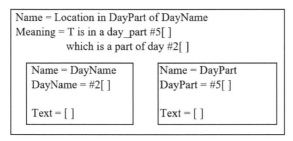

```
Name = Location in DayPart of DayName
Meaning = T is in a day_part #5[ ]
            which is a part of day #2[ ]

    ┌────────────────────────────┬──────────────────────────┐
    │ Name = DayName             │ Name = DayPart           │
    │ DayName = #2[ ]            │ DayPart = #5[ ]          │
    │                            │                          │
    │ Text = [ ]                 │ Text = [ ]               │
    └────────────────────────────┴──────────────────────────┘
```

Figure 24

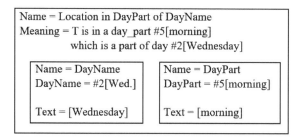

Figure 25

This construction is responsible for phrases like *yesterday afternoon*, *tomorrow morning*, *Wednesday night*, *Friday evening*. Syntactically the construction needs to state that the DN constituent can only be filled with a single lexical item. With phrasal indications of days—not treated in this paper—a different pattern is needed, giving us *the morning of the day before yesterday*, *the evening of August 15th*, *the afternoon of the day the baby was born*, etc.

6. *Pre-Emption*

The numerous possibilities for locating temporal Targets within calendar units and subunits, including lexicalization, have overlapping conditions, and to complete the story we need to see how choices are made in cases where they seem to compete. To make this easier, we can view the patterns from an encoding rather than a structural perspective.

Figure 26 shows three successive calendar units, the one containing 'now' in the center. The most general phrasal pattern for CUs is seen in Figure 26, where the LTN word indicates the calendar unit containing the Target. As we saw, this does not apply—is blocked—when the CU is 'day'; for that the pre-empting pattern of Figure 27 is called for.

last CU	this CU	next CU

Figure 26

yesterday	today	tomorrow

Figure 27

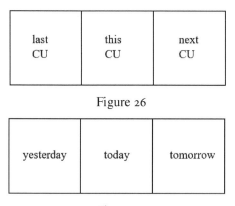

For CSUs the pattern is shown in Figure 28. This time the LTN word is followed by the CSU name, and the meaning is that the CSU in question is a part of the associated CU as identified by the LTN term.

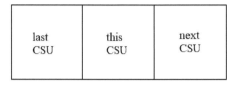

Figure 28

Thus, *this summer* is the summer in the year containing 'now'; *this Wednesday* is the Wednesday in the week containing 'now'; *this morning* is the morning of the day containing 'now'. But where the larger unit is 'day', the pattern is restricted as follows: it only works for the night of the preceding day (*last night*) and the morning, afternoon and evening of the current day (*this morning*, *this afternoon*, *this evening*). For *this night* a lexical form pre-empts: *tonight*. For the other deictic days we depend on the structure in Figure 24, giving the pattern seen in Figure 29.

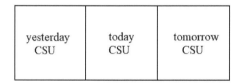

Figure 29

Summarizing, one of the LTN patterns, LTN+CU, shown in Figures 15 and 26, do not cover days; the arrangement in Figure 27 pre-empts. This means that *yesterday*, *today* and *tomorrow* are lexical day names, and should be available for participation in the DN+DPN pattern shown in Figures 24 and 29; but just in the case of four DN+DPN combinations, this is blocked, and the second of the LTN patterns, LTN+CSU takes over. Add to this the pre-emption of *this night* or *today night* by *tonight*, and we see that the question of what pre-empts what is not easy to answer.

The pre-emption we have seen is sometimes rigid and sometimes flexible: it is useful to make a distinction between hard pre-emption and soft pre-emption. With soft pre-emption, the pre-empted form is typically marked for a special registral effect. Thus *this day* and *this night* can exist alongside of *today* and *tonight*, but they have a limited registral quality. But *last day*, *next day*, *today morning*, *today afternoon*, *today evening*, and *today night* are instances of hard pre-emption: they do not occur at all. A suggestion that in the case of soft pre-emption one should rather speak of variation than pre-emption can be rejected from the fact that the pre-empting forms are more neutral in meaning and effect than the pre-empted forms.

7. *The Marking of Temporal Adverbials*

The calendar-unit expressions we have examined so far identify temporal locations, but not all of them can stand by themselves as fully-formed temporal adjuncts. One generalization seems to be that those expressions whose description includes reference to 'now'—these, then, are the purely deictic expressions—occur without any marking. This includes single-word expressions (*today*, *tonight*), LTN-based constructions (*this week, next year, last night*, as well as *this morning, last summer, next Christmas*), and complex expressions containing the deictic day-names (*yesterday afternoon, tomorrow night*). For these expressions, prepositional marking seems to be blocked.

Otherwise, there are certain generalizations concerning the selection of marking prepositions. For example, *at* is chosen with time point expressions (*at noon, at midnight, at dawn*, but *at night*); *in* is chosen for general time periods, like *in December, in the morning, in the summer, in 1941*. But the preposition *on* pre-empts *in* just in the case of day units and day parts that are explicitly connected with particular days, but this pre-emption does not override the zero marking of the deictic names. Thus, we get *on Wednesday, on Wednesday morning, on the next day*, etc. There are numerous puzzles here. When no actual day name is included, but the expression presupposes a context in which the succession of days is relevant, we still get *on*. Thus, *on the next morning*, but oddly also *on that morning, on the morning of the funeral*. Thus we have the strange discrepancies in the contrasts shown in Exx. 16, showing separate effects of *the*, *this* and *that*.

(16) a.   this morning, *on this morning, *in this morning

   b.   *the morning, *on the morning, in the morning

   c.   that morning, on that morning, *in that morning

This morning has no prepositional marking because it is one of the deictic time expressions; *that morning* chooses *on* because the demonstrative marks it as referring to the morning of a specific day; *the morning* (without any modification that would link it to the morning of a specific day) takes the default for time periods, *in*.[7]

Flickinger (1996), dealing with some of these same facts, explores the question of the dependency structure of the DN+DPN phrases. There is some initial reason to believe that in such phrases, the DN is the head. *Yesterday morning*, as with *yesterday* alone, appears without a preposition (as is the case with all instances of *yesterday* or *tomorrow* with *morning, afternoon, evening* or *night*); in American English, *Monday morning*, as with *Monday* alone, can appear either with or without prepositional marking (as is the case with all weekday names with daypart names). The argument would be that since the distributional facts of DN+DPN phrases are the same as the distributional facts of DN, DN must be the head constituent.

Temporal adjectives modifying DN+DPN structures clearly go with the DPN word. Thus, *early* and *late* in Exx. 17 clearly modify the DPN.

(17) a. early tomorrow evening (which is not early tomorrow)

 b. late yesterday morning (which is not late yesterday)

But the argument about the headedness of the DN loses support with phrases in which the DPN is clearly the syntactic head of its phrase, in 'DPN of DN' expressions, such as these taken from the British National Corpus.

(18) a. On the afternoon of Saturday, 27 July

 b. On the evening of the next day

One possible explanation for the occurrence of *on* in these phrases might be that the day part names have some of the features of 'transparent' nouns, in being transparent to selectional relations between prepositions and their complements. The word *part* is like that, being transparent to the relation between the preposition and its complement in *on this part of the shelf* versus *in this part of the room*. (The prepositions *on* and *in* go with *shelf* and *room*, respectively, and are not affected by the intervening *part*.) But it appears that *on* is chosen even when the complement of the day part name is not itself an expression that designates a day unit.

---

[7] It is interesting that the simple knowledge that a daypart belongs to a particular day is not sufficient; the connection has to be linguistically marked.

(19) a. On the night of the full moon

    b. On the morning of our departure

    c. On the morning of Dobson's funeral

    d. On the night of the fatal attack

Not so easy to determine from corpus evidence is whether a specific day unit is always implied: in example 19b–c, is it necessary to believe that our departure or Dobson's funeral took place in the morning, or, in 19d, to know whether the fatal attack took place in the night? If not, then there can be a semantic/pragmatic requirement that there is always an allusion to a particular day which justifies the choice of *on*. My intuitions fail me.

8. *Conclusion*

The phenomena examined in this paper have shown, I believe, connections between fairly subtle semantic facts and fairly subtle kinds of syntactic behavior. It should be noticed that the descriptions themselves have been purely semantic in nature, except for constituent structure. The phrases we end up with in the Vector Construction appear to be prepositional phrases, but that is because the words that show temporal directions are prepositions, and that *ago* and *hence* can be thought of as 'intransitive prepositions' because of their distributional properties. But of course the same abstract structures can be headed by adjectives (in particular comparative adjectives—*smarter, taller, heavier, later,* etc.), but that is because scalar relations are indicated with adjectives.

While the Vector Construction appeared to be at base an instance of an extremely regular syntactic pattern, the calendar-unit expressions were built up out of quite special material and in quite special ways, so much so that the question of the syntactic organization of the phrases could not always be established. For all of this it would seem that description in terms of grammatical constructions, in the sense of Kay and Fillmore, is quite appropriate and can for the most part be successful.

The phenomena of pre-emption, including a difference between hard pre-emption and soft pre-emption, were well illustrated with this material.

References

Fillmore, C. J. 1994. Under the circumstances (place, time, manner, etc.). *BLS* 20:158–72.

Fillmore, C. J. 1998. Deixis and context. *Context in Language Learning & Language Understanding*, eds. K. Malmkjaer and J. Williams, 27–41. Cambridge: Cambridge University Press,

Flickinger, D. 1996. English time expressions in an HPSG grammar. *Studies on the Universality of Constraint-based Phrase Structure Grammars*, ed. T. Gunji, 1–8. Ministry of Education, Science and Culture. Japan.

Kay, P. and Fillmore, C. J. 1999. Grammatical construction and linguistic generalizations: The *What's X doing Y?* construction. *Language* 73.1:1–33.

McCawley, J. D. 1983. The syntax of some English adverbs. *CLS* 19:263–82.

Quirk, R., Greenbaum, S., Leech, G. and Svartvik J. 1985. *A Comprehensive Grammar of the English Language*. London: Longmans.

Part 4

Constructions and Language in Use

13

The Pragmatics of Constructions[1]

1996
CHARLES J. FILLMORE

1.

I have been interested for some time in the kinds of decisions linguists have made in drawing boundaries in and around linguistics, by which I mean both the lines that separate one subfield of linguistics from another, and those that separate linguistics proper from impinging disciplines (Fillmore, 1984). Probably every linguist, while working through some puzzling collection of language phenomena, has had the experience of beginning with the assumption that a given problem will yield to the system of principles that characterize one particular field of linguistics, only to conclude in the end that the explanation really belongs elsewhere. What began looking like a morphology problem turned out to have a phonological solution; what started out as a problem in semantics received a pragmatics solution; or what began as a mystery of syntax proved in the end to be an instance of some semantic generalization. At times, of course, we find that the problem really belongs to cognitive psychology, or ethnography, or logic, rather than to linguistics. The problems that linguists deal with day-to-day don't always have labels on them telling us who owns them.

These surprises are usually not embarrassing, especially in the modern world where integrative results are praised and cross-disciplinary research is encouraged. But in those circles in which disciplinary boundaries are defined

---

[1] A version of this paper was read at the Kobe, Japan, meeting of the International Pragmatics Association in the summer of 1993.

in dogmatic or dictatorial ways, one sometimes feels pressure to be sure in advance that the outcome of an inquiry is going to be of the right sort, in the fear that one might not be seen as really working in one's declared field. It's one thing to face the occasional charge that what we are doing isn't really semantics, or isn't really grammar, or isn't really linguistics, but it's awkward to have our students, and it's dangerous to have our employers, overhear such judgments.[2]

When we read in the Levinson textbook *Pragmatics* the author's lengthy discussion of the problem of defining this field (Levinson 1983: 7–31), we become aware of two boundary problems: the boundary between pragmatics and sociolinguistics at one edge, and the boundary between pragmatics and grammar (including semantics) at the other. We read that the Anglo-Saxon linguistic world has tended to draw a sharp distinction between pragmatics and sociolinguistics, while much of the rest of the world does not, and we learn that a distinction between pragmatics and grammar is something about which some of the colleagues sometimes dispute quite feelingly. It's this latter boundary, that between pragmatics and grammar, that concerns me here. My goal in this paper is to explore some of the ways in which the study of grammar and the study of pragmatics necessarily overlap, and to suggest that in a grammatical theory that sees pragmatic function as one of the natural dimensions of grammatical description, this 'overlap' is not a cause for embarrassment.

On one influential view the main distinction we need to keep in mind is one which separates (a) knowing a language, from (b) putting that knowledge to use in everyday communication. This view yields a subtractive view of pragmatics, according to which it is possible to factor out of the full description of linguistic activities those purely symbolic aspects which concern linguistic knowledge independently of notions of use or purpose. A grammar of a language is defined as a repertory of semantically significant primary elements plus a combinatorial mechanism capable of creating and interpreting more complex elements in the understanding that it is the possession of such a repertory and such mechanisms which makes people legitimate speakers and interpreters of their language. The study of what people do with each other, employing these resources, when they speak is something different: this second area is *pragmatics*.

---

[2] This little preamble does not mean that I have any objection to scholars wishing to be clear about the assumptions they make on the kinds of phenomena they choose to deal with or the kinds of explanations they are willing to countenance. In any scientific field, if we are to make progress, we will need to formulate our findings on a shared foundation of well established and agreed-upon principles. But I have become convinced that, in the case of language in particular, there are so many layers of explanation for what we observe that we are not yet ready to tolerate exclusivist claims on any of its territories.

A relevant comparison is with the tools of a culture, on the one hand, and skills that members employ while using those tools, on the other hand. However, telling the difference between linguistic knowledge and the ability to function competently as a member of the community of people who share that knowledge, is not always easy, especially because knowing a language and knowing how to use a language can both involve *conventionality*. The pragmatic conventions can be said to presuppose the grammatical conventions: Descriptions of the resources of the language, on this view, do not, and should not, contain any reference to pragmatic purposes.

This understanding of the distinction is compatible with the view that many usage practices can themselves be institutionalized or conventionalized—as conventions of use rather than conventions of language. Given such a grammar-external view of language use, we find that the study of pragmatics needs to recognize two kinds of pragmatic inferences, those which involve locally special cultural conventions, and those which involve common sense reasoning. In the latter case, the explanations depend on members being rational and cooperative rather than, say, 'trained.'

My favorite example of a locally special pragmatic pattern is the Japanese letter-writing convention by which the first part of a personal letter is expected to comment on the current season. The force of this convention is demonstrated by the practice of using the word-sentence *zenryaku*, meaning 'first part omitted', when ignoring the convention for reasons of speed or space.

The kind of pragmatics that involves common-sense inferencing can be illustrated by considering the following (invented) conversation.

(1) Q: Waiter, can you bring me an ashtray?

  A: Sir, this is a smoke-free restaurant.

The customer's utterance sounds like a question about the waiter's ability to deliver an ashtray to the customer's table. The waiter's reply is a statement that is not, in the usual information-transmission sense, a proper answer to that question. Our second kind of pragmatics should enable us to explain the nature of this interaction and our ability to interpret it, without appealing to locally specific conventions. Given what is known about the functions of ashtrays, it is rational to assume that the customer's question was an opening move in a sequence of acts that was likely to end in the customer's doing something unpermitted (and loathsome); and the waiter's response can be heard as short-circuiting that process while offering an explanation of why it could not be carried through. The customer did not specifically say that he wished to smoke, and the waiter did not specifically say that the customer was not permitted to smoke.

Let's assume that the reasoning that goes on here is natural, not needing an explanation in terms of specifically linguistic conventions. In agreeing to that what we are not necessarily saying that the same communicative purposes could be served, equally naturally, with translations of these sentences in all languages. There could very well be culturally specific conventions for participating in such indirect communications. Our claim of naturalness amounts to saying that in those communities which lack special conversational conventions for covering such a case, it is easy to assume that nobody has to learn anything special to be able to figure out how the two contributions to this conversation fit together, or to be able to participate competently in similar exchanges.[3]

On the view just caricatured, pragmatics includes both conventions governing the use of language and a number of very general principles that do not need to be covered by locally learned conventions. These conventions and principles are distinct from, and presuppose the autonomy of, the grammar of the language in question.

2.

There is another, nonsubtractive, way of defining pragmatics, based on the idea that linguistic pragmatics concerns itself with any of the ways in which the resources of a language are put to use as tools in human interaction, at any level. On this view, it doesn't matter to what extent our understanding of the ability to perform particular kinds of interactionally relevant linguistic acts requires a prior isolation of what is 'purely linguistic.' It is possible that some elements of the repertory, some pieces of grammatical or lexical competence, so to speak, exist precisely for the sake of achieving pragmatic goals, much in the way that most tools were created for highly specific uses. The need for at least *some* such connections inheres in the concept of *conventional implicatures*. But while the literature that treats conventional implicatures generally limits itself to individual words like *but, therefore, even,* or *yet,*[4]

---

[3] I am quite prepared to believe that I am totally wrong about this example, and that there are special dedicated culturally specific conventions which govern this interaction in ways that I am culturally short-sighted to see. I ask the reader merely to assume that there are some cases in which nothing but rationality and cooperation are involved.

[4] See Grice (1975, 1978, 1981), Kempson (1975), Karttunen and Peters (1979), and Wilson (1975).

the view I am proposing is that pragmatic factors enter fully into the grammar and lexicon of a language.[5]

Linguists mainly concerned with having things come out right when attaching a theory of truth-conditional semantics to a generative grammar need a concept like conventional implicature to cover the problem areas. But linguists who emphasize the interactional aspects of language find much more to worry about. When it comes to acknowledging parts of grammar that are inherently pragmatic, even the purest separatists are likely to accept as belonging to such a domain the special category of words known as *pragmatic particles*. These are the little noises, occurring more abundantly in some languages than others, that have such conventional functions as signaling that the speaker is engaged in insisting or pleading, expressing dominance or hostility, marking the boundaries in and around speech events, signaling the difference between foregrounded and backgrounded information, and so on. Of course it was wrong of me to call them 'little noises,' since that might suggest that they belong in the class of intentional acts that includes hissing and whistling and clearing one's throat. On the contrary, the kinds of words I have in mind typically exhibit canonical phonological structure, they have well-profiled word-class features, they have fixed syntactic distributional properties, and they participate in precise ways in the rules of phrase-formation, etc.; in short, they are necessary to any description of the fundamental workings of the languages in which they occur.

Other sorts of lexico-grammatical entities which have uncontroversial pragmatic aspects can be found in expressive speech, more elaborated in some languages than others; in the wide variety of categories of deixis, including tense; and in the so-called moods, distinguishing statements, questions and commands, from each other, through verbal desinences, syntactic forms, prosodic patterns, etc., again, in ways that can differ broadly from language to language.

My interest here goes beyond these relatively noncontroversial cases. Here my concern is in grammatical constructions which—as I like to say it— are themselves 'dedicated' to particular pragmatic purposes. *Far from regarding this involvement of pragmatics in grammatical descriptions as evidence that the general theory of grammar doesn't work for the whole of a*

---

[5] Since the term *conversational implicature* occurs mainly in the context of the residue of problems that are not solvable by the well-behaved parts of grammar and semantics, suggesting in a trivializing way that it concerns that uninteresting corner of language where the regular theory fails, and since from my point of view the phenomena covered by this term fall out as the properties of particular types of grammatical constructions, the theory of construction grammar has no special need for this concept. (The basic ideas of construction grammar can be found in Fillmore and Kay [ms], Kay and Fillmore [ms].)

language, I wish to regard the pragmatic dimension as an inherent part of every grammatical construction.[6]

3.

For a detailed first illustration of the ways in which pragmatic information needs to be included in the description of a grammatical construction, we can draw from Fillmore, Kay, and O'Connor (1988), a study of the English *let alone* construction. Three varieties of pragmatic information are encoded in sentences built around this construction. First, we find that a *let alone* sentence requires for its interpretation that the hearer be able to call on (or create by accommodation) some background conceptual structure in terms of which certain semantic entailments must operate. Second, the analysis of a *let alone* sentence reveals something about its place in an ongoing discourse. And third, a *let alone* sentence gives information about the quality of its contribution to the ongoing discourse, in terms of Gricean relevance and informativity.

Here are three sentences exemplifying the construction I have in mind:[7]

(2) (a) He wasn't wearing a shirt, let alone a necktie.

     (b) I wouldn't give you fifty cents, let alone fifty dollars.

     (c) I didn't get up in time for lunch, let alone breakfast.

Each of these sentences can be seen as somehow posing two propositions: the first of these (the 'α' proposition) is completed with the material preceding the phrase *let alone*, the second (the 'β' proposition) by substituting what follows *let alone* for the focused constituent in the former part.[8] The semantic segmentation (at this level) of the sentences in (2) are shown in (3).

(3) (a) He wasn't wearing a shirt, let alone a necktie.

          α: he wasn't wearing a shirt

          β: he wasn't wearing a necktie

---

[6] The pragmatic dimension may be empty in some cases. That is, there may be some abstract grammatical constructions—very general typological word-order patterns, for example—which are themselves pragmatically neutral.

[7] We note that each of these sentences is negative; while this is the most common context for *let alone* it is not obligatory. I forego here an attempt to explain the strong preference for negation in such sentences.

[8] It's a *bit* more complicated than this, actually. For details, see Fillmore et al. (1988).

(b)   I wouldn't give you fifty cents, let alone fifty dollars.

α: I wouldn't give you fifty cents

β: I wouldn't give you fifty dollars

(c)   I didn't get up in time for lunch, let alone breakfast.

α: I didn't get up in time for lunch

β: I didn't get up in time for breakfast

The observation of the dual-propositional nature of the interpretation of a *let alone* sentence can be described as semantic, allowing us to think of *let alone* as a kind of coordinating conjunction.[9]

The first pragmatic observation to make is that the interpretation of these sentences depends on the hearer's being able to situate the two propositions in a particular *scalar model*, within which an entailment relation can be said to hold between the α proposition and the β proposition. Given the belief structure represented in such a model, wherever one could expect α to be true, one has even more reason to expect β to be true.

In situations in which normal standards of dress are accepted, one does not wear a necktie without wearing a shirt.[10] Given ordinary notions of selfishness and trust, if I am unwilling to give you fifty cents, I would certainly be unwilling to give you fifty dollars. And given the ordinary sleeping and eating patterns of people in my culture and the way in which we linguistically differentiate the meals that we eat during the day, if I woke up in time for breakfast, I was still awake at lunchtime; if I slept through lunch, I was necessarily asleep at the time when I might have been expected to make breakfast.

In all of the cases just given, knowledge of world and culture gives easy access to the assumed scalar model, so we might briefly think that the culturally 'normal' scalar positioning of the scenes presented as α and β in these sentences is itself what creates the understanding of a scalar entailment. But now consider sentence (4) and its interpretation.

---

[9] The interpretational asymmetry that goes with the left–to–right order of the two conjuncts is not a matter of conversational implicature, as we will see. Unlike what we find with *and,* in other words, it is not defeasible. With respect to its truth-conditional semantic interpretation as a coordinating conjunction (the 'α' and 'β' propositions are jointly asserted), *let alone* would figure in 'conventional implicatures.'

[10] One does indeed occasionally see a bare-chested man wearing a necktie, as a joke, but the judgements we make about such a scene support the scalar implications just suggested. In the world of expected behavior that the interpreter brings to this sentence, a man who is not wearing a shirt is not wearing a necktie.

(4)　I wouldn't hire Jones, let alone Smith.

α: I wouldn't hire Jones

β: I wouldn't hire Smith

This time, independently of whether the hearer knows anything about either Jones or Smith, or the speaker's feelings about them, the scalar interpretation is clear, and it is the construction itself which creates it: the world in which the speaker would not hire Jones is necessarily a world in which, *a fortiori*, the speaker would not hire Smith.

I repeat that the entailment relationship itself is naturally a semantic notion; but the appeal to the hearer to recognize or construct a scalar model on the basis of which such entailments operate is pragmatic.

A second and different kind of pragmatic observation is that a *let alone* sentence cannot easily be the first contribution to a discourse. There is always what Paul Kay has called a *context proposition* in the air, some proposition whose truth or falsity is at issue possibly by way of a question which an interlocutor has just asked, possibly in the form of a suggestion in the speaker's own preceding contribution, which in uttering the *let alone* sentence the speaker is reinforcing or contradicting. The β proposition in the interpretation of a *let alone* sentence is always taken as a direct response to such a context proposition. The utterance of a *let alone* sentence, thus, makes a pragmatic demand on the hearer to remember or reconstruct the context proposition.

The following three conversations are intelligible and interpretable, given such an assumption:

(5)　Q: What tie was Jimmy wearing at his wedding?

A: He wasn't even wearing a shirt, let alone a necktie.

(6)　Q: Could you give me fifty dollars so I can go to the races?

A: I wouldn't give you fifty cents, let alone fifty dollars.

(7)　Q: Did you make a nice breakfast for the kids today?

A: I didn't get up in time for lunch, let alone breakfast.

In all of these cases, the context proposition, derivable directly or by presupposition-detection from the preceding speaker's questions (Jimmy wore a necktie at his wedding, you might be willing to give me fifty dollars, you woke up in time for breakfast), was rejected by the β proposition in the *let alone* sentence.

By contrast, the following conversations, in which we pretend that the α part is responding to the interlocutor's question, are pragmatically ill-formed (bearing the prefix ≈)

(8) Q: What color shirt was Jimmy wearing at the wedding?

     A: ≈He wasn't wearing a shirt, let alone a necktie.

(9) Q: How about giving me fifty cents for a cup of coffee?

     A: ≈I wouldn't give you fifty cents, let alone fifty dollars.

(10) Q: What did you have for lunch today?

     A: ≈I didn't get up in time for lunch, let alone breakfast.

The requirement of a context proposition also means that a *let alone* sentence cannot easily begin an interaction. Nobody could make sense of the following first-contribution without working pretty hard to create a context—and that context would have to be one which determined in each case a very precise context proposition:

(11) Have you heard about Harry? He hasn't been married once, let alone twice.

(12) Guess what! You didn't get accepted at Harvard, let alone Yale.

Given all of these observations, what we see is that the β proposition is the relevant response to the context proposition, satisfying a Gricean Relevance (Relation) condition while the α proposition is a more informative statement, satisfying a Gricean Informativeness (Quantity) condition. In saying that the α proposition 'satisfies' an informativeness condition I mean that the speaker regards this news as giving that level of information that the hearer needs for making further inferences. These sentences have the function of responding to a context with a contextually relevant answer while at the same time indicating that an answer that is merely responsive to the context propositions falls short of being fully informative. The α proposition is more informative because, given the scalar model, α entails β. Our third pragmatic observation, then, relates the two parts of the *let alone* structures to judgments about informativeness and relevance. The sentence yields two components, semantically, and assigns to each of them information about the quality of its contribution to the conversation.

The *let alone* construction seemed to us to be a particularly clear case of a pragmatics-rich grammatical construction: It is not possible to derive any of the pragmatic observations in a straightforward way from the kinds of structures conjoined around *let alone*, nor simply from the propositions that can be built from unpacking these conjoined structures, let alone from any independent meanings that a clever semanticist could assign to the individual words *let* and *alone*.

4.

In the case of the *let alone* construction we have what seems to me to be a 'clear case.' For a number of other candidate constructions, however, the question of the degree to which its pragmatic interpretation involves special conventions, as opposed to general pragmatic principles, could be controversial. Let us briefly explore the pragmatic properties of *negative questions* in English. It would appear that negative yes–no questions express what grammarians have sometimes described as a *negative bias* or *negative orientation*. What does that mean, and how can we find out if it's true? Couldn't we derive the special force of a negative question from what we know about negation and questioning? If so, how would such a derivation proceed? If not, can we speak of a complex construction that is characterized by the combined syntactic-form features of negation and interrogation which has a pragmatic force which is not computable from the meaning of each of its structural components? The whole is greater than the sum of the parts, but how could we go about characterizing the function from those parts to that whole?

It is difficult to pin down the exact effect that negative yes–no questions have, but it has always been clear that there is a sharp affective-cum-interactional difference between, say, two sentences like (13a) and (13b):

(13) (a)   Did you like the dessert I made for you?

    (b)   Didn't you like the dessert I made for you?

Question (13b) clearly suggests that the speaker is expecting to be disappointed by the answer. On being asked the question in (13b), someone who liked the dessert (or wished to communicate that idea) would have to say something to mitigate the questioner's suspicions, since a simple 'Yes, I did' answer would not do. Better would be something like, 'Of course I did, it was wonderful.' And even such an expression of exuberance would probably be most naturally followed with an explanation for not eating more of it. In Quirk, Greenbaum, Leech, and Svartvik (1985:806–809), we read:

Negative questions are always conducive. Negative orientation is found in questions which contain a negative form of one kind or another: Don't you believe me? Have they never invited you home? Aren't you joining us this evening? Has nobody called? Hasn't he told you what to do?

Negative orientation is complicated by an element of surprise or disbelief. The implication is that the speaker had originally hoped for a positive response but new evidence now suggests that the response will be negative. Thus, Hasn't he told you what to do? means 'Surely he has told you what to do, hasn't he? I would have thought that he had told you.' Here there is a combining of a positive and a negative attitude, which one may distinguish as the OLD EXPECTATION (positive) and NEW EXPECTATION (negative). Because the old expectation tends to be identified with the speaker's hopes or wishes, negatively orientated questions often express disappointment or annoyance: Can't you drive straight? ['I'd have thought you'd be able to, but apparently you can't.'] Aren't you ashamed of yourself? ['You ought to be, but it appears that you are not.']

Quirk et al. also recognize that some negative questions are 'biased toward positive orientation.' It is hard to state precisely what that means, but one can recognize what they had in mind from their examples:

If a negative question has assertive items, it is biased towards positive orientation. Didn't someone call last night? Didn't he recognize you too? Hasn't the boat left already?

With some adjustments necessary for the last examples, it would appear that a grammatical construction that combines negation and interrogation invites certain special interpretation principles, roughly paraphrasable by saying that the speaker would like to hear a positive answer but the context appears to offer some reason to expect a negative answer. Let us consider the possibility that what we have here is best seen as a complex grammatical construction which is a composite of two other constructions, namely that of the yes-no inverted question and that of sentence negation, and that while this construction inherits some of the semantics of each of the other two, it has a package of interpretation principles that are, by separate convention, associated with the whole. Would it be upsetting to such a proposal if we found that not all negative questions have such interpretations? The answer, of course, is no. On the contrary, we would be relieved if we found that to be true. Then we could say that there is a negative question construction, which has the pragmatic functions just mentioned, and it coexists in the grammar with the two constructions that give us negative sentences and yes-no questions. Every such sentence could also be formed by combining the two constructions independently, and when that happens we do not get the special pragmatics.

This would be particularly satisfying if every negative question could be given both a compositional and a special interpretation.

But suppose that we do not find such differences? Suppose it's simply not possible to separate the special pragmatics we have been talking about from any negative yes–no question. That could mean that within the theory of grammatical constructions we have to devise some theory of blocking, or pre-emption, of the sort often discussed in morphology (see Aronoff 1976, Scalise 1984), guaranteeing that a given assembly of constructions cannot be formed, much in the way that certain structurings of morphemes, for an otherwise completely general and productive process, are ruled out.

The alternative is that we simply have to recognize that the special interpretation of negative yes–no questions is derivable from what can be independently known about negation and interrogation. There may be pragmatic dimensions to interrogation and negation, but the pragmatic force of composites of the two is compositional.

An approach to achieving compositionality for negative questions might be suggested based on Talmy Givón's theory of negation, in which he proposes a difference between negation in natural languages and negation in logic, in that a *sentence* with negation, independently of whether it's a statement or a question, 'presupposes' (in some sense) that the corresponding nonnegative speech act is a part of the discourse context (see Givón 1979:103–105; 1984:321–351; 1989:156). The task then, is to derive the special interpretation of negative questions compositionally, making it unnecessary to posit a special construction for negative questions.

An interesting consequence of accepting Givón's version of negation is that we would then have to say that there exists in English a very special, somewhat artificial negative construction with 'neutral pragmatics' and understood as requiring the sentence that contains it to be false just in case the corresponding sentence without it is true, and vice versa. The phrase 'neutral pragmatics' is in quotes because, from one point of view, this particular negative construction is highly specialized pragmatically. Its prototypical use is in providing natural-language pronunciations of certain of the logical propositions that we find in the exercises in logic textbooks. (What could be more context-bound than that?) This turns the 'subtractive' view of pragmatics on its head. Now, instead of saying that grammatical negation has the semantics of logical negation and that the pragmatics of negation involves considerations of the occasions when people decide to express propositions negatively, we would instead have to say that the semantics of logical negation, in those rare contexts in which it figures in natural language discourse, is associated with its grammatical form in a very special way.[11]

However suggestive this may be, I don't know of any way of accomplishing this rescue of compositionality for negative questions, since I don't know how to derive the interpretations that have been described for negative questions from the generalizations proposed by Givón. But before we give up on the idea that negative questions can be an argument for pragmatically functioning grammatical constructions, let's consider a new case, that of *requests* being grammatically expressed as negative questions. In English such requests sound quite rude, because of the biases we have just been discussing. Consider the reactions you might have to the questions in (14) and (15):

(14) Won't you give me some (any) more tea?

(15) Can't I have some (any) more tea?

Negative questions of these sorts, used as requests in English, would ordinarily be heard as including a complaint about the waiter's or host's inattentiveness or stinginess. It appears that whatever explanation we might come up with for English negative questions in general would cover the special feelings associated with negative questions, used as requests. There is scant reason for claiming special constructional status for the negative-question-requests in English. But not so for Japanese. In this language, by contrast, requests taking the form of negative questions—as in (16) and (17)—are quite standard.

(16) *Otya o moo sukosi kure.mas.en ka?*

[tea OBJ more a-little give.pol.not QUES]

(17) *Otya o moo sukosi itadak.e.mas.en ka?*

[tea OBJ more a-little receive.can.pol.not QUES]

These questions ask literally 'Won't you give me some more tea?' and 'Can't I receive some more tea?' but they are heard as polite—more polite, I am told, than the corresponding affirmative questions.[12]

---

[11] A similar reversal can be seen in Knud Lambrecht's treatment of the representation of subjects in colloquial French. Lambrecht proposes a number of syntactic devices for avoiding SVO structures in spoken French, and then isolates the special conditions under which lexical subjects are possible (Lambrecht 1987, 1988).

[12] Negative questions based on an alternative way of forming the negative would convey the rudeness of the English question, as I have learned from Professor Tetsuya Kunihiro (p.c.). Thus,

What are we to make of this? Is this a case of constructional pragmatics or regular pragmatics? Can we find a functional difference in negation itself between Japanese and English? Or could there be slightly different politeness rules distinguishing the two cultures such that the ordinary semantics of the constructions simply operates differently against a background of different politeness conventions? Maybe, for example, the polite character of these sentences in Japanese comes from the idea that by linguistically taking notice of the possibility of the host's unwillingness or inability to provide the tea we are acknowledging the imposition we are making and are revealing that we will have considerable reason to be grateful if our assumption is wrong.

As I said, I don't know what the final solution in these cases is going to be. But in any case, we are dealing with pragmatic questions. The possibility just suggested for examples (14)–(17) is that there are general compositional principles operating in each language, but that, most clearly in the case of requests, these principles interact with different rules of politeness. Another possibility is that in each language negative questions require special interpretations, but these happen to be strongly *motivated* (not *explained*) by facts about culture and politeness. To which we may add the possibility (preferred by me) that in Japanese, a special constructional status is given to negative questions used as requests, questions about the addressee's giving favors, or the speaker's possibility of receiving favors.

5.

I've looked at two cases in which something pragmatic is going on, one for which a constructional account cannot be avoided (the *let alone* construction), and one for which it is quite difficult to find out just what is going on (the putative negative question constructions). I will now look at another set of phenomena that I suspect belong to the latter type.

In a recently completed Berkeley doctoral dissertation, Seiko Fujii has come up with some insightful things to say about the differences between various types of English and Japanese conditional sentences (Fujii 1993). One pair of patterns that Fujii considers is the English *even if* construction and the Japanese *te mo* construction. The two are worth comparing, since each is the closest translation of the other, yet the assumption that they 'mean' the same thing is wrong, and language learners frequently make mistakes. These are the so-called concessive conditionals. Briefly the difference between the constructions in the two languages seems to be something like this. They communicate the idea that within a particular universe of possibilities identified

---

Otya o moo sukosi itadakenai no desu ka? would be heard as 'Is it the case that I cannot have more tea?' and would be rude.

by the *protasis*, or *antecedent* clause, the speech act performed via the *apodosis*, or *consequent* clause, is universally and unconditionally valid. The Japanese and English versions differ, however, in how they identify that universe of possibilities. In particular, for English the interpreter must call on a scalar model and scalar entailment (familiar from our discussion of the *let alone* construction), but Japanese has a more general means of identifying the universe of situations in which the proposition in the antecedent clause is universally true.

Consider sentence (18)

(18) Even if you paid me a million dollars, I wouldn't marry Louise.

This sentence suggests that the speaker can imagine a range of possible inducements that the addressee might come up with to get the speaker to marry Louise, and within that range, a payment of a million dollars is the extreme case. In speaking of this as 'the extreme case' I am not exposing my belief that 1,000,000 is the largest possible number; rather, I am claiming that the construction itself suggests that in the world of possibilities envisioned by the speaker, on this occasion, one million dollars stands for a big enough amount to express the speaker's unconditional refusal to marry the person known as Louise.[13]

In Japanese, the protasis of the corresponding sentences also gives information interpreted as exhausting the possibilities in a given universe, but this is not necessarily done by scalar entailment.

The Japanese expressions can exhaust the possibilities with a universal quantifier, morphologically an interrogative word coexisting with the particle *mo*. (The quasi-translations in parentheses pretend an equivalence between *-te mo* and *even if*.)

(19) *Dare ni kiite mo, wakaranai.*
No matter who you ask, you won't know.
(even if you ask anyone at all you won't find out)

The possibilities can be exhausted by pairing an affirmative and a negative condition.

---

[13] A person who follows (18) up with something like 'Of course, should you happen to come up with five million, I might be willing to reconsider,' from this point of view, should be heard as somehow 'switching frames' rather than simply choosing a higher figure within the originally imagined range.

(20) *Ame ga hutte mo huranakute mo ikimasu.*

   We'll go whether it rains or not.

   (even if it rains, even if it doesn't rain, we'll go)

The possibilities can also be shown by listing representative possibilities and allowing the interpreter to imagine other cases.

(21) *Niwa no kusa o totte ite mo, airon o kakete ite mo, ohuro ni haitte ite mo, anate no koto bakari kangaeru n desu.*

   Whether I'm weeding the garden, or ironing clothes, or taking a bath, I think only of you.

   (even if I'm weeding the garden, even if I'm ironing ...)

In these last cases, English would have to call on expressions with *whether* or *no matter*. In a recent sumo tournament in San Jose, California, a member of the troupe spoke in English to television interviewers explaining the various rituals associated with the sport, and contributed the information that 'Even if we win or lose, we always bow to our opponent.' In ordinary English, of course, it would not make sense to say 'even if we win or lose.' Given the meaning of bowing in general English-speaking cultures, it would only make sense[14] to say 'Even if we win, we bow to our opponent'.

Lastly, the protasis can merely set up a situation in which the event identified in the apodosis could relevantly take place.

(22) *Tanaka-san ni attemo, watasi no koto o iwanaide kudasai.*

   Don't mention me if you happen to meet Tunica.

   (even if you meet Mr. Tunica, don't speak about me)

Once again, the question we have to ask is, are we dealing with constructional pragmatics, conventional pragmatics, or regular pragmatics. Seiko Fujii has argued that while the various properties of the construction in each of the two languages is *motivated* by its constituents, it still needs to be described in constructionist terms. The 'motivation' has a lot to do with the word *even* in the English sentences (see Kay 1990), and with the word *mo* in the Japanese case. The 'pragmatic' part of it is that the interpreter is called on to create or recognize the relevant universe of situations within which the generalization stands as unconditional.

---

[14] In western culture the gesture of bowing is seen as symbolic of submission or subservience, so the occasion of bowing when victorious would be the unexpected extreme case.

6.

We began with the *let alone* construction, for which a constructional account is unavoidable. We continued with two kinds of constructions for which some pragmatic effect could be assigned to certain simple constructions, but it was difficult to determine whether the combination required a separately conventionalized description. In the first of these latter cases we worried, across English and Japanese, about the combination of yes–no questions and ordinary sentence negation; in the second situation we worried about the combination of *even* and *if* in English, and about *te* and *mo* in Japanese: These combinations yielded interpretations that were motivated by the constituent morphemes, but on the question of the interpretation of the whole, the jury remains puzzled.

In this section I give brief mention to several constructions which, though not as richly pragmatic as the English *let alone* construction, nevertheless show evidence of being grammatical patterns dedicated to specific pragmatic purposes.

6.1

The first of these is the family of presentational *there*–constructions treated in Lakoff (1986: 462–581). Sentences of this type are introduced by *here* or *there*, with subject–verb inversion in the case of full NP subjects, in which the main verb is limited to *be, come, go, sit, stand*, and *lie*, with precise constraints on permitted augmentation in the form of secondary predicates, or what Lakoff calls 'final phrases.' Examples are seen in (23):

(23) (a)   Here comes Harry (, all out of breath)

    (b)   Here I am (, ready to start working)

    (c)   There he stood (, with his hat in his hand)

For an important class of these sentences, present–tense uses have a deictic presentational function, as in example (24); past–tense uses have a narrative function, reflecting the point of view, with an implicit gaze direction assumed in the narrative, as in (25).

(24) Watch out everybody, here they come!

(25) … and there she stood.

Lakoff's discussion of this class of sentences shows them to reflect a complex motivated network of constraints and interpretations the details of which cannot possibly be seen as 'falling out from' ordinary principles of generative grammar and compositional semantics.

6.2

There are numerous clearly idiomatic constructions which have special pragmatics. One such example has been discussed by Bolinger (1977: 152–182) under the name 'Pseudo–imperative conditional.' Examples are:

(26) Show the slightest interest in what he's talking about and he won't let you go.

(27) Criticize him even a little bit and he bursts into tears.

These are disguised conditional sentences in which the first part looks like an imperative clause (except that real imperative clauses do not on their own create negative polarity contexts) and it is oddly conjoined with *and* to the consequent clause. This is not merely a variety of conditional sentence, however, since these sentences have a special interpretation: they are heard, as Bolinger points out (1977:162), as comments, often enough as complaints, about the nature of things, the foibles of life.

6.3

Another is the even more clearly idiomatic construction with the key word *time*, as in the sentences in (28), including (28c) which includes the special pragmatics of negative questions.

(28) (a)   It's time you brushed your teeth.

    (b)   It's high time you thought about getting married.

    (c)   Isn't it about time we started heading for home?

The special grammatical property of these constructions is the past tense on the embedded clause. Perhaps the most common use of such a construction is in suggesting action. It can also be used in the past tense, in a point–of–view narrative, but in such cases the past–tense form in the embedded sentence is not subject to back–shifting. That is, we do not find, in a narrative (I believe), something like (29):

(29) I was getting impatient. *It was time something had happened.

6.4

Another idiomatic construction with special pragmatics is what Knud Lambrecht (1986) has called the Incredulity construction. It is exemplified by

(30) (a) Harry, get married?

  (b) What? Me worry?

With these sentences the speaker is expressing surprise at someone's suggestion that a proposition that could be expressed as NP[nominative] VP[finite] might be true, with the form NP[accusative] VP[uninflected]. Not every sentence has a corresponding incredulity version, since the initial position is topical, and certain subjects cannot be topics.

(31) (a) *It rain?

  (b) *There be a problem?

  (c) *My foot being pulled?

6.5

One construction is the negative *why* question with head–verb *do*. With this construction one of the keys is the type of verb that accompanies *do*. Compare the following sentences:

(32) (a) Why don't you know your SSN?

  (b) Why aren't you the leader?

  (c) Why don't you try anything new?

(33) (a) Why don't you learn your SSN?

  (b) Why don't you be the leader?

  (c) Why don't you try something new?

I would like to claim that in these examples, the sentences in (32) are ordinary negative why questions, while those in (33) are instances of a special construction. The ordinary negative why questions lend themselves to a particular paraphrase pattern, suggested by the examples in (34):

(34) (a)   You don't know your SSN. Why not?

(b)   You aren't the leader. Why not?

(c)   You don't try anything new. Why not?

The sentences in (33), which exemplify what I consider a separate construction, do not accept such a paraphrase, as shown in (34).

(35) (a)   You don't learn your SSN. Why not?

(b)   You don't be the leader. Why not?

(c)   You don't try something new. Why not?

The difference in the sentences of (32) and (33) is the difference between states and acts, and since our construction is always interpreted as expressing what someone ought to *do,* verbs capable of expressing acts are more appropriate. In the (b) sentences, we know that except for certain imperative contexts, the verb *be* does not welcome *do*-support. The occurrence of *be* with *do* in (33b) is compatible with the idea that the addressee is being encouraged to take the leadership, to perform an act, and hence the context is directive. For the (c) sentences, the existence of negative polarity in (32c) corresponds to the presupposition that the negative sentence (concerning which an explanation is being sought) is true; the positive polarity form of (33c) is compatible with the notion that the sentence is a call to action.

7.

This chapter has discussed the need for incorporating pragmatic interpretation principles into the description of certain grammatical constructions, and hence has served as an argument in favor of a model of language which does not begin with the assumption that questions of language use and linguistic interaction can only be seriously studied if we first establish a pragmatics-free account of grammar.

Three distinguishable notions of pragmatics emerge from these considerations. First, there is the pragmatics which builds on reasoning about why such–and–such a message was presented on such–and–such a situation. (Mom asks Junior what time it is to make Junior realize that it's time to go to bed.) Second, there is the pragmatics which is based on conventions about what sorts of ideas people can express in given contexts. (One doesn't inquire into a stranger's age as a matter of small talk.) Third, is the pragmatics that belongs in the description of the language's grammatical structures.

The construction grammar principle according to which pragmatic interpretation features are intimate parts of grammatical description does not relieve the analyst of the need to distinguish what is 'compositional' and what is 'idiomatic.' For a structurally complex structure, we need to ask whether its interpretation can be analyzed as a compositional product of its constituent parts, or whether it is an instance of a complex structure with its own status as a separately functioning grammatical construction. The construction grammarian, fortunately, has reason to be pleased however things come out. If a complex structure can be seen as derivable from its component parts, then one can be satisfied that the grammatical structures one already has are sufficient to deal with the newly examined data. On the other hand, if it seems clear that there are special properties attending the whole of a complex construction, one is pleased to be working within a model in which such results are not an embarrassment.

References

Aronoff, M. 1976. *Word formation in generative grammar.* Cambridge, MA: MIT Press.

Bolinger, D. 1977. *Meaning and form.* London: Longman.

Cole, P. (Ed.).1978. *Syntax and semantics 9: Pragmatics.* New York: Academic.

Cole, P. (Ed.). 1981. *Radical pragmatics.* New York: Academic.

Cole, P., & Morgan, J. (Eds.). 1975. *Syntax and semantics 3: Speech acts.* New York: Academic.

Fillmore, C. J. 1986. Varieties of conditional sentences, ESCOL III (Eastern States Conference on Linguistics), 163–182.

Fillmore, C. J., & Kay, P. *Construction Grammar Coursebook.* Unpublished manuscript.

Fillmore, C. J., Kay, P., & O'Connor, M. C. 1988. Regularity and idiomaticity in grammatical constructions: The case of *let alone. Language,* 64: 501–538.

Givón, T. 1979. *On understanding grammar.* New York: Academic.

Givón, T. 1984. *Syntax: A functional-typological introduction, Volume I.* Amsterdam: Benjamins.

Givón, T. 1989. *Mind, code and context: Essays in pragmatics.* Hillsdale, NJ: Lawrence Erlbaum Associates.

Grice, H. P. 1975. Logic and conversation. *Syntax and semantics 3: Speech acts,* eds. P. Cole & J. Morgan, 41–58. New York: Academic.

Grice, H. P. 1978. Further notes on logic and conversation. *Syntax and semantics 9: Pragmatics,* ed. P. Cole, 113–128. New York: Academic.

Grice, H. P. 1981. Presuppositions and conversational implicature. *Radical pragmatics*, ed. P. Cole, 183–198. New York: Academic.

Haiman, J., & Thompson, S. (Eds.). 1988. Clause combining in grammar and discourse. Amsterdam: Benjamins.

Karttunen, L. & Peters, S. 1979. Conventional implicature in Montague Grammar. *Syntax and semantics·11: Presuppositions*, eds. C. K. Oh, D. A. Dinneen, 1–56. New York: Aacademic.

Kay, P. 1990. Even. *Linguistics and Philosophy*, 13: 59–111.

Kay, P., & Fillmore, C. J. *What's X doing Y?* Unpublished manuscript.

Kempson, R. 1975. *Presuppositions and the delimitation of semantics*. Cambridge, England: Cambridge University Press.

Lakoff, G. 1986. *Women, fire and dangerous things: What categories reveal about the mind*. Chicago: University of Chicago Press.

Lambrecht, K. 1986. *Topic, focus and the grammar of spoken French*. Unpublished doctoral dissertation, University of California at Berkeley.

Lambrecht, K. 1987. On the status of SVO sentences in French discourse. *Coherence and grounding in discourse*, ed. R. Tomlin, 217–262. Amsterdam: Benjamins.

Lambrecht, K. 1988. Presentational cleft constructions in spoken French. *Clause combining in grammar and discourse*, eds. J. Haiman & S. Thomson. Amsterdam: Benjamins.

Levinson, S. C. 1983. *Pragmatics*. Cambridge, England: Cambridge University Press.

Oh, C-K., & Dinneen, D. A. (Eds.). 1979. *Syntax and semantics·11: Presuppositions*. New York: Academic.

Quirk, R., Greenbaum, S., Leech, G., & Svartvik, J. 1985. *A comprehensive grammar of the English language*. London: Longman.

Scalise, S. 1984. *Generative Morphology*. Dordrecht: Foris.

Tomlin, R. (Ed.). 1987. *Coherence and grounding in discourse*. Amsterdam: Benjamins.

Wilson, D. 1975. *Presuppositions and non-truth-conditional semantics*. New York: Academic.

14

'Corpus Linguistics' or 'Computer-aided Armchair Linguistics'

1992
CHARLES J. FILLMORE

Armchair linguistics does not have a good name in some linguistics circles. A caricature of the armchair linguist is something like this. He sits in a deep soft comfortable armchair, with his eyes closed and his hands clasped behind his head. Once in a while he opens his eyes, sits up abruptly shouting, 'Wow, what a neat fact!', grabs his pencil, and writes something down. Then he paces around for a few hours in the excitement of having come still closer to knowing what language is really like. (There isn't anybody exactly like this, but there are some approximations.)

Corpus linguistics does not have a good name in some linguistics circles. A caricature of the corpus linguist is something like this. He has all of the primary facts that he needs, in the form of a corpus of approximately one zillion running words, and he sees his job as that of deriving secondary facts from his primary facts. At the moment he is busy determining the relative frequencies of the eleven parts of speech as the first word of a sentence versus as the second word of a sentence. (There isn't anybody exactly like this, but there are some approximations.)

These two don't speak to each other very often, but when they do, the corpus linguist says to the armchair linguist, 'Why should I think that what you tell me is true?', and the armchair linguist says to the corpus linguist, 'Why should I think that what you tell me is interesting?'

This paper is a report of an armchair linguist who refuses to give up his old ways but who finds profit in being a consumer of some of the resources that corpus linguists have created.

I have two main observations to make. The first is that I don't think there can be any corpora, however large, that contain information about all of the areas of English lexicon and grammar that I want to explore; all that I have seen are inadequate. The second observation is that every corpus that I've had a chance to examine, however small, has taught me facts that I couldn't imagine finding out about in any other way. My conclusion is that the two kinds of linguists need each other. Or better, that the two kinds of linguists, wherever possible, should exist in the same body.

During the early decades of my career as a linguist, I thought of myself as fortunate for having escaped corpus linguistics. Of course, I wouldn't have used the term corpus linguistics in describing my good fortune: maybe I would have called it statistical linguistics.

The situation was this. When I showed up as a beginning graduate student at the University of Michigan's linguistics program, a long time ago, the first person I considered as a possible dissertation director was the kind of professor I myself would like to be able to be, namely, someone with a well-articulated research agenda who asked each of the students who came under his wing to take on a predetermined assignment within that agenda.

If I wanted him to be my mentor, I was to carry out the following assignment.

First, I was to make extensive tape recordings—actually, at the time, it may have been wire recordings—of natural conversations in English and Japanese. After doing that, I was to choose and justify a set of empirical criteria for phonemic analysis that could be applied to each of these languages.

(Those were the days when, realizing that a single language could be given more than one phonemic analysis, people worried—correctly—that phonemic descriptions of different languages couldn't be considered comparable unless one applied, equally to each of the languages being compared, precisely the same set of decision-making criteria.)

Armed with a carefully justified phonemic analysis, for each language, I was then to prepare phonemic transcriptions of all of the conversations that I had recorded.

That was the first part—maybe a year, maybe a year and a half. The next and more important part of the job was to take from each transcript cumulatively larger samples—say, the first 200 phoneme tokens, the first 400 phoneme tokens, the first 600 phoneme tokens, etc., and with each of these growing samples, to plot out the relative frequencies of the phonemes. I was to continue doing this until I had determined, for each of these languages, the mean length of discourse samples, in terms of stretches of phoneme tokens, at which the relative frequencies of the phonemes stabilized.

If the results, using this measure, turned out to be significantly different for English and Japanese, and if I could argue that such a difference could be related to, say, phonotactic characteristics of the two languages, then the results of the research could be seen as contributing, to phonological scholarship, some practical guidelines on how large a corpus of spoken language needs to be for it to be considered an adequate reservoir of the phonological phenomena of the language.

I rejected the assignment. But now, having recalled it for the sake of the opening paragraphs of this talk, I find that it doesn't sound quite as bad to me today as it did thirty-some years ago. There have been times when I've regretted the missed opportunity, since I now know that in the process of moving carefully through a text, of any sort, I would undoubtedly have learned a great deal about both of these languages. I must admit, of course, that I can imagine languages for which the relative frequencies of their phonemes would stabilize long before all of their interesting phonological properties had checked in. The fact is, I couldn't really imagine myself becoming interested in such a project; nor could I imagine what I would be able to say in the section of the dissertation that was supposed to bear the title, 'The Significance of the Present Research'.

The year was 1957. I soon came to be subjected to other intellectual currents within linguistics; and, in fact, before long I was, without the encouragement of my Michigan teachers, converted to a way of doing linguistics which not only did not depend on the careful examination of corpora but whose practitioners often actively ridiculed such efforts.

There were two sorts of activities in those days that would have fit the category corpus linguistics: the first was the study of corpora that field linguists had gathered for poorly documented languages, with both descriptive–linguistic and ethnographic interests in mind; and the second was the study of the statistical properties of languages for which there was no scarcity of data. I was a good disciple, and I learned the correct things to say to linguists who pushed either of these kinds of studies on me. To the first I learned to say that the knowledge linguists need, in order to come up with an account of a language that met the requirements of a generative grammar, could not be derived from a corpus, however large. For that we need to appeal to the kind of intuitive knowledge of their language possessed only by native speakers, the people who know not only what one can say in the language, but also what one cannot say. And as long as we've got that, we don't need anything else.

To the second group of linguists I learned to quote the philosopher Michael Polanyi, author of *Personal Knowledge* (1958), who had said that if natural scientists felt it necessary to portion out their time and attention to phenomena on the basis of their abundance and distribution in the universe, almost all of the scientific community would have to devote itself exclusively to the study of interstellar dust. And I admired, and later shamelessly

imitated, Morris Halle's performance in a debate with policy makers in for-
eign language education who sought funding for corpus building so that it
could become possible to design programs in which one could teach a language's words and structures in the order of their frequency of occurrence in
natural texts. Halle said that if driver education were handled according to
such principles, nobody would be taught how to put an automobile into re-
verse gear, since the distance an automobile covers while moving backwards
is a hardly-noticeable fraction of the distance it covers when moving forward.

Later on I sometimes found myself arguing with people who were defending the superiority of corpus studies against those who kept pointing out
that there were many important features of English that simply were not to be
found in the corpora that were then available. I would hear my opponents say
that this is a pointless objection: all it means is that we need a larger corpus.
But the answer to that was easy: that the ability to judge that some corpus is
not large enough to be representative of the phenomena of the language, is an
ability based on the recognition that certain things which the linguist, as a
native speaker, intuitively knows about the language are not exhibited in the
corpus. In the end, there is simply no way to avoid reliance on intuitive
knowledge.

The most convincing part of the case for using a corpus was that it makes
it possible for linguists to get the facts right. Authenticity was the key word.
There was a lot of evidence that linguistic intuition, so–called, isn't always
reliable, but what one finds in a corpus more or less has to be taken as authentic.

On the question of the authenticity of one's data, I have in recent years
been given reason to believe that my own position in linguistics is a confused
one. A few years ago, my (I think) friend William Labov went around the
world giving a lecture in which something that I had written was offered as a
paradigm example of what he called 'woolly minded introspectionism'. In
attempting to demonstrate certain kinds of fit between linguistic form and
aspects of language use, I had suggested that a particular utterance form could
not be used over the telephone. My example involved the colloquial ges-
ture-requiring demonstrative *yea*, as in *It was about yea big*. For this sentence, the addressee has to be watching the speaker (Fillmore 1972). Labov,
master observer of language as he is, soon after reading my claim, heard
somebody use just that expression over the telephone. I am convinced that
the person Labov heard would have corrected himself instantly if he had realized what he had just said, but nevertheless I stand accused and convicted
as a woolly minded introspectionist. In a recent meeting with some Soviet
linguists I was informed that my work was admired in their group because I
always concerned myself with real language as opposed to made–up language; but shortly before that, at a conference of non-generative linguists,

after I had presented the results of some corpus-based research I'd been doing with Japanese, two different members of the audience spoke to me saying almost the same thing, something about how eye-opening it must have been for somebody like me to look at real data!

My own interest in corpora has so far been exclusively in respect to their ability to supply information about lexical or structural features of a language which the usual kinds of accidental sampling and armchair introspection could easily allow us to miss. The kind of work I have in mind proceeds like this. We extract, from a large corpus, passages exhibiting particular phenomena. We do manual processing of these examples: we record observations about them in some sort of structural database; we sort the examples by various criteria, we stare at the groups of examples we have collected, we speculate on relations among the phenomena that we observe, we consult the database in respect to our speculations, and so on. The basic rule is that we make ourselves responsible for saying something about each example that we find. This is similar in a number of ways to traditional lexicographic methods, working off of a collection of citation slips accumulated by the lexicographer or by members of the dictionary's reading program team. The difference is that—before COBUILD[1] at least—the citation slips the lexicographers examined were largely limited to examples that somebody happened to notice; the corpus work I am talking about here requires a principle of total accountability.

I have worked with on-line corpora on several projects, all of them fairly recently. One involves English conditional sentences, in which I am using mainly brochures from the U.S. Department of Agriculture;[2] another involves Japanese clause connectives, for which the corpus is a series of textbooks on science used in Japanese middle schools.[3]

But today I want to discuss two research efforts aimed at the lexical description of two English words, *risk* and *home*.

The *risk* work,[4] which was carried out in collaboration with Beryl T. Atkins, lexicographical adviser at the Oxford University Press, began with a

---

[1] COBUILD: Collins Birmingham University International Language Database; also a metonymic name for the *Collins COBUILD English Language Dictionary*, 1987 (Editor-in-Chief: John Sinclair).

[2] This is part of the DCI (Data Collection Initiative) corpus of the Association for Computational Linguistics; segments of the corpus were provided to the University of California at Berkeley through the courtesy of Mark Liberman of the University of Pennsylvania. (I am grateful to the Institute of Cognitive Studies for providing an electronic home for our campus's growing collection of linguistic corpora as well as facilities for accessing and processing them.)

[3] The corpus was provided by the Japanese Telecommunications firm NTT, in connection with an NTT-sponsored research project which I am directing.

[4] Two studies based on this work are soon to appear: Fillmore & Atkins forthcoming a, b. The summary presented here repeats material found in those articles.

comparison of the *risk* entries—for both the noun and the verb—in ten monolingual English dictionaries, both British and American, and noticing certain discrepancies among them. We decided to find out what a large corpus could show us about the behavior of this word.

In the case of the verb, we can notice that there are three different kinds of direct objects. To see the differences, consider a setting in which we are talking about the advisability of your climbing up a particular cliff. I might tell you that as far as I'm concerned, I wouldn't risk the climb. To give a little content to my worries, I warn you that since the cliff is steep and slippery, *You would risk a fall*. To convince you that the matter is serious, I might warn you that *You would be risking your life*. The *climb* names what you might do that could put you in danger. The *fall* is what might happen to you. And *your life* is what you might lose.

The *Collins Cobuild English Language Dictionary* listed all three uses, as did *Longman Dictionary of Contemporary English*, but all the others had only two of them, not always the same two.

Mrs. Atkins had the *risk* KWIC concordances from the Birmingham corpus, but it soon became obvious that to be able to sort the examples according to the senses they exhibited, we needed sentence-long contexts. From IBM Hawthorne we received all of the sentences containing the word *risk* from a corpus they had acquired from the American Publishing House for the Blind, representing a 25,000,000 word collection of edited written American English. The number of *risk* sentences was 1743.

Since I have been working on a method of semantic description which emphasizes the background conceptual structures for describing word meanings,[5] the first thing I wanted to do was to characterize situations involving risk.

All situations for which the word *risk* is appropriate are situations in which there is a probability, greater than zero and less than one, that something bad will happen to someone or something. In talking about such a situation we need to be able to identify the individual who is likely to suffer if things go wrong—call that person the Protagonist in a risk scenario—and we need to be able to speak of the bad things that might happen to this individual—let's call that Harm. All risk situations involve the probability that from the point of view of some protagonist something bad will happen.

The Harm could take the form of damage to or loss of something that the Protagonist cares about. We can refer to that as a Valued Possession of the Protagonist, meaning something that the Protagonist cares about which is endangered in the risk scenario.

---

[5] A discussion of this approach can be found in Fillmore 1985.

The probability that something bad will befall a Valued Possession of a Protagonist might, or might not, be the result of some act performed by the Protagonist. We refer to such an act as the Deed. The Protagonist's Deed might be performed in order to achieve some goal. We refer to the goal the Protagonist had in performing the Deed as, simply, the Goal.

We speak of the structure of notions lying behind a linguistic category as making up a 'frame', and of its elements as 'frame elements'. Since some of the frame elements were seen as present in all situations involving risk, and others only in some, we found it necessary to define three slightly different variants, or subframes, of the risk frame. The differences among them can be suggested by the following diagrams, adapted from a notation used in mathematical decision theory, in which branches in a directed graph represent alternative futures, and the nodes are either circles, representing chance, or squares, representing choices.[6]

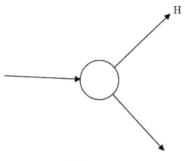

H

Figure 1

In Figure 1, we see a situation in which there is the possibility that some harm will occur, but not necessarily as the result of someone's action:

If you stay here you risk getting shot.

---

[6] For a representative work on decision theory, which uses the notation, see Raiffa 1970.

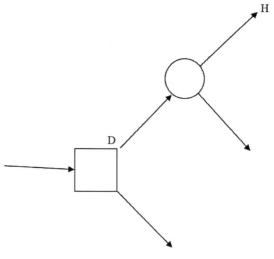

Figure 2

In Figure 2, we see a situation in which the Protagonist's Deed puts the Protagonist on a path for which there is the possibility of harm:

I had no idea when I stepped into that bar that I was risking my life.

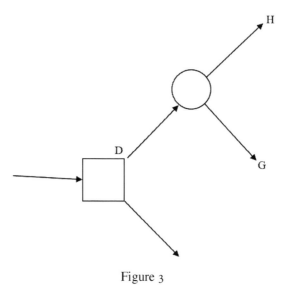

Figure 3

In Figure 3, the dotted circle—not a standard part of decision theoretic notation—is intended to represent the deliberateness of the Protagonist's decision to perform the Deed. The idea is that the Protagonist chose the path because it is a way of reaching the Goal, while knowing that same path might lead to Harm:

> I know I might lose everything, but what the hell, I'm going to risk this week's wages on my favorite horse.

Armed with this set of distinctions we went through all of the verb examples in the corpus and each frame element that got expressed in it. The following is an example of the kind of description this work yields (Figure 4):

When		
you talk like that	Deed	Subclause
you	Protagonist	Subject
risk		
losing your job	Harm	Gerund

Figure 4. 'When you talk like that you risk losing your job'

All of the examples of risk were transitive. We found NP objects of the verb representing Deed, Harm, or Valued Possession.

> Most of us decided to risk *the venture*. <D>
>
> You would risk *death* doing what she did. <H>
>
> Now he was prepared to risk *his good name*. <VP>

In the case of the Harm and Deed frame elements, we also found gerundial objects. In the Deed case the gerund was always a verbal gerund; in the Harm case there were also instances of clausal gerunds.

> He risked *committing grave mistakes*. <H>
>
> He had to risk *Pop getting mad at him*. <H>
>
> She risked *going to the pool alone*. <D>

Almost all of the sentences in the corpus could be accounted for, in the sense that we could fit all of their complements and adjuncts into our view of the risk scenario, but there were a few hold-outs, sentences containing syntactic units whose interpretations didn't directly or simply fit into the risk frame. It was the corpus that forced us to deal with these examples, because I am very sure we would not have thought of them on our own. I am referring to adjunct prepositional phrases with *in*, *on* and *to*. Examples:

> Roosevelt risked fifty thousand dollars *in* Dakota ranch lands.
>
> You risked a month's earnings *on* that stupid horse!
>
> The captain risked his ship *to* torpedo attack.

Risking money *in* something is interpreted as investing, and we note that the preposition *in* is appropriate for investing. Risking money *on* something is seen as gambling, and we note that the preposition *on* is appropriate for gambling. The example here involving risking something *to* something is interpreted as exposing, and we note that the preposition *to* is appropriate for exposing.

What we see operating here is a kind of metonymy. Investing, gambling and exposing all contain the notion of risk, so that *risk*, given the appropriate syntactic support, can be used to stand for each of them. Perhaps the ability of *risk* to participate in this metonymy is to be accounted for by the fact that this verb does not characterize any type of action on its own. It is the type of verb described by Yuri Apresjan as 'evaluative' (personal communication): it reveals the evaluated consequences of an action, but it has no other content. Most of the dictionaries we examined did not identify the three object types, and none of them contained any information, except in the examples they included, dealing with the gerundial complements. And of course none of the dictionaries had any way of relating the various individual senses to a single underlying semantic frame.

Turning briefly to *risk* as a noun, we note that the most frequent uses were as direct object of either the verb *run* or the verb *take*. *Running risks* and *taking risks* have meanings very similar to that of the simple verb *risk*, but they provide the possibility of expressing the evaluation only: since these phrases have no obligatory complement, it is not necessary to include mention of anything specific about the situation, whereas with the verb it is necessary to say something about either the Deed, the Valued Possession, or the Harm. These phrasal expressions welcome *of* + Gerund complements expressing either Deed:

> I took the risk of asking my boss for a raise.

or Harm:

> I took the risk of losing my job.

and they also accept a *that*-clause complement expressing Harm:

> Aren't you running the risk that your daughter will never speak to you again?

None of the dictionaries we surveyed told us anything useful about the difference between running and taking risks. Our conclusion was this: that when you speak of *running a risk* you have in mind the situation represented by Figure 1, but when you speak of *taking a risk* you have in mind a situation represented by one of the other two diagrams. Since Figure 1 is included in Figures 2 and 3, there are numerous situations in which either *run a risk* or *take a risk* could be used. In order to test the difference, you need to find a critical sentence which fits one of the diagrams but not the others. Such sentences can be imagined:

> The newborn babies in that hospital run the risk of hypothermia.

or

> A car parked here runs the risk of getting dented.

In neither of these cases can the version with *take* be used.

We are convinced that our analysis is correct, and that the existence of sentences with *run–risk* which do not allow substitution with *take–risk* supports our understanding of the contrast. However, we found no examples of that type in the actual corpus. And of course, even if we had found such sentences, we would still have to recognize that we cannot find corpus evidence that paraphrasability with *take* is impossible.

The work with *risk* convinced me of the value of a corpus, because, as I said, the simple requirement that we check all of the examples forced us to recognize things that we very probably wouldn't have noticed otherwise. But we could not depend on the corpus alone, since an important judgment that we wanted to be able to make did not receive support from the corpus.

The analysis of the data that we already have has not been completed, but it does in fact seem clear that we need more examples. There are mysteries with the count vs. noncount distinction with this word (*a risk* or *many risks*, vs. *much risk*). We are working with the hypothesis that the noncount form is compatible with *run* but not *take*:

> You won't be running much risk if you follow my instructions.

versus

> You won't be taking a big risk if you do that.

but not

> You won't be taking much risk.

There are also some mysteries having to do with the contexts in which verbs with the different types of complements can occur. It seems that *risk* when accompanied by the Deed complement occurs very often in negative modal form (*I would never risk swimming here* etc.), but we need more examples to see whether this tendency is a real part of the data. In short, I find myself in the end simultaneously convinced (i) that many decisions we have to make about the description of this word cannot be supported by direct corpus evidence, and (ii) that there are decisions that we will be able to make only if we get additional data, from a much larger corpus.

In connection with the next study, I should explain that I have been interested for a long time in words whose grammatical and semantic properties struck me as being completely unique; and *home* is one such word. So when, quite recently, I got my hands on the WSJ section of the DCI corpus (the text of the 1989 *Wall Street Journal*, approximately 8 or 9 million running words), the first thing I did with it was to extract from it all of the sentences containing the word *home*.

Colleagues with access to other corpora who heard about my interest, and who probably worried about the representativeness of my corpus, sent me great quantities of further examples, these taken from the *Grolier's American Academic Encyclopedia* and from online newspapers in and around Oxford.

Each of these sources, from written English, produced many hundreds of examples. I work in a third-world university, so except for the London–Lund Corpus, which we bought in better days, we have only corpora that we could get for free. I have access to only relatively small corpora of spoken-language data. I don't think that I will find big surprises when I take a careful look at the conversational data that I have, though there will undoubtedly be big differences in respect to relative frequencies of the usages I've found.

The word *home* has a number of distinguishable uses. Its central use is as a relational noun, seen in phrases like *my home, our home*, etc. where it can refer to any place where a person lives, with the resident or residents of the home indicated in a possessive modifier. It is in this central use that the phrase *my home* is to be interpreted as the place where I live, rather than, say, a home which I own.

For interpreting many of the uses of the word we need to appeal to a kind of prototype understanding of this particular cultural unit. A semantic prototype for *home* would probably run something like this:

- a home is a place where people live
- the people who live in the home are members of an intact family
- the home is comfortable and familiar
- each member of the family has unquestioned use of at least some of the objects and facilities in the home
- one lives in the home throughout one's childhood and early youth
- there are many reasons to go away from the home temporarily (shopping, play, travel, education, work, military service, etc.) but after these temporary absences, the natural and expected thing is to return home
- when one reaches the age appropriate for seeking one's fortune, one leaves home and, sooner or later, founds or becomes a part of a new home

A number of lexical and phrasal expressions containing the word *home* appeal to various aspects of such a prototype. A *homeless person* is someone who has no fixed place to go to after the day's wanderings. *Being homesick* is feeling bad when separated from the familiar and comfortable setting of home and from the people in it. If we remark about somebody that *she left home at age fifteen*, we recognize that this was out of the ordinary. We speak of children of divorced parents as coming from *broken homes*. If I say that I want you, as a guest in my house, *to feel at home*, I am inviting you to treat the objects in my home as objects you can use and enjoy, to relax in the way you would relax in your own home, etc. (We never actually mean just that, of course, but the phrase is intended to give that impression.)

The meaning of *home* that fits the prototype is very closely tied to the notion of family, and in this way *home* differs from *house*. The following contrast shows this distinction quite clearly. If I say that during the first ten years of my life I lived in five different houses, you will assume that my family moved a lot; but if I say that I lived in five different homes, you will assume that I was an orphan and that I lived with five different families, or that I lived in various institutional settings.

In addition to what I spoke of as the central sense of *home*, there are other relational noun usages with meanings that depart in a number of ways from the prototype. With slightly different meanings, two of the other usages can be reflected by their occurrence with the prepositions *to* and *of*; and a third, carrying a considerably different meaning, takes the preposition *for*.

> The Barbican Centre provides a permanent home to both the London Symphony Orchestra and the Royal Shakespeare Company.
>
> The African continent was the home of one of the world's oldest civilizations, that of ancient Egypt.
>
> He spent his final years in a home for the aged.

In addition to the necessarily relational uses, *home* also occurs as a plain noun. In this function, not requiring any mention of actual or intended residents, the word is used as a kind of up-market name for *house*. For the noun in this sense, a modifying possessive construction has to identify a relationship other than residence, for example, that of the home's creator. This usage is said to be an American development, and it is noticeable mainly in the speech of real estate professionals. We see it in sentences like

> Our construction company specializes in luxury homes.
>
> Our homes were built with the busy executive in mind.

The focus of my interest in this word has concerned its use without an article, especially when functioning as a locative or directional adverb. Examples of adverbial *home* and its typical contexts are the following:

> Let's go home
>
> when did you leave home
>
> I just want to stay home
>
> the school principal sent the kids home early today
>
> let's get out there and welcome the troops home
>
> would anybody like to take the leftovers home
>
> I usually work at home
>
> I keep expecting letters from home
>
> I wonder what the folks back home are doing

The adverbial use descends from early dative and accusative case forms, which froze into particular colligations before determiners became popular. The word has both locative and directional adverbial functions, at least in American English. It occurs with the prepositions *at* and *from*, but not *to* when it is a complement of a verb. (That is, we can say *go home* but not *go to home*. However, in structures in which *to* is independently required, the combination of *to* + *home* is possible: *from work to home*, *close to home*, etc.)

The adverb behaves—most clearly in the case of its occurrence with transitive verbs—like a verbal particle. That is, as with other particles like *off*, *away*, etc., we find alternations between Object + Particle and Particle + Object orders.

Would anybody like to take home the leftovers?

Would anybody like to take the leftovers home?

There are numerous reasons for my interest in adverbial uses of *home*. One is that they present a problem in cohesion semantics: in the case of the noun *home*, the 'resident' is identified by a possessive determiner, but in the adverbial use we have to figure out who lives in the house from the context. This fact is indirectly revealed in definitions of the word *home* through the use of the word *one*—and one of my interests in lexicographic traditions is the conventions for using the word *one* in defining phrases.

In the *Concise Oxford Dictionary* (1990) we find *home* defined as 'the place where one lives'; in the *Chambers Twentieth Century Dictionary* (1983) it is 'the residence of one's family'; in the *Collins English Dictionary* (1986), 'the place or a place where one lives'; in *Webster's Third New International Dictionary* (1986), 'one's principal place of residence'; in the *Random House Dictionary* (1987), 'the place in which one's domestic affections are centered'; and so on. This definitional pattern distinguishes *home* from *house*, where the definers never use the word *one*, but are more likely to speak of something like 'a structure in which people live' or 'a building used as a home'.

Because of the connection between the adverbial uses and the central sense of the noun, we can think of the prepositionless noun as meaning 'the place where one lives', the locative adverb as 'at the place where one lives', and the directional adverb as 'to the place where one lives'.

The felt appropriateness of the word *one* in these definitions reveals an anaphoric element in the meaning of the word. One part of the process of giving a semantic interpretation to expressions containing the adverb *home*, then, is that of establishing the cohesive link between this hidden anaphoric element and some other part of the text which can provide its antecedent.

When I go home it's to my home; when the factory boss sends the workers home, it's to their homes, etc. One of my interests was in figuring out whether there are any strict principles determining what controls or binds the hidden anaphor in *home* and whether what we know about the anaphoric properties of *one* allows us to use it in formulating the definitions of adverbial *home* in a way which predicts which cohesive links are possible and which are not.

A second interesting fact about adverbial *home* is its participation in multiple contrast sets. One of the discussions of *home* in Quirk et al. (1985) points out the quasi-antonymy relation the word has with *abroad* and *out*:

> We were *abroad* during the last few summers, but this year we're staying at *home*.

> I've gone *out* the last few nights, but tonight I'm staying at *home*.

One question I'd like to ask is whether we are dealing with clearly distinguishable contrast sets here. The adjective *short* has very similar meanings in the contrast set in which it is opposed to *long* and in the one in which it is opposed to *tall*, but it is quite clear that it has separate if related senses precisely because of its participation in these two antonymy relations. What can we say about *home* in this respect?

A third point of interest relates to certain differences between American English and British English. The usage notes in some dictionaries tell us that in British English *be home* is used only to refer to a situation in which someone has freshly arrived from elsewhere. I wanted to see if there are any traces of this distinction in the American English examples.

A fourth reason for being interested in *home* relates to my interest in deixis. Twenty years ago, as a part of a series of lectures on deixis, I read a paper in which I presented what I then believed to be a true account of the English verbs *come* and *go* (see Fillmore 1975). The connection with deixis is that in describing *come*, one has to say something about the presupposed location of one or both of the speech-act participants at the destination of the journey. Independently of that deictic feature, I claimed in my paper that a temporal adverb associated with a *come* expression identified the arrival time, whereas a temporal adverb adjoined to a *go* expression identified the departure time. To see what I mean, imagine Max at a late night party and people talking about his return home after the party. The sentence

> Max went home at midnight.

would be interpreted as telling us what time Max left the party, but

Max came home at three in the morning.

said by somebody in his home, would inform us of the time at which he arrived at the house. The generalization I proposed is that a time-phrase with *go* indicates the departure time, a time-phrase with *come* indicates the arrival time.

I believed, then, that the interpretation differences I reported had to be described as a difference in the semantic structures of *go* and *come*. If anybody had asked me about it, I surely would have said that the fact that I used the word *home* in my examples to indicate the destination of the journey was purely accidental. Anything else would have done just as well, I would have said.

Once in a while, in the intervening years, I worried about the fact that a sentence like

He went to the dentist's at two o'clock

Doesn't really mean the same thing as

He left for the dentist's at two o'clock

as my generalization would have predicted, but I tended to think that there must be some special problem with such sentences. I now believe, as you have guessed, that the difference has a lot to do with the word *home*.

There was still another reason for my interest in *home*. I have a general cross-linguistic interest in the concept of the 'home base' as a feature in lexical semantic systems.

A home base feature is present in the semantic systems of many languages, and sometimes the home base category interacts with or contrasts with the other deictic categories in the verbs of motion. I know of several such systems in the native languages of the Americas, but the phenomenon might well be much more widespread than that.

In Japanese the idea of going home, coming home, returning home, getting home, etc., is expressed using the verb *kaeru*, which is usually translated as 'return'. And the idea of sending somebody home, bringing or taking somebody home, is expressed with the causative form of *kaeru*, namely *kaeraseru*. These verbs usually occur in construction with some secondary verb indicating the difference between coming and going, or that between sending and accompanying.

I have always thought that the Japanese verb *kaeru* really means what the English verb *return* means, but that it is simply conventionally used in the context of talking about going home. This seems reasonable, since every journey to one's home is an instance of returning. I now think, however, that it really means 'to go home' and that its use in some contexts with more temporary starting places is a separate development. The difference can be seen in talking to Japanese or foreigners about going back to Japan. If I want to ask a Japanese person when he's going back to Japan, I can use the word *kaeru*, because he is going home. But if I am talking to a foreigner who may have visited Japan many times to ask him if he is ever planning to return to Japan, I cannot use the verb *kaeru*. I have to say something that means 'go again'. Japan is not that person's home, and so *kaeru* is not appropriate.

The idea that *kaeru* and return mean the same thing is not only a mistake made by English-speaking people who are learning Japanese. It works in the other direction too. I recently learned about an anti-American demonstration in Japan in which the protestors carried placards in English urging Americans to return. The addressees of this message might have found it quite friendly and welcoming, were it not for the accompanying shouting and clenching of fists.

The WSJ corpus yielded about 450 sentences with determinerless instances of *home*, and I'll briefly survey the collection now. The examples sort themselves into literal and figurative, and I begin with the literal. Of these, the examples can be divided into those expressing location, those expressing going away from the home, and those expressing returning to the home. The location examples can express location at the home or location away from the home. The examples of returning to the home are further divided into those that express arrival at the home, those that express setting out on the homeward journey, and those that express transit. Superimposed on these path differences is the distinction between intransitive and transitive, i.e. between plain and caused movement.

One group of the location examples simply described things that were at the resident's home, expressed as objects of the verb *have* or objects of the preposition *with*.

He believes every family should have a Bible at home.

According to the poll, 19% of respondents already have computers at home.

It would be nice if each of us had a wife at home to anticipate and meet our needs, ...

I remembered being fired at age 44, with five children at home.

Sentences about the resident not leaving home used the verb phrase *stay at home* and *stay home*. The latter possibility apparently does not exist in British English.

> Mothers who work should be subsidized more than those who stay at home.

> I don't have the personality to stay at home.

> If I stayed at home, I'd be looking at the walls. Friends criticized her for not staying at home.

> Then maybe I could stay home and have seven children and watch Oprah Winfrey.

> I think a lot of people got scared and stayed home.

> ABC wanted comedies that would appeal to the kind of people who stay home Saturdays.

> Kaye Myers challenges the view ... that men should work and married women should stay home with the children.

Stay specifically communicates the idea of not going out or away, but we also have expressions with *be*, simply indicating the fact of being at home. Both languages accept *at home*.

> The company's chairman ... and another top official were at home yesterday.

> Subscribers won't need to be at home during the day for in-home service calls.

There is a difference between the two languages when *be* is followed by *home* without a preposition. The usage notes tell us that there is no distinction in American English between *be home* and *be at home*, but that in British English *be home* is used only to express the idea of having freshly returned from somewhere. Another way to think about this is to say that in British English, *home* without a preposition is only a dynamic or directional adverb, never a static or purely locational adverb. Thus perhaps *he is home* has a structure that is a bit like *the ball is over the fence*, where we are indicating the location of something by saying that it just got there.

The following examples would presumably not be accepted by British speakers.

Japanese tradition says she should be home taking care of her two preschool children.

Because of her inability to be home to care for a kitten, she was counseled instead to adopt a cat.

'At least she can die knowing she is home.'

For the fresh-return sense, American English also prefers the preposition-less form.

'Mona, I'm home!'

'Will he be home in time for dinner?'

He barely had time to tell the news media 'I am happy to be back home' before one of his bodyguards tugged his elbow and said 'Comrade, let's move'.

If a speaker of American English comes home, sees nobody in the house, wants the people in the house to know that he is back, he will shout *I'm home*, and surely not *I'm at home*.

I am not sure, but I think we can summarize the difference by saying that in British English the prepositionless form requires the 'fresh arrival' meaning, and in American English the 'fresh arrival' meaning requires the prepositionless form.

There is another difference between *be home* and *be at home* in American English. The form without the preposition can only express the resident's location, the form with *at home* can express the location of some possession of the resident. Thus, it is possible for me to say that *my computer is at home*, but I can't say that *my computer is home*.

There are expressions talking about people not being at home. The most common phrase is away from home.

The children were away from home for 16 days altogether.

The ASPCA doesn't give young kittens, which are more in demand than cats, to people who are away from home during the day.

School administrators walk a tightrope between the demands of the community and the realities of how children really act when they are away from home.

The word *away* is interesting in this respect. Being *away from home* can signal a short absence or a long absence, but simply *being away* suggests an absence of at least one night. In this it contrasts with being *out*. Thus if some-body calls for my wife asking if she is at home—or, in America, if she is home—I could answer that she is away, the assumption being that she won't be back until at least tomorrow, or I could answer that she is out, the assump-tion being that she will return in the same day. The examples I mentioned from Quirk et al. (1985) earlier contrasted *at home* vs. *abroad* and *at home* vs. *out*, but I think that *away* is a third alternative.

When you are away from home you can still communicate with your fam-ily. The 'directionality' with the adverb *home* can also be that of a communi-cating act, as shown in two of the WSJ examples:

> You can always call home if you're lonely.

> In the spring of '40 they stopped writing home.

Another attested sentence, absent from the WSJ corpus, is *E.T., phone home*, illustrating the same point.

Leaving home can be for a short period or a long period. One can go shopping, one can go on a trip, or one can leave home for good. Examples of each type were found in the corpus:

> Many residents leave home without locking doors.

> Most travelers are leaving home for fun rather than business.

> If you'd rather have a Buick, don't leave home without the American Ex-press card.

> Miss Johns ran away from home to California at age 14, got a job as a battle teller, earned a high school equivalency degree and became a trading assis-tant at Drexel Burnham Lambert.

> At an early age, Wonda left home and married.

Verbs indicating arrival at home include *arrive*, *get*, *return*, and *come*.

> Warner arrived home to tidy the house and prepare a nourishing meal for the brats.

> Four months after he got home, he and his wife separated.

> 'I phoned my wife from there. 'Put on the coffee', I said, 'I'm coming home for good'.'

> 'You can come home from work at 6 o'clock, and they call it 'abandon-ment'.'

Verbs indicating 'going home' included simple *go*, the general directional verb head (*heading home* is going in the direction of home), and manner and means verbs like *hurry, run, drive, ride a bike*, etc. We find that *home* is also a possible complement for nouns designating journeys:

On the flight home she kept worrying about the children.

The journey home was to take three days.

The transitive verbs we find in the corpus include *bring, take*, and a number of verbs suggesting the idea of carrying, and *send, order, summon*, etc., suggesting the idea of giving orders.

The remaining examples were metaphorical, with *at home* used in the meaning of being competent (*The pianist was at home with Chopin*); *pounding, driving, hammering, nailing* or *pressing point home*, meaning something like 'try energetically to convince'; *hit home, strike home*, etc., meaning 'to affect one deeply'.

I turn now to the various semantic problems we left hanging. One was the question of interpreting the anaphoric element in *home*, and the appropriateness of the word *one* in the definition of home. Dictionary entries for idioms with variable possessive pronouns distinguish two types, along the lines of *to blow one's nose* and *to pull someone's leg*. The possessor, in the case of the idioms listed with *one's* is always the subject of the verb (*I blow my nose, you blow yours*), but in the case of the idioms listed with *someone's* it is distinct from the subject (*I'm pulling your leg, *I'm pulling my leg*).

I will allow myself to use the word 'control' to express the relation between the antecedent and the anaphoric element in *home*. In all of the examples of intransitive verbs in the corpus the controller was the subject. With the transitive verbs the controller was the subject with some verbs—for example *bring, carry, tote*, and *take*—but the object with others—for example *send, summon, order*, etc. In the case of *be home* or *be at home* it was always the subject. However, this is a case where the corpus has let us down. It failed to show that the subject with *at home* wouldn't have to be the resident of the home (since I can say that I left my computer at home), and it failed to show that with *bring* and *take* the object could be the controller. (Actually there was one example with *take*, concerning a limousine that was waiting to take some judges home.) It is certainly possible to say things like

A policeman brought my husband home last night.

It is also possible for *send* to be used with the subject, not the object, controlling the anaphoric element of *home*, as in

> If, when I travel, I buy books, I always send them home rather than carry them home.

But there's still more to say. In the case of both the intransitive verbs and the transitive verbs, there are contexts in which the resident of the home can be introduced with a *with* phrase: *My dog is so friendly he'll go home with anyone*. And we can imagine a sentence with three possible controllers of the anaphoric element of *home*. Consider the sentence *The teacher sent Jimmy home with Mary*. It could mean that she sent the kids to her own home; it could mean that she sent Jimmy to his home, in Mary's company; or it could mean that she sent Jimmy to Mary's home (in Mary's company). The context for this last case might be that Jimmy's parents had had a family emergency and had to leave town, and that Mary's parents had agreed to take care of Jimmy during their absence. *The teacher sent Jimmy home with Mary*, then, would mean that it was to Mary's home.

It seems clear that the relationship between the anaphoric element of home and its antecedent is not controlled syntactically but semantically. The controller can always be the subject, but otherwise you simply have to know who the travellers are. Furthermore, paraphrasing *home* with 'at one's home' or 'to one's home' will not make it possible to identify the antecedent of the anaphoric element of *home*, because the referential anaphor *one* is always bound to the clause's subject.

You have undoubtedly noticed that I resorted to made-up examples and imagined contexts. But that, of course, is because I'm pretty sure that what I am claiming about the fact of the matter is right, but the corpus didn't give any evidence on it one way or the other.

I turn now to the paradigmatic semantics of *home*. A part of knowing what function a word performs in a given context is knowing what it is being used 'in contrast with' in that context. Recall what we have already noticed about the ability of *at home* to be in contrast with *out*, *away* or *abroad*.

In the WSJ corpus a great many of the sentences contained explicit indications of the alternative to *at home*, either in a way in which the contrast was presented directly (*at home and abroad*, *at home or at work*, *in school but not at home*), or in some less direct way. In fact, in just this respect it is clear that in the case of *home* we need more than a single sentence to learn the facts, since we had some sentences like *At home, however, things were different*. To understand the scale of the intended contrast for this sentence we have to know what the preceding sentence was.

These contrasts show us that the English category of *home* involves considerable variation of scale.

> Advertisers claim virtues for their products overseas that they are forbidden by law to claim at home.
>
> Senators and representatives don't always say the same thing in Washington that they say at home.
>
> The yen is powerful overseas but has little purchasing power at home.
>
> Parents wonder if their children behave better at school than they behave at home.
>
> These children speak one language at school and another language at home.

In many cases the contrast was covert, discoverable only by figuring out why it seemed relevant to use the adverb *at home*. It is relevant to say that some parents teach their children at home, since the usual thing is to have children educated at school. It makes sense to talk about people who shop at home with a computer, or that in bad times people tend to eat at home, because these activities are understood as things that one could carry out in shops or restaurants.

A Bulgarian linguist, Svillen Stanchev, who has been visiting the Berkeley campus this year, went through my WSJ examples, and concluded that the English word *home* was a translator's nightmare. Most of the sentences could not be translated using a Bulgarian equivalent of *home*. There seem to be three reasons for this. One is that Bulgarian does not have the scale variations that English has, which allows us to use *at home* to refer to being in one's house, neighborhood, town, state, country, or planet. A second is that Bulgarian doesn't seem to allow the distributive interpretation of adverbial *home* with multiple travellers. In a sentence about the director of a factory sending the workers home after an accident, a translation with *home* would suggest that they all went to the same home, but a translation that made explicit that each worker went to his own home sounded silly, since the point was that the workers had to leave the factory and in the context there was no reason to make sure that each one ended up in his own proper home. The third reason—and this was the biggest surprise I got from the corpus—is that many English expressions with *home* appear to be simply negations of the other member of the contrast set. That is, to say that *Joe is at home sometimes* means simply that Joe is not at the other place where he might instead relevantly be.

It appears that with the word *home* a potential three–way alternation has come to be seen as a two-way contrast. If on a given day I could be expected to be either at home or at work, that sounds like a two–way contrast, but we know, of course, that in reality there is a third possibility: I might go someplace else altogether—for example, to the beach, to a coffeehouse, or what have you. But we find in the corpus lots of expressions about being at home or going home or being sent home that give the impression of only a two–way contrast. We read that *in a bad business climate customers stay home in droves*. (There aren't many homes large enough for people to assemble in droves.) Because of an accident the factory workers stayed home. One of the most striking examples of this that I have noticed—not from the WSJ corpus but from a recent news report—was a sentence which described non-voters as people who stay home on election day. Since elections in the United States are traditionally held on Tuesdays, when most people work, it is not at all likely that the people who didn't vote stayed home.

It is this use that I now associate with the 'departure time' interpretation of *go home*, since *go home* has to be interpreted as going away from the place where one is. Mr Stanchev tells me that the slogan YANKEE GO HOME would not work in direct Bulgarian translation, since it focuses on the wrong end of the journey.

A careful study of sentences with *risk* and with *home* has revealed facts about the uses and meanings of these words that have not been well described in existing grammars or dictionaries, and has given me reasons to be absolutely committed to the use of corpus evidence. But it is also true that in thinking through the consequences of the various hypotheses that observed corpus data evoked, other judgments needed to be brought in. Atkins and I think that we understand the difference between *run a risk* and *take a risk*, but we didn't find the critical examples in the corpus. But even if we had found sentences which worked with *run* but which wouldn't have tolerated replacement of *run* with *take*, we still have to face the reality that there are no corpora of starred examples: a corpus cannot tell us what is not possible. The cohesion problem with *home* is not syntactically resolvable, but almost all of the examples in the actual corpus did suggest that antecedents could be found in the subjects or the objects. The possibility that they could also be found in the objects of the preposition *with* was not shown in the corpus, and this seems to be an accidental gap.

As I said at the beginning, my concern with corpora is with the possibility of amassing enough examples to cover a particular domain more thoroughly than an armchair linguist could possibly manage without this sort of help. So one kind of corpus linguist should find this encouraging: there are really good reasons for building corpora, and as far as I'm concerned, the bigger the better. But what I have been saying is probably not encouraging to people who want to do most of their analysis without expecting anyone to have to sit down and stare at the examples one at a time to try to work out just what is the intended cognitive experience of the interpreter, what are the interactional intentions of the writer, and so on. Should it ever come about that linguistics can be carried out without the intervention and suffering of a native-speaker analyst, I will probably lose interest in the enterprise.

References

Fillmore, C. J. 1972. A grammarian looks to sociolinguistics. Georgetown University Monographs on Language and Linguistics 25: 275–287. Washington, DC: Georgetown University Press.

Fillmore, C. J. 1975. Santa Cruz lectures on deixis 1971, reproduced by the Indiana University Linguistics Club; the lecture *Coming and going*, under the title *How to know whether you're coming or going*, was revised and reprinted in Karl Hyldgaard-Jensen (ed.), *Linguistik 1971*: 369–379. Athenaeum.

Fillmore, C. J. 1985. Frames and the semantics of understanding. *Quaderni di Semantica* 6: 222–254.

Fillmore, C. J. & B. T. S. Atkins. forthcoming *a*. Toward a frame-based lexicon: The semantics of RISK and its neighbors. *Frames, fields, and contrasts,* (eds) A. Lehrer, E. Kittay. Hillsdale, NJ: Lawrence Erlbaum.

Fillmore, C. J. & B. T. S. Atkins. forthcoming *b*. Starting where the dictionaries stop: The challenge of corpus lexicography. *Computational approaches to the lexicon*, (eds.) B. T. Atkins, A. Zampolli. Oxford: Oxford University Press.

Polanyi, M. 1958. *Personal knowledge: Towards a post-critical philosophy*. Chicago, Illinois: University of Chicago Press.

Quirk, R., S. Greenbaum, G. Leech & J. Svartvik. 1985. *A comprehensive grammar of the English language*. London: Longman.

Raiffa, H. 1970. *Decision analysis: Introductory lectures on choices under uncertainty*. Reading, MA: Addison Wesley.

15

Border Conflicts: FrameNet Meets Construction Grammar

2008

CHARLES J. FILLMORE

1. *The Problem*

I count myself among the linguists who believe in a continuity between grammar and lexicon (Fillmore et al. 1988, Joshi 1985), and I entertain the common image that each lexical item carries with it instructions on how it fits into a larger semantic–syntactic structure, or, alternatively, on how semantic–syntactic structures are to be built around it. My remarks here specifically concern an ongoing effort to describe and to annotate instances of, non-core syntactic structures, and to see how the products of this work can be integrated with the existing lexical resource, called FrameNet (FN), which is a set of procedures, and a growing database for recording the meanings and the semantic and syntactic combinatorial properties of lexical units. The FrameNet project, which I have directed since 1997, has recently begun exploring ways of creating a *constructicon*, a record of English grammatical *constructions*, annotating sentences by noting which parts of them are licensed by which specific constructions.

The grammatical constructions that belong in the larger constructicon— that is, in a construction-based grammar—include those that cover the basic and familiar patterns of predication, modification, complementation, and determination, but the new project is concentrating on constructions that ordinary parsers are not likely to notice, or that grammar checkers are likely to question. Some of them involve purely grammatical patterns with no reference to any lexical items that participate in them, some involve descriptions of enhanced demands that certain lexical units make on their surroundings, and some are mixtures of the two.

2. *The Work, The Product, and The Limitations of FrameNet*

Since many features of the new resource are modeled on FrameNet, I think it useful to review FN's goals and activities, and the features of its database (Baker et al. 2003, Fillmore et al. 2003). FrameNet research amounts to

1. describing *lexical units* (LUs) in terms of the *semantic frames* they evoke, and describing those frames (i.e., the situation types, etc., knowledge of which is necessary for interpreting utterances in the language),
2. defining the *frame elements* (FEs) of each frame that are essential for a full understanding of the associated situation type (the frame elements are the props, participants, situation features that need to be identified or taken for granted in sentences for which the frame is relevant),
3. extracting from a very large *corpus* example sentences which contain each LU targeted for analysis (FN has worked mainly with the British National Corpus),
4. selecting from the extracted sentences representative samples that cover the range of combinatorial possibilities, and preparing *annotations* of them as layered segmentation of the sentences, where the segments are labeled according to the FEs they express, as well as the basic syntactic properties of the phrases bearing the FE,
5. displaying the results in *lexical entries* which summarize the discovered *combinatorial affordances*, both semantic and syntactic, as *valence patterns*, and creating links from these patterns to the annotated sentences that evidence them, and
6. defining a network of *frame–to–frame relations* and the graphical means of displaying these, that will show how some frames depend on or are elaborations of other frames.

2.1. *The frames*

The frames developed in FrameNet are the conceptual structures against which the LUs in the FN lexicon are understood and defined (Fillmore 1982, Fillmore & Atkins 1992, 1994). These can be as general as the location of some entity in an enclosure, or as specific as interest on investment.

One FN frame that is simple enough to describe completely, and just complex enough to be interesting, is the so-called Revenge frame, the nature of which requires understanding a kind of history. In that history, one person (we call him the OFFENDER) did something to harm another person (what he did we call the OFFENSE and his victim we call the INJURED_PARTY); reacting to that act, someone (the AVENGER, possibly the same individual as the INJURED_PARTY) acts so as to do harm to the OFFENDER, and what he does we call the PUNISHMENT. Thus, we have the frame Revenge, and the frame elements AVENGER, OFFENDER, OFFENSE, INJURED_PARTY, and PUNISHMENT. Other features of the Revenge frame include the fact that this kind of pay-back is independent of any judicial system. There is a very large set of verbs, adjectives and nouns that evoke this frame, by which we mean that when users of the language understand these words, their understanding includes all of the elements of that scenario. Among the verbs that evoke this frame are *avenge* and *revenge*, the nouns include *vengeance* and *retribution*, there are phrasal verbs like *pay back* and *get even*, adjectives like *vengeful* and *vindictive*, support constructions like *take revenge on*, *wreak vengeance on*, and *exact retribution against*, plus prepositional adverbials like *in retribution*, or *in revenge*.

FrameNet has developed descriptions of over 800 frames to date, and nobody is ready to estimate how many there are altogether. The list from the time of the last official release can be found at *http://framenet.icsi.berkeley.edu*.

2.2. The frame elements

The frame elements (FEs) are somewhat analogous to the deep cases of early Fillmore (Fillmore 1968, 1971), *thematic roles* in various generativist writings (Jackendoff 1990), *actants* and *circonstants* in the Tesnière tradition (Tesnière 1959). There are good reasons for not tying the frame elements into any of the familiar lists of semantic roles (agent, patient, theme, experiencer, instrument, etc.). Since annotators are asked to find expressors of frame elements in actual sentences, FE names that are memorable in respect to the frame itself will facilitate such identifications. Thus to take the case of the arguments of *replace* in a sentence like

[I] replaced [my stolen bicycle] [with a much cheaper one],

it makes more sense to refer to the phrases introducing the two bicycles as the OLD and the NEW than to try to figure out how well these roles can be accommodated in the 'standard' lists. (The missing bicycle, in fact, is not a participant in the event described by the sentence but is a necessary element of its meaning.) The recognition of FE commonalities across frames is made possible by the system of frame–to–frame relations.

We wanted to think of the frame elements as representing the kinds of information that could be expressed in the sentences and phrases in which the frame is 'active', and we wanted to be able to discover which parts of a sentence reveal information about which frame element. There is an important constraint on this task, distinguishing it from annotation practices that seek to learn everything about each event in a continuous text. Since the information we record is supposed to be relevant to the syntactic description of a given lexical unit, we require that the frame elements we attend to are in *grammatical construction* with the lexical unit being described. Annotators will ignore event-relevant information elsewhere in the text.

We make a distinction between *core* and *peripheral* FEs. The core FEs are those that are conceptually necessary in any realization of the frame by the nature of that frame; the peripheral frame elements are the adjuncts that fit the familiar description 'time, place, and manner, etc.', especially the 'etc.' (the core/periphery distinction can vary across frames; for verbs like *reside*, *elapse*, and *behave*, the locative, temporal and manner components, respectively, are not peripheral). A characteristic of the peripheral FEs is that they have essentially the same meaning and the same syntactic marking wherever they appear; whatever distributional limitations they have are explained by the fact that frames about *happenings* can take time and place modification, frames about *intentional* acts can take instrument and purpose modification, and so on. A third kind of frame element is what we refer to as *extrathematic*: these are expressions (like benefactives or phrases like *in revenge* or *in return*) that have the effect of situating the event signaled by the target's frame in some larger or coterminous situation.

The goal of FrameNet lexical descriptions is, for each frame-bearing word, to match the word's semantic combinatorial requirements with the manner of their syntactic realization. Reversing the point of view, we seek to recognize in the syntactic nature of the phrases around a given frame-bearing lexical unit, information about the participants in situation that is an instance of the frame. The resulting pairing of semantic and syntactic roles constitutes the valence description of the item.

2.3. *Example sentences*

The goal in providing examples was to have, for each lexical unit, a full set of illustrations of its basic combinatorial properties, and we preferred sentences whose content was clearly relevant to the meaning of the word being exhibited. If we were looking for an illustration of *knife*, we would prefer *the butcher sharpened his knife* than *the poet photographed a knife*. These example-selecting decisions were made in resistance to several kinds of pressure. Some members of the research community wanted to see sentences of the most frequent type; but for many verbs, the most frequent examples had mainly pronouns (*I risked it*). Some wanted us to include complex and distorted sentences as well as the simplest type; some wanted us to make sure we include creative uses of a word wherever we found them, scolding us for neglecting metaphor and other figurative uses: our view echoes that of Patrick Hanks (MS), namely, that we had the obligation to produce clear descriptions of the *norm*, leaving it to some auxiliary research to explore the ways in which speakers *exploit* the norm for creative expression. Where a metaphorical use was *lexicalized*, the LU resulting from that lexicalization was included in its appropriate frame.

2.4. The annotation

The original mission of FN was purely lexicographic: to annotate a variety of typical uses of each target LU and to seek to cover a wide range of relevant contexts for the LU (i.e., all of its *valence* possibilities and representative samples of its semantic collocates), and this meant creating a collection of sentences in which each was annotated with respect to one word in it. Thus a sentence like

> She smiled when we told her that her daughter had been nominated to receive an important award.

might be annotated for the verb *smile* alone, as a member of the Make_faces frame, where it belongs in the set *frown*, *grimace*, *grin*, *pout*, *scowl*, *smile*, *smirk*.

As the size of the lexicon increased, it became clear that there were sentences for which FN was prepared to describe many of the words in it, and ultimately we received a subcontract to look into the possibility of producing full text annotations. That meant annotating each word in the sentence—that is, each frame-evoking word. For the above example, that would mean showing the frame structure of the words *smile*, *tell*, *daughter*, *nominate*, *receive*, *important* and *award*. For our purely lexicographic purposes, we would have no reason to annotate the word *told* in this sentence—we already have more than enough examples of the lemma—but it would have to be done here again in order to prepare the semantic structure of the sentence as a whole. Obviously this need increased our eagerness to find ways of automating parts of the annotation process.

FrameNet has to date annotated a growing number of texts, some of them viewable on the FN website. Most of them are only partially annotated, partly because they contain lexical material FN has not yet worked through, and partly because they contain meaningful grammatical patterns that FN annotation has not been prepared to capture.[1]

The annotations themselves are presented in layered stand-off representation in multiple layers. For lexicographic annotations, one layer identified the target LU and its frame; another represented the FEs in the phrases that serve as its valents; one indicated the phrase types of the constituents so identified; one indicated the grammatical function of each valent; and a few other layers were dedicated to special features associated with individual parts of speech. The FEs were annotated manually, the GF and the PT labels were attached automatically and checked manually. Annotations viewable on the FrameNet website show only the frame element labeling, as in Figure 1.

[Fluid The River Liffey] FLOWS [Target] [Source from west] [Goal to east] [Area through the center of the city] [Goal to Dublin Bay].

Figure 1: FE annotation of a sentence.

Full text annotations consist of sets of layers, each corresponding to one target LU. It is virtually impossible to get a view of the full annotation of a long sentence, but there is some experimental work being done to derive dependency trees from these, with the nodes indicating lexical heads and their frames, the branches labeled according to the frame element represented by the dependent nodes.

One special feature of FN annotation is the recording of FEs that are conceptually present but syntactically missing. These are sorted into *constructional null*, such as the missing subject of an imperative sentence; *indefinite null*, such as the object of intransitivized *eat*, *sew*, *bake*, etc.; and *definite nulls* (*zero anaphora*), entailing that the missing element has to be recoverable in the context, such as the missing object of *we won* (what is understood but unexpressed is the contest—not the prize), the missing preposition phrase in *she arrived* (where the destination has to be known) or *mine is similar* (where the unexpressed comparand has to be part of the conversation), and so on. The last of these plays an important role in construction annotation as well. Such information is associated with the annotation of the LU that licenses the omission.

---

[1] The texts—chosen because other researchers are examining them as well—were taken from the Wall Street Journal section of the Penn TreeBank, the Nuclear Text Initiative website, and a selection of Berlitz Travel Guides that have been made available to the American National Corpus.

2.5. The entries

Each LU is identified by lemma, part of speech, and frame name. The LUs were chosen because of their membership in one of the frames being covered by FrameNet, and what that means is that in many cases the most common use of a lemma is not to be found: FN researchers have not reached that frame yet. Almost all features of the lexical entry are produced automatically: hand-made features include a simple definition.[2] For valence-bearing words, the entry contains a table showing the ways in which each frame element can match a phrase type, and a separate table showing the variety of ways in which combinations of FEs and PTs make up the valence exhibited by individual sentences. Viewers of the valence descriptions can toggle between core FEs only, or all FEs found in the sentences—core, peripheral, and extrathematic.

The entries for nouns that designate events or states of affairs also include information about the existence of *support verbs* and *support prepositions*; access to the sentences will reveal which FEs are represented among the arguments of the LU's verbal or prepositional support.[3]

2.6. Frame–to–frame relations

Since frames can differ from each other in granularity, and some frames are clearly related to other frames, it has proved necessary to create an ontology of frames, linked to each other by several kinds of relations. Figure 2 is a display of the frame relations centered on Commercial_transaction:

---

[2] The purpose of the definition is purely mnemonic, to aid the user in knowing which sense of a word is being analyzed in a given entry. Where appropriate the definitions were taken from the *Concise Oxford Dictionary 10*, with permission from Oxford University Press. Others were in-house.

[3] The current database shows no way of classifying support constructions along the line of the lexical functions of the MTT model of Igor Mel'čuk and his colleagues, though various researchers are seeking to derive such information automatically from the FN annotations. (Rambow et al., MS, Bouveret & Fillmore, MS)

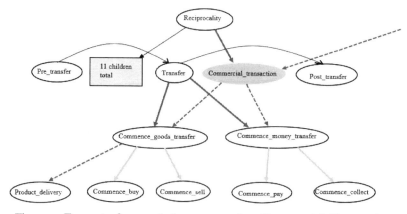

Figure 2: Frame-to-frame relations centered on Commercial_Transaction.

Several different kinds of relations can be seen in this diagram. Commercial_transaction has two components (related to the mother node by a *Part_of* relation as indicated by the broken line), and these are Commerce_goods_transfer and Commerce_money_transfer. Each of these is a type of (=has an Inherits relation to) the frame Transfer. The low frames Commerce_buy and Commerce_sell have separate *Perspective_on* relations to Commerce_goods_transfer, and the frames Commerce_pay and Commerce_collect have *Perspective_on* relations to Commerce_ money_transfer. Thus, a commercial transaction is an instance of Reciprocality, involving two cooccurring reciprocal transfers, one of goods and one of money. Buying and Selling are perspective-varying instances of goods-transfer, differing from the point of view of the buyer and the seller; and similarly with paying and collecting (=charging) and their relation to money-transfer.

3. *FrameNet Treatment of Multiwords So Far*

The constructicon-building work concerns itself with linguistic knowledge that goes beyond simple grammar and simple words, and hence it will include various kinds of idioms and other multiwords. There are many kinds of multiwords that already fall within the scope of FrameNet work.[4] Among the multiwords covered by current FrameNet[5] we find

---

[4] Josef Ruppenhofer delivered a paper on this topic at an earlier Euralex meeting (Ruppenhofer et al. 2002).

[5] FN treatment of compound words has more or less awaited the capability of constructional annotation. In the current databases, there are compounds that are simply treated as single unanalyzed units, and there are others in which the head is a frame-bearing word and the modifier is

1.   phrasal verbs, with particles, which are simply treated as two-part verbs that take a specific particle as a syntactic valent; the particle is more or less motivated, but can't be understood as simply contributing its own meaning
     a.   Intransitive: *pick up* (increase), *take off* (start flying)
     b.   Transitive: *take up* (consider), *take off* (remove)
2.   words with selected prepositional complements, listed with preposition, syntactically selects P-headed phrase
     a.   Verbs: *depend on, object to, cope with*
     b.   Adjectives: *fond of, proud of, interested in*
     c.   Nouns: *fondness for, pride in, interest in*
3.   support constructions—syntactically separate, treated as evoking a frame linked to the noun rather than the verb
     a.   Verbal heads: *take comfort in, take pride in, put emphasis on*
     b.   Prepositional heads: *at risk, in danger, under arrest*
4.   combinations—combining selected prepositional complement with particle or noun
     a.   *put up with* (tolerate), *break in on* (interrupt)
     b.   *take comfort in, place emphasis on*
     c.   *take into possession, take under consideration*
5.   transparent nouns—the first noun in [N of N] structures signifying types, aggregates, portions, units, measures, epithets, etc.; the motivation for recording these is to be able to recognize selectional or collocational relations between the context and the *second* noun
     a.   *my* gem of a *wife, in* a part of the *room, on* this part of the *shelf, wreak* this kind of *havoc*.

4. Full-text Annotation and the Confrontation with Constructions

In carrying out full-text annotation the goal was to end up with structures which could be the basis of the semantic integration of the whole sentence. Working with one of those linguist-invented sentences like

> The Secretary ordered the Committee to consider selling its holdings to the members.

we should be able to identify straightforwardly the participants in the *ordering* event: *the Secretary* gave the order, *the Committee* received the order,

---

labeled as an FE in the head's frame. FN has lacked the means of describing a compound word both as a unit on its own and as having an internal structure.

and *to consider selling its holdings to the members*, specifies the order. For the verb *consider*, the entity that was to do the considering was *the Committee*, and *selling its holdings to the members* was to be the content of such considerations; and the three participants in the *selling* event are to be *the Committee* as seller, *the members* as buyer, and *the holdings* as the asset destined to change ownership. The words *Secretary*, *Committee* and *members* are all relational nouns used without any indication of what the other term of the relation is, and that's possible if that other entity is understood in the context. A simple frame-annotated dependency tree will fairly well capture the meaning of the whole, with word-frame pairs making up the node labels, the branches labeled according to the semantic role, and with the missing entities in the relational nouns marked with the possibility of indexing them to contextually given entities.

One doesn't have to look far to find sentences containing structures that do not lend themselves to such simple treatment. Here are the first three sentences of a leader from the Economist newspaper of June 17, 2007, with comments on those features that go beyond simple lexicon and simple grammar.

> For all the disappointments, posterity will look more kindly on Tony Blair than Britons do today. Few Britons, it seems, will shed a tear when Tony Blair leaves the stage on June 27th after a decade as prime minister, as he finally announced this week he would do. Opinion polls have long suggested that he is unpopular.

1. *for all the disappointments*:
   for all X is a concessive structure with a meaning like 'in spite of X'; seems to be restricted to definite objects; not best treated as a complex preposition
2. *look kindly on*:
   a phrasal verb with the meaning 'judge positively'
3. *[posterity] will look more kindly on Tony Blair than [Britons] do [today]*:
   a comparative structure with a double-focus comparand—[Britons] [today], each accented, requiring the semantic unpacking of *posterity* as something like [the world] [in the future] (a contestable interpretation)

4. *few Britons*:
    not a vague indication of cardinality like *a few Britons*, semantically a negator (= 'not many'), creating a *negative polarity* context (see item 6)

5. *it seems*:
    an epistemic parenthesis, bearing no structural relation to the rest of the sentence but limited in the positions that would welcome it

6. *shed a tear*:
    a VP collocation of the *minimizer* type, appropriate to the negative polarity context created by *few*; similar in this respect to *drink a drop*, *lift a finger*, *give a damn*, *eat a bite*

7. *leave the stage*:
    metaphor, referring here to leaving the PM-ship

8. *on June 17th*:
    use of the preposition *on* with day-level temporal units (cf. *in March*, *at noon*, *in the morning*)

9. *June 27th*:
    one of various ways of pairing a date with a month name

10. *as prime minister*:
    as selecting 'role' name; requires context implying service in a role

11. *as he announced he would do*:
    relativizer *as* (consider replacing *as* with *which*)

12. *would do*:
    the form of VP ellipsis (including *do* after a modal) found in BrE, missing or rare in AmE (*as he announced he would*)

13. *this week*:
    an expression in which the first element is taken from the list *this/next/last*
    and the second is a calendric unit name like *week*, *month*, *year*, but not *day*

14. *have long suggested*:
    the use of *long* in the meaning 'for a long time' has numerous contextual constraints, difficult to pin down; here both (a) the position between *have* and the participle and (b) restriction to certain classes of verb meanings seem necessary (compare *I have long known that ...* with **I long knew that...* and **I have long lived in California.*)

5. *Constructions and the New Constructicon*

Section 3 offered a number of ways in which the behavior of multiword expressions can be incorporated into the FN lexicon and into FN-style annotations, that is, where the information recorded is mainly limited to a small number of requirements that lexical items impose on their immediate grammatical environment. Stepping outside of that is a definite new challenge.

5.1. The annotation challenge

How did FrameNet become concerned with such matters? First, with our efforts in full text annotation, we became interested in the possibilities of making better coverage of all of the linguistic properties of texts, not just those involving simple predicates and their valence structures. Second, it seems clear that while with support constructions we moved slightly beyond 'standard' valence projections, the view of syntactic structure within which we explained the syntactic concomitants of lexical selection needs to be expanded. Third, the community in Berkeley that got started with FrameNet is also a community that has an interest in the broader theory of grammatical constructions. Fourth, and most importantly, it seemed likely that *the same data structure and annotation software devised for lexical annotation could be assigned to the treatment of constructions*.

In 2007 FrameNet received a small grant for doing exploratory research on designing a constructicon, an inventory of 'minor' grammatical constructions, and to demonstrate a means of annotating instances of them. The parallels to ordinary FN lexical annotation were striking, as can be seen in Table 1.

The questions to ask for setting up an annotation system for constructions include: What is the constituent (the *construct*) within which a construction operates? What needs to be tagged within a construct? What are the functions of the elements of the construction? What if anything reveals to the reader/listener that there's anything special about the sentence?

In FN lexicographic annotation, we describe a frame and its components or participants, we annotate sentences by identifying the target lexical item and bracketing off the valents and labeling them with frame element names. In constructional annotation, then, we should be able to describe a construction and name the parts of sentences that are the constituents of the constructs licensed by the construction, and then to bracket off those components and assign them labels assigned to the elements of the construction. One important difference is that often there is no *target* LU to link the construction to.

Lexical FrameNet	Constructicon
Frame descriptions describe the frames and their components, set up FE names for annotation, and specify frame–to–frame relations; lexical entries are linked to frames, valence descriptions show combinatory possibilities, entries link valence patterns to sets of annotated sentences.	Constructicon entries describe the constructions and their components, set up construction elements (CEs, the syntactic elements that make up a construct), explain the semantic contribution of the construction, specify construction–to–construction relations, and link construction descriptions with annotated sentences that exhibit their type.
The FEs are given names according to their role in the frame, and provide labels for the phrases in the annotations that give information about the FE.	The CEs are named according to their function in the constructs, they provide the labels on words and phrases in annotated sentences.
The syntactic properties—grammatical functions and phrase types—are identified for all constituents that realize frame elements.	Phrase types are identified for constituents that serve as CEs in a construct; for constructions that are headed by lexical units, grammatical function labels will also be relevant.
Example sentences are selected that illustrate the use of the lexical units described.	Example sentences are selected and annotated for the ways they illustrate the use of the construction.
Annotations identify the LU, the FEs, and the GFs and PTs of the segments marked off.	Annotations contain labels for the CEs and identify, for lexically marked constructions, the relevant lexical material.
Valence patterns are identified, and linked to the annotations.	Varieties of construct patterns are identified and linked to the annotations.
Frame–to–frame relationships are documented and displayed in a separate resource.	Construction–to–construction relationships are identified and (will eventually be) displayed.

Table 1: Lexical and Constructional Description and Annotation Compared

Figures 3 and 4 show the similarity of lexical and constructional annotations, as they appear in the annotation tool. The lexical example represents the clause *one of them accused Mr Wisson of kidnapping*; the constructional example represents the sentence *None of these arguments is notably strong, let alone conclusive*. The list of labels at the bottom of each is the list appropriate to a single level: the FE level in the lexical example, the CE level in the construction example.

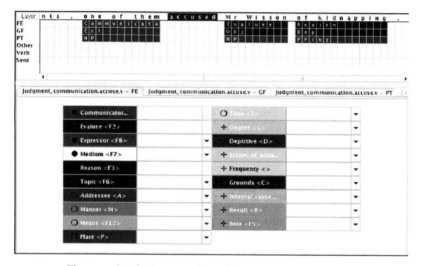

Figure 3: Lexical annotation of the verb *accuse* in the
Judgement_Communication frame.

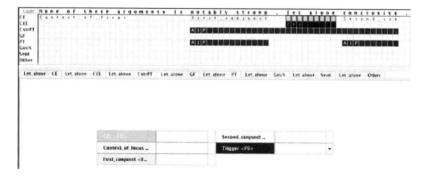

Figure 4: Constructional annotation of a phrase built around the
conjunction *let alone*.

5.2. The varieties of constructions needing annotation

The assumption that it would be easy to adapt the FrameNet annotation tool to construction annotation turned out to be false. Essentially the first half of the year of this grant passed by before a proper annotation tool was ready. Finally, in the spring semester, there are two graduate students working on the project, Russell Lee-Goldman and Russell Rhodes, with strong backup by Michael Ellsworth and Project Manager Collin Baker. By the time of the Euralex meeting, I expect to be able to give a coherent report on our accomplishments and their significance. In the meantime, however, I offer some hastily gathered notes on the types of constructions we need to cover. In the final report almost all of the construction descriptions will include references to the relevant literature, omitted here with apologies, including names like Boas, Borsley, Croft, Goldberg, Jackendoff, Kay, Lakoff, Lambrecht, McCawley, Michaelis, O'Connor, Pullum, Pustejovsky, Sag, Wierzbicka, Zwicky.

5.2.1. Lexical constructions

For an important class of cases, the grammar allows words with one meaning to be paired with the *combinatory affordances* that are common to a semantically defined class of words (in the case of verbs, this amounts to valence patterns; for nouns, the difference between proper and common nouns, or that between count and non-count nouns; for adjectives the difference between scalar and non-scalar adjectives). The word *coercion* is sometimes used to cover such relationship.

We can distinguish the words that are 'at home' with these affordances from the words that are their 'guests'. There is an obvious problem for a corpus-based lexicon-building effort like FrameNet, since there is no automatic way of telling the difference: should the derived behavior of 'frequent guests' be listed in the lexicon or merely recognized in context as an instance of the construction? It's a problem for lexicography in general, since the decisions that need to be made one way or another are not always clearcut.

EXAMPLES include the phenomena in much of the literature on Argument Structure Constructions, especially in the work of Adele Goldberg. The meanings created by these constructions involve specified relations between the meaning of the 'guest' and the semantic expectations of the 'host' pattern: *slipping someone a banknote* is using a slipping action to give someone a banknote, *wriggling into the swimsuit* is 'entering' the swimsuit (putting it on) with a wriggling motion; an event of *sneezing the napkin off the table* is one in which the air current created by a sneeze has motive force. With nouns, examples like *we had beaver for dinner* show the use of the name of an animal with the grammar of a mass noun, coercing a construal as the flesh of the animal prepared for human consumption.[6]

5.2.2. Verbs with contextual requirements outside of their phrasal projection

For the kinds of examples we have in mind under this category it should be possible simply to specify the greater context as part of the combinatory affordances—but there is no familiar formal way to do this within theories of valence. The most common cases are words that fit negative polarity contexts, contexts including negation straight on or other sources of general irrealis contexts, like questions, conditional clauses, and dozens of others (since we are mainly interested in identifying cases and annotating them, the kinds of careful formulation that a true grammar would need can be glossed over). Verbs that require contexts that involve both ability and negation allow various ways of expressing those contexts.

EXAMPLES include *can't stand, can't afford, can't tell, can't seem to...*, *can't help*. The contexts can be expressed in different ways: in *were you ever able to afford such luxuries?* the polarity is not triggered by a negative morpheme, and the ability is expressed by an adjective rather than a modal. In *it's too dark to tell what they're doing*, the semantics of 'not + able' is entailed in the meaning of *too*. In the case of the verb *brook* a first impression might be that its required negation is 'local'—i.e., in the determiner of the direct object—but the negation can be presented by an external negation with *any* replacing the *no* in the determiner position: *I will brook no interruption, I am too busy to brook any distraction.*

5.2.3. Templatic constructions

Some constructions seem to require a pattern of fixed positions with strict requirements on what can fill those positions: such is the case of the linguistic way of expressing proportions of the kind A:B=C:D; it is sufficient to think of the sentences as providing ways of pronouncing the symbols in such a representation.

EXAMPLES are often found in lower-grades test questions: *Six is to three as four is to two; blood is to red as snow is to white.*[7]

---

[6] The construction does not merely convert the animal name into the name of a continuous substance. A sentence like *the neighborhood fox likes beaver* is not licensed by this construction.

[7] These sentences could be given a somewhat tortured parse, involving the extraposition of the *as*-phrase: if we think of *as four is to two* as identical to *what four is to two*, and as naming a particular relation, then we can see the pattern by putting things 'back': *Six is [what four is to two] to three.*

5.2.4. A mere five dollars

There is a phrasing of numerical expressions that requires (a) the singular indefinite determiner, (b) an adjective that qualifies a number, and (c) a number, such that the combination demands a noun head that matches the number and can contradict the singularity of the article *a*. That is, for something like *a mere five dollars*, all three elements are required: **a five dollars* doesn't work, **mere five dollars* doesn't work, **a mere dollars* doesn't work. We see the construction as determining the prenominal phrase only: in the manner of an ordinary cardinal number, the noun can be deleted if its nature is understood in the context—as people or dollars, for example, in *a mere two million*.

EXAMPLES show adjectives with minimizing, neutral and maximizing senses: *a paltry twenty cents, an additional thirty pages, a whopping seven billion dollars.* An expression like *another $200* is a disguised instance of this construction, where *an+other* is analogous to *an+additional*, and *$200* is shown as *two-hundred+dollars*. The modifying adjectives that appear in constructs that instance this construction make up an interesting class.

5.2.5. Presentative constructions

George Lakoff has discussed a family of constructions using *here* and *there* which have important communicative functions. Formally, they begin with *here* or *there*, they have a verb which most typically is *be, come, go, sit, stand,* or *lie*, with the restriction that if the subject is a pronoun it precedes the verb but if it is a lexical NP it follows the verb, and utterances of them have the function of announcing something about the appearance or presence of something. In the complete version, they include some kind of secondary predicate, that can be an adjective, a preposition phrase, a participial phrase, or a with(out) clause.

EXAMPLES include *here comes that old fool; there she stood, with her hands on her hips; here comes Billy, crawling on his hands and knees; here I am, ready to serve.*

5.2.6. Wherewithal

There is a construction which uses the determiner *the* and a noun construed as naming a resource; it is followed by an indication of what the resource could be used for, expressed as an infinitival VP or a *for*-PP; and its governing context identifies someone as a POSSESSOR (or not) of a sufficient supply of the resources to carry out the purpose represented by the noun's complement. A parallel construction exists with the word *enough* in place of *the*. The name it's been given is due to the fact that the noun *wherewithal* occurs only in this construction!

EXAMPLES with physical resources include *I don't have the resources to landscape the garden, we lack the staff for such a project, who will provide me the wherewithal to accomplish this, they denied me the funds to complete the job, do we have the fuel to make it to the next town?* Nouns that designate spiritual resources that fit the same construction include *courage, spirit, will, guts, balls,* and several others. Arguments that this construction is needed include the observation that the combination of the nominal and the complement cannot serve as a self-standing NP: **we spilled the fuel to make it to the next town.* The purpose complement can be omitted in contexts where it is understood: A sentence like *Where did you find the cash?* can be an instance of this construction, addressed to someone who had just bought an expensive car, or it can be used simply to refer to some until-now misplaced amount of money. The existence of the *Wherewithal* construction explains that ambiguity.

5.2.7. Gapping and Right Node Raising

Some constructions are purely organizational, and have no lexical components beyond conjunctions or words that can function as conjunctions. Those referred to as Gapping and Right Node Raising (RNR) omit phrases whose meaning is shared against elements that are in focal contrast.

EXAMPLES of RNR include *John loves, but Mary hates, rock music,* where comma intonation separates the two truncated conjuncts from their common completion; gapping is seen when the shared element is between the focal elements: *John loves peaches and Mary apples.* Those are obviously made-up sentences, chosen for their brevity. An attested sentence that exemplifies both of these constructions simultaneously is *Bears have become largely, and pandas entirely, noncarnivorous.*

5.2.8. Let alone

Let alone is a conjunction whose combinatory potential and semantic-pragmatic interpretation are discussed in Fillmore, Kay & O'Connor 1988 [a.k.a. FKO] and some discussions following that. Briefly, the pieces that are in focal contrast can be[8] assembled with their surrounding contexts to form two

---

[8] For example:
> Context proposition spoken by interlocutor: *Can you give me a dollar?*
> Direct response to the context proposition: *I won't give you a dollar.*

propositions, one of these propositions is responsive to the context (i.e., to some assumed or expressed context proposition), the other is strongly asserted by the speaker, and it contextually entails the first.

EXAMPLES include the sentence in Figure 4, *None of the arguments is notably strong, let alone conclusive.* Numerous examples of multiple foci are found in the FKO article. *Let alone* sentences frequently exemplify RNR: *I wouldn't touch, let alone eat, anything that ugly* (Made-up sentence).

5.2.9. Verb one's way

A much-studied construction is a way of providing motion verbs by inserting a verb that indicates an action by which someone is able to move, or a path through which the mover moves, or an activity on the mover's part during which they moved. The structure is (a) verb plus (b) possessive pronoun co-referential to the moving entity plus (c) the word *way*: VERB one's WAY. The most neutral verb that is 'at home' in this construction is *make* (*Let's start making our way home.*) The verb *wend* exists *only* in this construction.

EXAMPLES that show the variety include *She pushed her way through the crowd, the river winds its way through the prairie, we dined our way through the south of France.*

5.2.10. In one's own right

A number of constructions depend on the extended reflexive possessive pronoun *one's own*: *he finally has a room of his own, you're on your own now,* but one we have examined is the adjunct *in one's own right.* A typical background assumption for its use is something like this: A is affiliated with B in some way (a relative, an assistant), B is already known for some property or accomplishment, the sentence asserts that same property or accomplishment of A, and the construction conveys the assumption that A's accomplishments are not due to the affiliation with B. The son of a poet can be *a fine poet in his own right,* the husband of a famous chemist can be *an accomplished chemist in his own right.* It would sound odd to say of the wife of right-wing radio commentator Rush Limbaugh that *she is a major intellectual in her own right,* without invoking a belief that Mr. Limbaugh is a major intellectual. (I don't even know if he's married—this is just an example.)

Response that strongly entails the context-relevant response: *I wouldn't lend my mother a nickel.*

Result: *I wouldn't lend my mother a nickel, let alone give you a dollar.*

Relevant scales for the triple contrasting foci: I'm more likely to lend money to someone than to give it away; I'd be more generous to my mother than to you; a dollar is a lot more than a nickel.

5.2.11. Rate phrases

The concept of rate is expressed in English with two adjacent NPs in which the first identifies a quantity of units of some type and the second introduces a unit of a different type across which the measurement applies, more or less as numerator to denominator. Typically the second NP is marked with *a* or *per*, but other types occur as well. These expressions express such notions as growth rate, frequency, fuel efficiency, speed, and the like.

EXAMPLES include *it grows four inches a day*, but also *four inches every three days*; *my Hummer gets seven miles a gallon*; *our committee meets twice a week*; *we were moving at 150 km per hour*. The type of rate can be calculated by comparing the two kinds of units, and can be supported by making note of aspects of the governing context, such as the items *grow, meet, gets*, and *at* of the examples.

5.2.12. Measurement phrases

Some scalar adjectives, but not all, support measurement qualifiers that indicate a quantity of units used for values on the scale.

EXAMPLES include *five meters long/wide/tall/thick*, and *seventeen years old*. Weight and cost values are expressed verbally, with the verbs *weigh* and *cost*; there is no **twenty pounds heavy* or **twenty dollars expensive*. Comparative expressions, however, can have measured 'gaps' across the board: *twenty pounds heavier, twenty dollars cheaper, three years older*, etc.

5.2.13. Deictically anchored calendar units

The lexical set this–next–last occurs in several constructions dedicated to locating a reference time to the present moment—the *temporal deictic center*— with respect to calendric time periods like *week, month*, and *year*. This makes reference to the period containing 'now'; *next* refers to the period following the period containing 'now'; and *last* refers to the period preceding the period containing 'now'. These patterns do not apply to days, however: at the day level the same functions are served by the lexical items *today, yesterday, tomorrow*.

EXAMPLES illustrating one of the constructions, simply identifying a period, are *next year, last month, this week*; a second construction uses these words to mark a recurring point or subdivision of a larger unit and locates the event within the lower unit with respect to whether the larger period is current, past, or future to 'now': *next Wednesday, last summer, this August*; the third construction uses *next* and *last* in a fixed pattern where the word is understood as picking up the immediately preceding mention of the time entity: *the week after next, the month before last,* and *the summer after next, the Christmas before last.*

5.2.14. The + Adjective

Expressions like *the rich* and *the poor* are usually thought of as showing these adjectives being 'used as a noun'. Instead of attributing a part–of–speech change to the adjective, it would seem that a better analysis is that the combination THE + Adjective-Phrase behaves like a full NP. How else could we understand *the very rich, the very young?* Not as *very* modifying a noun, presumably. The constraints seem to be that the adjectives designate some categorizing property of humans; the resulting phrase is human, generic, and plural. Certain adjectives—*poor, rich, young, old* —are 'frequent guests' of this construction, but the lexicographers' decision to identify them as actual nouns in those contexts does not seem helpful.

5.2.15. Adjective + and + Adjective

These same adjectives can be used, in roughly the same meaning, when they surround *and,* as in *he was beloved of rich and poor alike.* In this case the definite article is not needed, but the conjunction is necessary: **he was beloved of poor* does not work.

5.2.16. Degree modifiers of adjectives

It's difficult to decide how many constructions are needed for the intended family of constructions, perhaps several, with constructional inheritance connecting them. Some examples communicating sufficiency or excess have extraposable complements: *too* and *enough* go with an accompanying infinitival VP, *so* goes with a *that*-clause. Others question a scalar value posed in the context, require negative polarity, are accented, and do not have an extraposed complement.

EXAMPLES include *she's not that young, you can't be too hungry* or *you'd help us get dinner ready, you're too young to understand, he's so senile that he can't follow the conversation, I am hungry enough to eat a horse.* For *too* and *enough,* the complement can be omitted when the idea is contextually given: *she's too young, she's not old enough.*

5.2.17. Adjective comparison

Comparison makes up a huge topic, that will not be conquered during the time of this pilot study, but they're included here because of some further constructions that will include them. The comparative markers also carry extraposable complements: *more/-er* and *less* → *than;* [*not...*] *so* and *as* → *as.*

EXAMPLES include *She's much more intelligent than you said, are you as angry as you seem, it's less warm today than it was yesterday.*

5.2.18. Comparative Negation with no *rather than* not

If I say that *you're not more qualified for the job than I am*, I could believe that we are both well qualified, and that I should certainly be included among the candidates. On the other hand, if I say that *you're no more qualified for the job than I am*, it's assumed that we're both barely qualified, and (say) I'm complaining that they had no right to give you the job. Using this construction seems to suggest that both of the things being compared are at the low end of the scale. *Your puppy is no bigger than a mouse!*

5.2.19. NP-internal degree-modified adjectives

All of the adjective modifiers we've just reviewed can be used predicatively, but there is a construction that allows them to be used attributively, *but only in the case of a singular indefinite count noun.* Those that have extraposed complements allow them to be extraposed after the noun. The adjectival part precedes the indefinite article. (Compare [*an*] [*intelligent*] man with [*too intelligent*] [*a*] man.) A variant of the construction has an intrusive *of* which sounds more natural in some contexts than others. We have nothing to say about that just now.

EXAMPLES include *you're too intelligent a man to act like that, that's much bigger of a house than we need, that's as sensible a solution as we can expect, is it really that big of a problem, that's no bigger a problem than others we had in the past, that's so big a problem that we'll never be able to deal with it, is this big enough of a box?* The limitation to indefinite singular count nouns is striking: **it's not that hot of soup, *they're no older of people than my parents.*

5.2.20. One's every something

I once proposed that a particular expression with *every* was dedicated to talk about indulgence fantasies, but have learned from corpus data that it is also frequent in paranoid talk.

EXAMPLES of the former kind include *we are here to meet your every need, you will obey my every command, my every dream has been fulfilled, I've satisfied my every wish*; but the other kinds include *why are you dogging my every step, they watch my every move, he records my every gesture.* And there are neutral expressions as well, so it probably requires no more than a sense of extreme attentiveness. Whatever it is, the relationship between the

POSSESSOR and the noun has to be agentive in some way—it cannot be one of simple possession: *they stole my every donut* doesn't seem to work.

5.2.21. Plural-noun reciprocals as predicates

Some plural undetermined nominals can occur as predicates indicating a symmetrical social relation between two people. *We were best friends in high school* can be expressed from one member's point of view: *I was best friends with him in high school*. If the subject is singular, a *with* is needed to identify the other member of the relationship. This only works with nominals that indicate some kind of social relation that inherently is (like *cousin* or *friend*) or can be (like *brother* or *sister*) symmetrical: *we're siblings* can stand alone as a predicate, *we're sons* requires mention of the second term of the relationship, **I was foreigners with him in Japan* doesn't work: *foreigner* isn't a relation between two people

EXAMPLES include *we were colleagues in the post office, she is cousins with a very rich man*, and, from the web, *my theory is that Harry's mother is siblings with Voldemort*.

6. Opportunities for a construction–expanded FrameNet

The decision to enter constructional information and lexical information in the same database turns out to have many advantages. In particular, it's seldom necessary to worry about whether we're dealing with a lexical or a grammatical structure. Some products of a construction are simply lexical units in essentially every way, except in that they are 'generated' rather than requiring individual listing in a dictionary's wordlist: this is true of the products of argument structure constructions as well as a number of derivational patterns, morphological or 'zero' derivation. The lexicographer might now have a principled way of deciding whether a 'frequent guest' deserves inclusion in the lexicon's standing wordlist. Some constructs behave like ordinary lexical items in their external environment, and can then be annotated as equivalent to single LUs in their own right: the reciprocal *best friends* can be annotated as an ordinary symmetric predicate of the kind that permits both joint and disjoint expression of the paired participants. The phrase *to push one's way* in its external syntax works just like an ordinary motion verb and acquires the valence expectations shared by ordinary motion verbs and can be annotated as such. Many of the constructions produce constituents that fit their environment in normal ways requiring nothing special: a rate expression classified as indicating FREQUENCY, or SPEED, or UNIT_PRICE, or WAGES, can combine with whatever marking goes with the governing predicate and find its place in the annotations for that predicate. The zero anaphora facts that FrameNet has encountered in preparing lexical descriptions are similar to those that occur with constructions as well, and pose similar challenges to theories of anaphora. Thus, to take a sentence like *otherwise most members wouldn't have the funds*, a search for cohesion with preceding texts would have to include the condition implied by *otherwise*, the organization presupposed by *members*, and the purpose-indicating complement of the Wherewithal construction that the *funds* are needed for.

Whether parsers can recognize (and interpret) instances of special constructions will remain to be seen. It's possible that a very large sample of construction-annotated texts could provide the learning corpus for statistics-based parsers. An apparent number agreement failure could lead to interpretations that permit such possibilities: *she is friends with the president, a mere twenty pages*. In many cases there are overt markers of a construction that could initiate specific steps to find the components (the phrase *let alone*). A comma before a conjunction will trigger a search for discontinuities permitted by RNR and Gapping structures. And in some cases the failure to find, in the immediate context, a needed valent of a verb or head of a modifier should guide the search for explanations: the hanging *largely* in the sentence *Bears have become largely and pandas entirely noncarnivorous* should serve as a clue.

References

Fillmore, C. J. 1982. Frame semantics. *Linguistics in the Morning Calm*. Seoul: Hanshin Publishing Co. 111–137.

Fillmore, C. J.; Atkins, B. T. S. 1992. Towards a frame-based organization of the lexicon: The semantics of RISK and its neighbors. *Frames, Fields, and Contrast: New Essays in Semantics and Lexical Organization,* eds. Lehrer, A.; Kittay, E., 75–102. Hillsdale: Lawrence Erlbaum Associates.

Fillmore, C. J.; Atkins, B. T. S. 1994. Starting where the dictionaries stop: The challenge for computational lexicography. *Computational Approaches to the Lexicon,* eds. Atkins, B. T. S.; Zampolli, A., 349–393. Oxford: Oxford University Press.

Fillmore, C. J.; Kay, P.; O'Connor, M. C. 1988. Regularity and idiomaticity in grammatical constructions. *Language* 64 (3): 501–538.

Goldberg, A. 1995. *Constructions. A Construction Grammar approach to argument structure*. Chicago: University of Chicago Press.

Jackendoff, R. 1990. *Semantic Structures*. Cambridge: MIT Press.

Joshi, A. K. 1985. Tree-adjoining grammars: How much context sensitivity is required to provide reasonable structural descriptions?. *Natural Language Parsing,* eds. Dowty, D.; Karttunen, L.; Zwicky, A., 206–250. Cambridge: Cambridge University Press.

Lakoff, G. 1987. *Women, Fire, and Dangerous Things*. Chicago: University of Chicago Press.

Tesnière, L. 1959. *Élements de syntaxe structurale*. Paris: Klincksieck.

Subject Index to Volume III

Index of Constructions and Frames